YOUR MOVE

A NEW APPROACH TO THE
STUDY OF MOVEMENT AND DANCE

YOUR MOVE

A NEW APPROACH TO THE
STUDY OF MOVEMENT AND DANCE

Ann Hutchinson Guest

Director of the Language of Dance Centre
London

with
illustrations by the author

GORDON AND BREACH
New York   London   Paris   Montreux   Tokyo

Gordon and Breach Science Publishers

One Park Avenue
New York, NY 10016
United States of America

42 William IV Street
London WC2N 4DE
England

58, rue Lhomond
75005 Paris
France

P.O. Box 161
1820 Montreux-2
Switzerland

48-2 Minamidama, Oami Shirasato-machi,
Sambu-gun,
Chiba-ken 299-32
Japan

The notation in this book conforms to the Labanotation system as set forth in the 1970 textbook LABANOTATION, published by Theatre Arts Books, 153 Waverly Place, New York, N.Y. 10014. A booklet on recent Motif Description developments is available from the Language of Dance Centre, 17 Holland Park, London W11 3TD, England.

Library of Congress Cataloging in Publication Data

Guest, Ann Hutchinson.
Your move.

Includes index.
1. Movement education. 2. Dancing. 3. Movement notation. 4. Movement education — Study and teaching. 5. Dancing — Study and teaching. I. Title.
GV452.G83 1983 793.3 83-16304
ISBN 0-677-06350-4
ISBN 0-677-06365-2 (pbk.)

ISBN 0 677 06350 4 (Hardcover), 0 677 06365 2 (Softcover).
 Printed in the United Kingdom by Bell and Bain Ltd., Glasgow.

Dedication

To the memory of SIGURD LEEDER who first opened my eyes and understanding to the wonderful world of movement and also inspired me to capture the seemingly intangible nuances of dance through the medium of notation.

To the memory also of KURT JOOSS whose faith in my notation abilities and the commission to notate four of his ballets provided the practice and experience needed to make notation an automatic part of my equipment as a dancer and teacher.

Lastly, to the many dance teachers and choreographers with whom I have worked, in grateful recognition of the contribution each made to a rich and varied insight into the phenomenon of movement and the art of dance.

Acknowledgements

So many people have given me encouragement and assistance on this book that it is difficult to give adequate credit and expression of appreciation to each one. Long before it reached final production, many had contributed to its growth at the working type-script stage. As my assistant in the Language of Dance classes, Michelle Groves contributed many suggestions to the penultimate version developed for the Teacher Training College of the Royal Academy of Dancing.

Teachers in many different countries and fields of movement study generously took the time to read the typescript and to send in thoughtful comments and criticisms. My grateful thanks go to:

Ann Kipling Brown
Judith Chapman
Meg Abbie Denton
Bodil Genkel
Irene Glaister
Peggy Hackney
David Henshaw
Jennifer Holbrook
Mary Ann Kinkead

Welland Lathrop
Elfrieda Mahler
Sheila Marion
Barry McBride
David McKittrick
Patty H. Phillips
Ines Reisin
William Reynolds

Rhonda Ryman
Muriel Topaz
Lucy Venable
Varina Verdin
Mary Jane Warner
Joan White
Jean Williams
Peggy Woodeson

The 'nurturing' and production of the book would have been impossible without the devoted and patient work of the staff at the Language of Dance Centre. Renee Caplan typed the several editions of the text; Nancy Harlock produced the various versions of the notation examples, concluding with the ink autography. Gillian Lenton, Michelle Groves, Angela Kane, Judith Siddall and Nicola Whitehouse contributed to the assembling, checking, correcting, paste-up, proofreading, indexing and all that pertains thereto.

If the text of this book reads easily and clearly it is the result of the devoted care given to it by Juli Nunlist who, as a non dance or notation specialist, questioned the meaning and clarity of every sentence. To her I cannot give enough thanks. Nor to the resident dance historian, my patient husband, Ivor Guest, who ever gives encouragement.

Contents

x   Contents

xii   Contents

Introduction

YOUR MOVE is a book about *movement*. Its aim is to provide an exploration of movement based on a fundamental, universal approach applicable to all movement study. In this book the progression in exploration leads to dance. Movement is 'distilled' to its elements, which form a basic movement 'alphabet'. This alphabet is composed of the prime actions, movement concentrations and aims. These actions, concentrations and aims are: flexion, extension, rotation, direction and level, travelling, support, absence of support, balance, loss of balance, and relationship to the environment. Each of these elements has subdivisions, the various possibilities of which are combined to produce movement sequences. Progression develops from the simplest of examples to the more subtle. For example, a prime action such as flexion is explored first as any form of flexion for the body as a whole; later the specific forms of contracting, folding, and adducting (joining) are explored as they relate to various parts of the body, such as the torso, arm or hand. The focus in this book is on 'what to do', the basic movements and their derivatives. The 'how to do it' of timing and dynamics is touched on only lightly. Timing and dynamics need to be explored thoroughly in the context of specific structured movement sequences.

YOUR MOVE was chosen as the title of this book because it states directly and simply that the focus is on movement, and that each individual should make each movement his or her own. No movement study has achieved its ultimate goal until each particular movement is understood intellectually and experienced kinetically. The spirit of the movement, the content (intent) and the physical act must be blended into a unified whole.

Integration of Notation

Because this book contains notation symbols many people may assume that it is a book about notation, but it is a book about movement — the symbols are movement in written form. Any serious educational study in other fields automatically incorporates some form of notation — what better way to pin down the seemingly intangible aspects of movement than through this visual aid? And what better means than the highly developed, flexible and comprehensive system of Labanotation? Consider music. Music notation is introduced as an aid to understanding pitch, time structure, time values and manner of performance — the basis of the art. Music notation provides a visual aid which makes it possible to memorize and practice without the presence of a teacher; learning to read music also provides access to the literature of music and facilitates a professional career. The same is true of the use of notation in connection with movement studies.

To those who have never experienced the use of symbols to clarify explanations in a movement class, the introduction of notation may seem a time-consuming intrusion. The teaching of movement requires verbal explanations; drawing the symbols can accompany the verbal explanation of differences between movements and indicate what is specifically required. In YOUR MOVE the Motif Description is brief, direct. Class time is not taken up with writing; emphasis is placed not on acquiring writing skills, but on acquiring the ability to use signs as a speedy memory aid — so much faster than writing words.

The Place of Labanotation

As visual aids Labanotation symbols provide a means of clarification and communication. If one can write down what one wants to say about a movement, then one can communicate this information to others as well as remember it later for oneself.

In contrast to YOUR MOVE the Labanotation textbook was designed to explain the system itself. Even so, people have discovered that in the course of studying the system they have also learned a great deal about movement. But the textbook presentation is totally factual. It is not concerned with exploring any particular movement discipline, i.e., training for any particular physical skills, for example, any form of dance technique. It investigates facts concerning human movement, and delves into what must be covered if all forms of movement are to be recorded on paper.

YOUR MOVE gives only as much information on the Labanotation system as is needed for investigation of the prime actions and their many 'offspring'. The book concludes with a presentation of the transition from Motif to Structured Description so that the serious student can progress to the latter and, like a student of music, benefit from the available recorded literature.

Training the Eye

One cannot look vaguely at movement; one must look for specific factors. The novice must be given a guide, a pre-program of what to look for. Movement contains so much detail that one does not know where to start unless some guidelines are given. Should one be aware of the spatial pattern, or of what part(s) of the body are in action? Should the rhythm, the use of time be the point of focus, or is concentration to be on the dynamic pattern, the movement qualities used?

Analyzing the component parts of movement helps students to observe and to understand. The eye must be trained to see, the mind to comprehend. If details in a movement are not observed they cannot be understood and hence cannot be mastered. For most people aural training is a necessary part of music education; in art the student must observe many factors which go into the final effect of a painting. Such observation does not come naturally; guidance is needed and awareness must be developed. Those who are trained in one form of movement may have become extremely proficient in that form, but may not have developed an eye to observe specific differences in other forms.

The tumbler acrobat may not be able to identify swiftly what took place in a complex series of batterie in ballet, while the ballet dancer cannot immediately analyze an intricate combination of aerial revolutions. Intricate movement techniques can be acquired without total awareness of what takes place. Mastering physical skills does not necessarily include skills in movement observation.

Universal Approach to Movement

The material in YOUR MOVE is not based on any one form or style of movement, but itself provides a basis for movement of all kinds. After the first general exploration of the prime actions, however, further investigation which advances toward structured movement is bound to be directed toward one or another movement discipline. In YOUR MOVE the development is toward dance, dance of all kinds; no preference is given to any particular type. Because the exploration stops short of structured forms there is still much freedom. Once structured notation is employed with its greater precision in use of time/body/space, it becomes more difficult to avoid established steps and recognizable movement patterns of one kind or another, forms which can be given labels and which require technique for performance.

Variety in Choice of Movement Description

For movement study life would be much simpler if only one type of movement description existed, one type which would serve all needs. But how much poorer we would be! A lesson learned from studying systems of movement notation is that those with only one form of movement analysis, one type of movement description, do not faithfully serve all forms of movement. Often a description must be adjusted, 'tailored' to fit the limitations of the notation system; the true identity of the movement is thus lost. This is particularly true when one comes to expressive movement. Movement subtleties are not the invention of a theoretician or a notator, but are inherent in movement. Too often such subtleties have not been observed, awareness of them has not registered. If one is not to be limited in description of movement and in understanding subtle differences, one must welcome all concepts that exist. A concept may be in daily use but may not have been specifically applied. Awareness of what is actually taking place and why may not yet have become a familiar fact of life. The task of defining and codifying movement to a fine degree has only fairly recently been undertaken. Because it is now possible to distinguish between subtle differences and because there are now terms and signs for these differences, movement education can be that much richer. As one explores the by-ways of movement one has 'maps' (notated material) of known terrain and the means of charting new courses.

Terminology

The words we use are the key to understanding. If a universal movement terminology existed, much greater communication would be possible among all concerned with movement of whatever kind. There is far too little communication, particularly on the topic of terminology, among those concerned with movement studies which involve various dance disciplines. In the development of Labanotation those making decisions felt a strong sense of responsibility with respect to the adoption of specific terms. Terms from many different movement disciplines were considered with the aim of providing a logical and consistent terminology (see Appendix C).

Purpose of This Book

YOUR MOVE provides a framework for learning about movement. The approach presented in this book can be the first introduction to movement exploration given to children as young as four years old. Obviously for this age-group special books and practice sheets are needed. YOUR MOVE also offers a completely fresh look at movement to those already trained in one or another movement technique. The knowledge gained in understanding what one is doing and why one is doing it can help further mastery of technique and also enrich quality of performance. In addition YOUR MOVE provides an excellent basic introduction to movement composition and thence to choreography. It opens the eyes to a 'store cupboard' of movement possibilities.

YOUR MOVE presents a way of looking at and learning about movement which, to our knowledge, has never before been published. Both practical facts as well as expressive ideas are covered, starting with the most basic. The text explores each new topic first through a consideration of how this prime form of movement or basic concept appears in the world around us. Starting with familiar examples, movement exploration then concentrates on how the body can make use of that basic form or idea. Classroom work concentrates first on the physical experience, a free exploration of the material with direct interaction between teacher and students. Discussion and clarification through introduction of the appropriate symbols then follow. Improvisation leading to composition of movement sequences gives the opportunity for students to make this material 'their own' and demonstrate the degree to which the material and logical variations of it have been understood mentally and physically. Exploration and performance of the Reading Studies for each chapter can be introduced before or after students try out their own compositional ideas.

YOUR MOVE is not designed as a text to be read during the movement class; study of each chapter should be given as an outside assignment to reinforce what has been physically experienced in class. Each student should, therefore, have a copy of the book as well as a set of Exercise Sheets to be turned in for checking at regular intervals. Every effort has been made to keep the cost of the book down so that each student can afford a copy and thus derive all possible advantages from a full understanding of this exploration of movement as well as of the presentation of movement in notated form.

The Teacher's Guide

Detailed suggestions on how best to handle exploration of the prime actions, suggestions on devices to aid the students in composing their own sequences, further clarification and answers to the written assignments are included in the Teacher's Guide.

Application to Movement Exploration

The YOUR MOVE approach to movement exploration employing the basic 'alphabet' which YOUR MOVE provides has three important functions:

(1) as a first introduction of movement leading to dance for young children. At first only a single factor is imposed as a discipline so that freedom in interpretation is allowed. The element of time may be chosen as the discipline, movement exploration being centered around, let us say, a duration of three slow beats and a one-beat stillness. While experiencing this timing in movement the children may use any part of the body and any space and dynamic patterns. In another exploration, use of a particular space pattern may be demanded, while freedom in part of body, time and energy are permitted. Gradually as the child's physical coordination develops, the disciplines of time, space, part of the body and dynamics are combined and refined to provide the challenges needed. Although this book is designed for older students and does not concentrate on application of the material to teaching children, its basic approach and ideas allow the material to be used fruitfully in that area.

(2) as a broadening, enriching experience of movement, a re-evaluation and survey for teenagers and young adults who may already have had movement or dance training of some kind.

(3) as material for movement composition leading to choreographic study.

This book has been specifically designed for use with young adults. It is the result of much classroom exploration at the College of the Royal Academy of Dancing where the students, predominantly ballet trained, came gradually to see the relation of the balletic form to dance in general and, through the Language of Dance approach, were able to view their familiar movement vocabulary in a new light.

Language of Dance is the name given to the educational approach in which the movement 'alphabet' is learned physically and at the same time understanding is reinforced by the visual aid of notation symbols.

Origin and Meaning of Language of Dance

As a dancer and dance teacher, I discovered many years ago that there was no logical list of prime actions on which all dance (and other movement) is based. In painting there are three prime colors, in western music the octave — what exists for dance? This question led me into an investigation lasting many years. My background of study in ballet, modern dance (European and American) and various ethnic forms provided me with a broad view of dance, and my work with the system of recording movement, Labanotation, provided the tool through which findings could be pinned down. The results of this research were the establishment of the Prime Actions and Movement Concentrations and development of the Movement Family Tree.

All movement can be seen to be composed of a specific selection and combination of the many variations of these prime actions. What better way to begin education in movement study than by investigating this raw material? And what better basic education can be devised than combining the physical experience of movement with the written form, the visual aid which provides clarification.

For dance such introduction to the raw material of movement offers a greater understanding of dance as a language — not language in the academic sense, but in the expressive and communicative sense. How do the parts of a movement relate to the whole? To perform with conviction one must understand the content of a sequence and the 'value' to be placed on each component part. To interpret a passage one must have a concept of the meaning of movement, its 'kinetic sense', or its dramatic intent. Such understanding of movement is also necessary for the mastery of technique.

The act of dancing is a physical one, but behind it must be an intelligent awareness of what one is doing. The classroom and studio experience produces the professional dancer and teacher. Communication requires clarity based on a comprehensive understanding of the nature and facts of movement. The Language of Dance, like all languages, has the purpose of communication, communication through a common terminology and vocabulary supported by the written form. Full communication in dance should occur at all levels, at all stages and at all locations. Communication across the oceans of the world requires a common language, the use of symbols to represent the many 'building blocks' of movement on which all dance cultures are based.

To many people the idea of Motif Description for movement is not new; many teachers of young children start with general movement ideas and images. There are many years ahead in which to progress from the freedoms in interpreting Motif Description to the demands of structured forms. Motif focusses on the kernel of the movement, the central concept. As details are added to the bare framework, the desire to be specific in use of time, space, part of body, dynamics, etc., leads into Structured Description. This Structured Description can be a simple memory aid or details can be added until very precise instructions are produced from which a more exact performance should result. Leeway in interpretation then lies in the subtle nuances of expression.

Reading and Practice Studies

The Movement Alphabet

The prime actions and concepts of which movement is comprised.

Presence or Absence of Movement

1.   *Any action*   Movement of some kind, a change

2.   *Stillness*   Suspension of motion, sustainment of an arrested activity

An action may be concerned with or may concentrate on:

Anatomical Possibilities

3.   *Flexion*   Contracting, folding, closing in, making smaller, narrowing

4.   *Extension*   Lengthening, reaching out, enlarging, opening out

5.   *Rotation*   Any revolution, turn of the body as a whole, or of parts of the body

Movement Ideas or Concentration

6.   *Travelling*   Any path (straight or circular) moving from one situation to another

7.   *Direction*   Movement up, down, to the right, left, forward, backward, etc.

8.   *Support*   An action ending in a new support, transference of weight, a step

9.		*A Spring*	Any aerial step leaving the ground and returning to it
10.		*Balance*	Equilibrium, centering of center of gravity over a moving or static support
11.		*Falling*	Center of gravity moves beyond base of support

Specific or Relative Description

12.		*Destination*	Statement of ending situation, position or state to be reached, designation of aim
13.		*Motion Toward*	Approaching a person, object, direction or state to be reached, designation of aim
14.		*Motion Away*	Leaving, withdrawing from a person, object, direction, or state of being; a gesture away from oneself

Chapter One
MOVEMENT; STILLNESS; TIMING

What is movement? There can be dozens of answers to that question depending on the context in which the question is presented. Are we concerned with electric impulses from the brain which trigger muscular responses and thus produce physical movement? Or do we anticipate the reply "Movement is life!"? We need a simple, practical investigation of human movement which leads to recording the outcome of muscular responses. In this book, viewing and experiencing movement progress from a first broad introduction to a focus specifically on dance.

MOVEMENT

Perform one movement, then follow it with a rest, a moment of inactivity. Move again. Find variations without seeking a specific structure. Just move. Whatever the movement, it may have arisen from a thought (an idea which came to mind), or from a physical impulse (an outflowing from the center of the body). A movement may be just a simple spatial displacement rather than an arrival in a particular pose. As we are starting with the most basic, elementary movement concepts, let us take spatial displacement. From whatever position you are now in, make a change, move limbs and torso into a different situation. If sitting or kneeling, change by rising or lowering, move the head and arms away from where they were. If you focus on leaving the situation where you were, rather than on moving to a predetermined new spatial placement, the action is more likely to reflect true motion performed for the sake of moving, of enjoying the process, rather than of achieving a particular 'picture'. Before long we will be concerned with specific actions, and will be investigating the various possibilities of what these actions might be.

But first we need to consider the difference between movements which are just 'done', (such as those which are purely functional), and movements which are 'performed', (such as those in gymnastics, skating, swimming, or dance). Practical movements are presented with a heightening, be it ever so slight, of intensity in the manner of execution. One may 'walk through' the motions, marking them for memory, but for full benefit and enjoyment of the experience the innate expressive content of each movement has to be found.

What is 'performed' movement and what is not? In turning on the television one can distinguish in a moment between a panel discussion on some current topic and a comparable discussion occurring in a play. The difference lies in the manner of presentation.

Indication of an Action

The most simple statement regarding movement is that an action, a movement of some kind occurs. For such a basic statement an equally basic notation indication is provided, Ex. 1a. This vertical line, called an action stroke, makes no statement about the movement other than that it occurs. When no movement takes place there is no action. A blank space indicates no movement, i.e. no change. In Ex. 1b an action is followed by no change (read from the bottom up). Note use of a double line: ==== to indicate both the start of action and the end of the example. Ex. 1b provides the most rudimentary movement theme - an action followed by inaction.

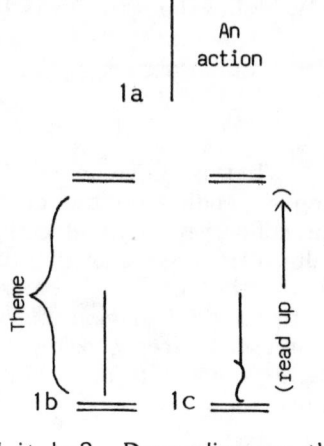

1a An action

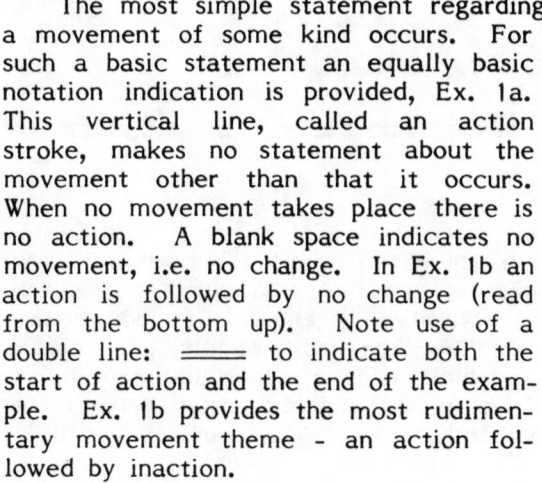

1b   1c

So we have one movement. What could it be? Depending on the context, the accompanying music, the dramatic situation, the proximity of and relationship to other persons, it could be an appropriate, expected movement, appropriate to the context in which it occurs, or it could be any kind of movement at all, the performer having total freedom of choice. The sign for ad libitum: (is placed at the start of the action stroke, Ex. 1c, when total freedom of choice of movement is allowed. The range of such movement can be from a general fluent spatial displacement of the body as a whole to an isolated finger movement. Focus on isolated actions will come later.

The Basic Staff

In the writing of Motif Description (indication of the basic movement idea), no staff, as such, is used. The 'column' which runs up the page from the double starting line to the end, as in Ex. 2a, represents the body as a whole. No distinction is made yet regarding use of one body part or another. Later on movements of the right or left side of the body will be indicated as well as actions of specific parts of the body.

Simultaneous Actions

Two or more actions may occur at the same time; one part of the body may perform an action at the same time as another part. A double action may have occurred in your previous movement exploration; now two simultaneous actions are consciously being performed as such. Experiment

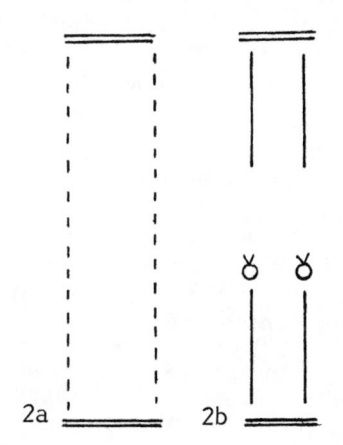

2a   2b

with different possibilities, perhaps both arms, or one arm and one leg. Try moving the torso with both arms in unison performing a different action. Many possibilities can be explored.

Actions which occur at the same time are written side by side. Ex. 2b indicates two simultaneous actions followed by stillness which is itself followed by two more simultaneous actions - possibly quite different from the previous ones, possibly relating to them.

STILLNESS

What is stillness? Basically it is the passage of time when movement does not occur. It is absence of movement, absence of action, but not in a negative sense. It is not 'stop'; it is not 'blankness', a 'deadness', a 'minus', though these may be wanted at times for special effect. As Agnes de Mille has observed: "A tacit in music is not a silence. It is a suspension. In a play that tacit is called a pause, and all too often, God knows, the pause in question is a dead, dulling silence, a break in the continuity, a gap, an on-stage nap, empty air. Unless a pause can make tension, it's sheer dereliction of duty." Absence of movement should be enjoyed by both performer and viewer; it should be a positive experience. In stillness there may be repose, not the blankness of people sitting still waiting for a bus, but rather the stillness of listening as in listening to a symphony. Such stillness catches the eye. Because so much emphasis is placed on actions, on techniques of moving, it seems important to give full value here to the concepts behind stillness. If there is a pause between actions, the previous movement must terminate in a position of some kind, but the line of the previous motion may still project into the stillness in that a fragment of it lingers on beyond the arrival point. The movement is 'arrested' but the flow escapes — as though it intended to continue. It may be that it is the energy that continues even though the body has arrived at a spatial destination. Despite the position a sense of transience exists. This is particularly true of shorter pauses, comparable to commas in a sentence; longer pauses suggest full stops for which the stillness can express the idea: "Here I am. This is where I belong." Arrested action may be intended, a strong positive statement, or it may be a pause from which emerges a new movement, itself the result of a new movement idea.

Because stillness contains meaning and expression a special sign is used. The sign for 'hold': O is used in many contexts to retain a state or condition. For the special state of stillness the sign: V for outflowing is added to form the sign for stillness, Ex. 3a. The gap following the stillness sign indicates the length of time the stillness continues. Ex. 3b shows the movement theme of Ex. 1c but with stillness specifically asked for.

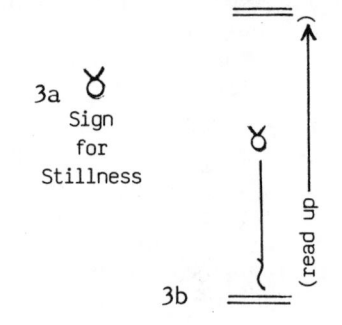

3a Sign for Stillness

3b

(read up)

TIMING

Timing is such an integral part of movement that, although it can be ignored and a neutral attitude to time can be taken, we want early on to be aware of it and to enjoy it.

Sustained Movement

Choose a simple movement and concentrate on the passing of time. If a gong is played, begin moving at the moment the gong is struck and continue until the sound dies away or someone stops it. Find a movement which the sound inspires. You may think of a word to say inwardly which supports your movement idea: for example, the word "S--T--R--E--A--M--I--N--G" sustained for as long as needed. The question will arise: "how long is that?" No statement has been made yet of specific length; you still have freedom in duration. Each person may have a different concept of the time span Ex. 4a represents.

Now try a contrasting movement, but still very sustained; indulge fully in time, enjoy the slowness of it, relish the sustainment, the feeling of never wanting it to stop.

Indication of Sustained Actions

The extension of movement in time is represented on paper by the length of the vertical line, the action stroke. In Ex. 4a the action extends in time from the start of the stroke to the end. As we all have slightly different innate attitudes toward time, each person will have a different idea of the duration Ex. 4a should represent. This does not matter as long as we are solo performers; it is when unison movement is needed that a basic beat must be established and kept constant. Music provides just such 'regimentation'; in a ballet such as Jerome Robbin's *Moves*, which is performed without music, the dancers must count inwardly to maintain a regular beat (and that takes a lot of rehearsing!) or must take visual cues from each other.

For Ex. 4a the chosen movement may spatially cover a long or a short distance. Length of time is quite different from distance, that is, space measurement. Walking can be performed as one long line of motion, but steps tend to punctuate and so gestures of the limbs and body are usually more suited to express sustained movement.

(end)

(one continuous movement)

(start)

Time passing by

4a

4

Only one movement was stated in Ex. 4a; 4b provides three sustained actions one after the other without a break. Note that the three are separate actions, not one very slow movement.

When a movement sequence continues beyond the top of the staff, a single horizontal line is used both at the top of the page and at the start of the next 'staff'. For movement exploration, Ex. 4b provides greater scope than 4a in that it offers a choice of three movements which can appropriately be linked together, each very slow. If moving so slowly seems difficult, find an image which will support each movement: for example, underwater plants swaying through the gentle motion of the water.

Continuity of Movement

While experimenting with performing these three movements, you may have stumbled on the question of how to determine in spatial terms what is one action and what becomes two or more. When a pause occurs, it is clear that separate actions are taking place. But if there is no pause the space pattern is the determining factor.

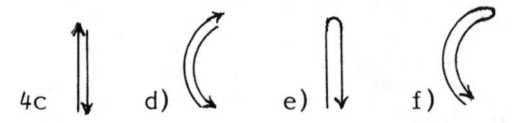

Ex. 4c illustrates a space pattern of two movements. You move out on a straight line and then reverse direction. Ex. d) shows two movements using an arc. But e) and f) show only one action. The curved transition produces one continuous line of movement. Ex. 4g represents one long line of movement. Though this line covers a great deal of space and may contain a variety of 'coloring', it may, in fact, represent one main movement 'thought', comparable to a sentence. If one part of the body is featured, try involving the whole body for an overall harmonious effect.

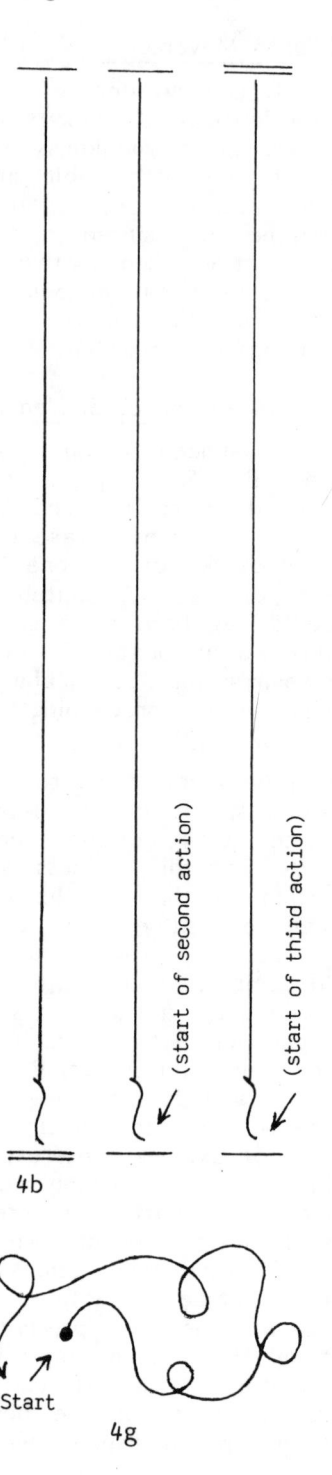

4b

4g

5

Sudden Movements

It is now time for a complete change of mood, of intent, of inner experience - an 'about face' into the world of no-time-to-spare, of haste, speed, quickness, suddenness. Choose an action and execute it at the fastest possible speed. It could be the same movement which you chose before, but the chances are that something quite different will be more suited to the speed now demanded of you. Try one very fast action, then another and another. Continuous performance of sudden actions can become very tiring. You and the audience long for stillness. Stillness provides a 'frame' for an interesting sudden action, making it memorable.

Indication of Sudden Actions

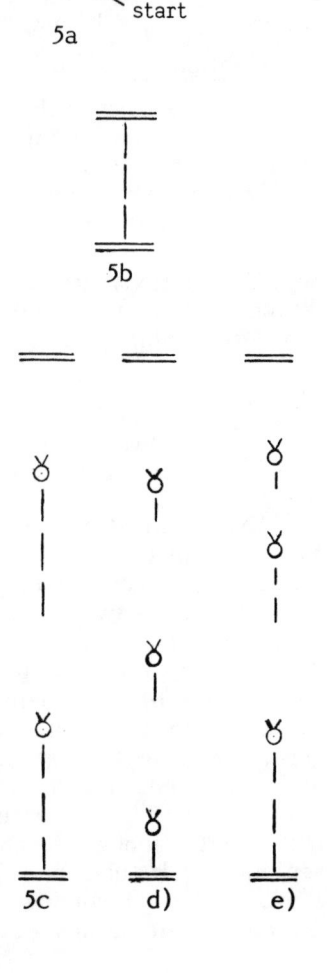

A sudden action is shown by a short line, Ex. 5a. The movement has barely started before it is ended. Ex. 5b shows a brief movement phrase composed of three very quick actions, one immediately after the other. A suitable accompaniment could be three percussive sounds such as three drum beats; the movement could be claps, stamps, or jabbing actions in the air, twitches or dabbing motions.

This 'theme' of three sudden actions will be more interesting if combined with stillness. In Ex. 5c between each set of three quick actions there is a stillness. Note that this stillness is of the same duration as that of the three actions; the sign for stillness plus the space following it are considered a unit in time duration. In complete contrast to this Ex. 5d shows three quick actions but with a considerable separation between each. These could be the same three actions used for Ex. 5b, but how different the effect now that they are so separated in time! The time pattern of Ex. 5e is interesting since it starts like 5c but develops differently. The movement pattern progresses from three swift actions one after the other without a break, then two actions, then one. The total number of actions is the same as in 5c but they are presented differently in time. From such simple material many interesting variations can result involving various parts of the body in smaller or larger spatial displacements.

6

Organization of Time

How much time is actually taken for the examples on page 5? No indication has as yet been given regarding counts, beats, seconds, or other time measuring devices. We have been dealing with free, un-measured time. Within the span of time indicated on the paper be-tween the double horizontal lines on page 5 and 6 the movements are proportionally spaced. For Ex. 5c, d), and e), the same overall amount of time was allowed so that the contrast between the three examples could be seen. If relative timing is understood and performed, it does not matter if one person's choice for the overall timing is longer than another's. Some forms of dance use time freely; only at key moments do all performers have to coordinate. For many kinds of actions no formal organization of time is needed. In many sports time can be personal; its use rests on what functionally produces the desired result. In dance it is common for time to be strictly organized, largely be-cause of the physical enjoyment of a rhythmic beat, but also because of the organization of the accompanying music.

In this book we are concerned with the nature of movement and its different forms; no deep investigation of time will be undertaken. An exploration of time as used in dance is a study on its own. But even in the first exploration of movement time cannot be ignored. We cannot move without involving time, without using it in some way. For our purposes here we will deal only with general organization of time.

Indication of Regular Time Spans (Measures)

As you read up the page, horizontal bar lines marking the measures (bars) provide a time structure. The measures are numbered for reference. The passage of time is always read from the bottom up. Ex. 6a shows spans of time which cov-er eight equal measures. Note that each measure is a span of the same length. For this ex-ample any piece of music or drumming in spans of 8 can be used and any tempo set. A basic structure has been provid-ed for which tempo and the number of basic beats for each measure have been left open.

Measure numbers are writ-ten on the left, just above the bar line at the start of the measure which is identified by that number.

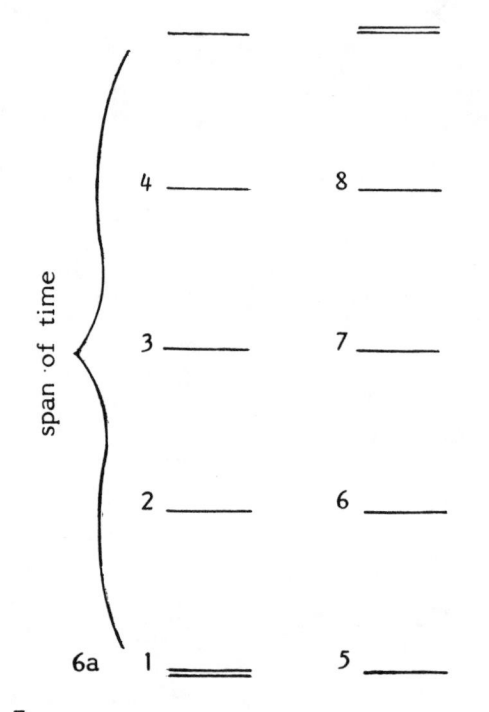

Indication of Meter

The next step in organization of time is to specify meter, that is, the number of beats in each measure, 3/4, 4/4, etc. The statement of meter is placed on the left before the start of movement. In Motif Description the individual beats in each measure are not usually indicated. In the examples below the beats have been marked in the first measure so that this organization of time can be understood. Ex. 6b has three quarter notes (crotchets) in each measure, while 6c has four. Counts, if shown, are written with smaller numbers, as illustrated in the first measure of 6b and 6c. Statement of meter is only a very general guide as to what kind of music may be used.

The tempo (speed) is still left open. In the early stages of exploring movement patterns, ample time is needed to experience the material and so a slower tempo is advised.

Listen to music in 3/4 and, as it is being played, run your finger up the page, following the passage of time, coordinating the music measures with those marked on this page. Do the same with the 4/4 example.

8

Reading Study No. 1

MOVEMENT PATTERNS IN TIME

A study in actions of different time values producing specific patterns in time. Find your own series of movements to express the time patterns given.

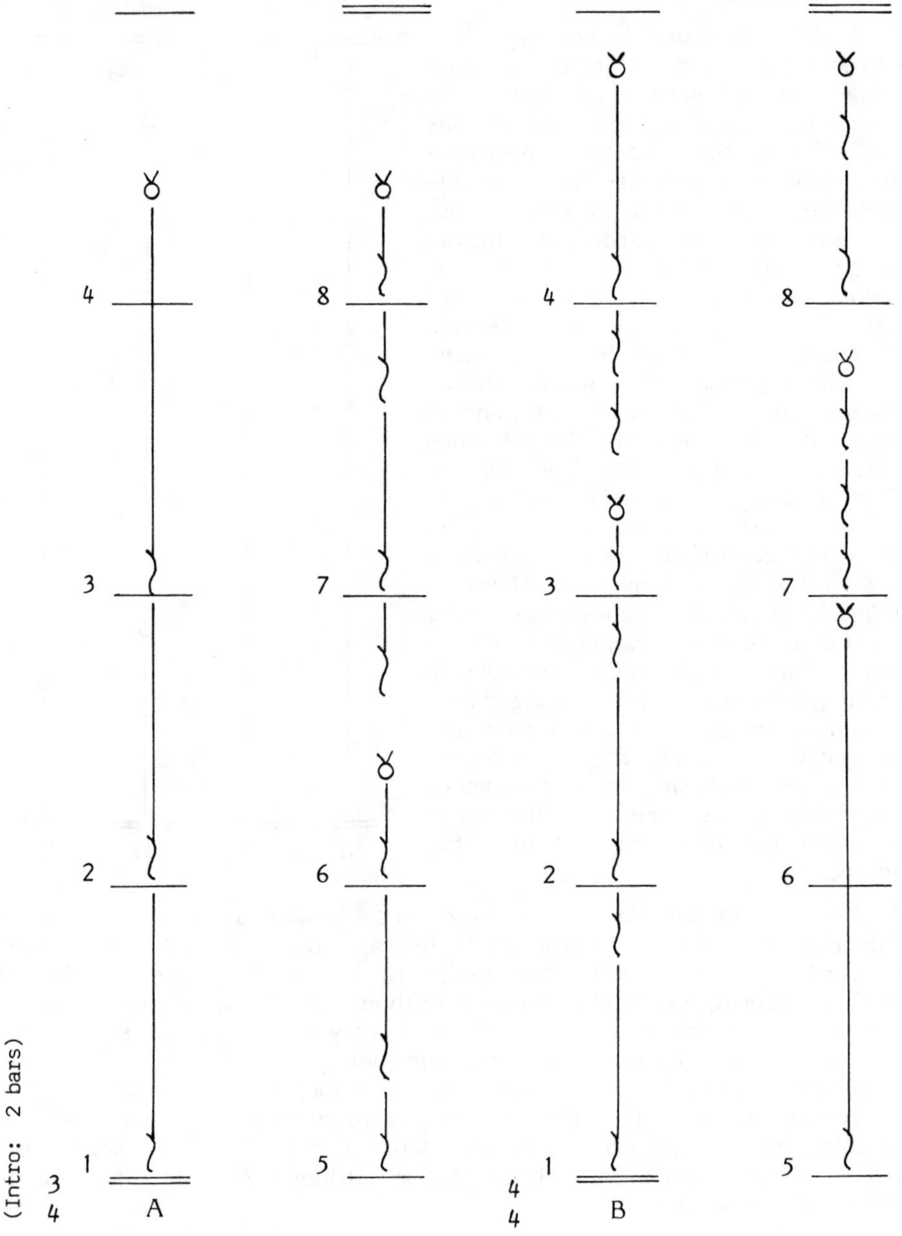

B

Breath Pause

A most expressive use of time for what would otherwise be purely legato movement is the breath pause. The term may be unfamiliar but the idea is not; it is used daily in speech as well as in movement. The following examples can help the reader visually to establish the change in performance which results from an increasing amount of time between movements.

In Ex. 7a there is no separation between the action strokes, only enough of a break to show the movement is not one continuous line. These tiny gaps only separate the actions; they have no time significance. Ex. 6b shows slight pauses between the sustained movements; they produce an effect not unlike commas in a sentence, very slight breath pauses in the absence of which movement flows on without any 'punctuation'. When sentences are completely devoid of punctuation, the listener or reader becomes irritated and loses the meaning of what is being said. The meaning in spoken or written words can be altered by placement of pauses, and so it is with dance. If movement flows on endlessly it is like cooked spaghetti; you can't find the beginning or the end. The breath pause provides a fleeting moment of rest during which the audience can see a clear image, an arrival point, and thus it is essential to good phrasing in performance. This moment of arrival is the point at which the photographer snaps the picture.

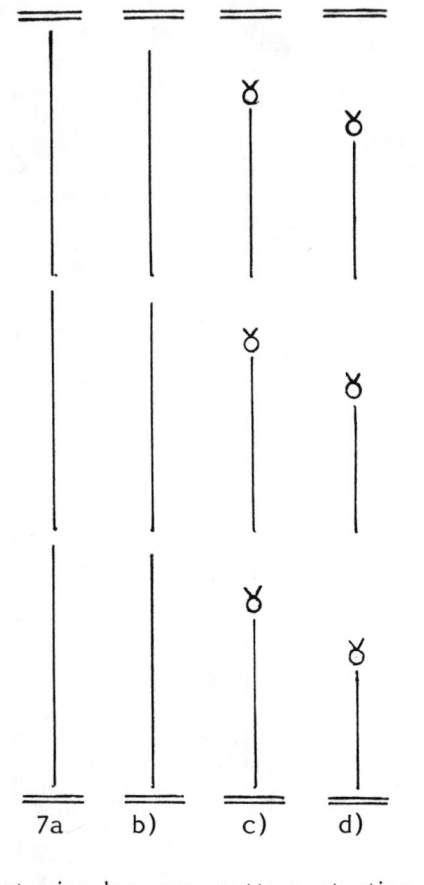

7a   b)   c)   d)

For Ex. 7a take a simple three-part circular arm pattern starting with the arms down. Raise them forward for the first action, open sideward for the second, then lower to the starting position for the third. Perform this simple pattern without any pause at all, as in 7a, then with a breath pause as in 7b, a slightly longer pause as in 7c and then with equal time for moving and being still, as in 7d. As the movements quicken and the pauses become longer you will be performing 7e and 7f, in which the movements to each point are as swift as possible, quite staccato, separated, with the rest of the time filled with stillness. Note that the sign for stillness: ☿ is included in the length of the stillness.

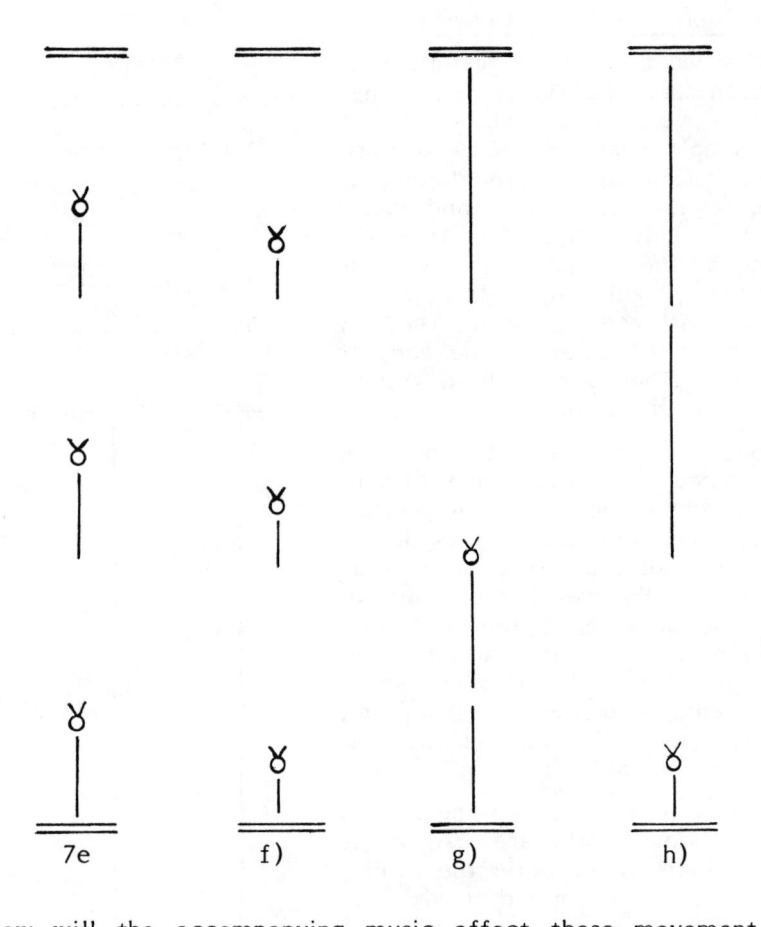

7e   f)   g)   h)

How will the accompanying music affect these movement examples? Each of the sequences above takes the same amount of space
on the page, so each takes the same overall span of time, the same
amount of music. But within this time span (from ▬ to ▬) the
organization of the actions and stillnesses has provided much variation.
If you are still using the same arm pattern, how would Ex. 7g come to
life? Bear in mind that the overall time is still basically divided into
three parts; therefore 7g shows the forward and sideward part of the
movement pattern occurring within the first third of the time span. A
stillness of the same length follows; the lowering then occurs on the
last third. In 7h the arms are raised forward swiftly. Then there is a
pause. They open to the side during the whole of the second part of
the time span, and then are lowered during the whole of the last time
span.

Many choices for musical accompaniment could be made; obviously
something flowing would be suitable. The music need not 'spell' out
the timing of the movement; it is more interesting if your movement
relates but retains its rhythmic independence.

Time Division of a Space Design

The speed at which a gesture travels through space can vary. As a first exploration we will be concerned only with a simple example. Ex. 8a illustrates a horizontal pattern moving to and fro, starting at the left and ending at the right. The black dot marks the beginning of the design. Try this pattern with the right arm in front of the body, then with the left arm. Then try it with the head, allowing the body to participate. Then with a foot, tracing the design on the floor.

Though this design, one long line, can be traced at an even pace with no change in the speed of the movement, different time durations for its different sections will produce a more interesting result. By the simple device of dividing the drawing of the path with cross lines we separate it into segments. In 8b the design is shown in five segments identified as a), b), c), etc. Now the following variations in performance can be indicated:

Ex. 8c. In this version the longer, horizontal movements are shown to take very little time, while the turning of the corners is performed slowly.

Ex. 8d. Here the longer lines of the movement are performed slowly while the turning of the corners is done swiftly. Neither of these two examples includes a pause, a stillness.

Ex. 8e. This rendition introduces equal motion and stillness to begin with, then continuous motion, becoming slower with each section. Many other variations may be tried.

Speed in travelling can also be enjoyed in walking and running. Try the same space pattern as above walking at an even pace; then try it with variations in speed, breaking into a run if you wish. Find movement motivations to underly the change of pace.

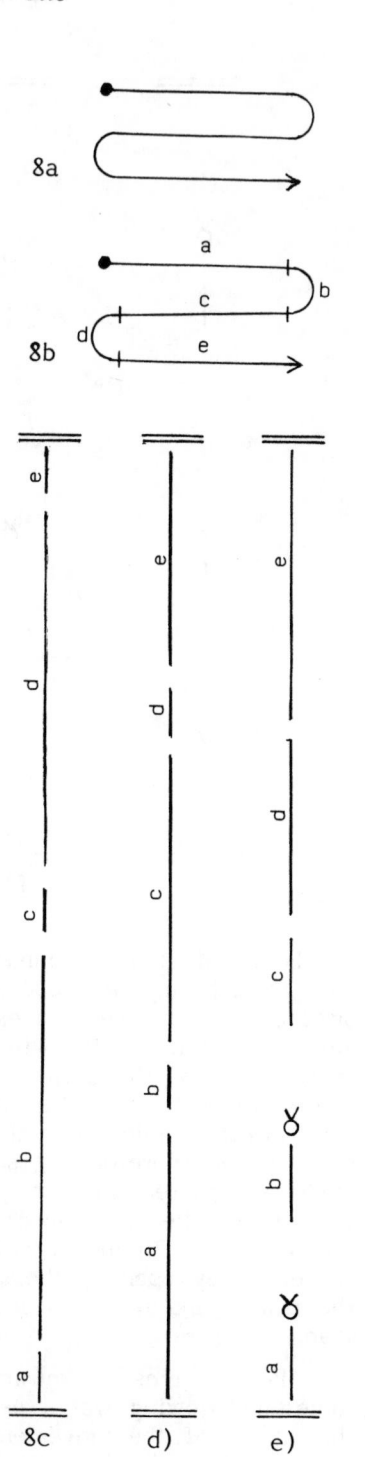

Spatial Continuum

Have you ever thought of how we move in space - the wonderful range of choice, and yet the limitations involved in never escaping the spatial continuum? It is impossible to move from point 'x' to point 'y' in space or on the paper here without going through all the points between. Music can jump octaves, intervals of all kinds, but movement is by nature chromatic: we must pass through the intervening space.

By the way we perform the movement we can give an impression of 'jumping' from point 'x' to 'y'. A swift, unemphasized transition and a clear arrival which is held momentarily will produce this effect. Thus by speed and intensity we can give the impression of darting from point to point, position to position, without intervening links. This impression of darting can deceive the eye, thus creating an illusion of escape from the spatial continuum. Ex. 9b illustrates the picture which a very sudden, sharp rising will produce in the viewer's eye.

A very different effect is achieved by the deliberate use of chromatic movement - movement which consciously progresses through all the intervening spatial points. Such movement cannot be extremely fast; by moving more slowly, indulging in time, so to speak, one has the opportunity to enjoy the passage through space. This passage is now often captured by rapid photography in multi-image pictures. Moving with a chromatic image in mind, as depicted in Ex. 9c, d), produces a fullness, a richness of gesture in motion that is missing in actions designed to move to distant destination points. Full awareness of the passage through space happens naturally in swimming where the resistance supplied by the water provides a consciousness of the fact that there can be no sudden darting from point to point.

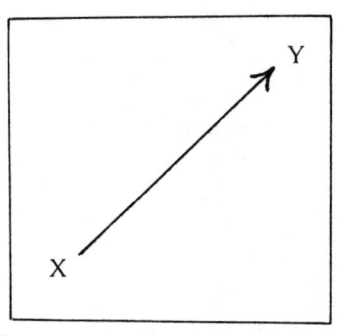

9a   A spatial 'leap'

9b

9c   Awareness of
passage through space

9d

Chapter Two
TRAVELLING

Travelling!   A familiar activity, but what exactly does it mean in movement terms?   How much are everyday meanings carried through into dance?   The dictionary states: "To journey, to proceed from place to place, to move from point to point, to be transported, to pass by, pass along, passage from one location to another, to move in a given direction or path, or through a given distance; to traverse, to travel across, to cross over (as over a river); to advance or retreat, to run back and forth. "

Two main ideas emerge from the above: 1) that of location, a particular place away from or toward which one moves, and 2) that of 'passage', the act itself of travelling.   Both ideas apply directly to dance, but in addition dance is concerned specifically with the nature of the path travelled, i.e. whether it is straight or curved.   Also to be considered are the speed of travelling and the mode of locomotion. Note that locomotion is defined as 'locus', Latin for place, plus 'motion', progressive movement, hence travel.   Locomotor steps are steps which travel.

What initiates travelling?   It could be said to be "Get up and go!" The aim may be to leave where you are, to put as much distance as possible between you and the point from which you started.   The next point of arrival may also be undesirable, and off you go again - away, away!   Or the motivation may be the reverse: to arrive somewhere, trying one place after another, searching endlessly for the right one. Or the motivation may be neither of these, but simply the sheer joy of moving through space, across the room or stage wherever empty space is waiting - the simple enjoyment of the 'going'.

If the emphasis is on departure, there may be a dramatic reason, perhaps an escape from imaginary alien space-creatures, or inner de-mons as in Anna Sokolow's | Rooms.   A dramatic reason for emphasis on arrival at a destination may be reunion with a loved one.   Who has seen Ulanova in *Romeo and Juliet* flying to Friar Lawrence for help? Or seen Rudolf Nureyev in the ballet *Marguerite and Armand* running swiftly like the wind when he finally discovers that Marguerite really loves him and is dying? It was so beautiful a run because an emotional impetus carried his limbs, thrusting him forward. He, his center had to be there. There was no thought of his feet stepping, of how his arms were held. These things did not exist. An inner force swept him across the stage; there was only one aim, one thought which propelled him forward.

When does one travel for the sheer joy of it? Such travel is rare in classical ballet since the feet are usually busy performing 'steps' of some kind. I once saw Irma Duncan perform and imagined the use which Isadora must have made of such free flow surging through space. Nadia Chilkovsky composed for a ten-year old an exquisite dance based only on running with variations in speed and dynamics. Paul Taylor captured this special feeling of exuberance in a dozen different patterns, all fleeting and travelling, in his ballet Esplanade. It is exhilarating to watch, and both exhilarating and exhausting to do for it is never ending, there is always more space to conquer.

Every room has 'awaiting space' to be filled. It is there to be used, and, as we use it, the awaiting space changes, it calls, challenges. Lucky the performer who is alone on the ice rink with the chance for gliding, skimming, travelling at will. The solo dancer on stage has similar freedom of spatial choice, but the presence of other performers makes the use of space more interesting because of changing patterns of relationship.

Does travelling have to be fast? Must it be a run? What of a walk? A crawl? The slower the kind of action used, the less the idea of travelling is directly expressed. Walking occurs for many reasons and can be a means of expressing several movement ideas, amongst which is travelling. That travelling is the focus of a walk must be expressed by the carriage of the body. An exhausted person crawling expresses both the desire to travel and a limitation in doing so. On the other hand we see babies crawling at amazing speeds. The intention to travel may be expressed clearly even though travel itself is barely achieved.

Improvise on travelling using changes in speed and energy, and also variations in the general carriage of the body, use of arms, head, etc. Since travelling is the theme, all complementary movements must be merely 'coloring' for the main theme; they must not become important in themselves. Too easily the accompanying music can call forth a variety of steps, foot patterns which embellish and become the focus of attention so that travelling becomes incidental.

FORM OF THE PATH

Starting with the least structured, the least specific mode of travelling, we have random travelling, which expresses the enjoyment of progressing with no destination in mind, no aim, no concern for the kind of path taken. Random travelling may occur while one is in a mood of day dreaming. If one is uncertain, or drifting, it is likely that curved, irregular paths will result. The inner motivation for the path dictates the form it will take. Determined people with goals in mind will choose straight paths.

Random travelling is expressed by the idea of 'any path', Ex. 10a. The sign: ∼ at the start and finish of the indication means 'any'; it is the ad lib. sign drawn horizontally. The length of the vertical line indicates how much time is spent travelling. In Ex. 10a a longer time is spent in random travelling than in 10b. In general one can say that a longer time will produce a longer path, but this need not be so. Distance (measurement of space) has a separate indication not needed for our first explorations.

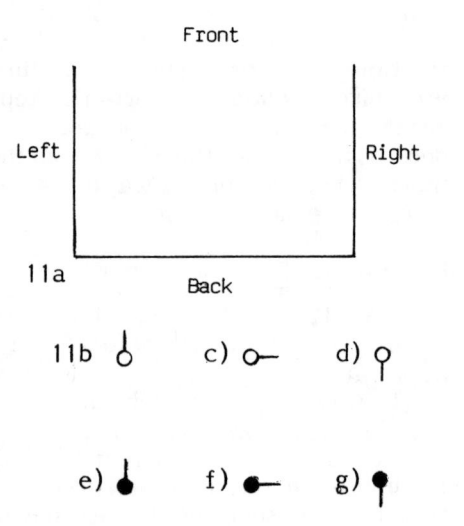

10a   b)

Any kind of path

Once random travelling has been improvised, a pattern should be established which can be repeated and performed. The resulting floor pattern can easily be written down.

Floor Plans

Paths traversed across the floor can be shown on a floor plan, Ex. 11a. This plan shows a bird's-eye view of the room or stage, the open end being the chosen front (the audience), and right and left sides and the back as illustrated. Indication of performers in this area is by means of pins. A white pin represents a girl (a female), the point of the pin pointing into the direction she is facing. In 11b she is facing front, in 11c the right side wall of the room (stage right); and in 11d she is facing the back (upstage). A boy (a male) is represented by a black pin. Ex. 11e-g show the same facing directions for a boy. Where the pin is placed on the floor plan shows the location of the performer in the room, i.e. the starting position. It may be that more than one floor plan is needed if the path is complex. Each plan must start where the previous plan left off.

Front

Left   Right

11a   Back

11b   c)   d)

e)   f)   g)

17

Straight Path

Travelling on a straight path must inevitably end when we come to the edge of the performing area. At some point an angular turn must take place to allow for the next straight path. Such paths may be of short or long duration and may be punctuated by pauses or may follow one right after another.

By nature we are built to walk and run forward, Ex. 12a, but a performer must meet the demands of greater variation, particularly in dance; thus running backward, sideward and in the directions inbetween must be practiced. Fluent change of step direction as well as of room direction provides interesting and enjoyable patterns. Zigzagging, for example, is the result of a series of short straight paths with quick changes of direction.

The resulting floor design for a series of straight paths might be something like Ex. 12b, short paths being combined with longer paths. Although it is comparatively simple the plan of 12b can be performed in many different ways if steps of different directions and timing are used. Try this design and try contrasting ways of peforming it. First follow the floor design only using forward steps. Then try it always facing front, changing the step direction as needed to keep travelling on the given path. For the third version use forward steps on the first part, side on the second, back on the third, side on the fourth, and so on, always travelling on the same design.

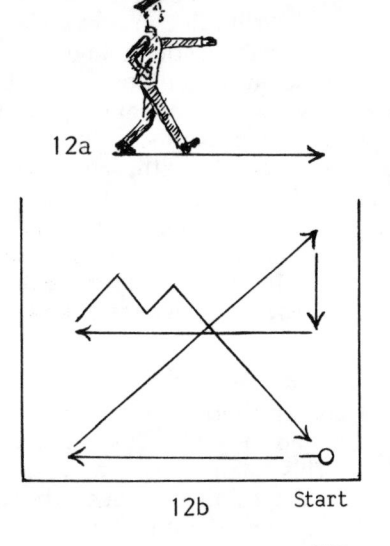

12a

12b   Start

Duration of Path

Ex. 12c is the sign for a straight path. As mentioned before, the length of a path sign indicates its duration, how much time is taken for that path, and not distance travelled. The number and size of steps taken affect the distance travelled. Experiment with many steps travelling a short distance, short steps on half toe or with bent knees, stamping on each step. Then try to achieve a great distance through very few long steps which really cover space — the seven-league boot effect.

duration

12c   d)

Straight path

Reading Study No. 2

STRAIGHT PATHS

This dance starts in the center of the room. Perform it facing the front of the room all the time. Then explore travelling along the same lines but facing into any room direction you choose.

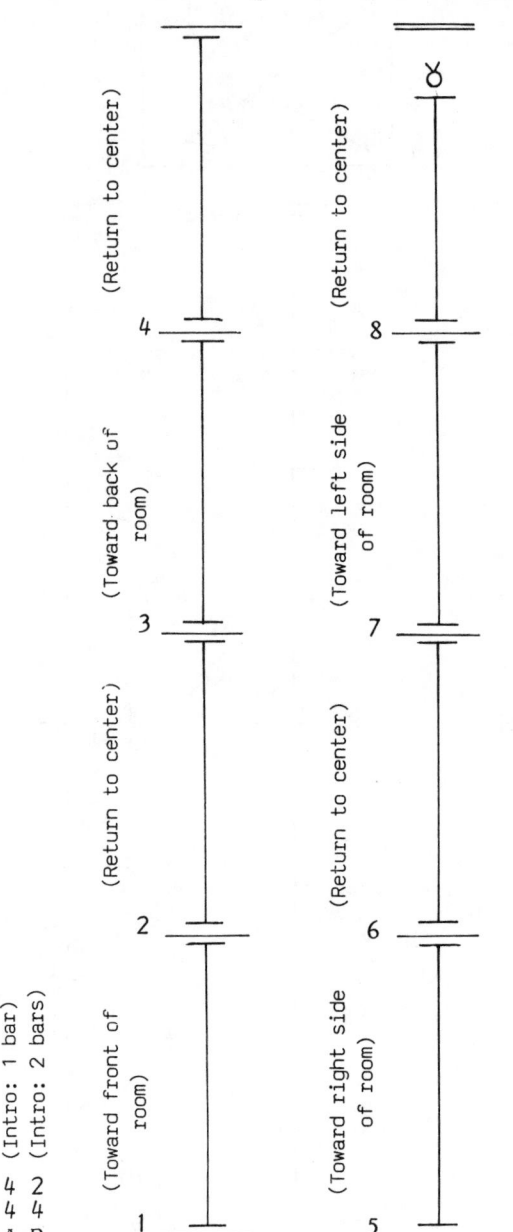

(Return to center)

(Toward back of room)

(Return to center)

(Toward front of room)

(Intro: 1 bar)
(Intro: 2 bars)

4 2
4 4
A B

4

3

2

1

(Return to center)

(Toward left side of room)

(Return to center)

(Toward right side of room)

8

7

6

5

Version A. Dance the sequence to slow music.

Version B. Dance it swiftly, running, galloping, skipping, as you choose.

For each version find a theme, an idea to make your movement logical and appropriate, e.g. giving out or collecting objects, pulling out streamers from the center point to make the design of a cross.

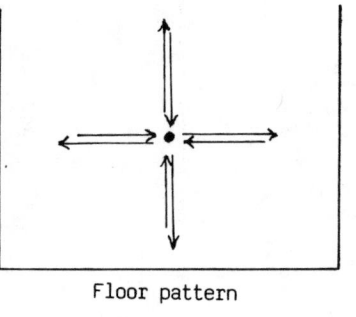

Floor pattern

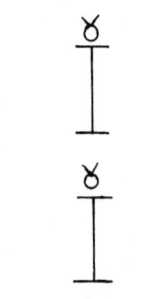

Try a change in timing for the above ideas, e.g. a pause between each change of direction. Note the resulting change in expression for the sequence.

19

DURATION OF PATHS; FLOOR PLANS

Guided by the floor plans, find a way of performing these straight paths in the timing given.

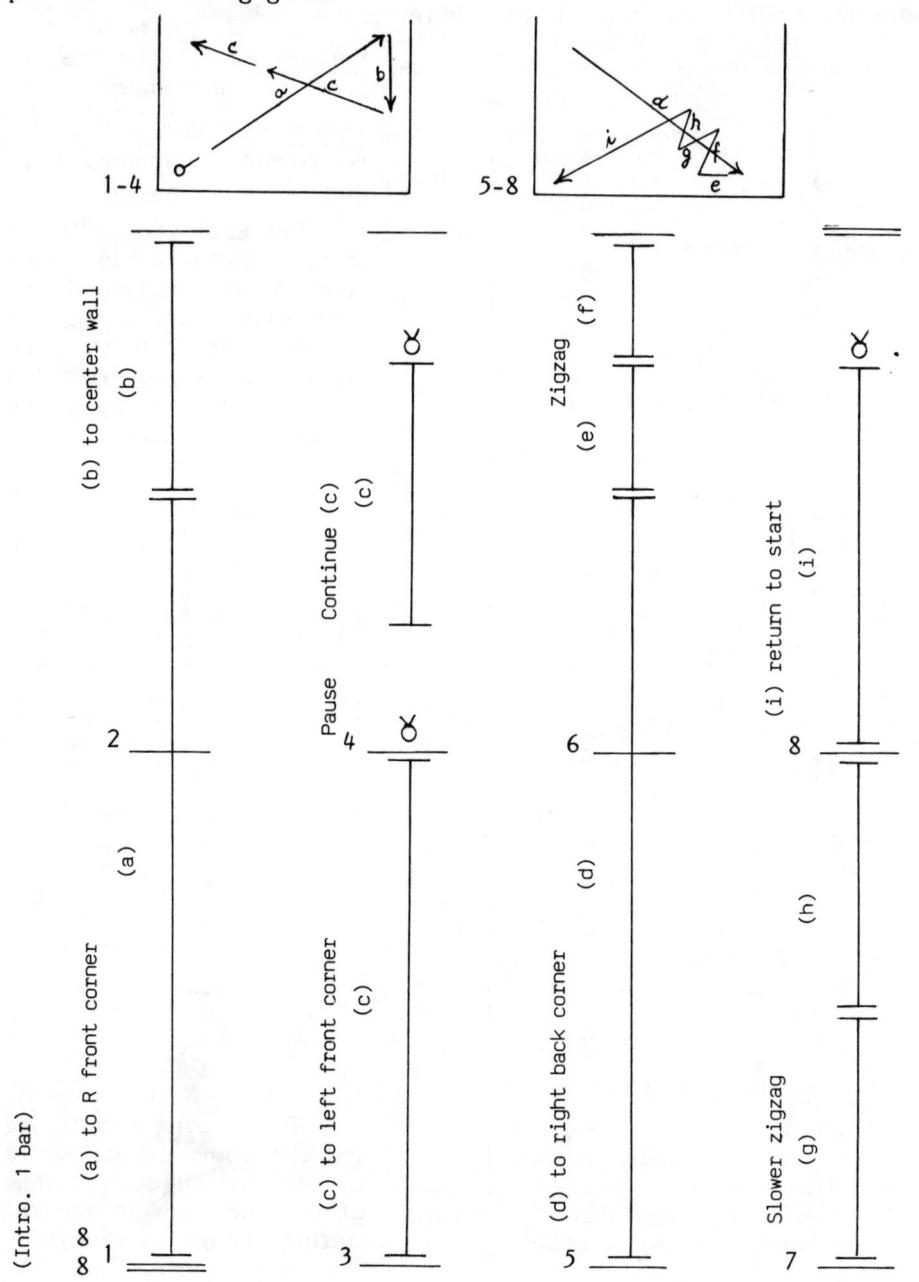

Meandering

Curving progressions have quite different expressions from straight paths;
other moods and movement ideas may e-
merge. Whether one is travelling across
the floor or making gestural paths in the
air (particularly with the arms), curving
paths allow endless movement without a
break; an uninterrupted flow of movement can result. Instead of a sharp
corner, as with straight paths, a larger
or smaller curve or loop can effect the
change of direction, as in 13a.

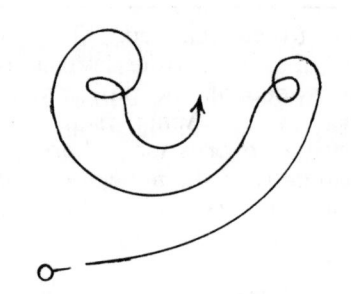

13a

While straight paths cut through
space using as little of it as possible -
the direct 'bee-line' - the greatest indulgence in space can occur in unpremeditated meandering. The symbol for
any curved path, i.e. without regard to
the kind of curve or the degree, is Ex.
13b. The wandering pattern of 13a is
well expressed by this sign. It serves
the mood of the wanderer who is not
concerned with the design of a path but
with freedom in the 'going'.

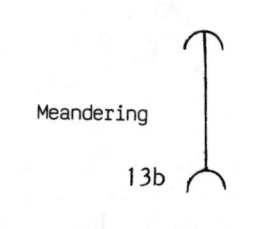

Meandering

13b

Circling, Circular Path

In contrast to 13a Ex. 13c shows
circular paths which require an awareness of circling as a clear space design
to be described on the floor. These circular pathways stem from a very different feeling and aim. In Ex. 13c a
figure 8 design is followed by a large
complete clockwise circle. To achieve
this design one must be aware of the
shape and plan ahead. Ex. 13d appears
to meander and to be closer in intention
to 13a, but in fact the path clearly is
two quarter circles leading into a half
circle.

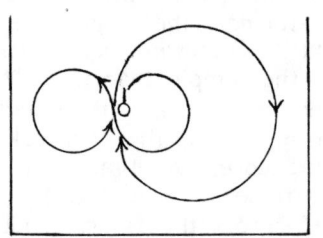

13c

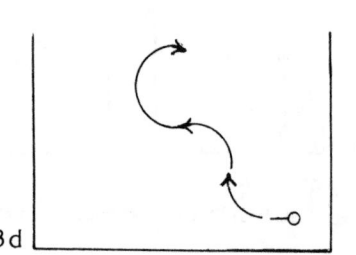

13d

The Nature of Circling

A straight line is spatially economical and is also usually economical in
time. Travelling on a straight line usually expresses purpose; there is usually
a clear intent, an aim, a clear destina-

13e

The Nature of Circling (continued)

tion to be reached. In circling there is a greater indulgence in the use of space; time is usually not important. A physical enjoyment of the sweep of the path as it curves, the constant change of front, may take over. Apart from any dramatic motivation, what is the innate physical expression inherent in the circular form? Anyone can mechanically walk a circle. Such movement produces a circle but has no expression as such. What is the basic nature of a circle? How does it get born?

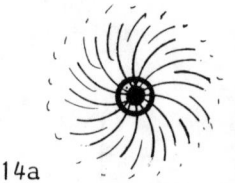

14a

Catherine
wheel

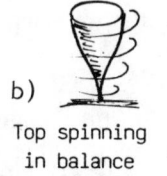

b)

Top spinning
in balance

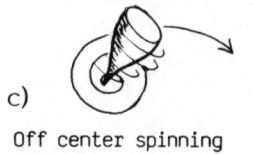

c)

Off center spinning
producing a spiral

A circle is an extension of a turn on the spot into space; a turn around one's own axis changes into curving while travelling, that is, a circular path. In a circular path the axis of the circle lies outside the performer; the larger the circle, the farther away the path is from the axis. Different possibilities exist for curving while travelling; circling is the simplest form. Think of objects which start pivoting around a centre point and then move out into space. One example is the Catherine Wheel, the firework in which sparks fly out from a central spinning core, Ex. 14a. Another is a spinning top. When centered it will continue to spin, Ex. 14b, but if it becomes lop-sided it is likely to fly off across the floor, producing a spiral path, as in 14c.

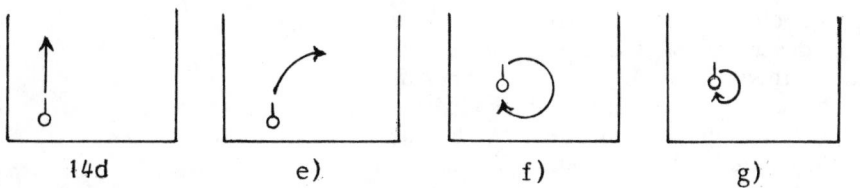

14d   e)   f)   g)

The 'pull' of a straight path into a curve and finally into a full circle.

A circular path can also be experienced as a straight path which veers constantly to one side as though the person is drawn by a magnet. The stronger the magnet, the sharper the curve. This magnet (which, in fact, is the center of the circle) is an outside influence; an inner source for circling can occur within the torso where only a very slight twist will start the center of weight on a curve. Whatever the image, the straight path of 14d becomes a partial circle, as in 14e, the 'magnet' lying to the right of the performer. The inner body energy initiating the rotation is greater in 14f, producing a circle. In 14g a 'tighter' circle is produced as the feeling of rotation comes closer to pure turning on the spot, i.e. a very small circle is produced.

Direction of Circling

As we have seen, the action of turning, of change of front, is an integral part of circling. When a large circle is performed we may not be aware of this turning; it is more obvious in a small circle. If condensed as much as possible, circling becomes turning on the spot.

Circling clockwise

Circling counter-clockwise

15a

b)

In circling, as in turning, there is a choice of two directions: clockwise (to the right), Ex. 15a, and counterclockwise (or anticlockwise, if you prefer, to the left), Ex. 15b. The abbreviations CW for clockwise and CCW for counterclockwise will be used from now on. Details on the size of the circle or arc, the number of circles and the possibilities of spiralling in or out will be dealt with later.

If you do not see at once the direction of circling in the circular path sign, let your eye follow the slanting line as you glance up the sign. This points the direction as the arrows in 15c and 15d illustrate. Note the indication of 15e which expresses circling either way; the choice is left to you.

= Clock-wise

= Anti-clock-wise

15c

d)

Travelling may combine straight paths and circling. On a path to a new destination the performer may have a change of mind and veer off course by curving into another direction. An obstacle, perhaps imaginary, may be in the path and need to be avoided. Just as decisiveness in selecting an aim, a destination, produces a straight path, so other ideas, other inner motives, may cause one to move on curved paths. A circular path might be used to creep up on someone, this aim being hidden until the last moment.

Circle = either way

15e

Pure enjoyment of passage through space, of the act of travelling itself, requires neither a sense of destination nor a need for departure, only a wish to go, to explore freely the space available. Such is the feeling of the open road, of the wanderer setting off on his travels with no planned route. In dance such freedom of traversing space is often enjoyed through running, but other modes of locomotor steps which allow ground to be covered may be used. Just as in daily life the traveller stops to rest, so in dance there will be pauses, 'punctuations' in the 'sentences' of travelling. Such rests occur because the momentum or energy has temporarily been spent, not because this spot, this location, was a destination chosen beforehand.

STRAIGHT AND CIRCULAR PATHS

Explore this study first with forward steps. Once you have worked out an overall design for the travelling indications, vary the space pattern by using backward and sideward steps as well.

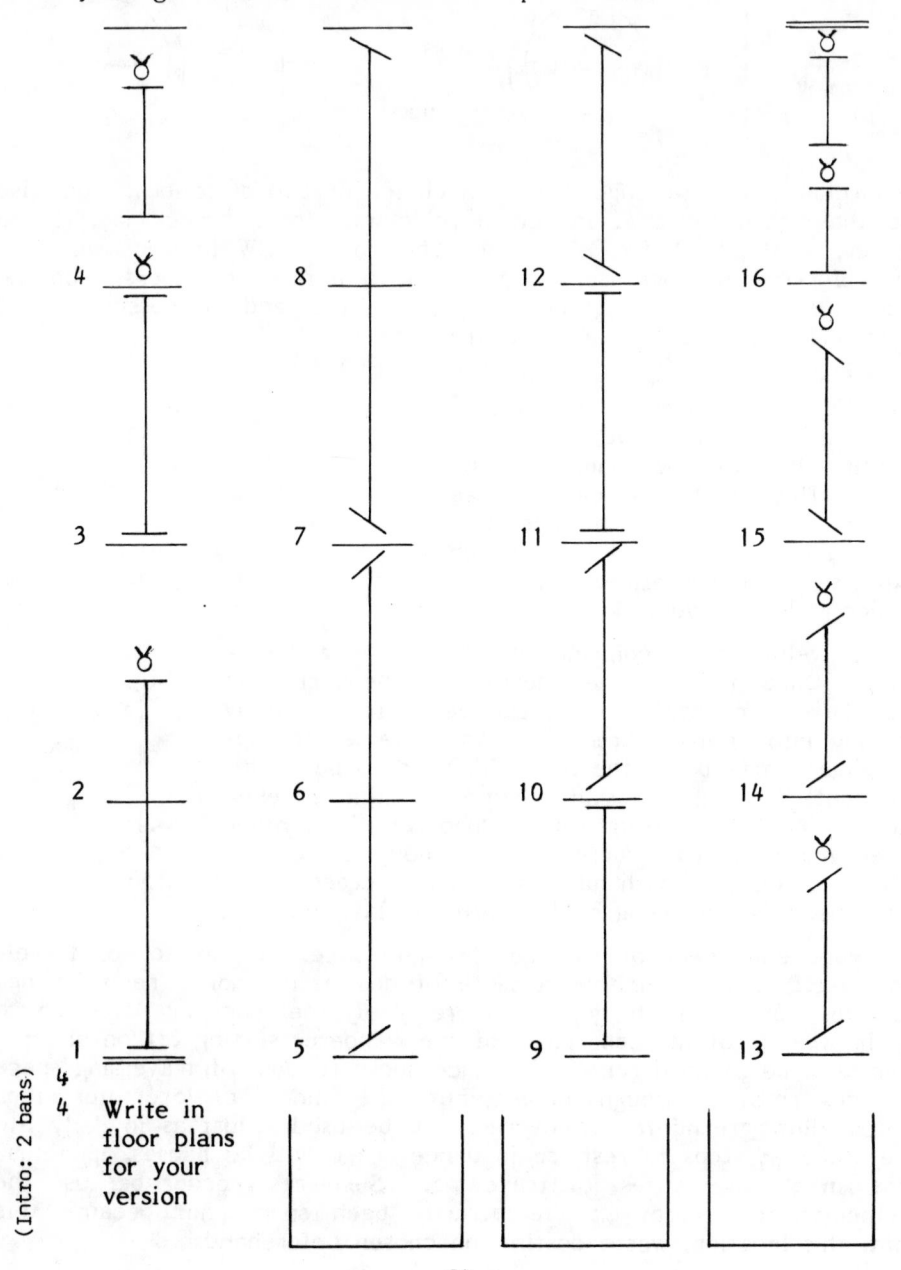

(Intro: 2 bars)

$\frac{4}{4}$

Write in
floor plans
for your
version

REVIEW FOR CHAPTERS ONE AND TWO

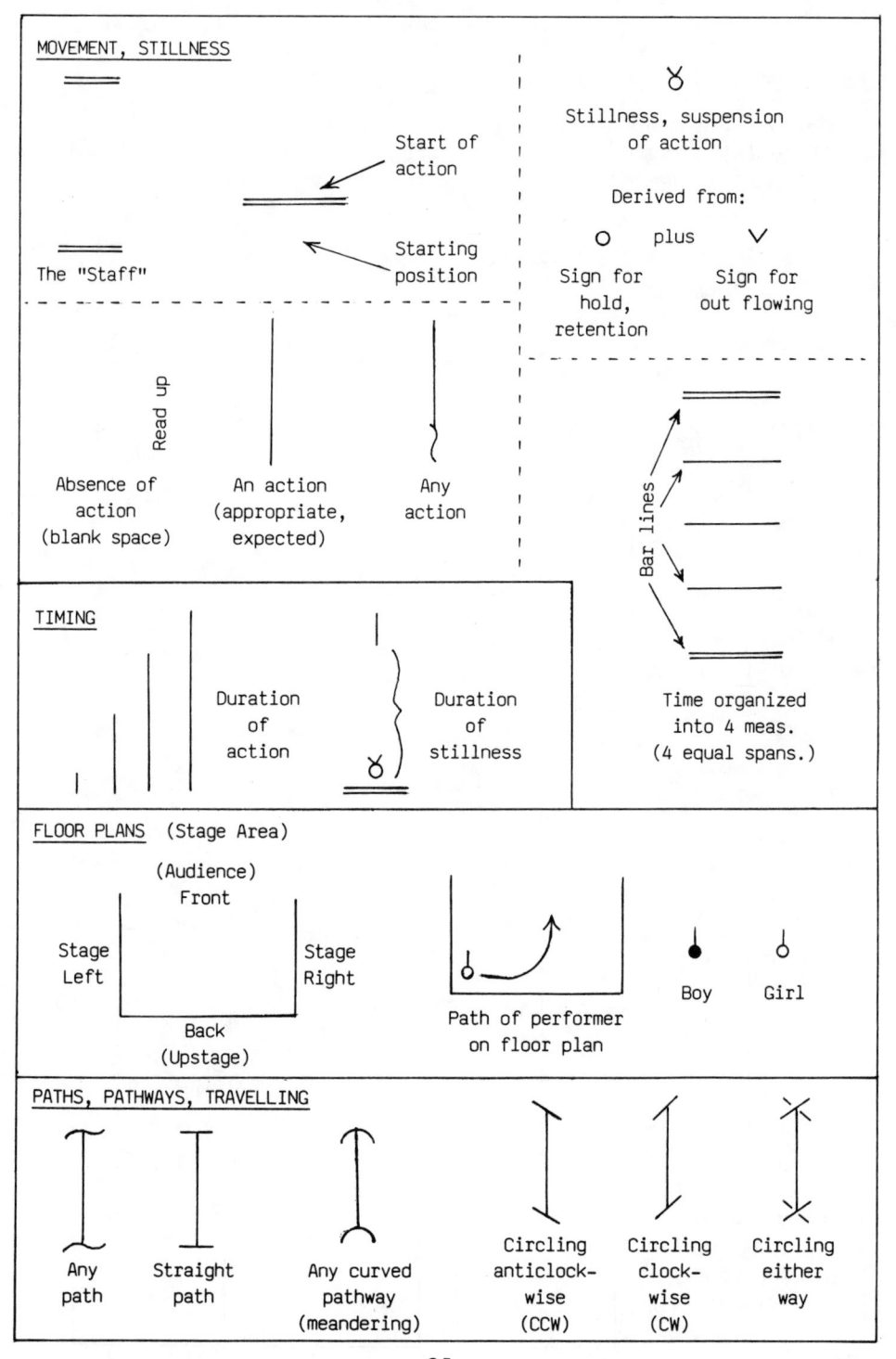

MOVEMENT, STILLNESS

Start of action

Starting position

The "Staff"

Stillness, suspension of action

Derived from:

◯ plus ∨

Sign for hold, retention

Sign for out flowing

Read up

Absence of action (blank space)

An action (appropriate, expected)

Any action

Bar lines

TIMING

Duration of action

Duration of stillness

Time organized into 4 meas. (4 equal spans.)

FLOOR PLANS (Stage Area)

(Audience) Front

Stage Left

Stage Right

Back (Upstage)

Path of performer on floor plan

Boy   Girl

PATHS, PATHWAYS, TRAVELLING

Any path

Straight path

Any curved pathway (meandering)

Circling anticlockwise (CCW)

Circling clockwise (CW)

Circling either way

25

Chapter Three
VARIATIONS IN TRAVELLING

THE MAIN DIRECTIONS FOR TRAVELLING

From the starting point travelling may occur forward, backward, sideward, or into the diagonal directions between. The signs for direction are derived from the rectangle, Ex. 16a, which represents the central point where the performer is. This basic shape is modified to 'point' pictorially into the appropriate direction; see Ex. 16b - e.

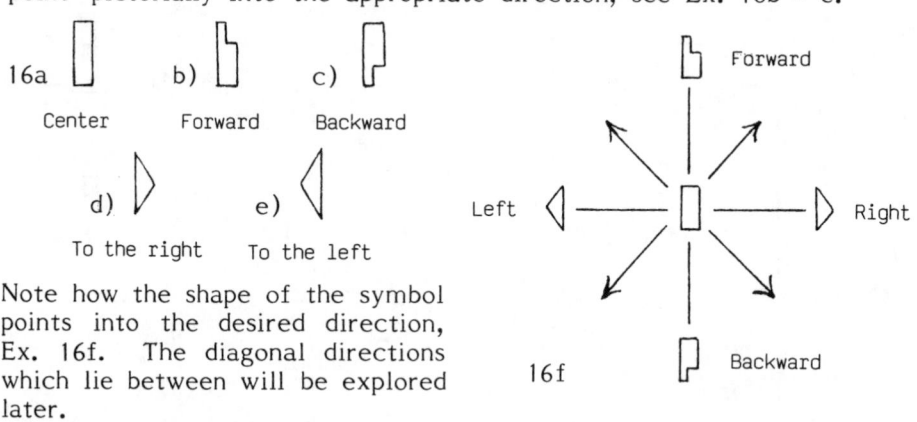

16a   Center   b) Forward   c) Backward

d) To the right   e) To the left

Forward

Left   Right

Backward

16f

Note how the shape of the symbol points into the desired direction, Ex. 16f. The diagonal directions which lie between will be explored later.

Directions for Straight Paths

These same direction signs are used also for other movements of the body. When placed within a path sign they indicate the direction travelled as judged from the performer's front, i.e. where the performer is facing.

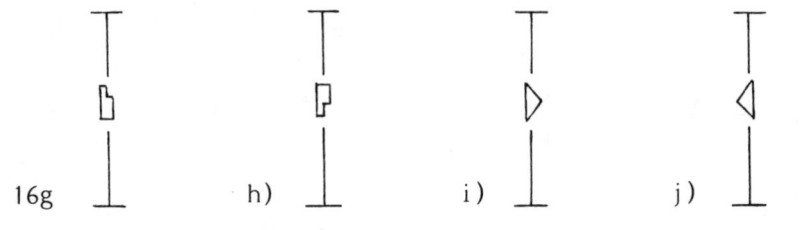

16g   h)   i)   j)

Ex. 16g shows a straight path travelling forward; 16h is travelling straight back; 16i states travelling to the right side of the body; 16j is travelling to the left side. These direction symbols state nothing concerning the kind of steps used or even what part of the body is supporting; travelling could be on all fours, as mentioned before.

27

Reading Study No. 5

TRAVELLING IN DIFFERENT DIRECTIONS

An appropriate ending to a sequence may be lowering, Ex. 17b, or rising, 17c. Full exploration of directional movements is given later. As degree of circling has not been given yet, follow the floor plans.

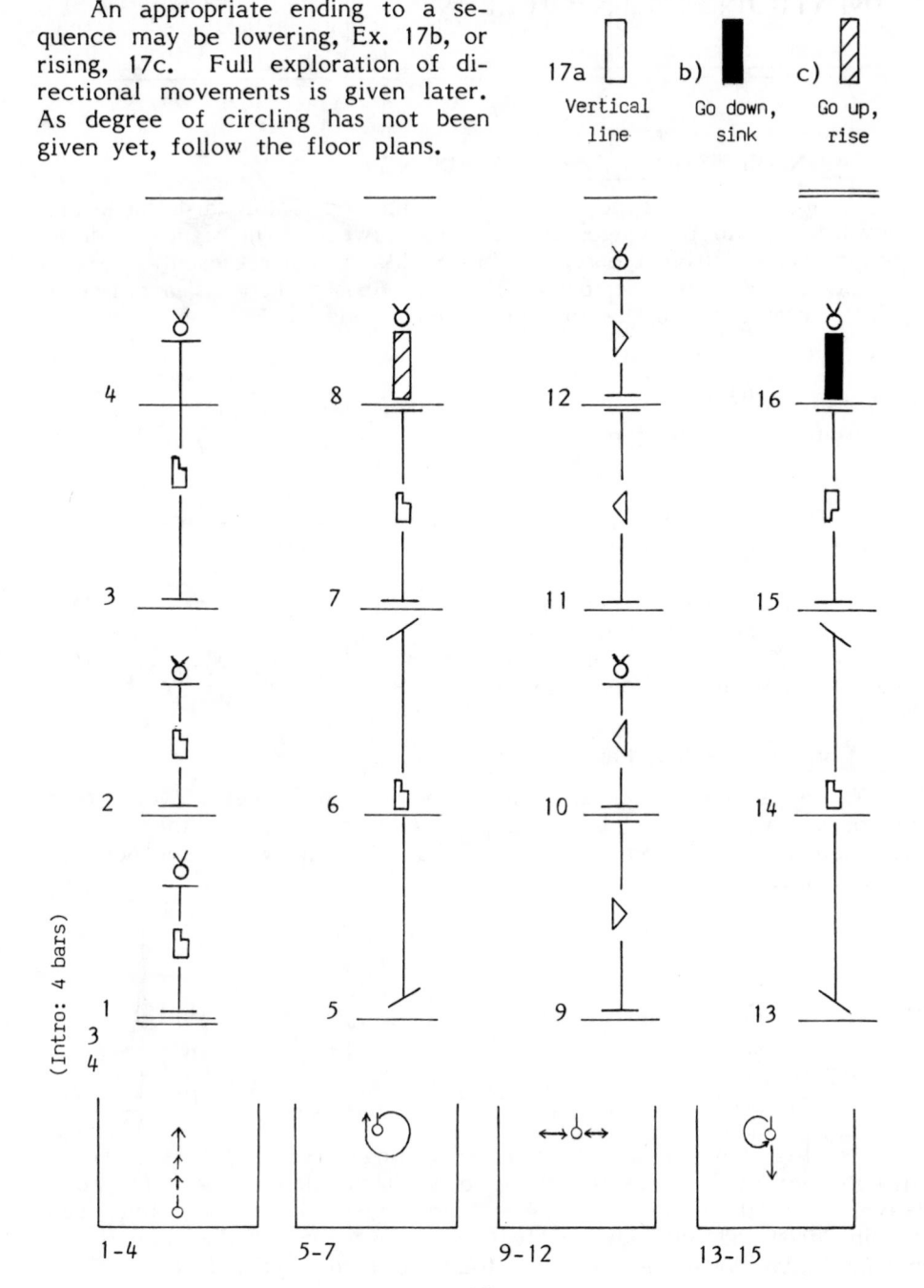

17a   Vertical line   b) Go down, sink   c) Go up, rise

(Intro: 4 bars)

1-4   5-7   9-12   13-15

Variations in Travelling

Directions for Circular Paths - Merlin's Magic Circle

When circling starts from a feeling within the body, circular paths of unpremeditated size and design may result. The movement impetus is free, is of the moment. In contrast, circling can be based on real or imaginary circular patterns on the floor. To begin with a circle may need to be chalked on the floor so that its size and placement is quite clear; later the performer can express this circle in movement, keeping exactly to the same circle without it actually being visibly there. An image which helps to develop such awareness of the circle and the ability to stay on it is that of a magic circle laid down by Merlin, the magician in King Arthur's Court. This circle is a narrow path surrounded by water, the opposite of a moat around a castle, and the performer is bound by a spell to travel only on that path, around and around, Ex. 18a.

18a

What are the ways in which you can travel on this path? What variations exist? What are the limitations? In creating a movement sequence on this path, what ingredients are at your disposal? First, there is the direction of circling, CW or CCW. Then there is the direction of the steps.

The natural tendency is to take forward steps along the 'rim' of the circle, the center of the circle lying at your right, as in Ex. 18b which produces CW travelling. Or, keeping the same relationship to the center of the circle, you can circle CCW travelling backward.

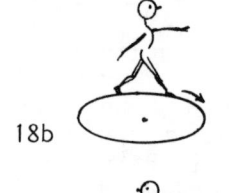

18b

To travel forward and be circling CCW, the center of the circle must lie at your left, Ex. 18c, and this is true for backward steps circling CW.

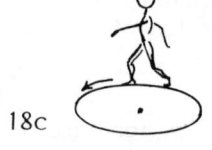

18c

If you face out from the center of the circle, that is, with your back to the center, you must take sideward steps to the right to circle CW and sideward steps to the left to circle CCW, Ex. 18d.

Finally, facing in to the center of the circle, as in Ex. 18e, also means travelling with sideward steps — steps to the left to circle CW, steps to the right to circle CCW.

18d

By combining the appropriate step direction sign with the appropriate circling sign we can indicate all these possibilities, as illustrated in the examples on the next page.

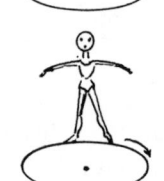

18e

Merlin's Magic Circle (continued)

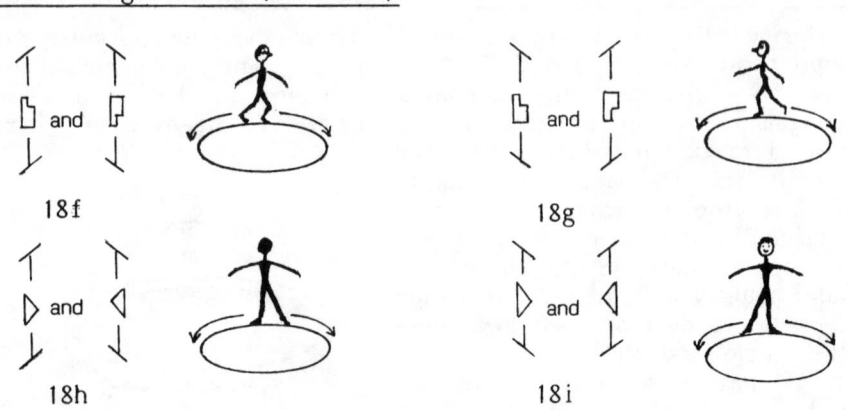

18f	18g
18h	18i

With use of the right amount of right or left turn as a transition, you can change from one of these possibilities to another, in each exploration, when there is no visible circle to guide you, keep awareness of the presence of the circle, its center and size, as a strong force within you.   Once this awareness is established, different step patterns and accompanying arm and body movements can enrich the progression; the accompanying movements should contribute to achieving the path by bearing some relationship to the circle.   Not yet discussed are the exact degrees of turning and circling.

Group Circling

Awareness of a circle is more easily achieved when one is dancing in a group which takes a circular formation.   The other participants provide the size and placement of the circle and there is a strong sense of the center (the focal point) of the circle to which the performers relate.   This relationship to the focal point determines the direction of the steps which will be taken.

When performers face the center of the circle, Ex. 19a, steps will be ▷ for circling CCW, and ◁ for circling CW.   Note that when pivoting (turning around the vertical axis) we speak of turning to the right or left.   When such turning evolves into circling, the description 'right' or 'left' is often confusing.   Think of the Square Dance caller: "Everybody circle right!", and off we go circling

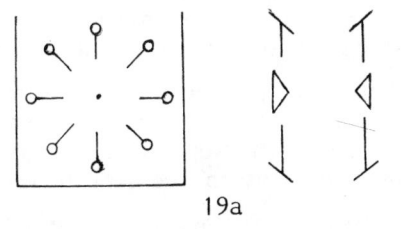

19a

Facing the center of the circle
(Facing the focal point)

CCW.   What he should say is: "Step to your right and circle left."   He calls the direction of the steps rather than the direction of the circling but from his words this fact is not apparent and confusion in determining direction of circling results.   Hence the preferred terms: CW for clockwise and CCW for counterclockwise (anticlockwise).

Reading Study No. 6

CIRCLING - RETRACING PATHS

As degree of circling is not indicated, the floor plans indicate one possible interpretation.

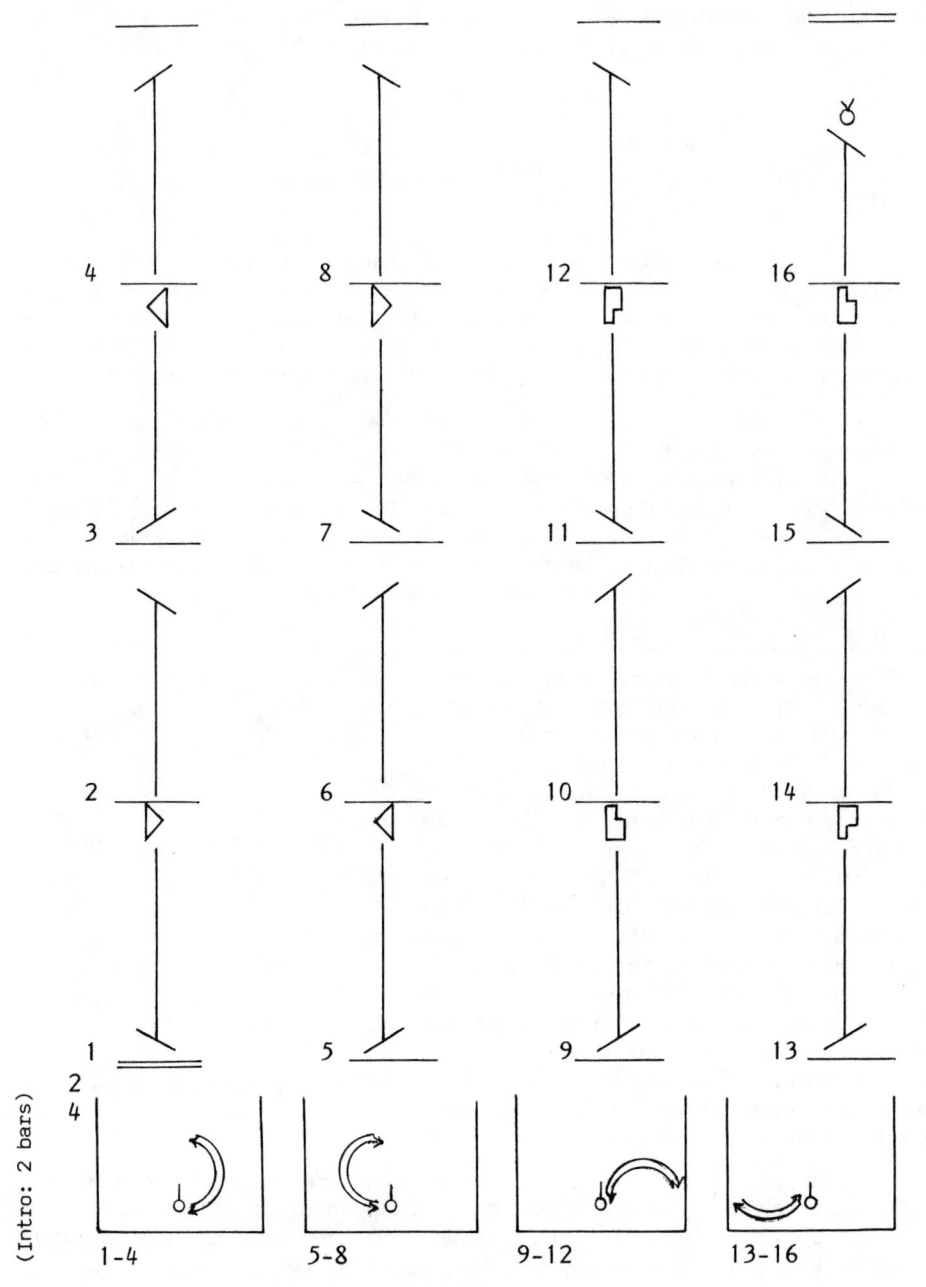

TURNING INCLUDED WHILE TRAVELLING

Turning around one's own center, the vertical axis, was introduced briefly on page 22. Turning has the function of changing the direction faced so that one can progress into another direction on a straight or circular path. But while travelling, there can be the enjoyment of a sudden whip around, a quick turn which does not impede progress but adds to the enjoyment of being in action, of being 'on the go'.

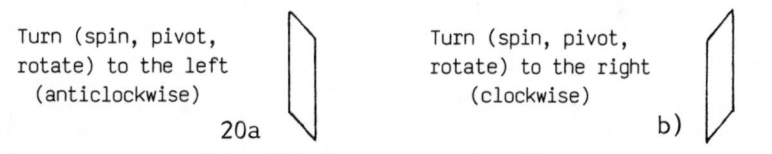

Turn (spin, pivot, rotate) to the left (anticlockwise)   20a

Turn (spin, pivot, rotate) to the right (clockwise)   b)

An empty turn sign means that the amount of turn is left open to the performer. At times it is welcome to be able to choose a slight degree of turn, at other times a greater degree, even several turns. The amount of turn will depend to some extent on how much time is available; multiple turns take longer even when swiftly executed.

For the reading study on the next page, specific floor plans have been provided as suggested interpretations of the movement material. For a specific performance much information needs still to be spelled out — degree of turning, degree of circling, whether circling spirals in or out, distance covered, and so on. Many of these questions are answered by the floor plans, since to achieve the stated floor design certain degrees of turning and distances covered must occur.

Turning Indicated on Floor Plans

In the next Reading Study, Part D includes a turn at the start of the circular path and another about half way through. Such turns occur on the line of the path, the intention being that the turn is an embellishment, not a change of direction for the path. As they do not affect the line of travelling such turns should not, strictly speaking, be shown on the floor plan. However, a tiny loop attached to the path line indicates clearly three factors we need to know: the existence of the turn, the direction of the turn, and where it occurs on the path. This device is therefore used as a convention for practical purposes, as illustrated in Ex. 20c and 20d.

20c   or

A turn to the right near the start

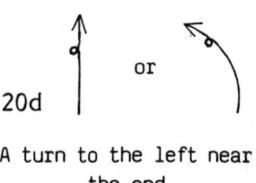

20d   or

A turn to the left near the end

In reading Study No. 7, first sense what the material expresses in movement terms, then work out how to organize it in the room. As soon as possible dance it. Remember you are free to take as many steps as you wish, and may walk, run, galop or skip.

Variations in Travelling

Reading Study No. 7

TRAVELLING WITH TURNING

Instructions for this study are given on the previous page. Note inclusion in meas. 29 and 32 of 'an action' combined with a slight accent, shown by the sign: ◇ . Learn the study phrase by phrase. The music is in the form of a fugue.

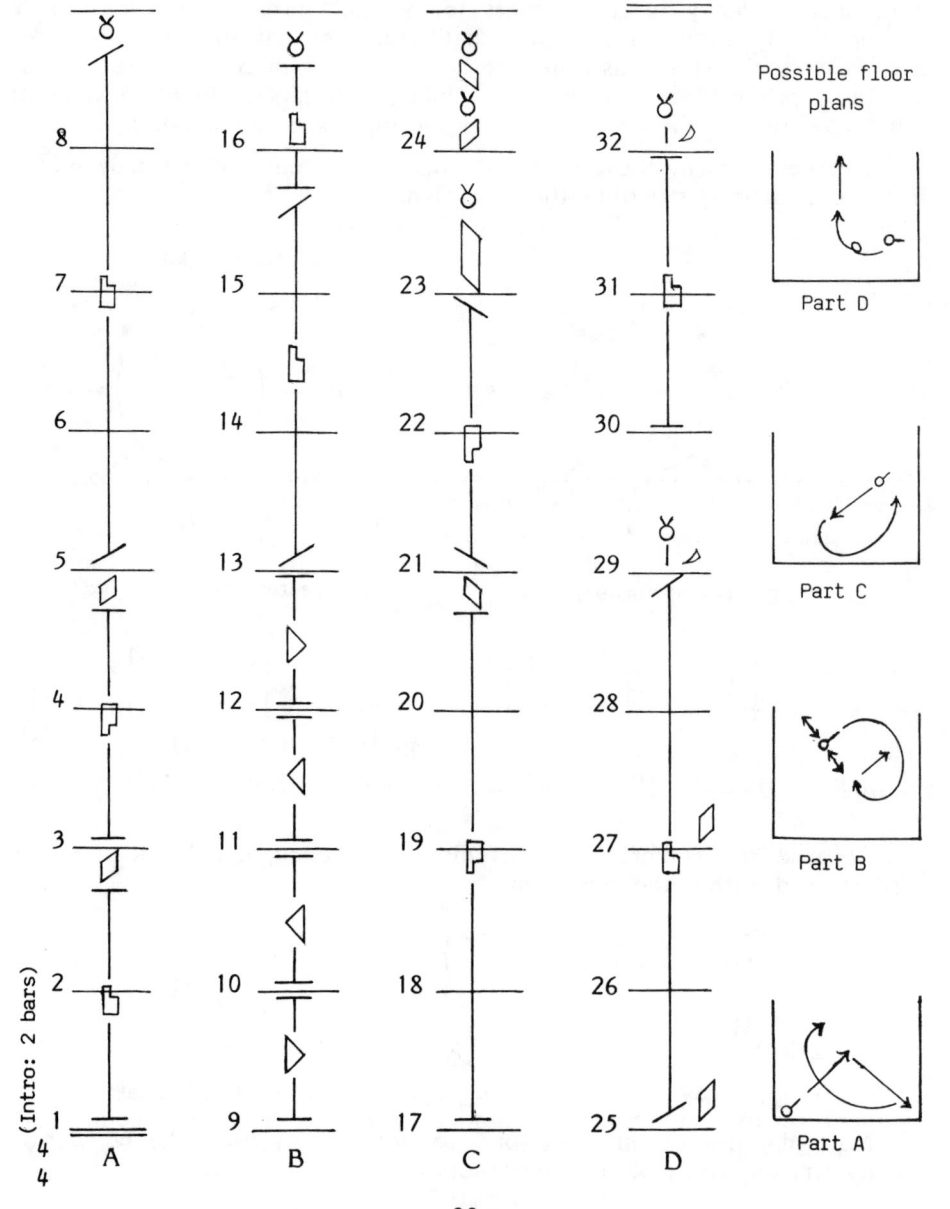

Possible floor plans

Part D

Part C

Part B

Part A

Degree of Turning

A turning action may be slight, the purpose being to face into an- other direction, i.e. to change front. In the case of 'about face', the new front is implicit in the instruction, a half turn being the means of achieving it. However, one may also be aware of having made a half turn. In a full turn the action of turning is in itself important. Re- turning to the previous front provides a sense of accomplishment. It is interesting to note that when degree of turning is left open there is a natural tendency for performers to use full turns, since returning to the previously established front (usually the front of the room) provides a satisfying, perhaps reassuring, sense of clarity in orientation. Multi- ple turns provide an opportunity to indulge in this form of movement; the faster the turning, the more the turning sensation is heightened.

Degree of turn, the amount of change of front, is shown by place- ment of a black pin within the turn sign.

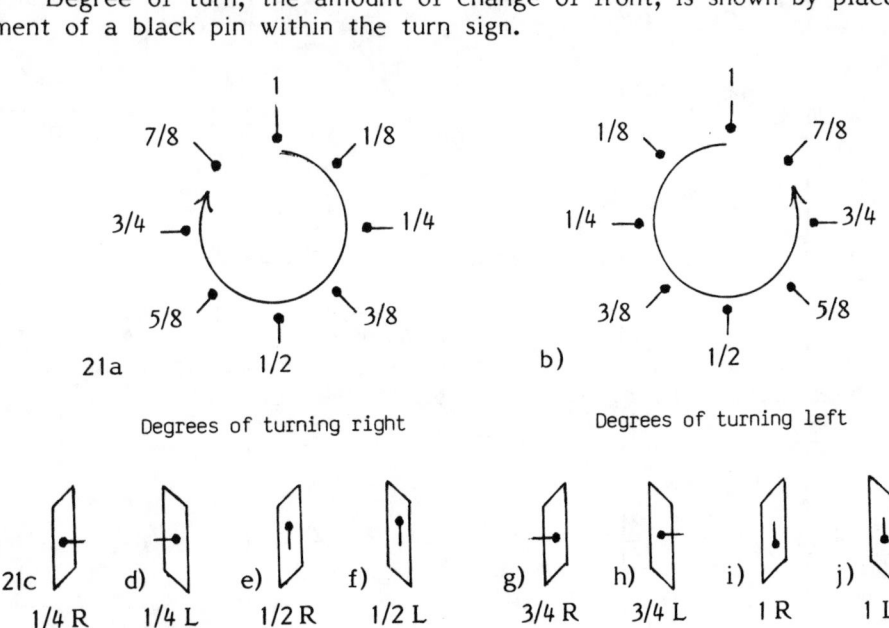

21a Degrees of turning right

b) Degrees of turning left

21c d) 1/4 R 1/4 L
e) f) 1/2 R 1/2 L
g) h) 3/4 R 3/4 L
i) j) 1 R 1 L

Because the numeral 1 is not distinctive enough, a black pin: ♦ is used instead within the turn sign.

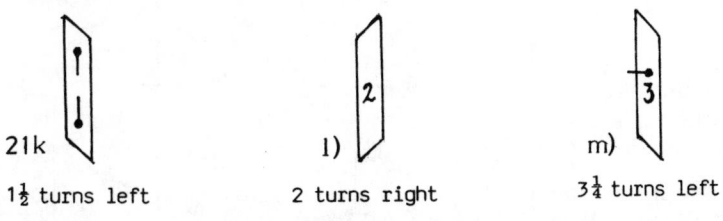

21k 1½ turns left

l) 2 turns right

m) 3¼ turns left

Note the use of numbers for two or more turns. The number is usually written first, before the fraction.

Degree of Circling

Degrees of circling are shown in the same way as for turning. In walking one full circle there is a complete change of front, as in one full pivot turn. In performing a half circle, one ends facing the opposite direction, just as with half a turn, and so on. The black pin is placed in the center of the path sign, the vertical line being broken so that the pin shows clearly and can easily be read.

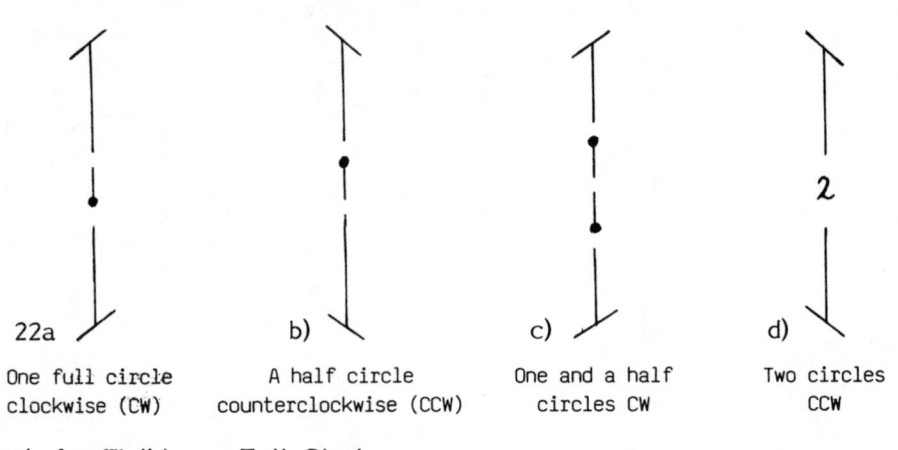

22a	b)	c)	d)
One full circle clockwise (CW)	A half circle counterclockwise (CCW)	One and a half circles CW	Two circles CCW

Path for Walking a Full Circle

Walking a true full circle with forward steps is not as familiar an action as one might suppose. There is a natural tendency to anticipate the circular path by turning and thus starting the actual circle from a different front. Starting as in Ex. 22e, facing front, the performer will usually make a quarter turn to the right so that the actual circling to the right starts facing the right side of the room. Only three-quarters of a circle is then performed to end facing front again. The performer often modifies the path so that it ends on the spot where it started. Note the different drawings of plan 22f and 22g. In 22f a true three-quarter circle is performed; in 22g an adjustment has been made to end up where one started. Ex. 22h is the correct path for a complete circle clockwise with forward steps for which no preparatory turn has been made.

Such preparatory turns result from the mistaken idea that to walk a circle one should start at the center of the circle; it starts of course on the 'rim', the periphery.

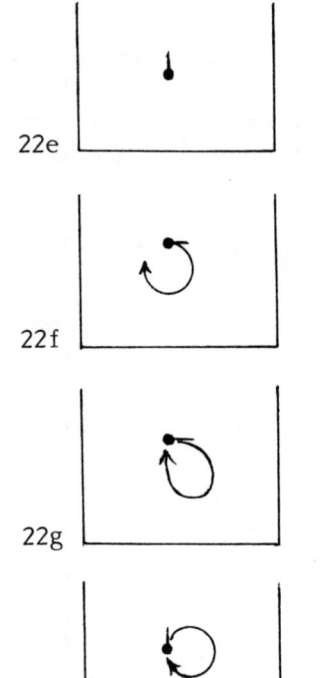

22e

22f

22g

22h

Reading Practice

DEGREE OF TURNING, CIRCLING

On the plans for A and B the wedge: △ shows where the dancer is facing at the end of a phrase.

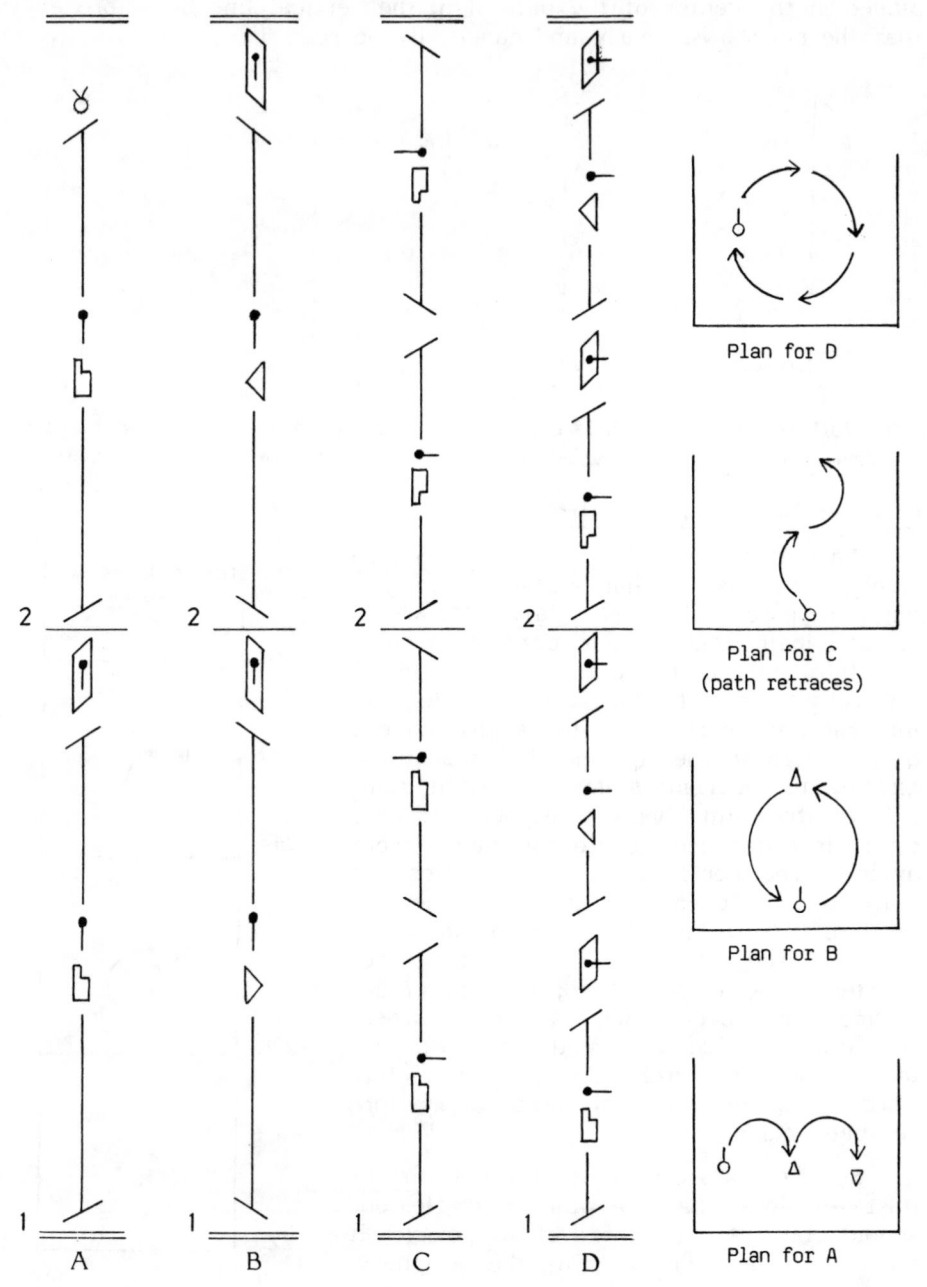

Plan for D

Plan for C
(path retraces)

Plan for B

Plan for A

A   B   C   D

ENDLESS CIRCLING; SPIRAL PATHS

A straight path in a room or on stage must inevitably come to an end as the wall (or a wing) is reached. A change of direction, a turn, must occur for another straight path to be achieved. But a circular path may continue forever with no change of direction needed, no turning to face another direction. Think of the poor slave attached to a millstone, endlessly tramping the circular path. Turns and a resulting change in step direction enrich circular travelling when the progression is constantly on the same path.

The monotony of continuing on the same size circular path in a solo dance can be avoided through enlarging or diminishing the size of the circle. To enlarge the circle the performer veers away from the center of the circle (the focal point) until the limits of the available space have been reached. To diminish the size of the circle the performer approaches the center of the circle. When this center is reached, circling has ceased: it has become turning on the spot.

Motivation for Spiralling

Spiralling in to the center may result from a gradual desire to end the aimless circular travelling and find a central spot to call 'home'. It could come from a petering out of movement motivation, hence also of the path. Diminishing energy may produce a smaller and smaller circle until one arrives at the center. Conversely, an outward spiral may result from setting off on an exploratory trip in which the adventuresome spirit gradually grows with confidence and the circles widen as more territory is encircled. Group spiralling makes the design more visible and has its own expression; for example, spiralling in increases the spatial tension.

For the solo figure a typical example of spiralling in occurs when a performer starts at the outer edges of the room and ends in the center, covering as much ground as possible on the way. Conversely, spiralling out may occur when rotation at the center starts to expand spatially, becomes more and more extended in space and ends with the performer exiting as though to explore larger realms beyond the stage. For groups such paths occur in line formations, as in some Farandoles.

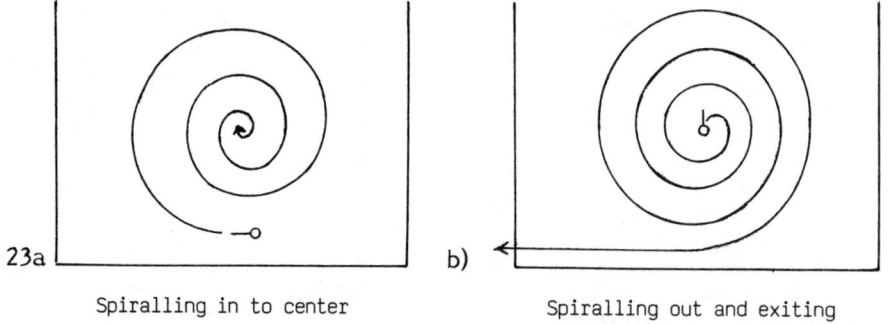

23a   b)

Spiralling in to center   Spiralling out and exiting

37

Indication of Spiralling

Circling occurs around a center, like the hub or axle of a wheel, Ex. 24a, b). This center is the focal point of the circle. As you spiral in you approach this focal point and gradually your distance from the center diminishes. Conversely, as you spiral outward you move away from the center, and the circling becomes larger. Note the shapes below:

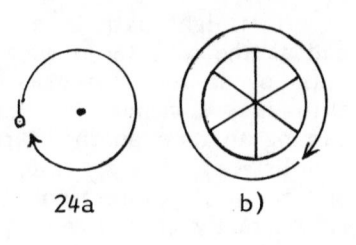

24a   b)

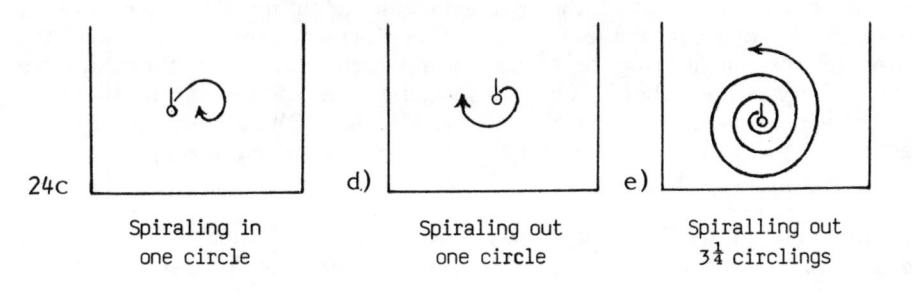

24c   d)   e)

Spiraling in   Spiraling out   Spiralling out
one circle   one circle $3\frac{1}{4}$ circlings

The following signs are needed to indicate spiralling:

The sign for   The sign for   The sign for   Toward the   Away from
focal point   approaching   going away   focal point   focal point

Amount of Circling for Spiral Paths

As can be seen in Ex. 24c and 24d a single circle does not give a clear impression of spiralling; one just ends farther away from where one started. Thus most spiral paths consist of two or more circlings which are indicated by appropriate numerals. Additional fractions, 1/4, 1/2, etc. are shown with the appropriate black pin.

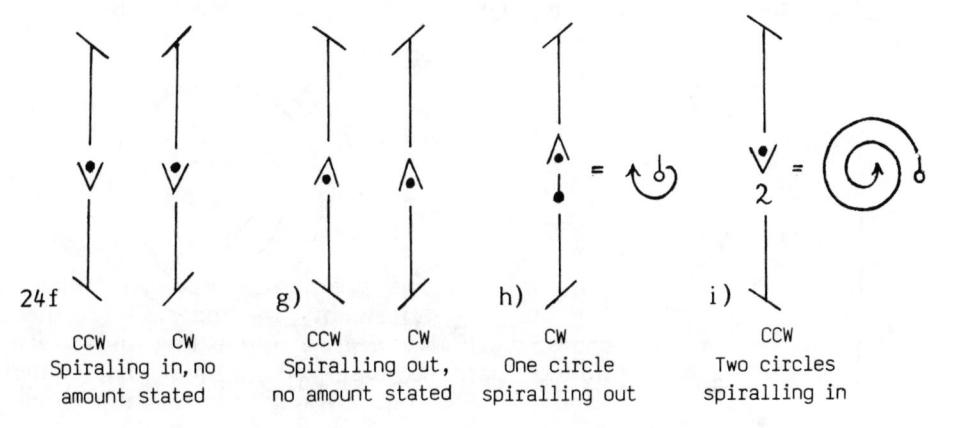

24f   g)   h)   i)

   CCW   CW   CCW   CW   CW   CCW
Spiraling in, no   Spiralling out,   One circle   Two circles
amount stated   no amount stated   spiralling out   spiralling in

SPIRAL PATHS

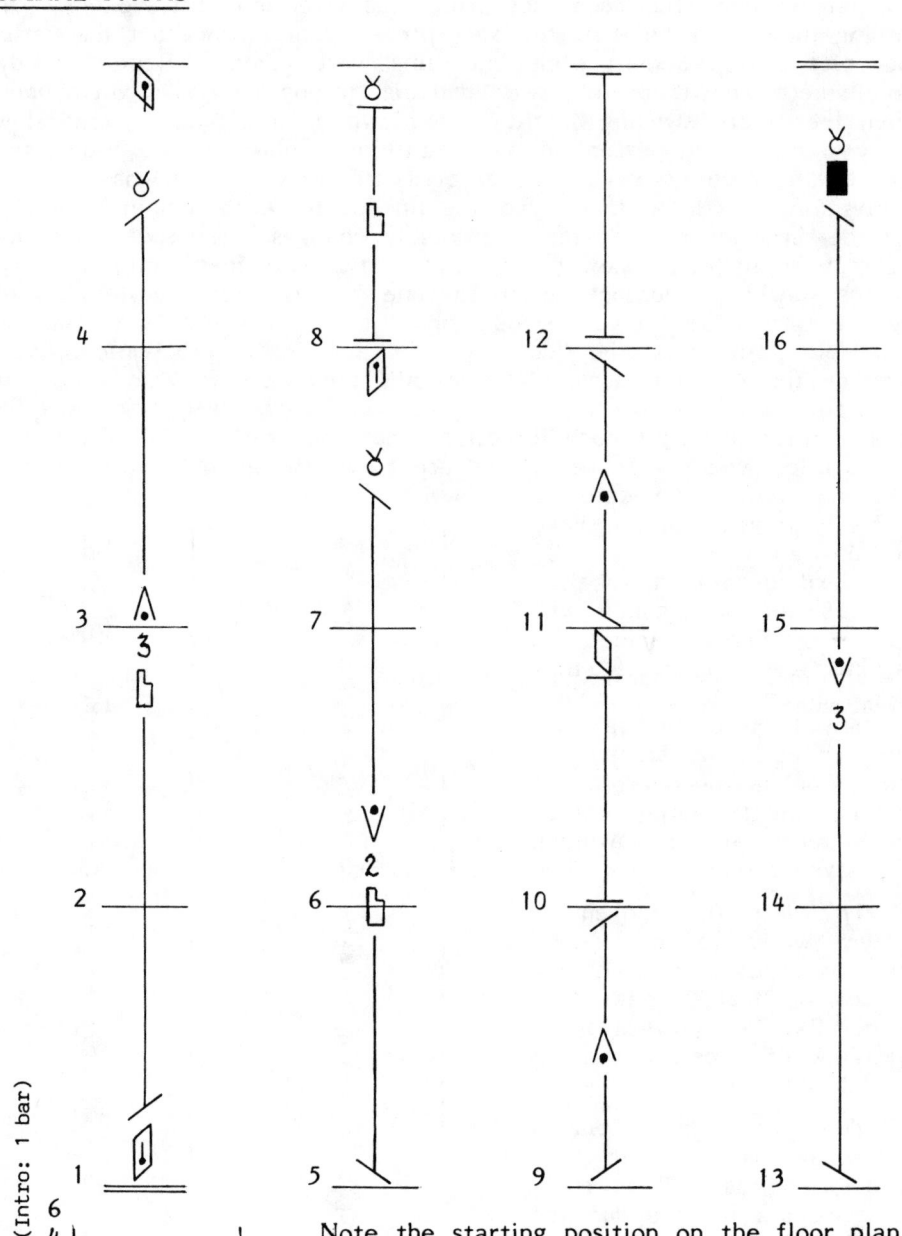

(Intro: 1 bar)

6
4

Note the starting position on the floor plan.
Try out the movements for meas. 9-12, then
choose your own degree of circling and direction of path so that you allow room for the
large outward spiral which concludes the study.

CONTINUOUS REVOLVING WHILE TRAVELLING

A turn which occurs while travelling may be just a sudden spin, a whipping around which does not affect the direction of travelling. Or turning may be more sustained and spread evenly throughout the path. Examples of swift spins while travelling were given in Reading Study No. 7; here we will explore slow, drifting turning such as might happen when leaves are swirling as they are blown along a path, or the slow graceful revolving performed by a fashion model as she progresses through the room, showing off her dress at every angle. Whatever the motivation, it will be found that the line of the path remains constant but the direction of the steps continually changes. The speed of turning may be faster or slower. To master this combined form, first try turning slowly on the spot, let us say one full turn with 15 steps, making the turning action very smooth and even. Then with 15 steps walk a straight path across the floor, observing the line of progression. Now combine these two actions. Whereas all steps were forward when you were not turning, now, to keep on the same path, each step must be in a slightly different body direction, changing gradually all the time. If you allow yourself to be carried around as though by a soft breeze, the steps will take care of

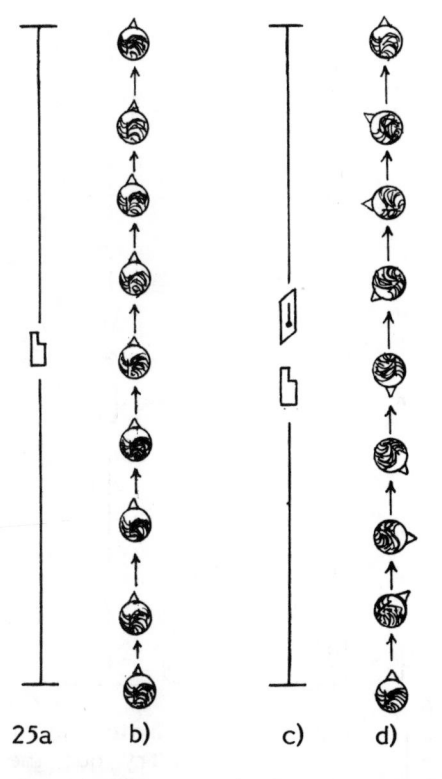

themselves; you will not have to think about each one. By the third or fourth practice the desired performance will be there. Try the same path varying the number of steps and the amount of turning. If many turns occur, say one turn for each two steps, then the action has become one of spinning and the enjoyment of the gradual, slower revolving will have gone.

To write this movement pattern we state the desired path, as in Ex. 25a which indicates a straight path forward. Ex. 25b shows a bird's eye view of a person walking on this path.

The turn sign is placed within the path sign to show that turning as well as travelling occurs for the duration of the path sign. Degree of turning is placed within the

25a   b)   c)   d)

turn sign, 25c. Ex. 25d illustrates a person gradually turning on this path. Direction for the path is always judged from the starting point.

Reading Study No. 9

REVOLVING WHILE TRAVELLING

Note whether the movement is one of revolving or circling and also the difference between measures 5 and 6 and measures 7 and 8.

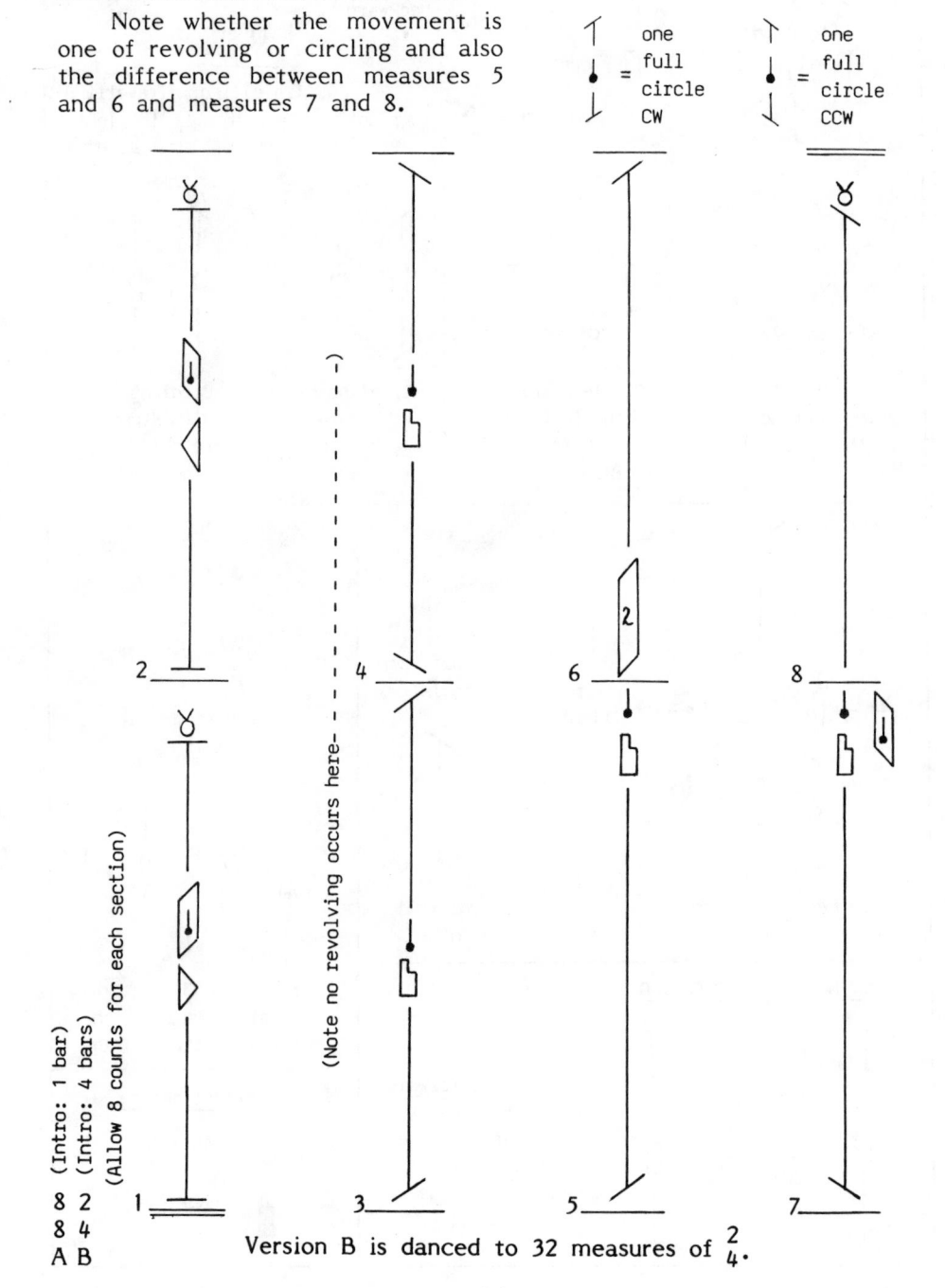

Version B is danced to 32 measures of $\frac{2}{4}$.

c

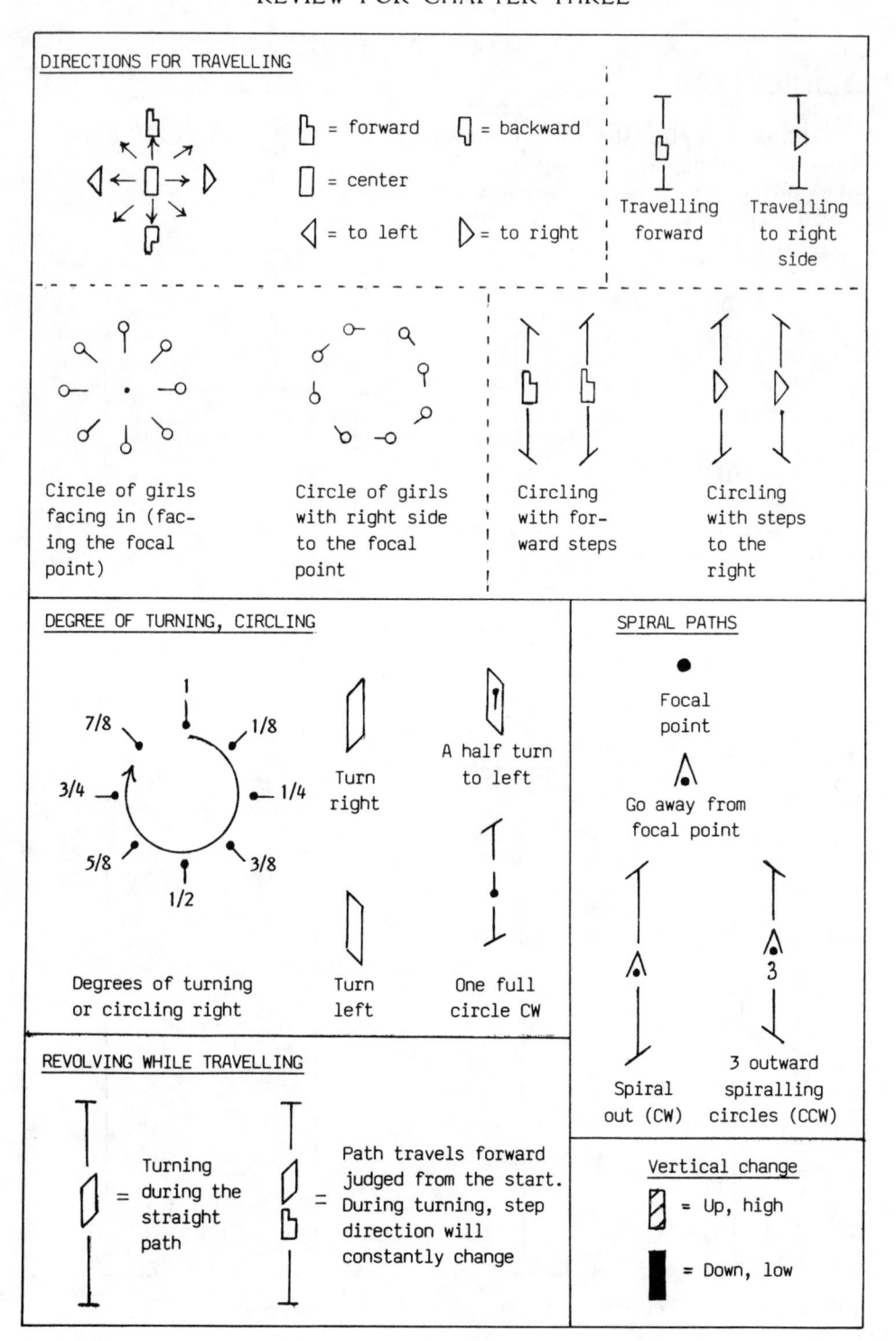

DIRECTIONS FOR TRAVELLING

⌐ = forward   ⌐ = backward

☐ = center

◁ = to left   ▷ = to right

Travelling forward

Travelling to right side

Circle of girls facing in (facing the focal point)

Circle of girls with right side to the focal point

Circling with forward steps

Circling with steps to the right

DEGREE OF TURNING, CIRCLING

7/8   1   1/8

3/4   1/4

5/8   3/8

1/2

Degrees of turning or circling right

Turn right

Turn left

A half turn to left

One full circle CW

SPIRAL PATHS

Focal point

Go away from focal point

Spiral out (CW)

3

3 outward spiralling circles (CCW)

REVOLVING WHILE TRAVELLING

= Turning during the straight path

= Path travels forward judged from the start. During turning, step direction will constantly change

Vertical change

= Up, high

= Down, low

Chapter Four
ABSENCE OF SUPPORT: JUMPING (ELEVATION)

What is jumping? Why do we spring into the air? We are concerned here with intentional absence of support, neither a momentary absence when someone trips and then falls nor that glorious (though at first strange) total absence of support experienced by astronauts in a weightless state. Think what tumblers and dancers could do with that state! How many somersaults? How many cabrioles or entrechats? We must, however, come down to earth, as every spring into the air must, and deal with everyday realities.

Nature provides us with many examples of jumping actions. Birds 'hop' from twig to twig, frogs 'leap' into the air, so do fleas. The Mexican jumping bean may not have been observed by everyone, but jumping fish are familiar, as are grasshoppers.

Children jump around from mere high spirits. They enjoy bouncing like a ball: it is an automatic reflex, a natural way of expending surplus energy. The desire to spring into the air must, therefore, be caused by or coupled with a rise in energy. He who has no energy cannot jump. The reason for excess energy may vary. It may be joy, it may be anger, rage, or even desperation. In the case of desperation the performer flings himself in the air, fighting Fate. Let us look at some everyday examples of 'springing' actions related to high energy level. An aggressive person will literally (or figuratively) 'leap' at a person or at ideas. An activity which is going 'by leaps and bounds' indicates progression with extraordinary rapidity — again high energy level. If someone is told to 'hop to it' he is expected to move with alacrity. The robber who 'skips' out on his mates uses speed and energy. Excessive energy, as in anger, may cause a person to perform stamping jumps on both feet — an expression of extreme frustration.

26a   b)   c)

Anger   Thief on the run   "Stop thief!"

There may be practical reasons for jumping, such as clearing a big puddle or avoiding a falling brick. Our concern with this kind of movement is with man's desire to overcome gravity. Rising into the air is an extension of an upward movement, a movement away from gravity. To get higher we spring into the air, enjoying a moment of freedom, of exhilaration, of flight, an escape from our earthbound lives. This desire to develop the body to surmount and defy the force of gravity, together with the inborn pleasure of jumping and the different forms it can take, led to tumbling and the stylized exercises featured in gymnastics and acrobatics. In these forms jumping is combined with revolutions to produce a great variety of aerial 'tricks', the range of which is augmented by use of trampolines, high bars, etc.

AERIAL STEPS

A word about terminology for this basic form of movement may be helpful here. A general term is needed as well as specific terms for the five basic forms of leaving the ground and returning to it, i.e. one foot to the same foot; one foot to the other; two feet to two; one foot to two; and two feet to one. These will be discussed specifically later on. In the meantime we need to be able to be general, to use terms which do not identify a particular form.

The general term most widely used is 'jumping'. But a 'jump' is the name given for springing from two feet and landing on two feet; to avoid confusion care must be taken to distinguish between "jumping" and "a jump". Better general terms are 'springing', a series of 'springs', or 'steps of elevation' and 'aerial steps'. Some of these terms are less familiar than others; in this book they are used interchangeably so that readers may become acquainted with them all.

Use of Aerial Steps in Dance

What purpose or effect does jumping have in dance? Marking the rhythm through springing is common in many kinds of folk dances. In many instances the music invites a bouncing reaction. The addition of elevation, of steps going into the air, heightens everything beyond the normal in theatrical dance, thus adding greatly to exaggeration and to stylization. Leaving the ground allows both legs to perform gestures at the same time, thus providing opportunity for interrelated actions of leg flexion, extension, spreading, closing and beating in different directional placements. All these possibilities can be further embellished by including turning.

26d

Rhythmic springs

e)

Aerial tricks

Absence of Support: Jumping (Elevation)

How are aerial steps used by choreographers? They may be for display, mere tours de force, or for movement design. There may be dramatic motivation, moments of ecstasy or despair. Elevation provides highlights, climaxes. The energy of surging emotions is well spent defying gravity, rising above our earthbound existence. Exuberance is well expressed through jumping.

26f

Spatial Expressiveness

Apart from the enjoyment it imparts of momentarily being suspended in the air, springing may have as its impetus a specific spatial idea.

27a   b)   c)

Ex. 27a is a spring away from the floor; 27b shows springing up to reach toward the ceiling or sky. In a warrier's dance of triumph over an enemy, these two might be combined as in 27c. These examples are concerned with vertical space. Ex. 27d below expresses freedom in use of lateral space while in the air, while 27e shows diving in the forward sagittal direction, an exciting moment for performer and observer alike.

27d   e)

Springs which mark the musical beat tend to be performed more or less on the spot; travelling, covering ground rapidly, can be achieved through leaps. In dance the various forms of springs become stylized to produce different effects; in athletics style is based on a necessary functional streamlined use of the body.

While the legs do most of the work in jumping off the feet, concentration should be on lifting the body mass, the center of weight.

Spatial Expressiveness (continued)

Some dancers think only of the feet in jumping, and not, as one well-known teacher used to say, of "lifting your bottom!" All parts of the body must coordinate to achieve lifting the center of weight.

Experiment with basic bouncing, rebound springing into the air with no thought of limb placement or body design. The basic sensation of such springing should be discovered and mastered; later the shape and style of movement can be developed without losing the basic dynamic force of jumping. Coordinated lifting gestures of arms and the free leg help to overcome gravity by providing needed momentum. In a jump from two feet both legs working together have greater strength, so the spring is likely to be higher. Timing and impetus are essential.

When we spring our energy may be directed to vertical travel, jumping as high as possible off the ground, or to propel us horizontally across the floor. The need to travel fast, to cover ground, automatically produces running. Ordinary walking easily merges into running when an increase in energy and speed occur. A slight lift off the ground occurs between each step. Competitors in a walking race are disqualified if at any moment both feet are off the ground at the same time. As a result the effort not to run produces a grotesque spectacle, an unnatural mode of walking. Running at a slow tempo develops easily into leaps.

Indication of Springing

Though acrobats spring from their hands and Russian folk dancers jump from their knees, and even from sitting, let us consider the ordinary forms based on springing from the feet.

Ex. 28a shows the symbol for any form of springing into the air. The three-part sign represents:
- (x) the support on the ground before the spring.
- (y) the moment in the air, legs off the ground.
- (z) the return to the ground.

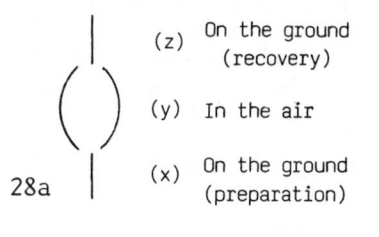

(z) On the ground (recovery)

(y) In the air

28a (x) On the ground (preparation)

Each of the movement examples which follow may be explored and performed in several different ways. If one possibility comes immediately to mind, perhaps a favorite form, then try another, and yet another. Different expressions will result from your choice, particularly if arms, body and head are allowed to take part, to add coloring to the form chosen for the legs without dominating it and becoming over-important.

We still have not begun to be specific as to which foot steps on which beat, what the legs do as you spring into the air, or on which foot you land. As with all these explorations, we go from the general to the specific. Find out the various possibilities, then focus on the specific form of your choice.

JUMPING COMBINED WITH TRAVELLING

Let us look at how springs can be combined with travelling:

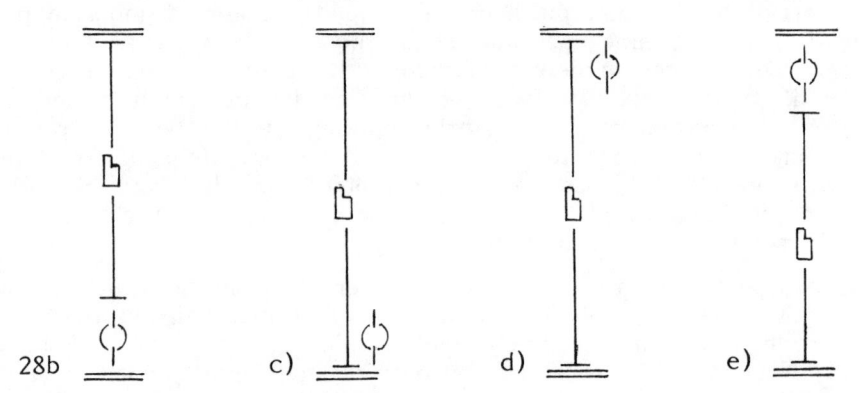

28b   c)   d)   e)

A spring can occur before starting to travel, giving the effect of an exclamation before a sentence, Ex. 28b. A spring can occur at the start of travelling, acting as a burst of energy, an impetus to send you on your way, Ex. 28c. In 28d the spring comes at the end of travelling, a burst of energy to stop, a conclusion. If the spring comes after the traveller has finished, as in 28e, it is like an afterthought.

A spring may occur in the middle of travelling, as in 28f. In 28g there are three springs. Placement of the sign for springing indicates when that action occurs.

Through trying out the different forms of jumping — one foot to the other, one foot to two, etc. — you can discover which lend themselves best to the start of travelling, which to terminating travelling and which to moving far across the floor.

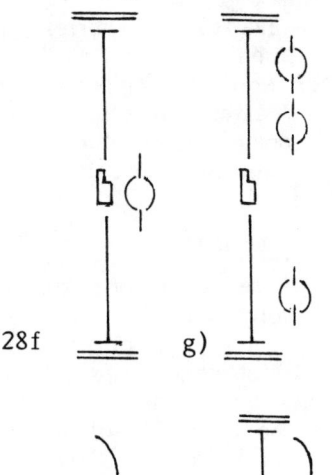

28f   g)

In the early stages of planning a movement sequence you may prefer to state that though jumping is to be included, just when or how often is to be left open. This idea is expressed by use of a vertical bow, the 'inclusion' bow, which has curved ends and a straight center, Ex. 28h. What is to be included in the main movement is written within the vertical line. Ex. 28i states that at some point jumping is to be included as you travel forward.

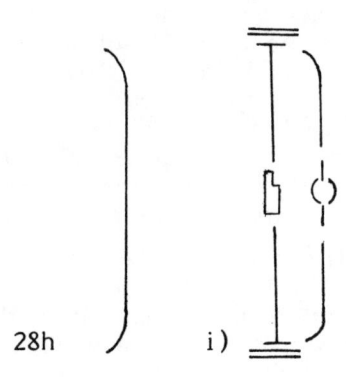

28h   i)

Size of Spring

When springs occur, what size will they be? How much time will be spent in the air, how much on the ground? Unless distance in travelling is involved, time spent in the air equates with the height of the spring. Differences in height markedly affect function and expression of aerial steps. Springs of short duration in the air may be little bounces of excitement or a gentle marking of the beat or rhythm. Small springs from foot to foot occur in running. In contrast, a high spring is needed to grasp an overhead object which is out of normal reach or to jump over an object without touching it. Such jumps obviously spend more time in the air.

When performed to an even beat, a series of springs can keep time and yet vary considerably in height. Lower springs will absorb the extra time by remaining on the ground, cushioning the landing. A higher series of springs will use a rebound pattern, the landing being an immediate take-off, as though from hot rocks. Between the two extremes of low and high springs is the comfortable resilient spring in which the same amount of time is spent in the air as on the ground.

Because the sign for a spring includes indication for being on the ground as well as in the air, it is possible to show the proportion of time spent on the ground and in the air. Thus the size of the spring, larger or smaller, can be indicated.

Ex. 29a shows a brief take-off and a longer time in the air, while 29b shows the reverse: more time spent on the ground before and after the spring itself which has only a short time in the air. Ex. 29c illustrates an ordinary 'healthy' size of spring, not especially high nor earthbound.

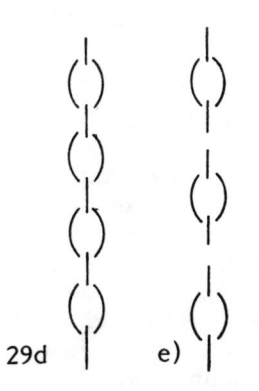

29a   b)   c)

Variation in height
of spring

Series of Springs

In a sequence one spring may follow immediately after another in a rebound pattern, or a new preparation may occur for each subsequent spring. Is the landing from one spring the take-off for the next, or is there a closing of the feet or a step in-between? Ex. 29d shows a series of rebound springs in which, like a bouncing ball, each landing is the take-off for the next spring. Compare this with 29e which indicates a new preparation for each spring, quite separate from the landing.

Try each of these examples varying use of one or two feet for take-off and landing; then experiment with combining these with travelling and turning.

29d   e)

Series of springs

48

Absence of Support: Jumping (Elevation)

Reading Study No. 10

AERIAL STEPS

In this study an inward spiralling path and later an outward spiral-ling have been given. Note how these are clearly represented on the floor plans. The sign: 凸 means face the audience.

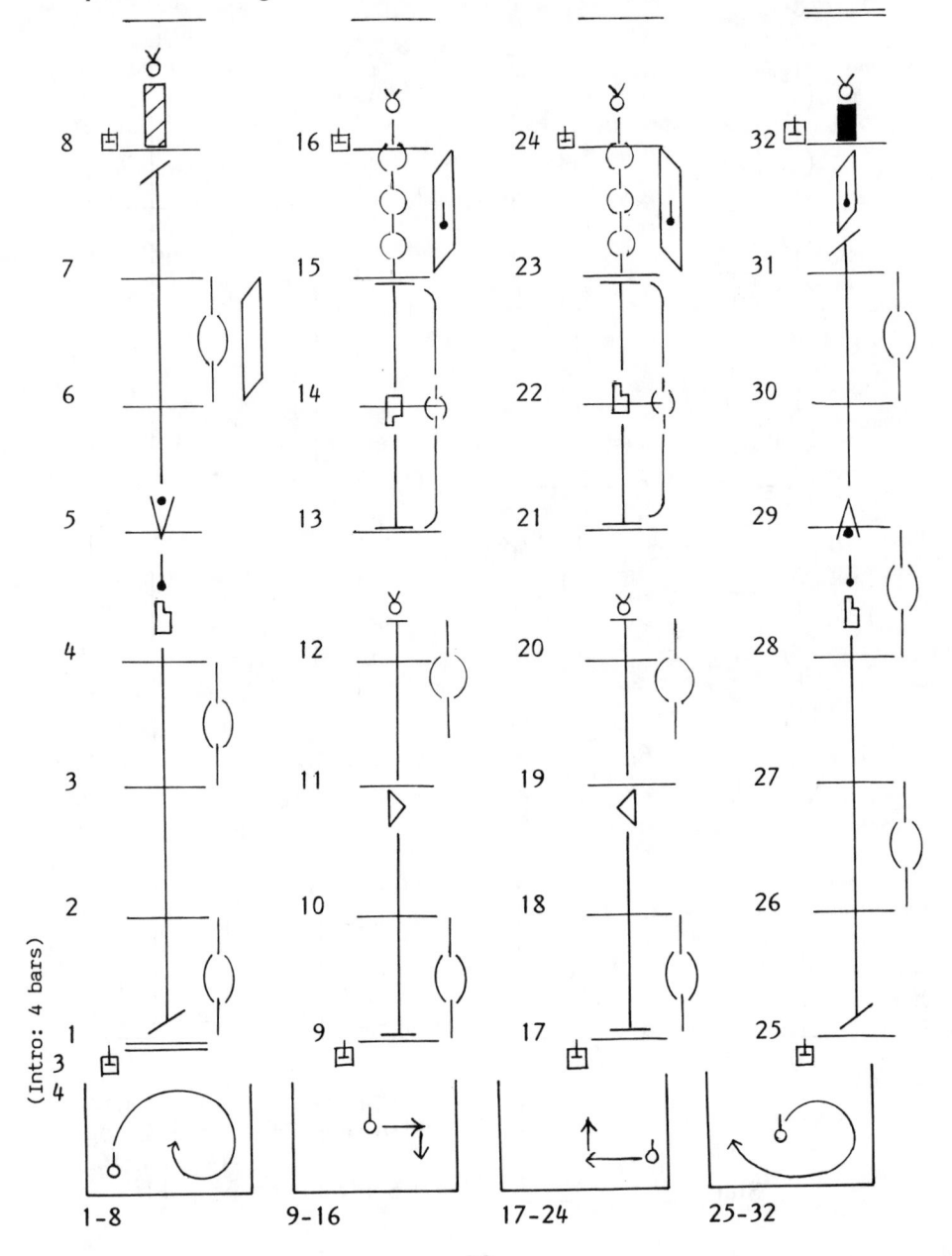

1-8   9-16   17-24   25-32

49

Reading Study No. 11

VARIATIONS IN SIZE OF SPRING

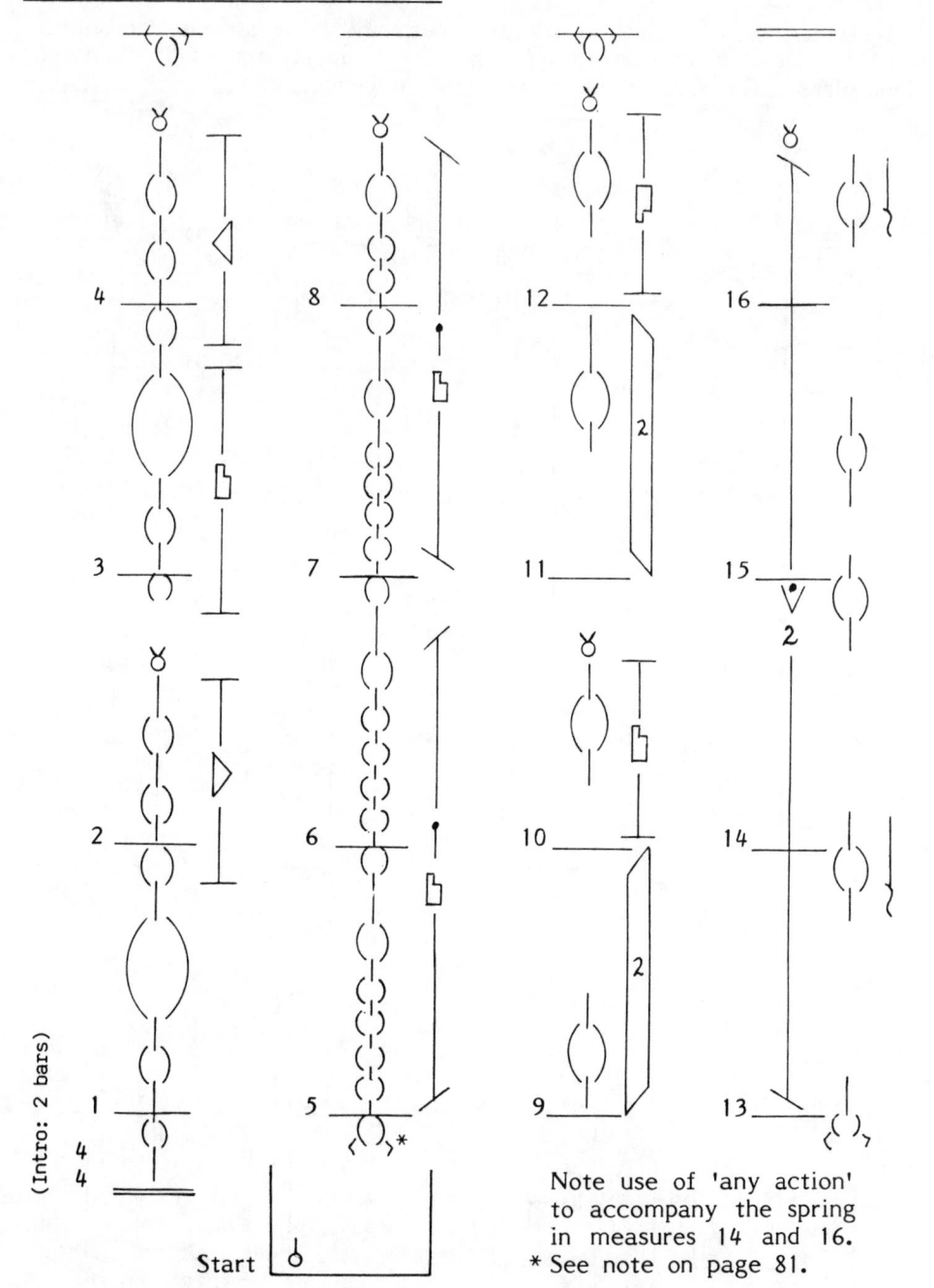

(Intro: 2 bars)

Start

Note use of 'any action'
to accompany the spring
in measures 14 and 16.
* See note on page 81.

Chapter Five
DIRECTION — DEFINITION OF SPACE

The cardinal directions of forward, backward, side right and side left, have already been introduced briefly to provide specific statements in relation to travelling. Though we grow up knowing the main directions, including up and down, for our purposes here we need to take a fresh look at the whole subject of direction, of the space around us. There is not just one way of looking at spatial directions, not just one way of experiencing them or of referring to them. Space is defined for us by the build of our bodies, by the buildings in which we live, and by the universe which we inhabit, the earth and the sky.

By nature we do not like to exist in a void. The astronauts illustrated this in their need for a 'floor', 'ceiling' and 'walls' to which to relate in their orbitting space. When performing in a field, a group is perfectly happy if it is dancing in a circle and the dancers can relate direction to that circle. But dancing alone, performers will usually choose a landmark, perhaps a tree or hill, as the point to which to relate. As a rule we move in the defined space of a room or a stage in which there is an established set of directions, Ex. 30a. For theatre in the round, reference points 30a are established for orientation.

In life, a baby becomes aware first of its own personal space, directions based on its own body — the fact that it has a front, a back, right and left sides, head and feet, even though it cannot identify them at that stage. Much later it begins to relate to the room around it.

30b

In daily life as well as in sport, gymnastics and dance we orient ourselves according to our personal directions, to gravity, to the room, and to focal points such as other people and objects. Each of these possibilities will be explored and clearly defined through appropriate terminology and signs.

51

In dealing with space there seem to be infinite points in space toward which we can move or through which we can pass. Such richness may seem overwhelming. The human eye is limited, however, in discerning minute differences in spatial placement, and performing subtle differences in directional placement is physically difficult. Other than with very small vibrating movements, slight displacements from an established point, it has been found that a 15° difference in arrival at a destinational point is the smallest degree with which we need be concerned. For our present movement exploration only two degrees are being considered: major changes of 45° and minor displacements.

DIRECTIONS - VARIETY IN EVERYDAY LIFE

Starting from the general and moving to the specific, let us consider what concepts concerning direction exist in daily life and how we relate to them.

East, west, north and south are familiar relative directions. But note that a location that is north to some people is south to others. The idea of being 'East of the Sun, West of the Moon' has poetry. 'Go west, young man!' has an open challenge. It speaks of freedom, the open road, the west stretching out,

31a

endlessly, as does the imagination. In movement many gestures and paths of the body as a whole have such a feeling toward space. A general, free sense of moving in space may be personally satisfying, but it is not practical for most purposes. For our daily living the establishment of locations is necessary. On earth a fixed point is defined through specific degrees of longitude and latitude. One may "head south" when driving and may take any road one fancies, but at some point, from practical necessity, one must find the destinational point of a town or village and orient oneself from there. Thus for travelling, east, west, etc. are general terms, relative to where one starts. A destination may, of course, subsequently be added.

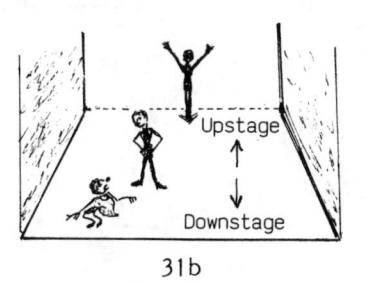

31b

Some cities are laid out with specific division into N, S, E and W, the dividing lines emanating from a designated point. In New York City, Fifth Avenue divides East and West. In that city there is no 'north' or 'south'; the general terms 'uptown' and 'downtown' are used, but with changing results. What is still marked as 'The Uptown Dispensary' is now far downtown. These terms are merely relative.

In the theatre 'upstage' and 'downstage' are also relative. One performer may be upstage of another and downstage of a third. Two dancers may both move downstage while one remains upstage in relation to the other. The terms 'upstage' and 'downstage' came from the raking (slanting) of stages toward the audience, designed to make performers located at the back of the stage more visible to the audience. Some European stages are still raked and dancers have to adjust to a different physical balance.

Upstage and downstage lead us to 'up' and 'down', the inescapable (on earth) pull of gravity. No doubt this needs no explanation, up being toward the sky or ceiling, down toward the ground or floor. Many objects, however, have an 'up' and 'down', as the expression "up-side-down" makes clear. This applies also to humans. Consider the child's delight on first seeing a man upside down, Ex. 31c.

31c

31d   e)   f)

Up and down lead us to 'front' and 'back'. Many objects such as houses and many types of furniture have a front and a back. Boats, cars and planes, indeed most (moving) objects are built with a definite front and back and hence a right and left side. On a boat the front is the bow (prow), the back is the stern, with starboard the right side and port the left. Boats and cars are designed to move forward, with backward motion used when necessary. Few objects, as indeed few creatures, move sideways. Certain crabs are an exception as is the sidewinder snake for which sideward and slightly forward is its natural direction of progression, Ex. 31g. Unnatural but splendid are the Lippizaner horses trained to walk sideways as a special gait in dressage, a skill required for the horse ballets of centuries ago which is still admired today.

31g

Sidewinder

Each person's own front, back, right and left may relate in different ways to the front, back, etc. of objects. An everyday situation may have its counterpart on stage in dance movements. The house we live in has a front and a back, etc. One may enter the front door walking sideways because of holding an awkward package, or even walk backwards if helping an infirm person through the door. The direction we are facing and the direction of our steps in relation to an object or person may encompass a wide range of possible combinations. In dance, movements are performed for other than practical reasons, but the basic facts of direction remain.

Directions - Variety in Everyday Life (continued)

Consider the comedian sitting on a horse facing backward while the horse trots forward down a one way street, going in the wrong direction. The clown here is being carried backward but is facing forward in relation to the street direction.

31h

31i

The words 'right' and 'left' provide a slight problem since they refer both to the right and left sides of the body and also to the right and left directions in space. The right foot may step to the left side of the center line of the body and the left arm may move across to the right side of the body. Thus we must be clear as to whether the words 'right' and 'left' refer to a direction or to one or other side of the body.

These are some references to direction met in daily living. Many similar usages arise in all kinds of movement studies. Directional descriptions may refer to destinations, to points or situations in space, or they may refer to motion, the 'going' of movement. We have already discussed the turning directions, clockwise and counterclockwise; these are relative directions in the same sense that 'east' and 'west' are. Circling is also relative; no specific path can be undertaken until the direction of travelling is known as well as the degree of circling.

THE SPHERE WITHIN WHICH WE MOVE

When moving around our center without changing location (known as 'axial' movement), we find that we are in the center of a sphere. It is our 'reach' space, the zone within which our arms and legs can move, flexing, extending, and describing large sweeping circles. The torso can also incline, twist and circle within this sphere.

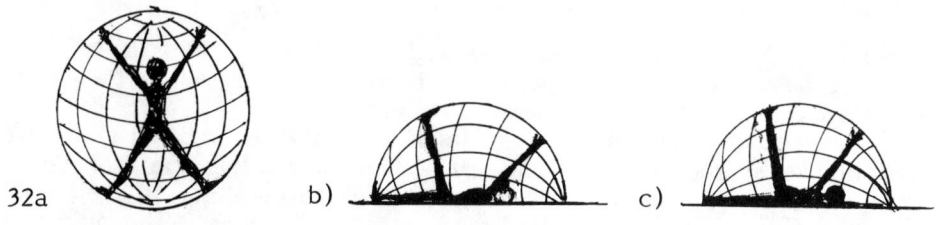

32a   b)   c)

Ex. 32a illustrates this sphere surrounding a performer. When we are lying on the ground, this sphere (called the kinesphere) is cut in half. When lying on the back, 32b, only the front half of the kinesphere is available. The reverse is true when we lie on the front. Lying on the right side, 32c, gives the left half sphere for movement, and so on. When we travel this sphere moves with us. It is our own individual area, our 'personal space' which we share only with friends.

Explore the range of movement possible within this sphere, for the arms, legs, and torso, and for combined arm and torso, and leg and torso movements, trying all the possibilities without changing location. There is 'near' space, the area close to your center. There is 'far' space out at the periphery of the kinesphere, and, of course, the area between these two. To explore near space the limbs must bend and probably also rotate; to explore far space they must extend, and this extension, this reaching out, may involve torso inclusion. Several forms of body inclusion are possible, but none should lead to travelling. Axial movements have their own statement to make; this may be augmented by travelling, but in many cases travelling may diminish the statement.

Experiment with lying on the ground, with changing from standing to lying and to standing again. Imagine the sphere as a great balloon filled with air and you, like the wind blowing leaves before it, moving that air, causing dust particles to rise, to float, to swirl and to whirl. Another image is to think of this space as a volume of water in which you are fully immersed. Every part of the area within the kinesphere can be 'felt' as you move through the 'water'.

SPECIFIC DIRECTIONS

There are many ways in which movement can be described; direction is so much part of life in general that it can't escape being an important part of dance as well. The daily instructions 'get up', 'back up', 'put it to one side', 'lay it down', 'keep to the left', and so on have their counterpart in dance. Different forms of movement and different styles of dance relate in different ways to space, to direction. In one dance, within one movement phrase, direction may be viewed from one point of view and then from another. We relate to gravity, to our own body directions, and, as mentioned before, to the fixed directions provided by the room, the stage or performing area.

Any Direction

Before analysing specific directions and how we relate to them and what they in themselves express, let us consider the first, broadest statement regarding direction, i.e. any direction. This is indicated by a rectangle, the basic shape for direction, combined with the sign for ad lib.: ⌒ i.e. 'any', thus expressing 'any direction', Ex. 33.

33

Any direction

How is 'any direction' used in movement? In travelling the absence of a directional indication meant that choice of direction was open, any direction was allowed. In springing, the legs will have made some use of direction without any being specified. The sign is needed when a directional action is to accompany other actions.

55

The Dimensional Cross

We live in a three-dimensional world, and are ourselves built in three dimensions. These dimensions - the vertical, lateral and sagittal - meet at a center point, and extend in two directions: up-down, right-left, and forward-backward, Ex. 34a.

The symbols for the six dimensional directions are as follows:

34b Vertical line   c) Center   d) Up   e) Down

34a   Up   Left   Forward   Backward   Right   Down

Ex. 34b represents the vertical line. A dot inside, 34c, shows the center point. Up is indicated by stripes, 34d; down by the symbol being shaded black, 34e.

The forward, backward and sideward signs, as was explained earlier, are indicated by modifying the shape of Ex. 34b, the basic sign for direction. Thus the signs become indicators pointing to the appropriate direction, Ex. 34f. Level for the horizontal directions in the dimensional cross is shown by the addition of a dot.

34f

Sagittal and lateral directions

A blank direction symbol, for example ⌐ , means a movement forward in the sagittal plane with no level stated. Level is left open to give the performer freedom of choice, Ex. 34g. By adding level we provide a more precise statement of the desired direction. Ex. 34h shows gestures slanting upward, forward high; 34i illustrates a horizontal gesture, forward middle, parallel with the floor. Ex. 34j shows slanting downward, forward low.

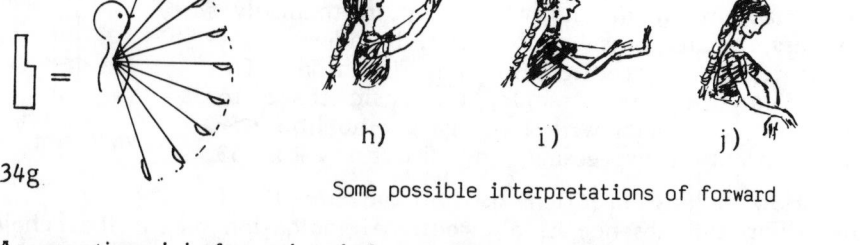

34g   h)   i)   j)

Some possible interpretations of forward

As mentioned before, level for a direction is indicated by shading the basic shape. By adding the appropriate shading we show level for all twenty-seven of the main directions (see page 68).

We are pleased to present you with a review copy of our new book:

Title: **YOUR MOVE**
        A New Approach to the
        Study of Movement and
        Dance

ISBN: **Hardcover: 0-677-06350-4**
        Softcover: 0-677-06365-2

Author/Editor: **Ann Hutchinson Guest**

Price: **Hardcover: $39.50**
        Softcover: $24.95

Please send two copies of your review to the Marketing Department of GORDON AND BREACH at the address below. Thank you for your interest in our publications.

Gordon and Breach, Science Publishers, Inc.
One Park Avenue, New York, NY 10016

MEMO

Date: 11-23-83

To: Connie Woodford   From: Jon Dahl

Re: <u>Your Move</u>

Enclosed is softcover
version, plus exercise sheets
which are shrink-wrapped
in with each copy. Cassette
tapes now being prepared.
Your order will presumably
be for hardcover, I believe.
Let me know.

Jon

The Areas of Direction

In going from the general to the specific, let us explore the areas which lie around the main directions. A gesture forward may be anywhere in the area directly in front of the body. Backward gestures occur behind the body. The sideward areas lie at the right and left sides of the body. Ex. 35a is a bird's-eye view of these areas.

Experiment with gestures which move in these areas, not aiming for a clear destinational line, but for an awareness of how gestures which take place in the forward area differ in expression from those which use the side or back areas. Also to be explored are the upward, overhead area and the downward area, as illustrated in 35b.

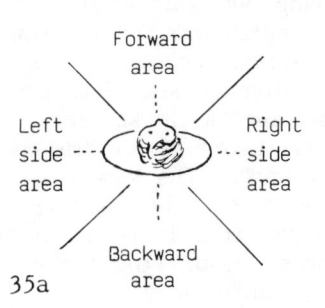

35a

The horizontal areas

As an aid in exploring all these areas of direction, imagine yourself to be in the dark in a strange room. You tentatively extend your arms, you reach out with your foot to find out what is there. What is at your right? At your left? Behind you? Is there an obstacle? Is there space in which you can move? Gradually all areas are tested and found to be free.

You can explore these directions simply for the enjoyment of moving in all these areas, or to produce air designs in each area in turn. A scarf or ribbon as a visual aid in seeing movement within these areas can increase the enjoyment of discovering the full range in each.

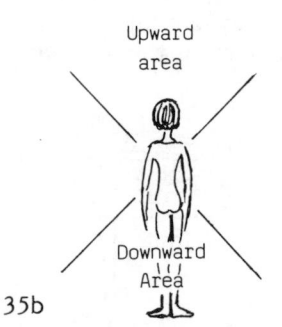

35b

The vertical areas

Exploration of High Level (Upward) Area

Upward movements may be actions in the process of rising, or actions in which the body as a whole - support, torso and limbs - has arrived up. Destinational gestures in the high area slant up. Movements upward may express great longing, joy, ecstasy, perhaps praying, reaching for the unattainable. Up is the direction of pride. Up is away from the fetters of gravity. Heaven is above, not below, and upward gestures suggest lofty thoughts, communication with higher beings, spiritual ideas. In all directional actions, use of the head, where you are looking, may strongly change the expression.

36

Movement in the upward area

Looking up or looking down while gesturing upward affects the meaning.

Exploration of Low Level (Downward) Area

Downward is the direction of gravity, the direction of repose, of rest. It is also the direction of despair, of sorrow, of humility; we lower ourselves as we bow, we hang our head in shame. It is the direction of earthiness, or relating to the earth in a practical or expressive way. It is the direction of stability, produced by downward pressure as in karate. It is the direction of assurance, as in "He has his feet on the

37

Movement in
the downward area

ground". The expression of downward can be achieved through bending the torso only slightly; it need not be lowered completely. With torso movements it is often not the directional line achieved which is expressive, but the movement, the motion the torso makes toward a direction or level.

Exploration of Middle Level (Horizontal) Area

Horizontal gestures suggest reality. They relate to the plane of the earth, the distant horizon, the calm surface of untroubled waters.

38a   b)

Movement in the horizontal area

For gestures of the limbs, middle, horizontal movements are parallel with the floor (or nearly so). Gestures may be circular or may flex and extend toward or away from the torso on a horizontal plane. A horizontal tilt of the torso avoids a downward expression by the focus of the face, by looking forward as in Ex. 38b. Horizontal placement of the body may suggest suspension, as in floating on water. Indeed arm gestures may be reminiscent of those used in breaststroke.

Exploration of the Forward Area

The two areas in the sagittal plane, that is, the forward and backward areas, provide very different movement possibilities. The build of the body favors forward movements, particularly for travelling. What range is there for gestures in the forward area, what is their expressiveness? What design or shape can they take? Has the movement a feeling of motion or destination? Is there movement within that area? Is it near the body or extending out? Is it arriving at one of many

39

Movement in the
forward area

possible forward points? Is it a one-sided movement? Is it an isolated gesture, of an arm perhaps, or is the arm gesture 'supported' by other parts, perhaps augmented by a body inclusion, an inclination of the torso? Does a leg gesture accompany the action, or is it the focal point of the action? In a forward movement is the weight shifting into that direction? If torso, arms and a leg move forward, how is balance maintained?

The forward direction is very expressive in that this is our habitual, comfortable and functional direction. We advance toward a person to greet him; we approach in the forward direction to give or to accept something. We are confident, assured about what is in front of us; we 'face facts'. We face the person toward whom we are sympathetic. We ask, beseech in the forward direction. It is the direction of greatest communication.

Exploration of the Backward Area

What movement possibilities exist in the backward half of the sagittal plane? Mobility is much more restricted than for forward actions. Backward arm gestures often require rotation in the shoulder joint, a chest inclusion of some kind or a slight turn in the upper body. Any turning action for this purpose is not a change of front; the rest of the body maintains the previous forward/backward direction. Backward torso tilts may need to be balanced by one leg moving slightly forward. Such a leg action should not be given importance; the emphasis should still be on the backward motion.

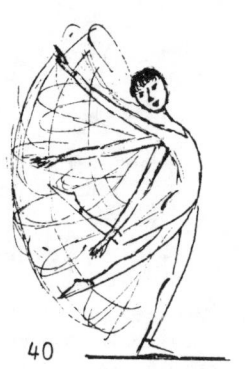

40

Movement in the
backward area

What do backward movements express? For the body as a whole it may be withdrawal, the desire to retreat. This withdrawal could be to get a better view, as in admiring a picture or an arrangement of flowers. It might be from surprise, from reluctance, for self protection, or perhaps from suspicion (if the body has a marked turn). A gesture reaching backward may be to find a support, the arm of a chair, or it may be a surreptitious reaching for something without drawing attention to the action. Many backward dance gestures have no direct everyday counterpart since, for practical purposes, we would turn to face that direction. Therefore they are used for design, to balance a forward action and to provide expressive stylized movements. Flinging the limbs backward can express abandon.

Exploration of the Sideward Areas

The vertical center line divides the body into right and left sides, a natural symmetry which makes open double-sided gestures of arms and legs (when both legs are free from weight bearing) comfortable to perform and pleasing to the eye. Let us first explore use of one side.

In exploring the sideward areas you should discover the many possibilities for gestures using the open side of the body - the right side for the right arm or leg, the left side for the left. Then explore the closed gestures, those in which the limbs have to cross the center line of the body. There is a world of difference between use of the open or closed sides, not only in the physical freedom of the open side and in the limitations or restrictions of the closed side, but also in the contrast in expression.

41a

Movement in the
open sideward area

b)

Movement in the
closed (crossed) side area

Ex. 41a illustrates gestures into the open sideward area, the left side in this case. Torso tilting may be the central sideward movement or it may accompany an arm or leg gesture. Tilting the head or turning it to look in that direction can be expressive by itself or may be an accompaniment to other lateral movement. Slight shifting movemets of torso, head, or general body weight can express the open sideward direction.

In contrast to 41a, 41b illustrates use of the closed or crossed side. Though physically not so easy to perform, such actions are very expressive and, because they are less natural, are often used in an exaggerated form in comic and grotesque dances or for unusual body design. To achieve such exaggeration, the dancer may have to include a slight turning in part of the torso, a hip or a shoulder inclusion. Such action should not destroy the sense of retaining the previously established front. If too great a turn is used and the head is included, the movement will become gesturing forward, forward of the torso. Some part of the body must hold the previous front when the crossed sideward direction is used exaggeratedly. When the dancer is reaching far out laterally, the torso may need to incline in the opposite direction to maintain balance. Such tilting should not be emphasized; it is only an accompaniment, not the main action.

Indication of Directional Areas

Several stages exist in the progression from a general use of direction to the specific, and they must be physically experienced as well as clearly indicated on paper. If you have trained in a movement discipline which demands directional precision it may be a new experience to be comparatively vague. For others vagueness is commonplace, as in certain African dances where jabbing actions occur in a general directional area. Similar spatial uses occur for gestures in other cultures.

The sign for an area: □ is combined with a direction sign to represent the space around a directional point in which gestures can occur Let us clarify on paper the various stages of refinement in definition to help in observing and experiencing the differences.

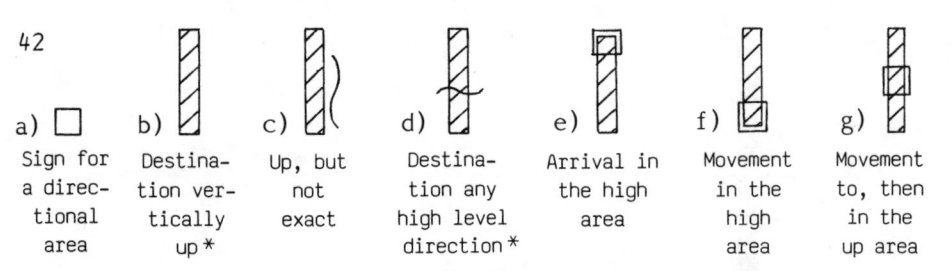

42

a)	b)	c)	d)	e)	f)	g)
Sign for a directional area	Destination vertically up *	Up, but not exact	Destination any high level direction*	Arrival in the high area	Movement in the high area	Movement to, then in the up area

Ex. 42b indicates movement to the destination vertically up. In the first general movement explorations flexibility in interpretation of this indication was permitted, however, its true meaning is movement to that particular destinational point. Ex. 42c allows a slight leeway in the destination up. Ex. 42d states any high direction, thus a destination somewhere up. Ex. 42e shows a movement which ends in the high area. The concept is different, but the result may be close to 42c. For full value in motion within a directional area we need to have the limb or limbs in that area at the start. Ex. 42f indicates the area at the start of the sign; thus the duration of the movement is within that area. In contrast 42g shows movement to the upward area which then continues in that area.

The illustrations here show the progression from general to specific in the forward direction. Ex. 42h states leeway in use of all levels in the forward sagittal direction plus some lateral divergence. Ex. 42i allows freedom within the area around forward middle. In 42j the destination is inexact, a little above, below or to one side of true forward middle. Ex. 42k shows movement to the true forward horizontal direction.

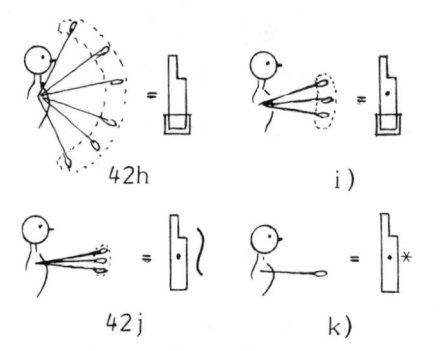

42h

i)

42j

k)

* See note on page 260 re exact direction in Motif Description

Reading Study No. 12

AREAS OF DIRECTION FOR GESTURES

At the start of this study a quick upward movement is followed by movement within that upward spatial area. Find a style of movement which suggests enjoyment of such general spatial usage. Note the addition of a slight accent: ⊳ to conclude the piece. At the start of meas. 5 and 6 there is a swift movement to the side horizontal area which provides time for gestures in that area.

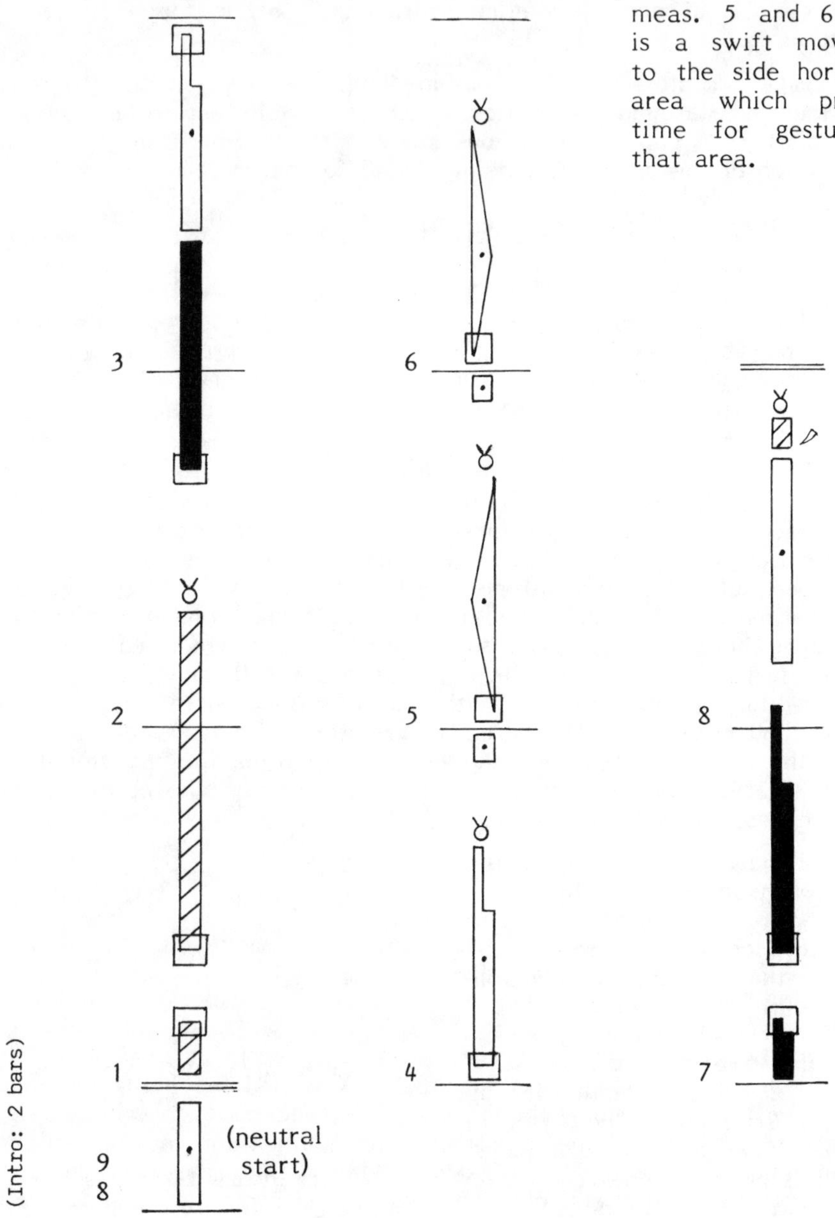

(Intro: 2 bars)

1

2

3

4

5

6

7

8

9
8

(neutral
start)

62

PERFORMANCE OF DIRECTIONAL MOVEMENTS

A directional movement need not be an isolated action; to add expressiveness other minor actions may occur simultaneously. However, these must not be so dominant that they become the focal point.

43a   b)   c)   d)

Variations on a forward movement

In Ex. 43a the gestures, posture and face are all forward, a unity in directional expression. But what of 43b? One arm is backward. Has this detracted from the forward 'message', or is it a choreographic embellishment to add style and interest? What about 43c compared with 43a? Have the arms moving backward weakened the forward expression? In 43d the forward leg gesture requires a backward lean to maintain balance. Does this leaning destroy the forward expression? Not if the emphasis of the movement is clearly placed on the forward gestures, the balancing action being unstressed. Try out various possibilities to discover how far accompanying directional actions can go before the main idea is overpowered and destroyed.

Symmetrical Gestures

Arm gestures in the backward direction are more restricted than in other directions. Symmetrical backward gestures are particularly limited and finding variations in performance can be a challenge.

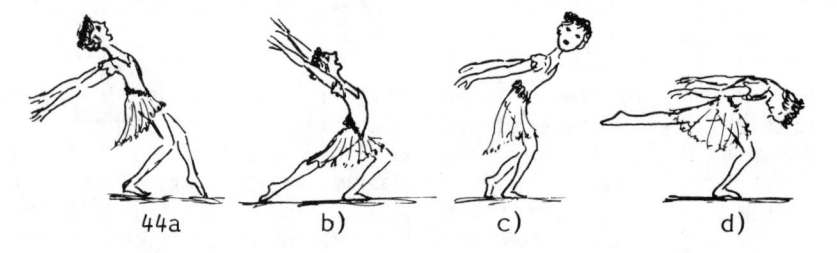

44a   b)   c)   d)

Backward movements with symmetrical arm gestures

By stressing the arms in 44a the movement can express a backward low (downward) direction. If the torso lean is stressed and the arms minimized, backward high (upward) can be expressed. In 44b the leg gesture reinforces the backward direction, arms and leg being of equal importance. In 44c turning the head to look backward contributes significantly to the backward expression. The head action in 44d can add the impression of looking backward, though, in this case, the unity in direction of arms and leg strongly establishes backward horizontal.

Interpretation of Directional Actions

How should a forward horizontal directional instruction be interpreted? If one is concerned with, let us say, the right arm, how many different kinds of gestures into the direction of Ex. 45a are there? Is there a range of expression in this direction?

45a   b)   c)   d)

As the body is built to walk forward, the face is normally to this direction and so is the chest: in short, the whole front of the body which we present to those we trust. Forward is the direction of communication. Ex. 45b shows a man moving toward someone; the forward arm gesture is accompanied by a forward inclination of the torso, a postural change which is in harmony with the gesture. In 45c there is no postural forwardness, only an isolated arm gesture. We see at once that this position produces a much weaker forward expression. In 45d a reverse postural action has accompanied the forward gesture. The turning away of the torso and head produces an expression of distrust, of unwillingness, of fear, some form of negative, withdrawal feeling.

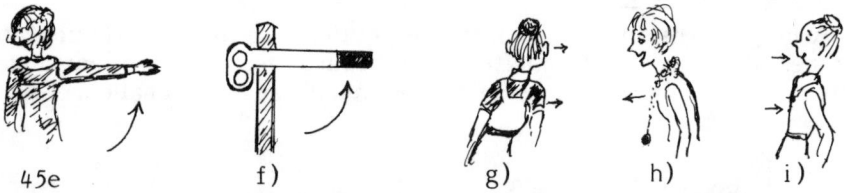

45e   f)   g)   h)   i)

The intensity of the expressiveness of any directional movement need not lie in the degree of spatial extension. A stretched arm extended sideward, as in 45e, may give more the impression of a railway signal, 45f, rather than an expressive arm gesture. In contrast a slight leaning or shifting of the body may convey a much stronger directional message. Compare 45e with 45g. Much rests on the manner in which the action is performed, the stress, emphasis, etc. which is easily observed in the movement but cannot be shown so readily in illustrations on paper. Ex. 45h shows a small but expressive postural leaning forward, while 45i shows a person taken a-back.

Use of Double Directions

Use of oppositional directions can produce strong countertensions, each direction being given full value. The directions up and down can both be stressed at the same time; perhaps one arm is extended up, the other down, or downward gestures can be counterbalanced by the face looking strongly upward.

Sagittal Double Direction

Ex. 46a states movement forward and backward at the same time, an equal pull in both directions. An arabesque used in skating as well as in dancing is a familiar example, Ex. 46b. Even if both arms as well as the free leg are gesturing backward, the forward extension of the torso and the face looking forward can provide sufficient emphasis to produce the double directional pull, Ex. 46c.

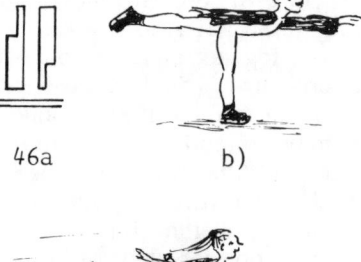

46a   b)

46c

Lateral Double Directions

The laterally symmetrical build of the body makes balanced sideward movements more comfortable and easier to perform than movements in sagittal directions. This is particularly true of the open sideward directions. The following examples illustrate the expressiveness of these seemingly simple positions. Note the change in expression when the feet are also opened sideward and also the differences resulting from the level of the arms. Some common interpretations are given below.

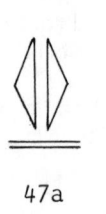
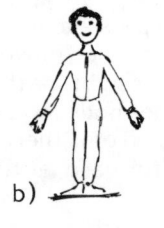

47a   b)   c)   d)

Ex. 47b: Simplicity, modesty: "This is what I am."
Ex. 47c: "Welcome!" or "There it is!"
Ex. 47d: "Marvellous news!" or perhaps "Please! Please be quiet!"

47e   f)   g)

Ex. 47e: "At your service"; "This is what I am, I have nothing to hide."
Ex. 47f: "Here I am!"; presentation, self assertion or in command.
Ex. 47g: "Success!" "We are the victors!"

The open stance expresses confidence, stability, the establishment of self. A different use of the head and of palm facing could change the meaning of the above.

Lateral Double Directions (continued)

A lateral oppositional pull can occur with a torso tilt, as in Ex. 48a in which the free leg extends in opposition to the torso and arm. Such a position is comparable to the sagittal arabesque in that the arms may extend in the same direction as the leg and the face may be used to augment the sideward expression. Ex. 48b is a similar position but the change from supporting on the leg (a vertical support) to lying on the ground affects the overall statement.

48a

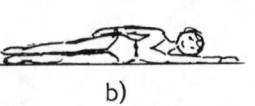

b)

Crossed Lateral Double Directions

The crossed lateral double directions, Ex. 49a, contrast strongly with the open. The legs and arms cross the center line of the body, thus expressing concealment, self protection, a shutting out of the rest of the world, furtiveness, Ex. 49b. This

49a   b)

is particularly true when the crossing involves a twist in the torso, a turning away from the viewer.

Pathway of Directional Movement

A directional action is most strongly expressed when a direct path is taken. This action can best occur when the movement originates near the body center and moves out on a straight path, as in Ex. 50a. A kicking leg gesture can have more of the body weight behind it if the foot starts near the hip and thrusts out from there, 50b. Ex. 50c shows use of center in preparation for the forward action.

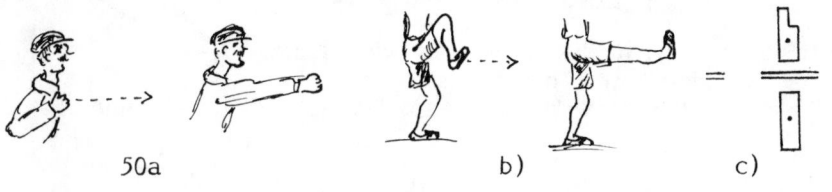

50a   b)   c)

Experiment with such gestures, comparing the differences between them.

The curved movement line of Ex. 50d has a very different expression and function. Starting down, the motion is one of rising and, until it stops, there is no way of knowing the aim, the directional destination. The curved path might be enjoyed for its own sake, the destination being unimportant. In the case of a leg movement such a curved path is functional for a football kick, the curved action lifting the ball into the air, 50e. Where this leg gesture will terminate is not known.

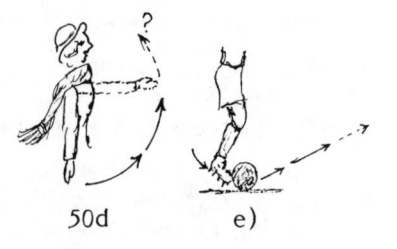

50d   e)

Reading Practice

DIMENSIONAL STUDIES

Placement of the accent sign, ◁ or ▷ , states the moment when an accent should happen - at the start, in the middle or at the end of a movement. Note that the white accent sign indicates only a slight, i.e. light accent.

What is consistent in the structure of Ex. A? In what way does the last measure of B vary from the rest of the study? Describe any ideas you derive from C. Note double sided directions in B.

THE 27 MAIN DIRECTIONS

The Diagonal Directions

Between the sagittal (forward and back) and the lateral (side to side) dimensions lie the four diagonal directions, Ex. 51a. The slanting line coming to a point visually indicates the directions in question.

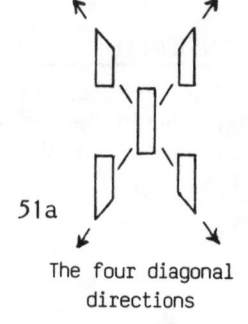

51a

The four diagonal directions

Left front   Right front   Left back   Right back

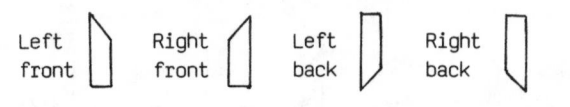

By adding the four diagonals of Ex. 51a to the cross of 34f we have the circle of directions of 51b all emanating from the center point. Each of these directions may be at low, middle (horizontal) or high level; specific information on these possibilities is given later. First we will explore how these main directions can be used in a general, more flexible way.

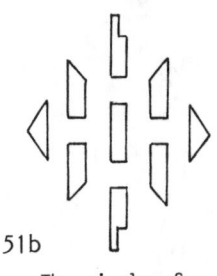

51b

The circle of directions

Below are the circles showing all of the twenty-seven main directions, the range for high level, middle level and low level. The center point, 'place', is included as a direction since it is a point to which the extremity of the limb can move, for example the hand moving to the shoulder which is the center point of direction for the arm. These cardinal directions are those featured in most styles of structured movement.

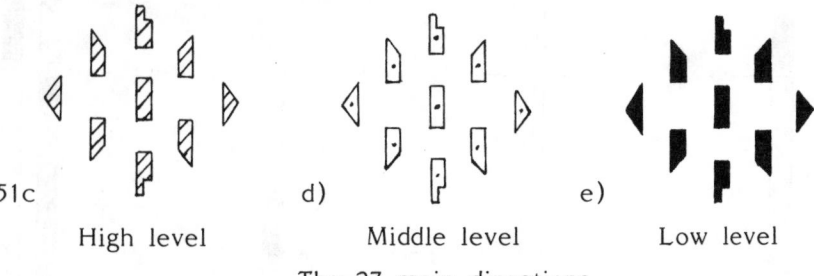

51c   d)   e)

High level   Middle level   Low level

The 27 main directions

For structured description of movement it is often necessary to indicate intermediate directions. Many styles of dance take intermediate points as their norm; for example in ballet the arms are not held in a true horizontal line in the sideward and forward directions, but somewhat lower. In Spanish dance the arms overhead are held slightly behind the head. Many other examples of such directional variation can be cited. For our purposes here no such specificity is needed.

Directional Actions While Travelling

Travelling may be accompanied by directional actions. In this case the two indications are placed side by side. Such travelling may or may not have the direction of travelling stated. Try out the following variations of directional gestures combined with travelling.

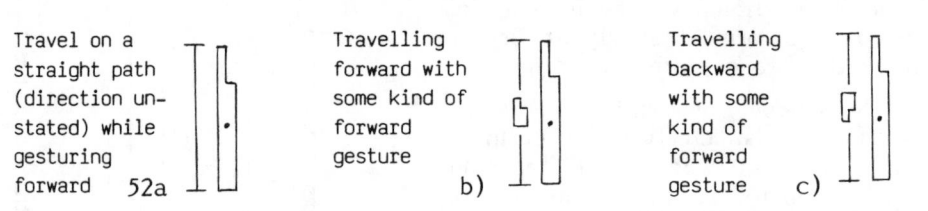

Travel on a straight path (direction un-stated) while gesturing forward   52a

Travelling forward with some kind of forward gesture   b)

Travelling backward with some kind of forward gesture   c)

The same can be applied to circular paths:

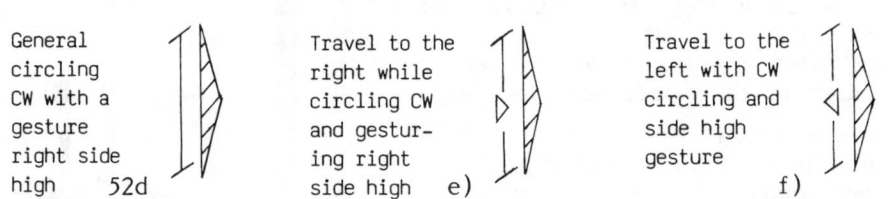

General circling CW with a gesture right side high   52d

Travel to the right while circling CW and gestur-ing right side high   e)

Travel to the left with CW circling and side high gesture   f)

A lowering or rising of the body as a whole is written outside the path sign.

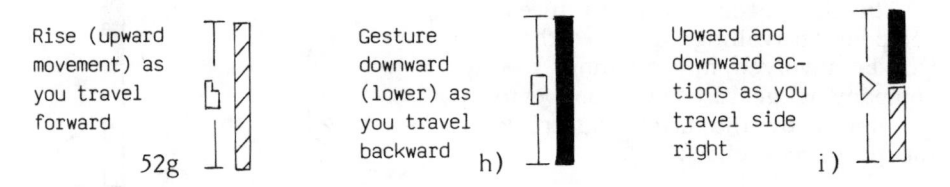

Rise (upward movement) as you travel forward   52g

Gesture downward (lower) as you travel backward   h)

Upward and downward ac-tions as you travel side right   i)

Such rising and sinking will affect the level of the steps because they are movements of the body as a whole. Change of level just in the legs (high and low steps) is a specific movement dealt with later. Indication of level within the path sign refers to the path itself. In the following examples no accompanying general body movement takes place.

The path is forward and downward (as in walking down stairs or on a downward slope).   52j

The path is forward and upward (as occurs when one walks upstairs or uphill).   k)

The examples above are only a few of many possible combinations involving travelling, directional gestures, and changes of the body as a whole. Variations in timing and use of stillness provide contrast and interest. Compose a dance using these movement ideas.

READING STUDY No. 13

DIRECTIONAL GESTURES

This simple study may be performed with many variations, yet the basic instructions will have been followed. Perform it slowly at first to allow time to explore the actions.

Some questions will come up regarding how much freedom in interpretation is allowed. Is a step sideward permitted to accompany the axial movement? Would such a step be considered travelling? No significant moving away from the original spot should occur; a shift of weight or a small step may, however, be added to augment the directional movement.

The result of movement into a direction is retained during stillness. A new movement produces automatic cancellation, so the downward destination of measure 3 will disappear as the backward travelling starts.

In the second staff gestures accompany travelling. Since the feet will be involved in travelling, the accompanying gestures will be performed mainly by the arms and trunk, as the performer chooses.

How is center ([·]) to be interpreted? It is the neutral standing position which expresses no other direction. For this the arms may hang down naturally, or they may be in a relaxed, resting position somewhere close to the chest. It is important that they express center, neutral in the directional sense, and not a flexion of the arms.

When performing this study has become comfortable and enjoyable, develop a variation of it, keeping the basic material as it is, adding travelling where it has not been given and directional gestures when none is stated. Notate your development to compare with others and, in the comparison, observe which version provides good kinetic flow.

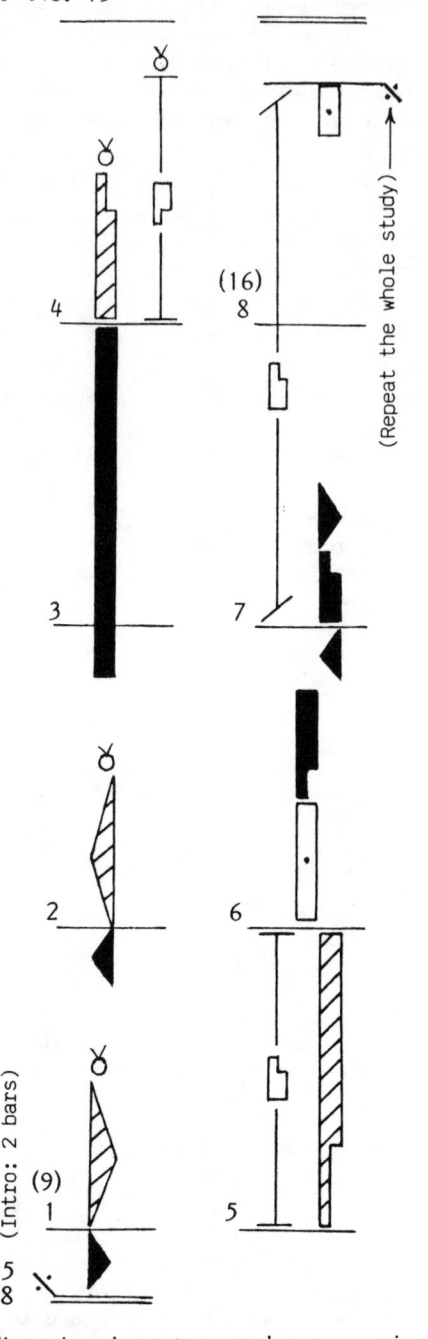

SPRINGING COMBINED WITH DIRECTIONS

A directional action may happen as an accompaniment during a spring. The action may or may not affect the spring itself. In combining direction with the spring itself, we can indicate direction for the take-off support, for the landing support, and also for the legs while in the air. Appropriate placement of the direction sign indicates which is being specified. Note the following examples:

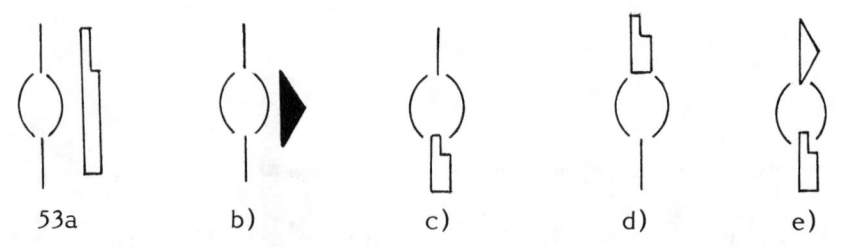

53a   b)   c)   d)   e)

Ex. 53a indicates a forward action during the whole springing process. The level of the forward gesture accompanying the spring is left open. In 53b a side low gesture occurs while the dancer is in the air. If a direction symbol replaces the action stroke at the start of the symbol for a spring, it states a preparatory directional support, usually a step. In 53c this step is forward. As yet no indication is given as to whether it is a step on the right or left foot. Ex. 53d states landing forward; again, no statement is made as to whether it is on one or two feet. In 53e the preparatory support (step) is forward but the landing is to the side. This movement may be performed taking off from either foot and landing on one or both.

In the sign for a spring the right curve represents the right leg in the air, the left curve the left leg. The take-off and landing supports do not, as yet, indicate right or left; specific use of right, left or both supports before or after a spring is given in Chapter Fourteen.

If one of the curved vertical lines is replaced by a direction sign, it indicates what that leg is doing while you are airborne. Ex. 53f shows the right leg gesturing forward during the spring; while 53g states that both legs open sideward away from each other while in the air.

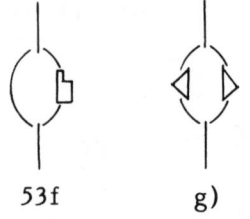

53f   g)

Such indications for one leg or both often dictate which basic form of aerial step will be used.

The addition of directional indications to springs leads into specific statements which begin to approach a full description of what is taking place. Since there is much material yet to be explored in a general way it may be as well to avoid becoming too specific in one area until we have 'caught up', so to speak, in other areas.

DIRECTIONS WITH TRAVELLING AND SPRINGING

⊞ means face front of room, audience.

⊟ means face the back of the room (stage).

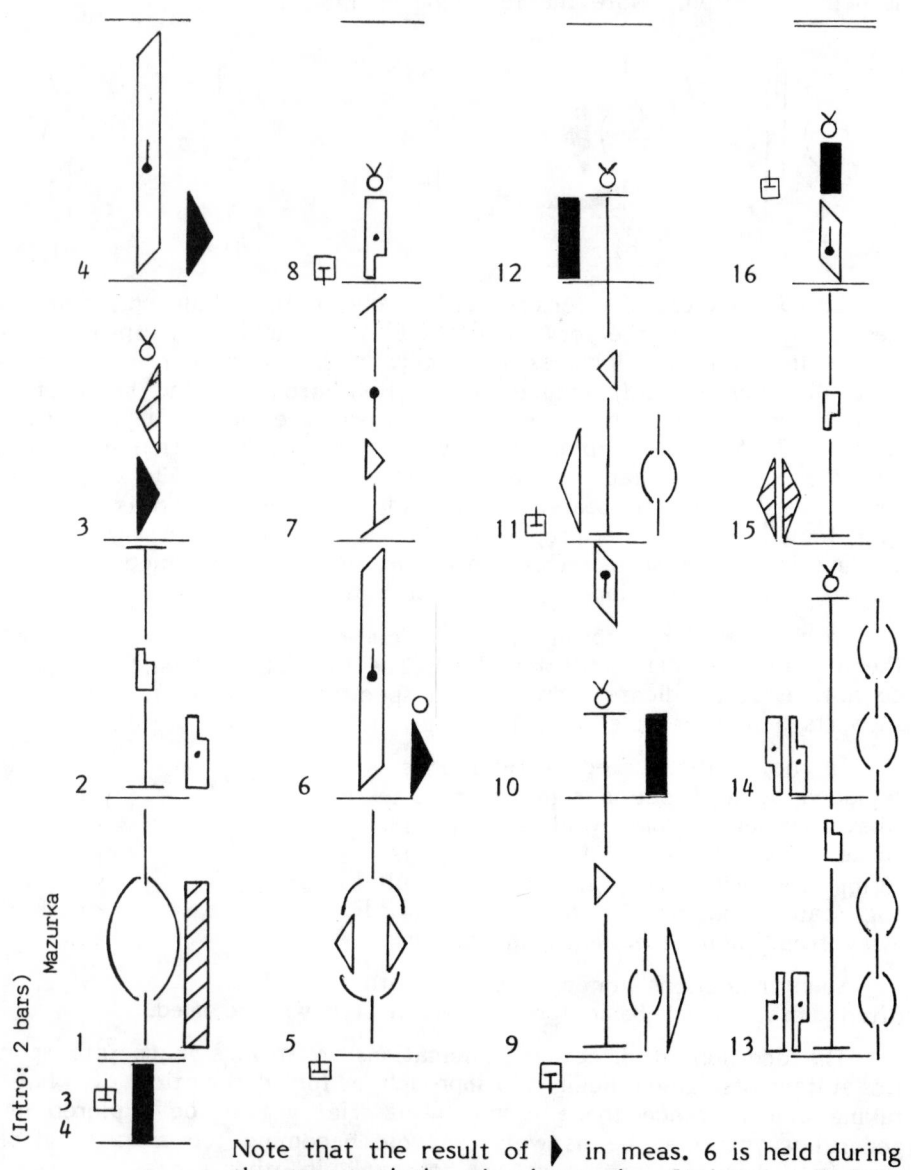

Note that the result of ▶ in meas. 6 is held during the turn and the circular path. It is cancelled by the next directional movement.

REVIEW FOR CHAPTERS FOUR AND FIVE

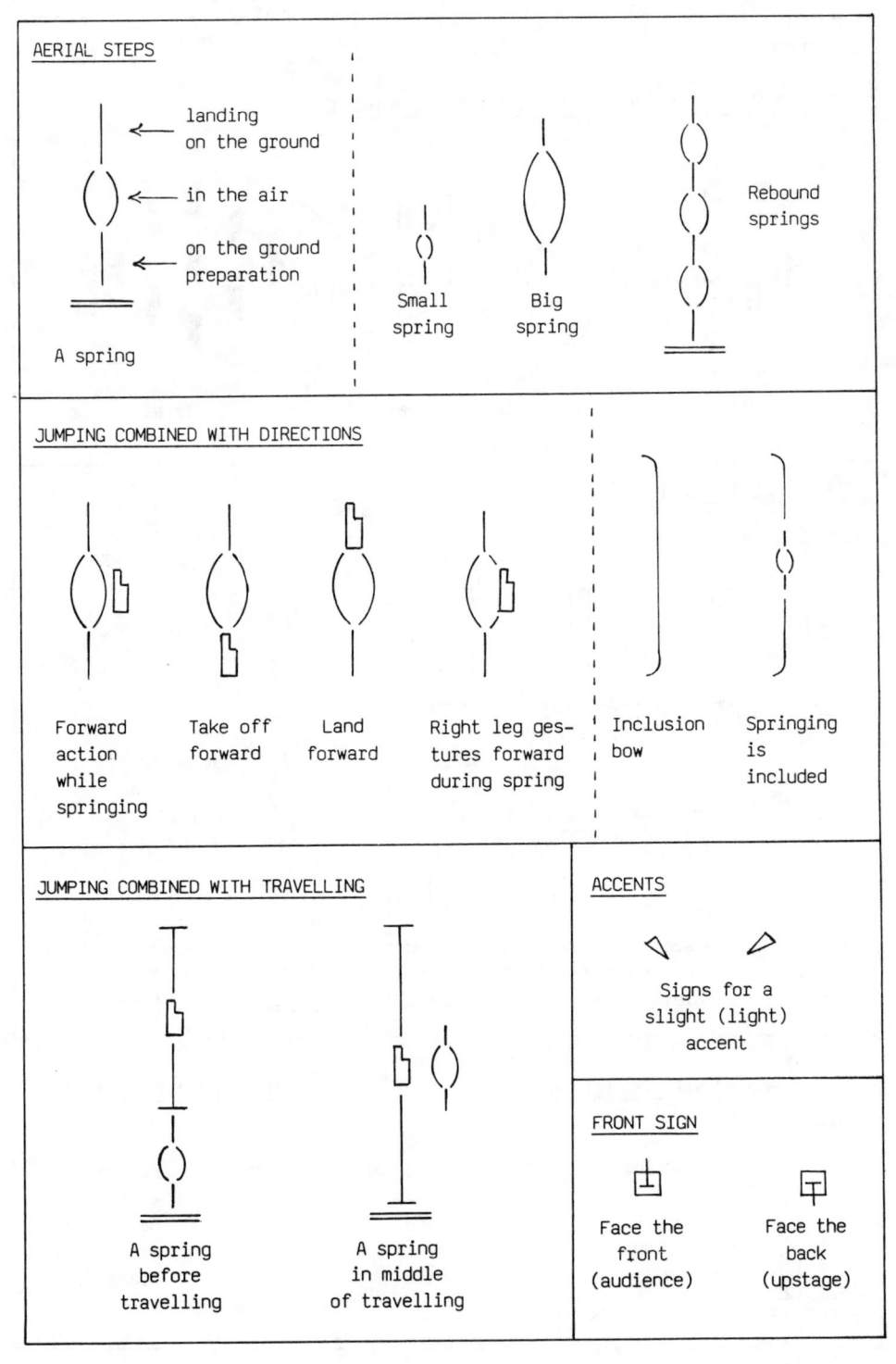

AERIAL STEPS

landing
on the ground

in the air

on the ground
preparation

A spring

Small
spring

Big
spring

Rebound
springs

JUMPING COMBINED WITH DIRECTIONS

Forward
action
while
springing

Take off
forward

Land
forward

Right leg ges-
tures forward
during spring

Inclusion
bow

Springing
is
included

JUMPING COMBINED WITH TRAVELLING

A spring
before
travelling

A spring
in middle
of travelling

ACCENTS

Signs for a
slight (light)
accent

FRONT SIGN

Face the
front
(audience)

Face the
back
(upstage)

DIRECTION

THE MAIN DIRECTIONS (Specific Destinational Points)

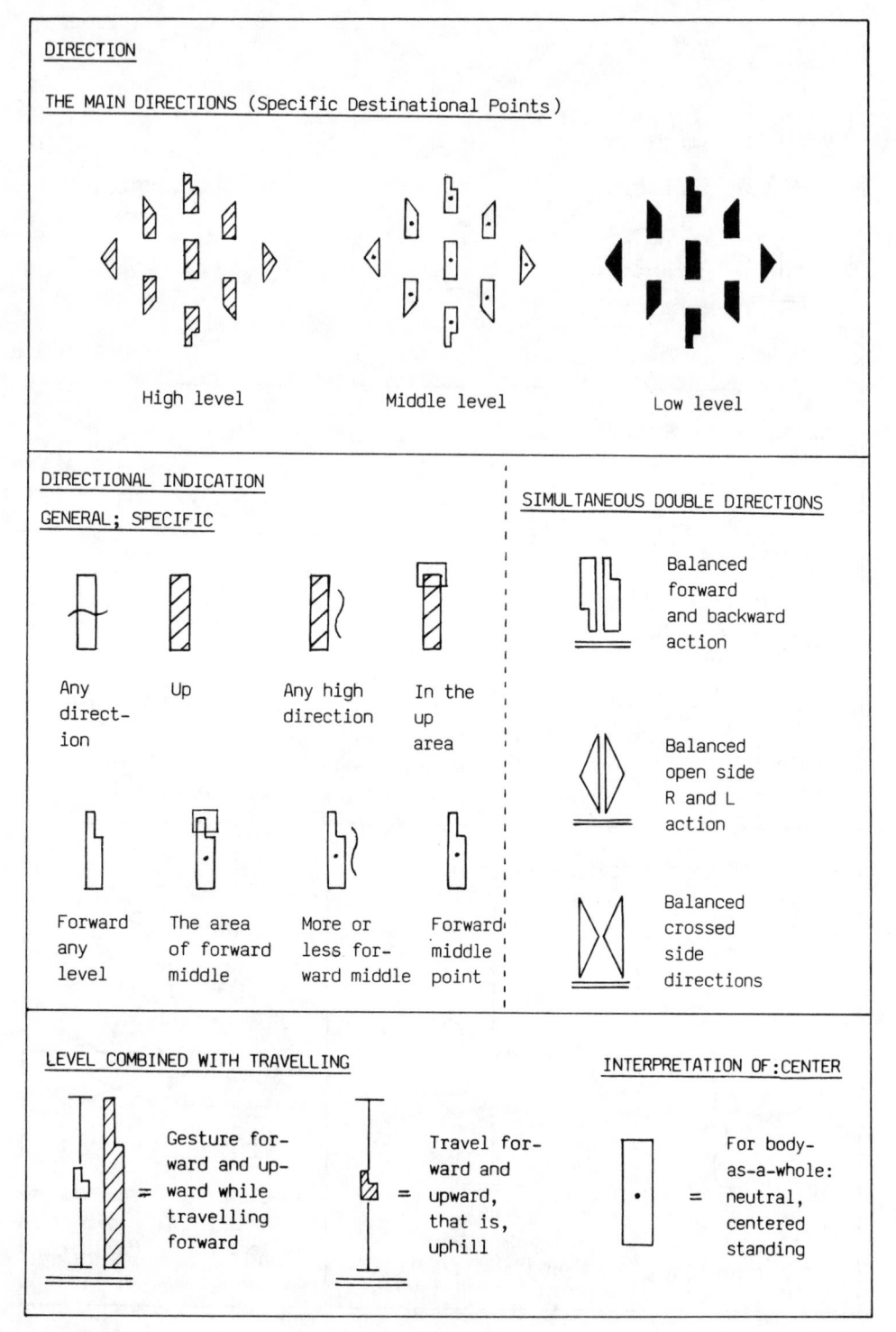

High level   Middle level   Low level

DIRECTIONAL INDICATION

GENERAL; SPECIFIC

Any
direct-
ion

Up

Any high
direction

In the
up
area

Forward
any
level

The area
of forward
middle

More or
less for-
ward middle

Forward
middle
point

SIMULTANEOUS DOUBLE DIRECTIONS

Balanced
forward
and backward
action

Balanced
open side
R and L
action

Balanced
crossed
side
directions

LEVEL COMBINED WITH TRAVELLING

= Gesture for-
ward and up-
ward while
travelling
forward

= Travel for-
ward and
upward,
that is,
uphill

INTERPRETATION OF:CENTER

= For body-
as-a-whole:
neutral,
centered
standing

Chapter Six
FLEXION; EXTENSION

Perform the simplest action and, though you may have thought of it in other terms, you will doubtless have involved two or three of the three 'anatomical' prime actions. Because of the nature of the joints in the body and the sets of muscles which move the limb segments, it is possible to flex and extend the joints and to rotate (twist) the limbs. These basic actions — flexion, extension and rotation — are so much a part of our daily functioning that we have to make a special point of thinking about them and observing when and how they are used in various movement forms.

FLEXION

What is the nature of the action of flexing? Flexion incorporates the following movement ideas: drawing in toward the center, becoming smaller, folding up, contracting, bending, closing in, adducting, narrowing, pulling in to a central point, retracting, shrinking, curving, curling up, imploding.

Each of these movement ideas evokes a different image — a snail retracting, a cat curling up, a flower folding up, and so on. In most instances the manner of performance is slightly different, and therein lies a whole world of exploration of the differences in expression. The degree of flexion may be partial or full. The action may involve several joints, or only one. The movement idea may be body-oriented (body-centered) or concerned with moving away from something, or with occupying less space. An action of drawing in may result from the intention of moving toward the center of the body or drawing in away from some outside person, some danger, perhaps.

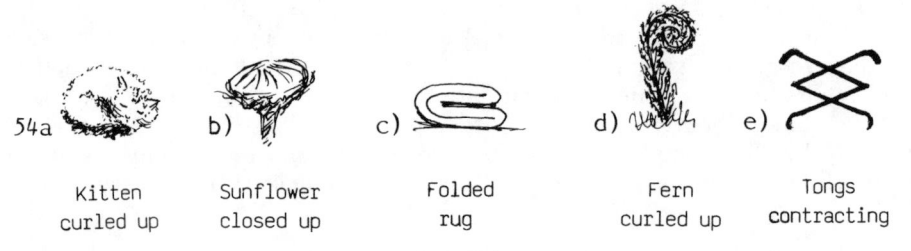

54a	b)	c)	d)	e)
Kitten curled up	Sunflower closed up	Folded rug	Fern curled up	Tongs contracting

For the moment we are concerned with the kind of action, not the specific degree. However, for the general statements needed at this point, two degrees will be distinguished — a little and a lot.

75

Flexion (continued)

The sign for the basic movement of flexion, Ex. 54f, includes the sign for 'any': $\sim$ (ad lib.) thus giving complete freedom as to which form of flexion may be used. Specific forms will be explored later. By doubling the sign, as in 54g, we show a greater degree of flexion. This greater degree is generally used in this book to produce a more emphasized action.

54f g)

EXTENSION

Extension can take several forms and involve different movement concepts. What ideas, intentions, or aims belong to this category of movement? Reaching out, lengthening, stretching, elongating, opening out, separating, broadening, widening, expanding, moving out from the center, becoming larger, growing. Again, each of these terms evokes a different image.

Flexion and extension are partners in that frequently use of one is followed by the other. We reach out to grasp an object, then bring it in close for inspection. The curled sleeping position is followed by the morning stretch. Breathing in, inflating of the lungs, is followed by breathing out, deflating, compressing the lungs. One action may be a preparation for the other. The body enjoys the sensation of closing in or opening out — think of lying in the hot sun on the grass or beach. Countless practical examples can be found.

55

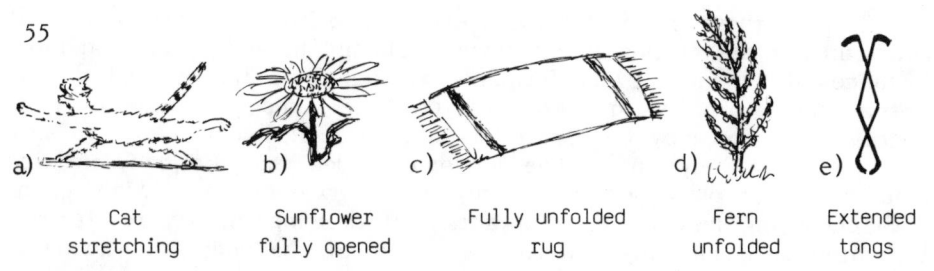

| a) Cat stretching | b) Sunflower fully opened | c) Fully unfolded rug | d) Fern unfolded | e) Extended tongs |

How do these actions relate to dance movement? How are they used artistically? In dance the two opposite actions are often enjoyed for their own sake. Consider the kind of physical delight evoked by the music of *The Afternoon of a Faun*. In the Jerome Robbins version, the boy stretches languidly and then closes in. Many of the subsequent movements in the ballet concentrate on the body actions of extension and flexion, subjective, body-oriented, physically based actions. But let us first be concerned with simple, more naturalistic movements which perfectly express these ideas. Stylization, which can be very subtle, comes later.

The sign for any form of extension is Ex. 55f, which includes the symbol for 'any' to give freedom of choice at this stage. The greater degree, very extended, is shown by 55g.

55f g)

Flexion; Extension

In extension of a limb, the degree of extending is limited. There is less distance to go in achieving extension because our limbs are normally 'straight', that is, not flexed. Of course extension of a limb can in an expressive movement be combined with participation in an adjoining part of the body, as for instance, in reaching out to grasp an object the torso inclines in the same direction. By such means the act of extending is augmented. But within the limb itself there is little range. Extension may often occur as the <u>act of extending</u>. From a very closed up position, the body and limbs may start reaching out, begin to stretch, <u>feel</u> that they are stretching, and yet stop short of actually arriving at normal extension. The effect of stopping short, of not arriving at a goal, which occurs in many forms of movement, will be discussed later. The point being made here is that the intention, the feeling of stretching, elongating, can occur without a stretched position (destination) being achieved. (See terminology note, page 80.)

A simple, basic movement pattern is illustrated in Ex. 55h in which flexion is followed immediately by extension, then by stillness. If repeated several times, each performance could be different spatially, in emphasis, etc. Ex. 55i starts with extension and the stillness follows flexion — a very different result. This pattern also has many possible interpretations, even without significant changes in timing.

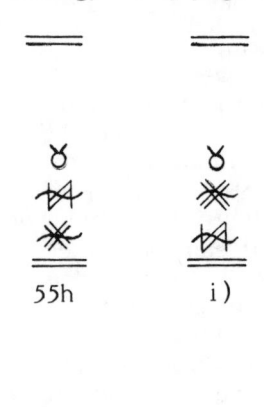

55h   i)

Duration of Flexion, Extension

The actions of flexing and extending may be sudden or sustained. The symbols themselves occupy only a small amount of time but swiftness is not stressed. If a sharp, sudden movement is wanted, an accent: ◁ or ▷ is added. Thus Ex. 56a shows a sudden extension followed soon by a sudden flexion.

The signs ✕ and ✕ are not elongated to show extension in time. The vertical line of the action stroke is attached and the length of this line indicates the length of time taken for the flexion or extension. Ex. 56b shows a slow flexion. By attaching the action stroke to a specific movement indication, we state what the action is to be. The vertical line retains only the meaning of length of time. For this reason it is often called the 'duration line' indicating as it does the duration of the stated movement. Observe how the following patterns vary in their use of time.

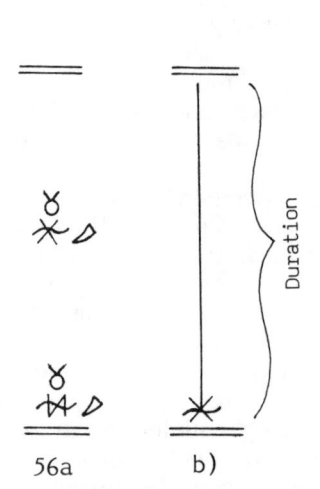

56a   b)

77

Duration of Flexion, Extension (continued)

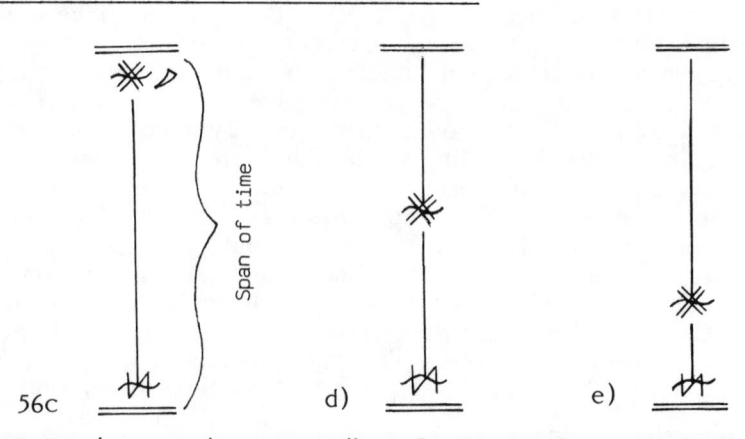

56c   d)   e)

Perform each example repeatedly. In 56c a slow, sustained extension is followed by a sudden, accented flexion. In 56d the duration of the two actions is equal, rather like breathing in and out without a pause between. Ex. 56e shows a brief extension changing to a prolonged, sustained flexion. In describing these examples only the basic terminology has been used. The ideas listed under 'flexion' and 'extension' offer opportunities for many variations. Ex. 56c could be a slow reaching out toward someone, then sudden retraction, a response to threatening behaviour. Or the idea could be that of a balloon blowing up gradually, only to pop (sudden deflation!). Ex. 56e could be a movement equivalent to throwing a line far out to catch a fish and then slowly drawing it in toward you, perhaps because of resistance met. Find ideas which will give substance to performance of this simple material. Then find enjoyment of the sequences in pure movement, movement for its own sake, no story, no specific dramatic content.

Flexion, Extension Combined with Other Actions

Flexing and extending can be added to the range of movements already explored — travelling, springing and directional actions. In Ex. 57a you move sideward and extend, then downward and flex. The extension need not be part of the sideward action; it may be general with no particularly spatial placement. The reverse instructions are given in 57b: flexion occurs with the sideward action and extension while lowering. For this the torso and one arm might close in while the other leg and arm gesture sideward. In lowering you may extend the arms down or the elbows out, or use any spatial arm extension. Lowering usually involves leg flexion, but the movement expression is not one of flexing since the intent is different.

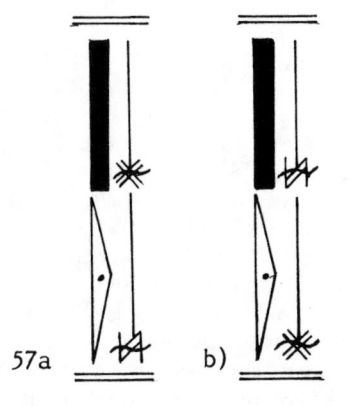

57a   b)

FLEXION, EXTENSION

Find an interesting interpretation for this study for music 'A', then find a contrasting one using the alternate more jazzy piece 'B'. Slight accents: ◁ or ▷ are used to highlight the sequence.

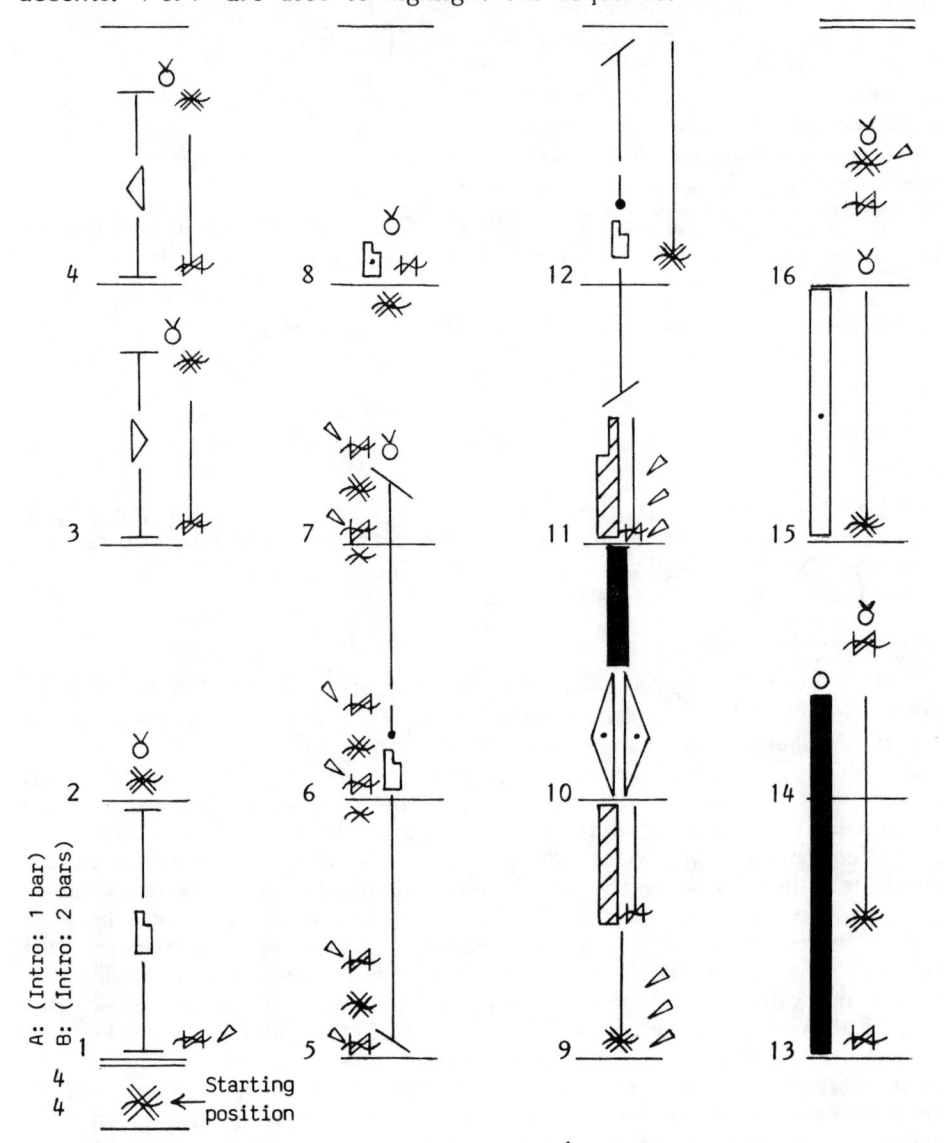

Remember ⋈ means extended and ⋈ means reaching far out with the body being included. In measure 9 the flexion is performed with three accents. Note use of double-sided directions in measure 10, and retention of the low situation while extending in measure 14.

Springing Combined with Flexion, Extension

During a spring flexion or extension of one or both legs can occur. The legs may be extended, spread, or perhaps pulled in, contracted, or a mixture of these possibilities.

Ex. 58a shows a spring during which an accompanying general extension occurs. This action will probably involve the arms and body as well as the legs. In 58b flexion accompanies the spring, again a general indication for the body as a whole.

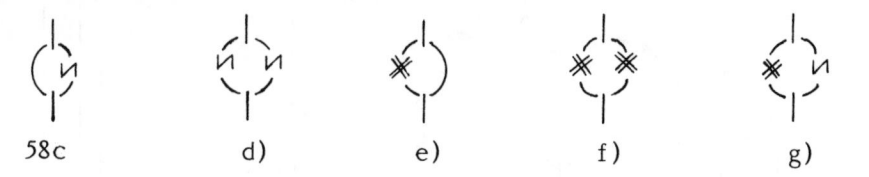

58a   b)

By placing the appropriate sign on the actual spring indication, we can show what happens to the right or left leg while it is in the air.

58c   d)   e)   f)   g)

Ex. 58c states that the right leg is extended while in the air; in 58d both legs are extended. In 58e the left leg is flexed, contracted, while in 58f both legs are flexed. Ex. 58g indicates that the left leg is bent while the right is stretched.

Extension: Terminology

The word 'extension' is used in this chapter and in Chapter Sixteen with the general meanings of lengthening, stretching, elongating, reaching out, expanding and spreading. A different meaning is given to 'extension' in anatomical terminology; there it is employed to mean the reverse of 'flexion'. For example, bending the wrist forward (toward the inner, palm side of the wrist) is called 'flexion'; what is commonly called bending the wrist backward (toward the outer surface of the wrist) is called 'wrist extension' in anatomical studies. Similarly, bending the torso forward is called 'flexion', but a backward torso bend is called 'extension'. This special meaning for the word 'extension' can be confusing for students who are studying anatomy and are also encountering other forms of movement analysis such as presented in this book. Consistency and logicality in use of terminology is important. It is interesting to note that a backward torso bend can be performed as a relaxed curve (a flexion) and can also be performed as an extended backward curve in which the actions of elongating and of curving are combined in one movement.

Reading Study No. 16

SPRINGS WITH FLEXION AND EXTENSION

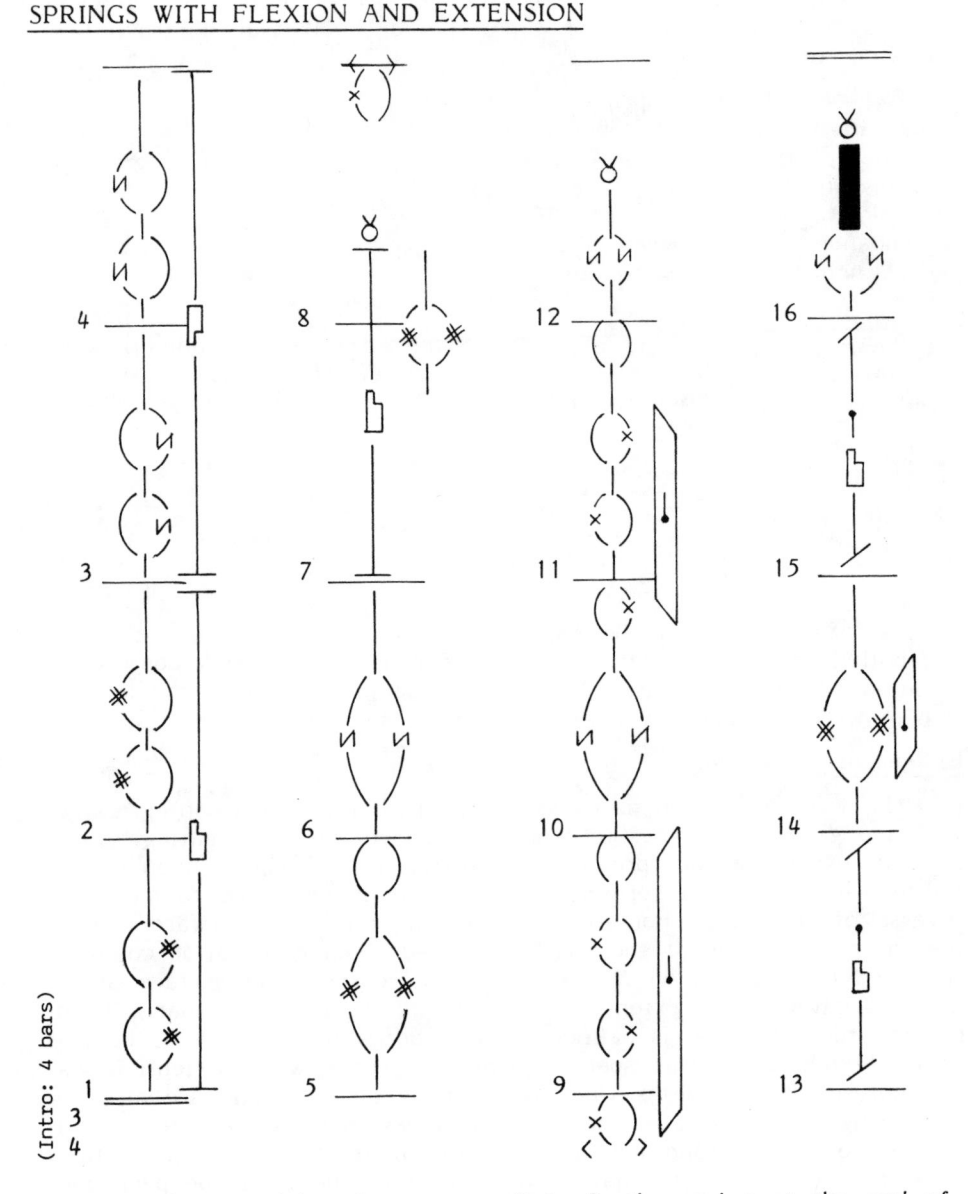

Note the transition from meas. 8 to 9: the spring at the end of meas. 8 is repeated below the bar line at the beginning of the third staff to facilitate reading.

The signs: $\langle$ and $\rangle$, called carets, have the meaning of 'the same' and are used here to show that the spring written before meas. 9 is the same as that written at the end of meas. 8.

Chapter Seven
ROTATIONS, REVOLUTIONS, TURNS

Before investigating this topic, let us check terminology. A rotation? A revolution? A turn? Are they all the same? To all intents and purposes the words are interchangeable, though for certain movements one term may seem preferable to another. The synonyms for turning, revolving, are full of descriptive movement - swivelling, whirling, wheeling, rolling, swinging, etc. Many of these suggest a circular path, in whole or in part. Certainly, when a pivot turn is performed with a limb extended, the extremity of the limb describes a circular path in the air. But we will come to paths for gestures later.

Is there something to be learned from our daily use of words such as 'turn', 'rotate'? What sort of 'movement' do they suggest? For instance we 'turn away' from an unpleasant sight. This may be a partial pivot (swivel on the supporting foot), or a turn (twist) in the body. In illness we 'turn the corner', a dramatic change (a new 'direction' is understood, though no real direction as such is involved). We 'turn the tables', a reversing which suggests a half turn. We 'take turns', a sequence of involvement in an activity which repeats after returning to where it started. To 'turn over in one's mind' also gives the idea of a circular pattern where there is a return to the same thoughts. 'Turn the pages of a book' usually involves a semicircular arc. To 'turn' on the enemy suggests an about-face, a half pivot turn.

ANY ROTATION, REVOLUTION

What is a rotation? Let us first consider this type of movement for the whole body. It can be rolling if one is lying on the floor, just as a pencil can roll. It may be spinning if one is on one's feet, just as a top can spin. Turning fast is an exhilarating sensation. Prolonged turning can bring on a state of trance as intentionally experienced by the whirling Dervishes. Their counterclockwise turning alternates between slower and faster but they never stop until they fall in a trance-like state. Turning should be experienced at different speeds. Speed affects not only the expression but also the functional use of the different forms of rotating, revolving. These forms include cartwheels, somersaults, walkovers (forward cartwheels), etc. The basic forms are mixed in gymnastics, acrobatics, tumbling and diving. But these are special skills; let us first deal with the common forms using just the floor. The other forms will be explored in theory but not physically; proper training is essential for aerial forms. The basic facts, once understood, are applicable to all forms. Certain body areas make use of partial rotations of a somersault or cartwheel nature.

83

Before we become specific, let us enjoy the freedom of any kind of rotation. Ex. 59a is the symbol for 'any rotation', 'any revolution'; the choice of form is left open. Try the following sequence of continuous rotation: while standing, start turning slowly, then keep on revolving while lowering to the floor, turning perhaps on one foot, then down to a knee and onto the hips while swivelling or rolling, and keep turning as you lie down until you begin to rise. While rising continue to turn constantly.

59a

Any form of rotation, revolution

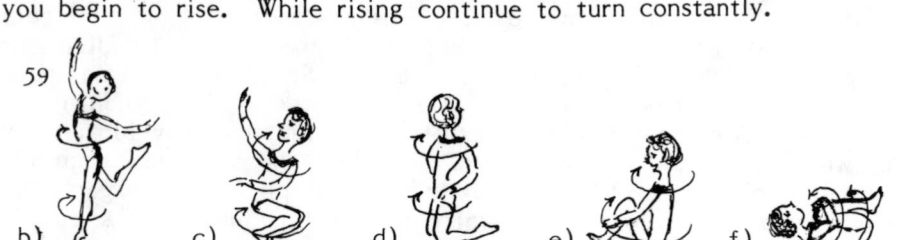

59

Find another way of descending and rising with continuous turning, changing from faster to slower, incorporating flexed and extended body states and using different devices to keep the turning action going, e.g. pushing with a hand or foot. Once on the floor, change the revolving into a somersault and from there into rolling with the limbs closed in. Then try rolling with the limbs extended, the whole body in one line. The basic turning, rotating action can be greatly colored by other actions which accompany it. Each variation provides its own expression and feeling. Discover these and enjoy them.

In a standing situation turning may be on one foot, on both feet, or a mixture between the two, changing from one foot to the other. A few steps or many may occur while turning. For pure rotation one should stay on the spot without travelling. Other contributory actions may occur, such as use of head, torso, or accompanying gestures, as long as none of these becomes dominant and overshadows the main rotary action. The featured movement must still be clearly observable.

What movement facts have we unearthed? Rotation occurs around an axis. When one is standing, turning (pivoting) is around the vertical axis, but the same physical activity performed while one is lying on the floor becomes logrolling. Continuous rolling of one kind produces travelling. Turning is directly related to circling, to circular paths in space. From the point of view of expression a turning action may have a dramatic origin, for example to face another person, an object or another room direction. It may occur merely to progress along another path; in this case the path and not the turning is important. Or the turning action may occur for its own sake. Spinning, once discovered, is much enjoyed by young children. It becomes an art when a skater climaxes a sequence with a dazzling series of spins. "When in doubt - turn" is the advice given to dancers who suddenly have to improvise in a performance when they mentally go blank for a moment.

ANY REVOLUTION

This study is so general it could be performed in a number of different ways. It starts in a neutral, middle level, so the first rotation is likely to be on the feet (but need not be). After lowering occurs some form of rolling on the floor is likely, though swivelling (pivoting) could occur. Note use of the hold sign: ○ to show that low level is to be maintained until the return to neutral on the 6th measure.

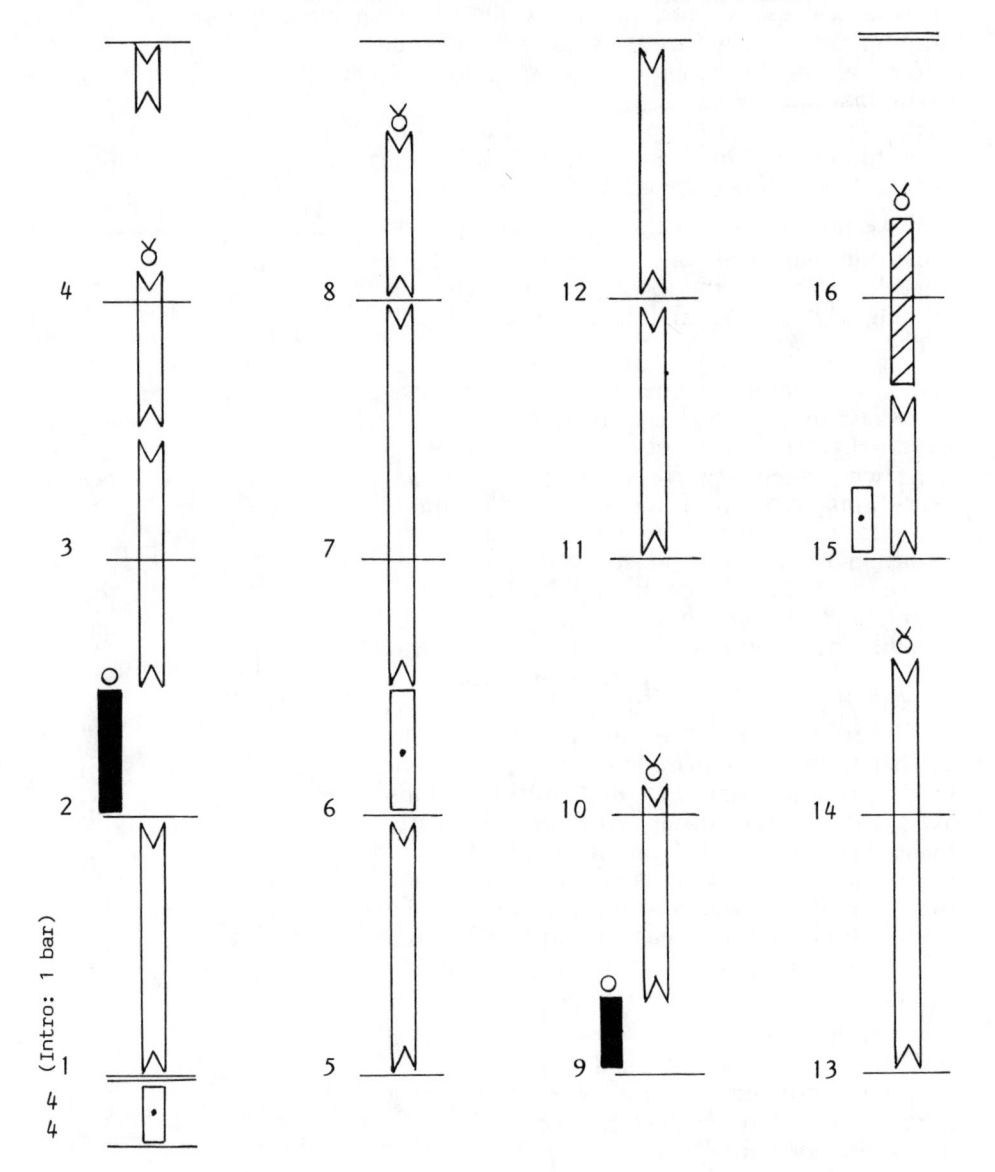

SPECIFIC FORMS OF ROTATION: PIVOT TURNS

All too often turning, pivoting, is thought of as a mechanical action or device, perhaps because so many inanimate objects in life, such as a turntable, rotate rigidly. For movement it is important to realize that the first 'notion' of turning, the origin of the motion (as with all movement), takes place in the brain. The thought, image of a turn to come, is followed by a reaction in the trunk, the center. Let us consider a turn while standing on one foot. The turn starts in the trunk and <u>only at the last</u> comes the swivel on the foot. In that sense it is a <u>successive movement</u>. Only when an outside force initiates a turn can the body rotate totally in one piece. The 'birth' of a turn occurring in the trunk is more obvious when turning stems from an emotional desire to turn, perhaps to express anger. Dramatic situations allow internal motivation to be evident. In classical ballet elegance dictates that torso preparation be unseen.

As discussed earlier on page 32, the most familiar form of turning is around the vertical axis of the body. The signs for turning right (CW) and left (CCW) are already familiar.

The simple sequence of Ex. 60a combines turning, extension, flexion and stillness. Perform this sequence first lying on the floor, then try it standing. Find different interpretations for this simple set of instructions. Remember the automatic cancellation rule: the extension is not expected to be held during the next turn. Try 60b first standing, then lying on the floor. Remember that degree of turn has not yet been stated. There is, however, always a tendency to want to make it a whole turn (an inborn desire to return to an established front) but this need not be so; 1/4 turn or 1/2 turn will just as well fulfill the instructions. Try using different amounts, make each turn the same amount or make each turn a different amount. Here you have freedom. The action (a turn) and the timing (swift) have been dictated, but you still have much leeway to do as you wish.

Turning on both feet, i.e. swivelling, is limited in degree; the legs become crossed and turning ceases. If as a preparation the feet are crossed on the correct side a greater degree of swivel can be achieved - a favorite step in Spanish dance.

Left turn (CCW)   Right turn (CW)

60a   b)

The timing of accompanying actions may vary. Ex. 60c illustrates completely simultaneous actions; in 60d there is partial overlap. In 60c turning to the right is accompanied by flexion, closing in. After a brief stillness turning to the right occurs again, but this time accompanied by extension. In 60d the slow turn is halfway through before flexion starts; extension occurs more rapidly at the start of the second turn, the turn continuing on. It is likely that the extension will be retained though no such retention is stated. This set of instructions could be done with one slow turn, or with multiple turns. It could be performed by a folk dancer, a skater or a ballet dancer. For the latter two the extension might take the form of an arabesque. Or the whole sequence could be performed lying on the floor - with a very different result. Swivelling on the hips and turning on the knees are also possibilities. Mode of support is unstated.

Choice of Right or Left Turn

When it is desirable to leave the turning direction open, to give a choice, then the composite turn sign of Ex. 61a can be used. This sign, in which the right and left turn signs are written one on top of the other, gives the reader the choice of turning, either right or left. In 61b as you extend you may turn either way; then, after the pause, you may again turn right or left as flexion occurs. Freedom in the choice of direction may occur in an otherwise defined movement sequence; its use is not limited to movement exploration.

Ex. 61b provides an interesting timing when repeated; the closing in at the end becomes the preparation for the extension at the start. Impetus must be found for any sudden change of turning direction.

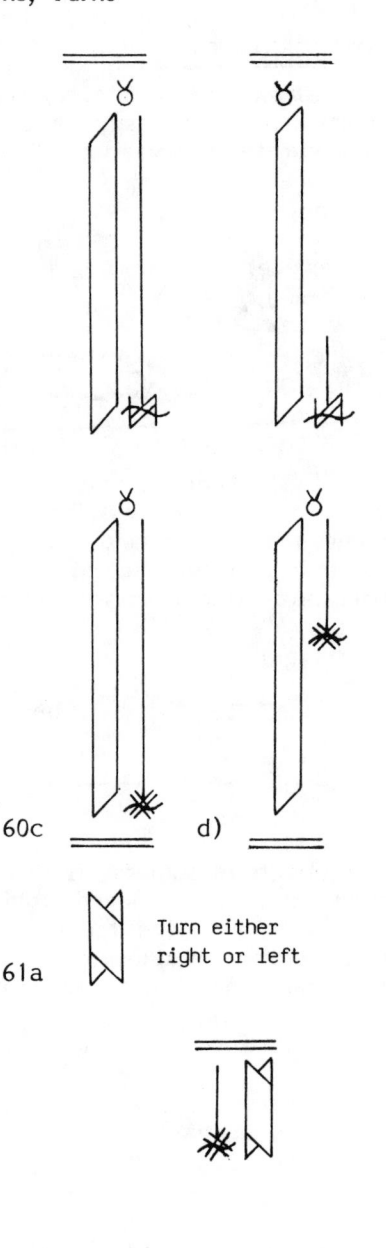

60c   d)

61a   Turn either right or left

61b

SOMERSAULTS

Revolutions in the sagittal plane, i.e. forward or backward somer-saults (rolls), are familiar to most people from childhood. Like wheels of a car these revolutions have a lateral, side to side axis.

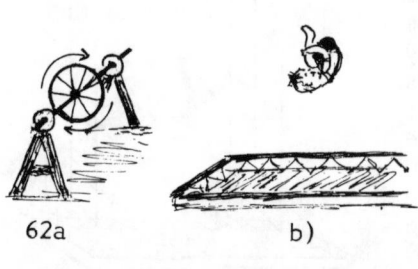

Ex. 62a illustrates a wheel revol-ving while remaining in the same lo-cation; it is spinning around itself, but does not travel.

Ex. 62b shows a tumbler perform-ing a similar revolution in the air having sprung up from a trampoline. There has been a vertical rise but no horizontal change of location.

62a   b)

If a wheel has contact with the ground, as is usually the case when it is a means of transporting a vehicle, as in 62c, then it rolls along the surface and travelling occurs. The same is true of somer-saults on the ground, 62d; you will not end up where you started. A backward somersault will result in travelling backward, 62e.

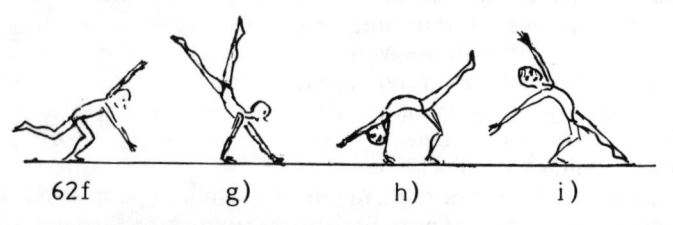

62c   d)   e)

The term somersault commonly means the form in which the body 'tucks in', i.e. is flexed, folded up. But the same form of revolution can occur with the torso and limbs extended. The usual form of this is a forward 'walkover', a sagittal cartwheel in which each hand and then each foot 'walks' into the forward direction, Ex. 62f - 62i.

62f   g)   h)   i)

Indication of Somersaulting

The choice of somersaulting either forward or backward is shown by the composite sign of Ex. 63a. A forward somersault (forward roll) is specified by Ex. 63b, and a backward somersault (backward roll) by 63c. These signs are pictorial and have a logical basis.

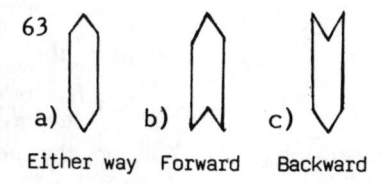

63

a)   b)   c)

Either way   Forward   Backward

CARTWHEELS

While in a somersault we have our front or back toward the direction of the revolution, in a cartwheel it is the right or left side which is toward the direction of progression. Our relationship to the image of a wheel has changed: now we are flat against the wheel, as in Ex. 64a, and the axis of rotation becomes a sagittal axis through the center of the body.

64a
b)

A cartwheel type of revolution can occur without horizontal travelling during a spring in the air. Such cartwheeling may be in a tucked-in position or with the torso and limbs extended, as in 64b. The familiar form is that which travels along the ground, 64c.

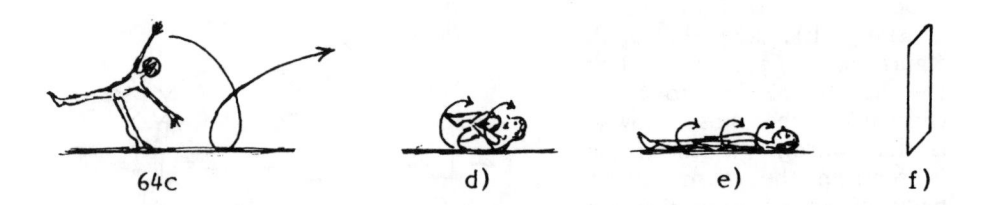

64c
d)
e)
f)

If the body is lying on the ground folded up, 64d, a lateral rolling can occur. Such rolling is usually experienced as folded up log-rolling, 64e. It could, however, be viewed as a cartwheel action if the axis is judged from the cross of directions established when the person was standing. Thus in 64d, if the feet are toward the front of the room, a 'cartwheel' revolution will result in a roll toward the right side of the room. Most forms of revolving are experienced and judged from the Body Key; therefore 64d-e are usually written with the sign of 64f.

Change of Front during a Cartwheel

Cartwheels are very deceptive in that many people do not realize that a full cartwheel also contains a full revolution around the vertical axis of the body. In a full cartwheel there is a return to the original front. But when half a cartwheel occurs there is a change of front. This fact is difficult to demonstrate with a doll, since the front surface of the doll remains toward the same direction all the time. But when half a cartwheel has been accomplished the body has also rotated a half turn around its own axis and so will be facing into the opposite direction. Ex. 65a on the next page shows a cartwheel starting with the back to the reader; 65b shows the completion of half a cartwheel.

Change of Front during a Cartwheel (continued)

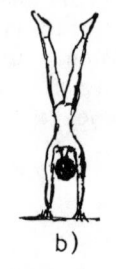

65a   b)   c)   d)

The performer's front appears still to be away from the reader. But note the difference impression made when the head is held up and the back arched, as they usually are in such activities. Because in 65c the face and also the hands are toward the reader, you may begin to see that the performer is now facing you. When the legs are dropped to the ground, either toward the reader or away (it makes no difference to the resulting standing position), the performer is then clearly seen to be facing the reader, 65d.

It is easier to see what happens if the figure is in profile. Ex. 65e shows the figure up in a straight line, the hands pointing toward F (forward), the nose toward B (backward). If the figure is seen in the more natural body curve of 65f, the forward direction is emphasized. In 65g the legs have been lowered over forward (a half forward somersault) and the performer is about to straighten up, facing F. In 65h - j the legs are lowered backward (a half somersault backward) and the performer is again seen to be facing F, 65j. Thus in 65e the indications F and B are correct, even though at first glance they appear to be wrong.

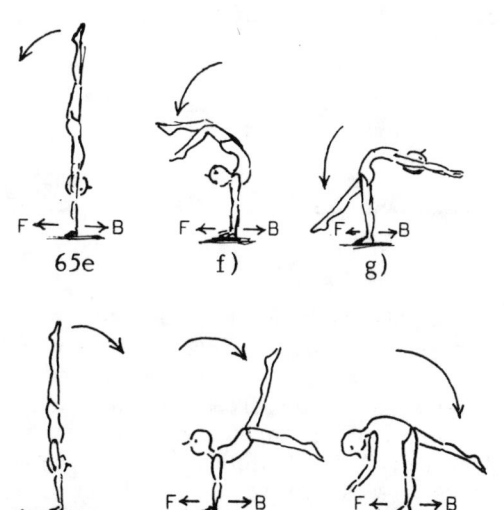

65e   f)   g)

65h   i)   j)

The change of front for a half cartwheel takes place at the moment that the first hand takes weight and the second foot is released. In 65k the body may be nearly straight down, but front is still considered to be away from the reader until the moment when all weight is transferred to the hand.

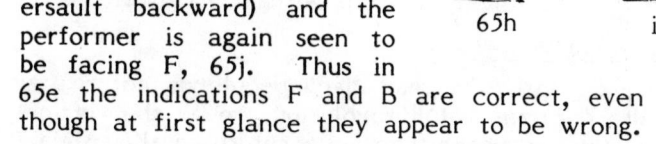

65k

Indication of Cartwheeling

As we have seen, a cartwheel contains within it a rotation around the vertical axis of the body; thus the sign is based on ⟦ or ⟧. Pointers at the top and bottom of the cartwheel sign indicate the lateral rotation. In 66b and 66d dotted arrows illustrate how the extremities of the sign act as indicators, as arrowheads.

The sign for cartwheeling either way, Ex. 66e, contains the composite turn sign for turning either way, but, for practical purposes, only one set of lateral pointers. To stress that 'either way' is intended the ad lib. sign: ∿ may be added as in Ex. 66f. In planning a movement sequence we soon make a decision regarding right or left, but on paper the choice may still be left open.

66a b)

Cartwheel to the right

66c d)

Cartwheel to the left

66e or f)

Cartwheel either way

HORIZONTAL WHEELING

In a pivot turn, even if three limbs are extended, as in 67a below, the turn is still around the vertical axis. One is aware, however, of the extremities of the limbs describing a horizontal circle, like the rim of a wheel placed horizontally.

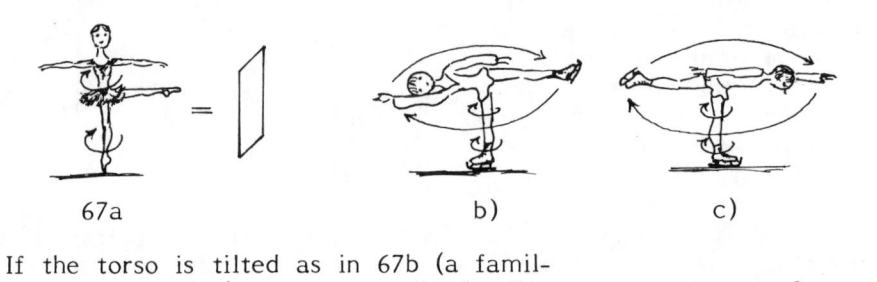

67a   b)   c)

If the torso is tilted as in 67b (a familiar action in skating), the sense of wheeling is increased, but the action is still described as a pivot turn, the vertical supporting leg retaining the vertical axis. Ex. 67c shows a similar turn but in an arabesque line. Again the extremities describe a wheel-like path but the vertical support retains the vertical axis.

67d

Even in swivelling on one knee, 67d, the vertical line still dominates.

When one is lying on the back, the side or the front, total body wheeling can occur. There is no longer any vertical support, but the axis for such wheeling is still the vertical line of gravity. To be able to wheel while lying, the performer needs a slippery floor and must usually push with the feet and/or hands to get around, or have outside

Horizontal Wheeling (continued)

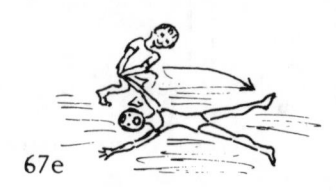 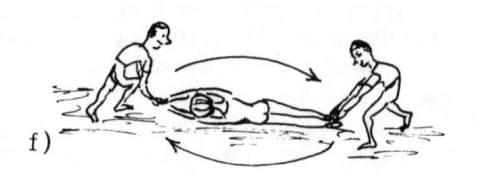

67e   f)

help, as in the examples above. In 67e a person lying on her back is being rotated clockwise by a partner. In 67f she is lying on her left side and two people, one grasping her hands, the other her feet, are rotating her clockwise. The axis of both rotations is the vertical line. Both are seen and experienced as horizontal wheeling, but it is of interest to note that Ex. 67e could be viewed from the cross of directions in the body. The axis would then be a sagittal one and the rotation cartwheeling to the left, which indeed it would be if the performer were standing. Similarly, 67f could be viewed or experienced as a forward somersault, but this is less likely. In general, body revolutions are described according to the body axes.

Indication of Horizontal Wheeling

Because from experience it has been found confusing to use a body reference for wheeling, this form of movement is written as horizontal circling on the spot.

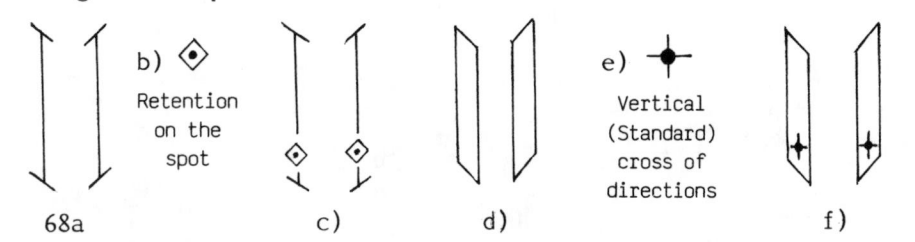

b) Retention on the spot

e) Vertical (Standard) cross of directions

68a   c)   d)   f)

Ordinary circling, Ex. 68a, involves travelling, a progression across the floor. The sign for retention on a spot, Ex. 68b, is added to indicate that no progression takes place, that the revolving is on the spot, Ex. 68c. Since this action is related to pivoting, as we saw in 67e-f, it can be expressed as turning around the vertical axis. As the signs of 68d mean log-rolling when one is lying, the key for the vertical cross of directions, Ex. 68e, must be added to these turn signs, 68f, to show wheeling. The signs of 68f have the same meaning as 68c; they provide a different choice of description. Such choices may seem unnecessary but they are, in fact, both practical and expressive.

The range of variation provided by these rotations enriches movement in many ways. In gymnastics, diving, etc. these revolutions often appear in combined forms. As aerial forms require special training we will not investigate them here. An understanding of the specific forms will help in later exploration or rotations and twists within the body.

Reading Study No. 18

REVOLUTIONS, ROTATIONS

This study may be interpreted in several ways. Note the separated turning in measure 11 and the differences between the following signs:

any extension.   stretch lengthwise.

spread as well as extend (three-dimensional extension).

Did you interpret measure 1 as a roll forward and measure 2 as wheeling?   This study could have included revolutions while springing but not everyone is a tumbler!

PHRASING OF MOVEMENT SEQUENCES

It is one thing to read and perform a series of movements; it is another to produce a sequence which has cohesion, kinetic logic and expression. When one movement follows another, are they related? Is there a link or is the second action a separate 'thought', in no way a development of what went before? Timing can give some indication; a definite break in the movement flow usually means a new start, a new idea. Let us investigate a simple movement sequence to discover the possibilities.

In Ex. 69a turning is followed by a circular path and then a straight path. Ex. 69b illustrates a possible interpretation of the path travelled. Ex. 69a can be interpreted as turning around the center which enlarges in its use of space to become a circular path. This then becomes spatially more direct, going off on a tangent, so to speak, to produce travelling on a straight path. In itself this material has a kinetic logic whatever accompanying gestures, dynamics, etc. may be used. It has a sense of space in its development from turning around the central core, the vertical axis.

Each kind of movement has its own kinetic logic. For a movement phrase to have its own logic, there must be a line of development; each new action must have its 'birth' in the preceding one. The germ, the seed of beginning to circle, must already be there by the end of the turning action; the seed of travelling on a straight path must already be in the body before the end of the circling. This germinating of a new idea is a small dynamic change which takes place usually in the center of the body, the torso. We do not want to spell out how to achieve this development; it takes place within, organically, and may not be evident to an observer. In the early stages it is best for these productive minor dynamic changes to be obvious, to be performed visibly; subtlety can come later.

Ex. 69c takes the same material as 69a, but the gaps between the actions show enough of a pause to break the thread of the 'movement thought'. Each action has its own start, each is a new 'idea'. Each must overcome the moment of inertia which preceded it. Such a kinetic pattern, three separate thoughts, may be just what is wanted. It is important that the difference be clear in movement as well as in the notation, the expression of the movement ideas on paper.

94

Rotations, Revolutions, Turns

What do we mean by 'one movement thought growing out of the previous one'? Let us take a verbal sentence to draw a parallel. "I enjoy writing poetry as a gift for your birthday." This statement carries the message that the pleasure of writing the poetry springs from the fact that it is to be a gift. This thought progression is missing in the following: "I enjoy writing poetry. I plan to give you a gift for your birthday." Movement has a comparable logic in its progression from one movement to another. But one cannot easily put into words just how or why one action grows out of another. A kinetic sense needs to be developed physically.

Complete separation of movement ideas can be intentional in a movement composition; this is particularly true of contemporary choreography. Just as modern music, poetry and prose, may juxtapose unusual, unexpected ideas, sounds and words to achieve a particular effect, so contemporary choreography may juxtapose unusual, non sequitur movements for a similar reason. In any study it is wise to master the traditional forms, to progress from the known to the unknown. Discover fully the simple forms, the usual, logical transitions and make them your own before becoming too adventurous.

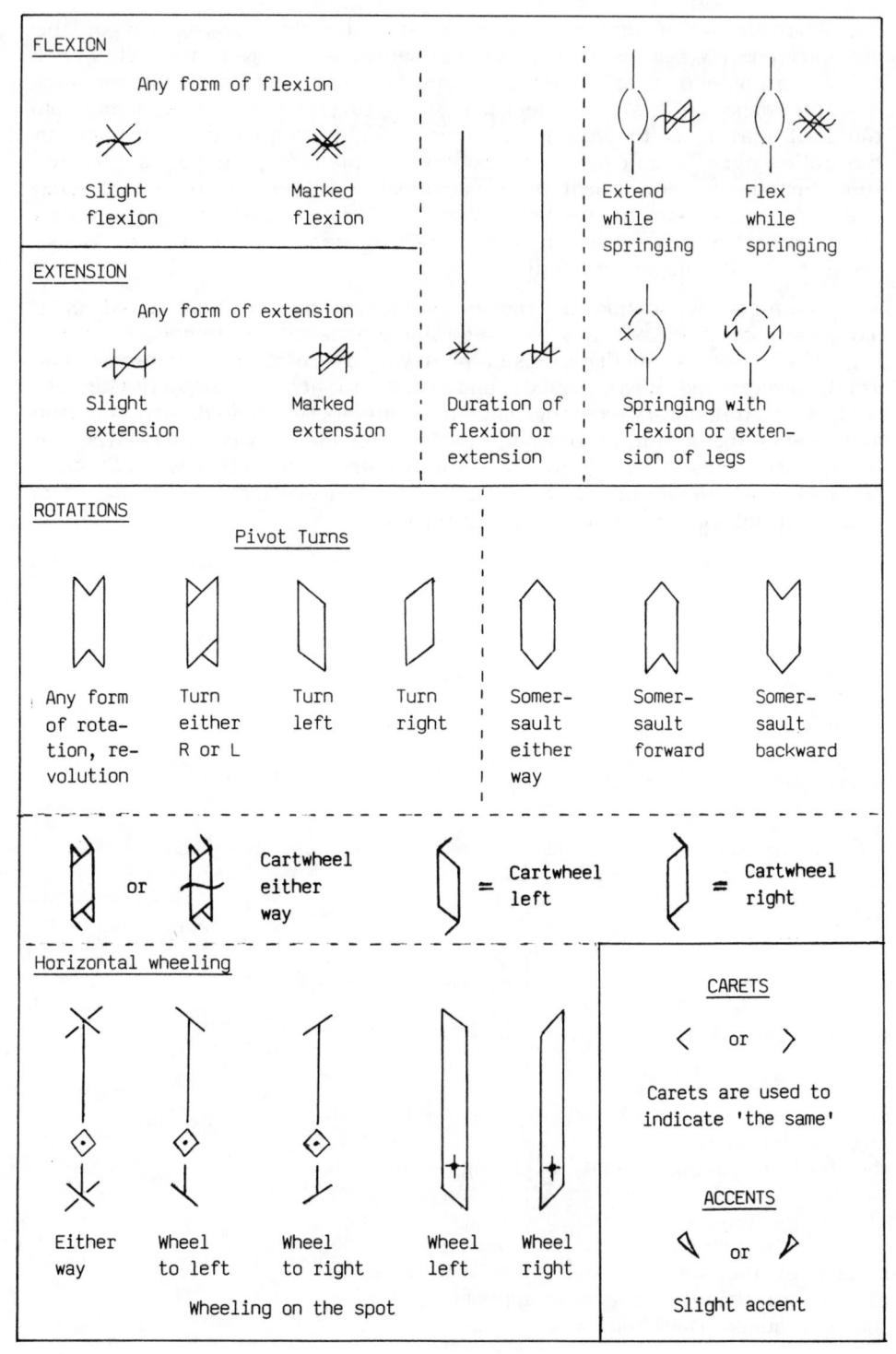

Chapter Eight
SUPPORTING, CHANGE OF SUPPORT

Because of gravity we spend virtually all our lives resting on one part or another of our body on the floor or on furniture of some kind. This state is so natural and common that we do not even think about it.   Under certain conditions we are aware of how we are supporting and consciously make a change.   The chair is too hard; we shift our weight to ease one part and take the weight on another.   Parts of the body get tired of being weight bearers; aching feet are a commonly shared experience.   Lying on the beach, reading or sunning, we make frequent shifts from sitting, leaning, lying, etc. by rolling over.

Many of the possible modes and changes of support belong in the category of gymnastics or acrobatics, particularly in conjunction with use of different apparatus.   For aerialists in a circus the part supporting is often the armpit, the crook of the knee, even the crook of the ankle.   Here we will stick to more everyday, non-specialist examples.

Weight may be supported on only one or on several parts of the body at the same time.   A single support may be one foot, one knee (not so easy, the knee cap not having been built as a weight bearing part), a single hip, the shoulders (a shoulder stand), the head alone, one hand, and, at one time, a single finger as performed by an acrobat named Mr. Uni.

Double supports can range from two feet, one foot and one knee, foot and hand, foot and shoulder, to foot and head, knee and hand, knee and head, and so on.   Triple, quadruple, and even five point supports are possible.   All these need to be explored to experience not only the moment of achieving such supports but also the transitions between.   Many interesting variations can be experienced without great physical skills.   On the next page is illustrated a selection of possibilities progressing from single to quadruple supports.

Indication of Supporting

The sign for supporting, taking weight, an angular horizontal 'bow', Ex. 70a, states only the fact of taking weight, of being supported. An action stroke is used as a general indication of the movement which produces the new support, i.e. which ends in a new support, Ex. 70b. Length of the action stroke shows the duration of the transition to the new support. Ex. 70c shows a quick transition.

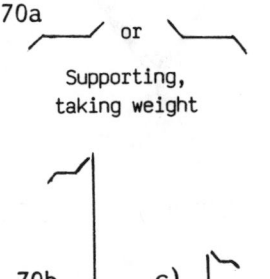

70a   or

Supporting,
taking weight

70b   c)

Number of Supporting Parts

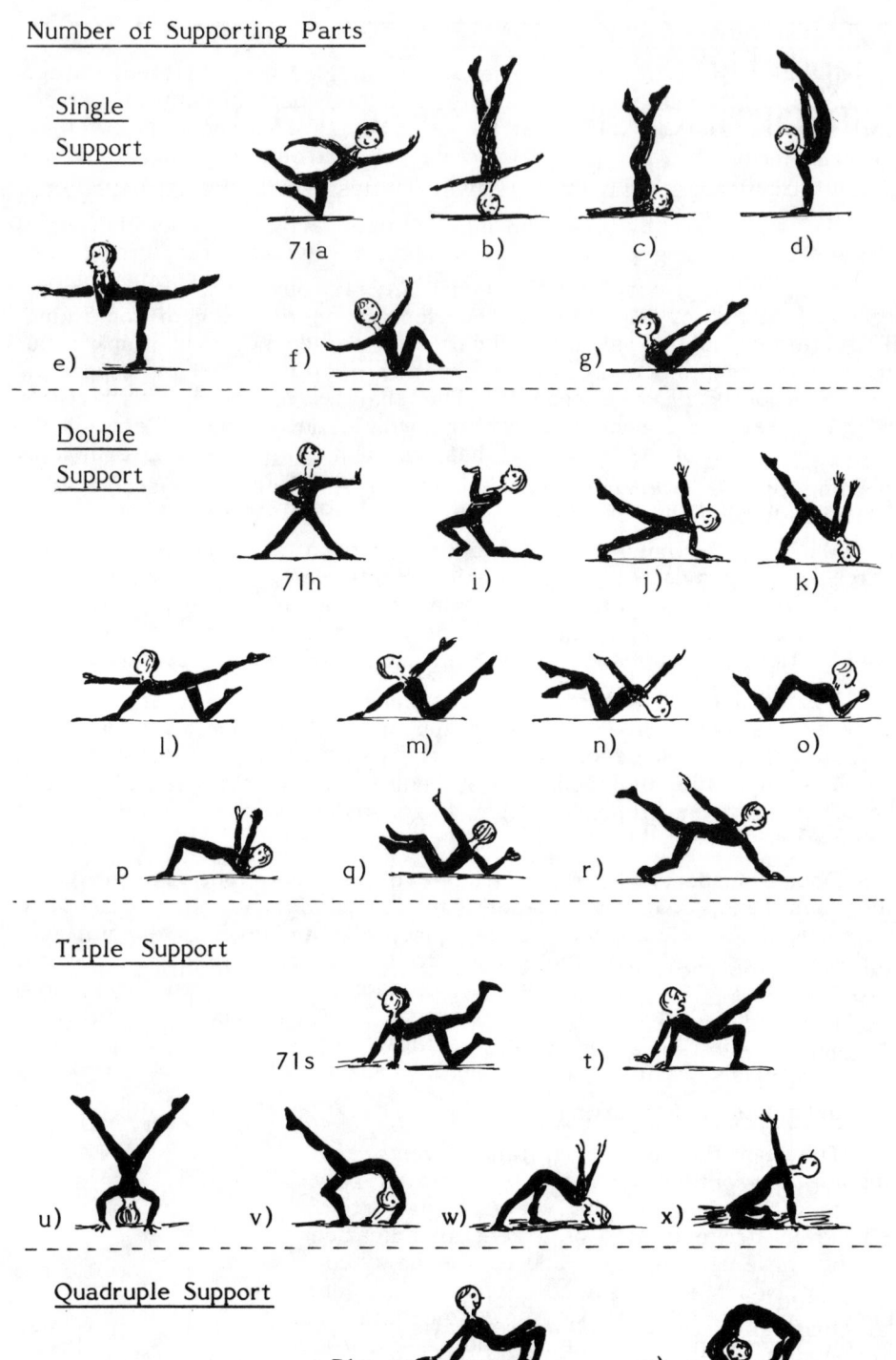

Single
Support

71a b) c) d)

e) f) g)

Double
Support

71h i) j) k)

l) m) n) o)

p q) r)

Triple Support

71s t)

u) v) w) x)

Quadruple Support

71y z)

Transition between Adjacent Parts of the Body - Rolling

In the matter of transference of weight two very different categories exist: 1) Weight transference to a distant part (usually an extremity) such as foot to foot, foot to hand, etc. This mode is given the general term of 'walking'. 2) Transference from one part to an immediately adjacent part, as in rolling, 'rolling' being the term used.

We will start by investigating rolling. A good experience is to move from kneeling to sitting on one hip, the weight transferring along the thigh until it reaches the hip. Then roll over to the other hip and along up to the other knee. Once the torso is on the ground the comfortable, easy way of transferring weight is through rolling, be it log-rolling or somersaulting. For somersaulting the body needs to be curled up. Because the feet are then near the hips, a smooth rolling between hips and feet can take place.

Different forms of rolling may require control and strength depending on the type and speed. In general, rolling is 'comfortable' in that no problem of loss of balance, of falling, exists. An interesting roll, the 'monkey roll', results from grasping both ankles, feet together, legs turned out, and the back rounded.

72a   b)   c)   d)   e)

Indication of rolling is based on the appropriate revolution sign. Ex. 72a gives the indication for any revolution around the axes of the body. Support signs are added to this indication to show rolling. Ex. 72b shows many changes of support while rotating. This notation is simplified by using one support sign at the beginning and one at the end to express continuous supporting, i.e. that rolling occurs from beginning to end, Ex. 72c. This indication is further simplified by abbreviating the supporting line, as shown in the log-rolling of Ex. 72d. The supporting signs may be drawn on either side of the symbol; there is no change in meaning.

72f   g)   h)

A somersault either forward or backward rolling on the floor is expressed as 72f. Ex. 72g specifies a forward roll; the performer will automatically curl up as a preparation to accomplish it. A forward somersault in the air is written as 72h. This is, of course, only the bare statement with no instructions as to how it is to be achieved.

99

Reading Study No. 19

LYING ON DIFFERENT PARTS OF THE TORSO

Lying on the front, the back or the side is indicated by stating the surface on which the body is supporting. A small 'tick' or line is added to the appropriate side of the torso sign: 🔲 to indicate the surface.

The front surface The back surface The right side The left side

In the following study changes in supporting on one surface or another are achieved through rolling. See p. 102 for other parts of body.

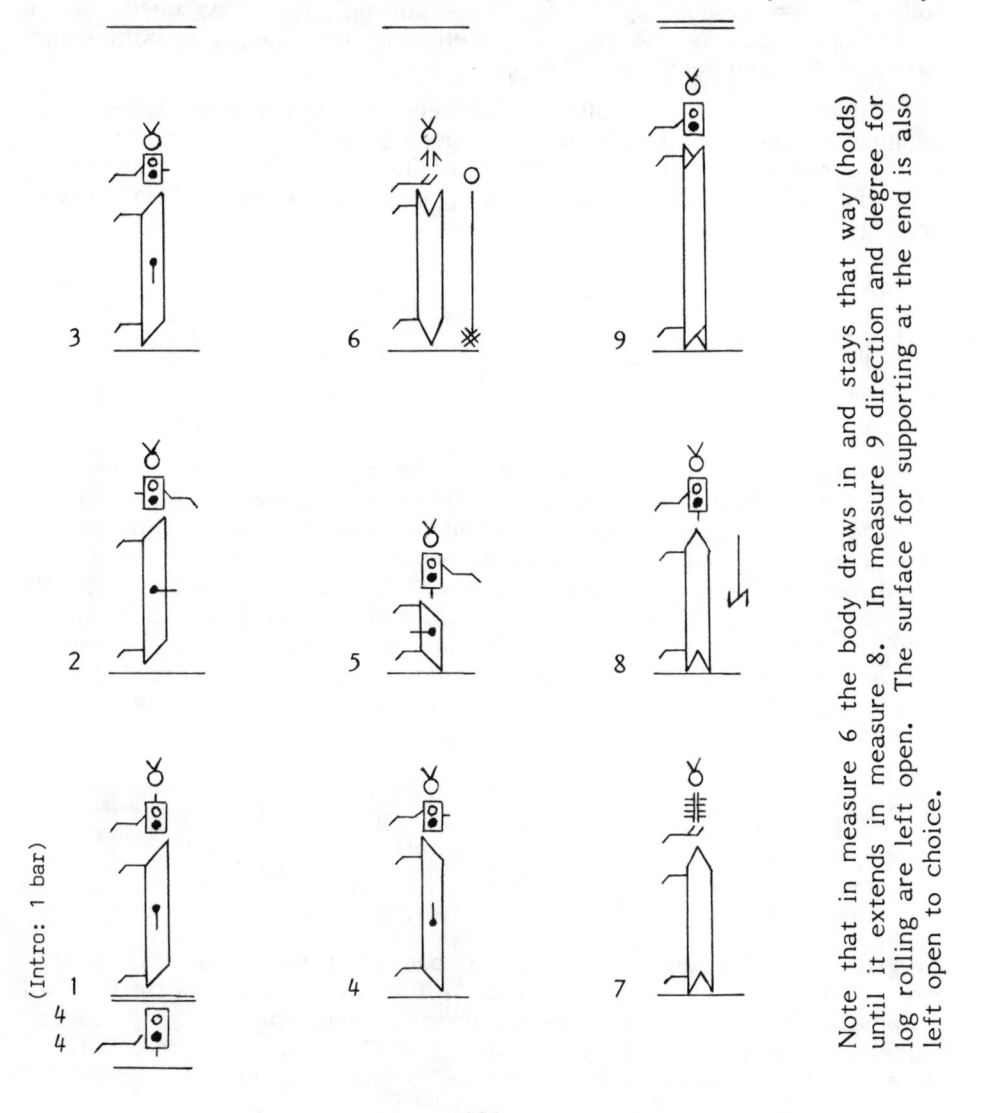

Note that in measure 6 the body draws in and stays that way (holds) until it extends in measure 8. In measure 9 direction and degree for log rolling are left open. The surface for supporting at the end is also left open to choice.

Supporting, Change of Support

Transition between Distant Parts of the Body - 'Walking'

As mentioned before, 'walking' is the general term given to transferring the weight from one 'extremity' of the body to another. Walking usually occurs on the feet, but we also 'walk' on the knees, on the
hands, from hands to feet as in a walk-over, and so on. In sitting we
can inch forward or backward by 'walking' with our hips. Of the less
familiar forms there is transference from foot to head, from knees to
lower arms, etc. In such contexts the hips, knees, lower legs and lower arms act as 'extremities'; no rolling occurs.

Transference of weight, complete or partial, may be onto an object. Partial transference occurs when leaning against a tree or
when one legs takes weight on the barre, the
other still being on the floor, as in certain
classroom stretches, Ex. 73a. In work with a
partner or apparatus many variations occur.

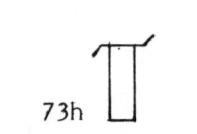

73a

The basic indication for an action taking
weight, 73b, is modified to show a 'step' of
some kind, 73c. It is expected that in much
improvisation such stepping will take place
on the feet, but other possibilities should be
tried out. In Ex. 73d a turn CCW is accompanied by three 'steps'. Try this first with
foot supports; then find a variation using a
knee. The instructions of 73e, moving sideward low with two transferences of weight,
suggest use of knee and hand. While a step
should eventually be a complete transference
of weight, at this stage sharing of weight is
allowed as long as weight is really taken and
the action is not just a slight lean to maintain balance.

73b   c)

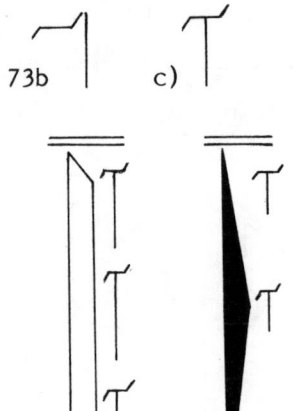

A direction sign and the supporting sign
can be combined to show the direction of a
new support. Ex. 73f states that the forward action results in a new support, i.e. a
forward transference of weight. In 73g the
low backward action results in a new support,
perhaps on a knee or hand. Ex. 73h indicates
transference of weight in place, i.e. not into
any direction, therefore on the spot. Gradually indications for movement possibilities are
combined to spell out more specific instructions for a desired sequence.

73d   e)

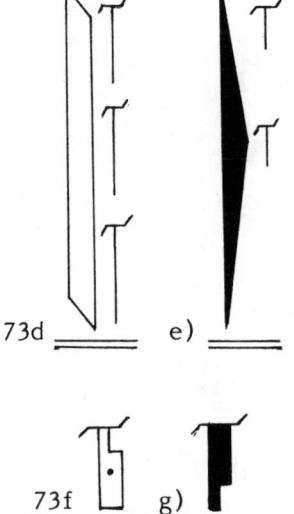

73f   g)

The next step, to specify which part of
the body is taking weight, is done by combin-
ing the appropriate part of the body sign with the support indication.

73h

SIGNS FOR THE MAIN PARTS OF THE BODY

Below are the signs for the main parts of the body, the areas and the joints. Indication of 'either hand', 'either foot', etc. is given on the next page.

C̆	= head
⌐↑↑⌐	= shoulder section
☐	= chest
⊠	= waist
☒	= pelvis
☒	= whole torso

74

For the Arms	Left		Right	Both	
↿ ↾ (Left Right) ⇑ (Both)	⌐	shoulder	⌐	↑	shoulders
	⌐	elbow	⌐	⋏	elbows
	⌐	wrist	⌐	⋏	wrists
	⌐	hand	⌐	⋏	hands
	⌐	fingers	⌐	⋏	fingers

For the Legs	Left		Right	Both	
⫪ ⫪ (Left Right) ⫪⫪ (Both)	⊣	hip	⊢	+	hips
	⊣	knee	⊢	‡	knees
	⊣	ankle	⊢	‡	ankles
	⊣	foot	⊢	‡	feet
	⊣	toes	⊢	‡	toes

Signs for Both

Use of both hands or both feet, etc. is indicated either by writing both left and right signs, Ex. 75a, or by combining them into one sign, 75b. The signs for both shoulders must be drawn:  so that it does not look like an arrow:  . For many years there were no separate signs for right and left parts of the leg (unlike the parts-of-the-arm signs for which right and left signs have always existed). The previous meanings in Motif Description for 75d, 75e and 75f were 'either foot', 'either knee', and 'either hip'. The change has resulted from standardizing usages in writing. Since this change is recent, in this book the double signs are used, as in Ex. 75g and 75h as these indications are self-explanatory. Note modification of the sign: 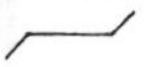 to: 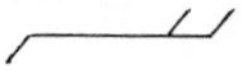 for supporting on two parts at the same time.

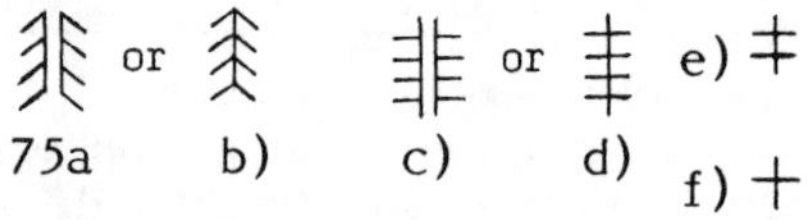
or
or
75a
b)
c)
d)
e)
f)
Both hands
Both feet

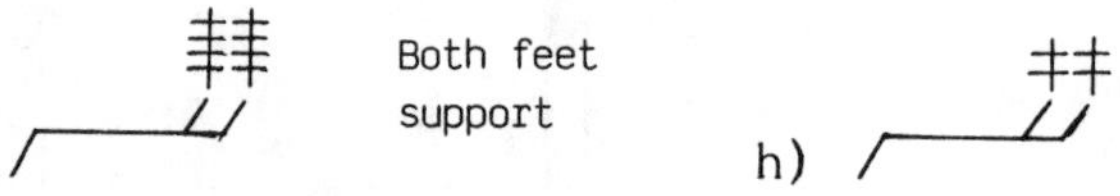
75g
Both feet
support
h)
Both knees
support

Sign for 'Either Side'

When choice should be left open to the reader to decide which hand, foot, etc. to use, the 'either side' sign, Ex. 76a, is added to the double part-of-the-body sign. The 'either side' sign is composed of a short vertical line (representing the vertical line in the body dividing right and left) and the horizontal ad lib. sign meaning 'any'; thus 'any side'.

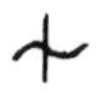
76a
Sign for
either
side

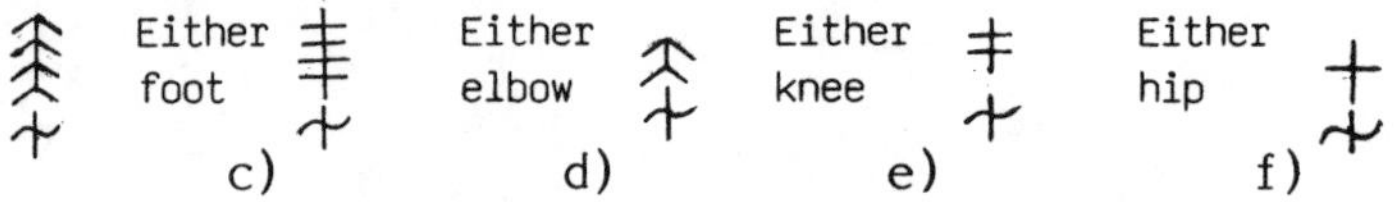
Either
hand
76b
Either
foot
c)
Either
elbow
d)
Either
knee
e)
Either
hip
f)
etc.

Part Supported; Part Taking Weight

There is logic in having the weight-bearing sign slant downward. At the top end of the sign is written the part being supported (knee, hand, etc.) and at the bottom end of the sign is written the indication of the object on which the supporting takes place. When nothing in particular is shown a support is understood to be on the floor. Ex. 77c shows kneeling on a chair ( = a chair); 77d shows sitting on a chair.

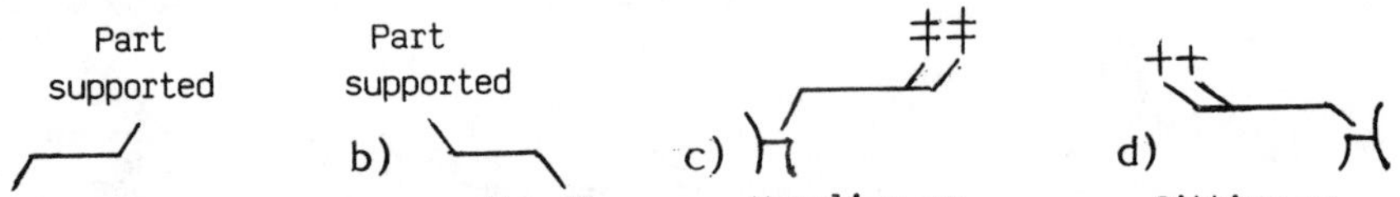
77
Part
supported
a)
the floor
Part
supported
b)
the floor
c)
Kneeling on
a chair
d)
Sitting on
a chair

Reading Practice

SUPPORTING ON DIFFERENT PARTS OF THE BODY

This study in changes of support progresses from a step (support on a foot) to kneeling (support on one knee), sitting on one hip, weight on one knee and one hand, weight on foot and hand, weight on foot and head, weight on both knees, and finally with weight on both feet. Transitions between these supports are up to the performer; many variations are possible. Note use of sign for 'either': ⊁ .

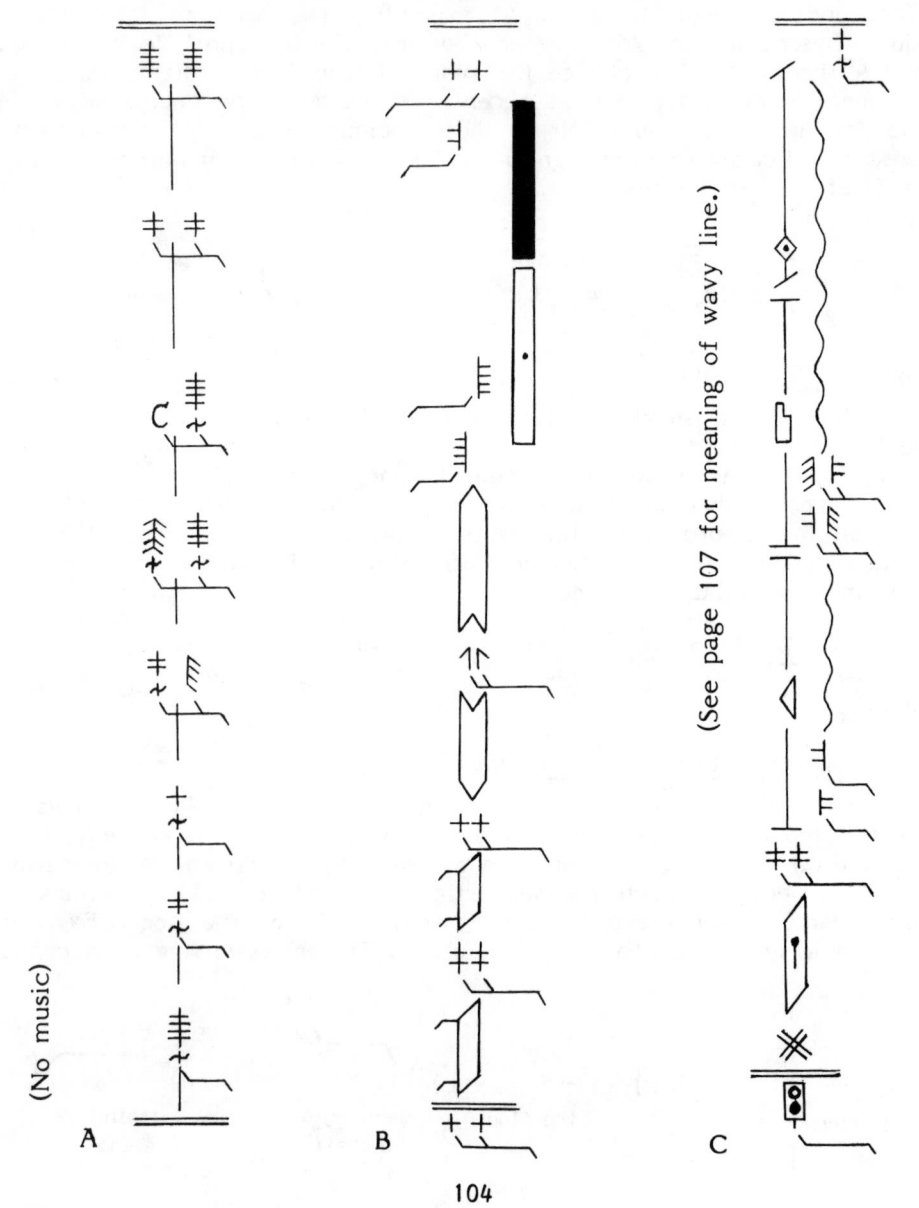

(No music)

A

B

C

(See page 107 for meaning of wavy line.)

PERFORMANCE OF A SINGLE STEP

Transferring the weight from foot to foot, that is, taking steps, walking, is such a familiar action that we are often unaware of the process. Do we really know what is happening and can we therefore modify performance of steps as needed in a movement sequence? How actually is a simple step, a transference of weight, achieved?

Where does a single step start? Where does it end? Except for steps in place (on the spot) the working leg has to move out in the direction into which the step is to be taken. Let us say that this will be a forward step.

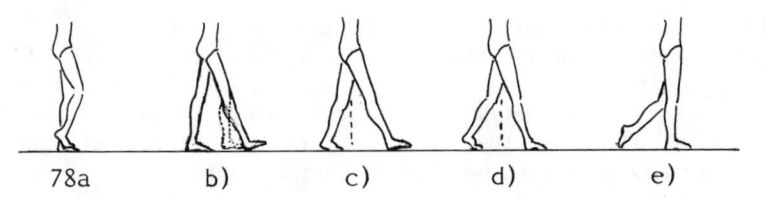

| 78a | b) | c) | d) | e) |

Ex. 78a shows the right leg free and ready to take a step. In 78b it has moved forward and is touching the ground; at the same time the weight has shifted slightly forward. But this leg gesture (touching the ground but free of weight) need not lead into a step. Many such gestures occur without a step following. In 78c it is clear that a step will take place because the weight has been shifted forward beyond the toes of the supporting left foot. This is a normal preparation for the transference of weight to the right foot. As the weight is transferred forward there is a moment of double support, as in 78d. In a forward step the back heel usually comes off the floor at this moment. The weight then moves completely onto the new support, Ex. 78e, and the left leg, released of weight, is free to leave the ground and to begin the preparation, the gesture, that leads into the next step. A full step is a total transference of weight and has not been completed until all the weight is on the new support. Moving into an open position on two feet, as in 78d, is only a half step.

Try a series of slow steps and sense the weight continuously moving. What happened? Did you pause before starting the next step? Did you perform a favorite variation of a step, rather than keeping it completely simple? Was an ornamental preparatory leg gesture included, an unnecessary flourish? Was importance given to the leg being released, bringing it, perhaps, conspicuously into place beside the other leg? Or did the leg gestures occur only to make the steps possible, that is, having no importance in themselves? This last is the correct performance of the basic action of walking.

The expression of walking can vary enormously according to how the body is held, how the legs flex, extend, their state of rotation, how the feet are placed on the floor, their use in transferring and releasing weight. Even in a simple walk a keen eye will spot significant variations in performances by different people.

E

Indication of Walking

Because ordinary walking on the feet is such a familiar mode of transporting the body, of travelling, it is indicated in a simple way in both Motif and Structured Description.

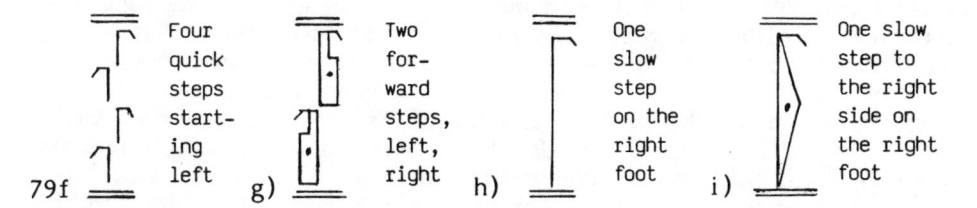

| 79a | Step on the right foot then on the left foot | b) or c) Basic sign for walking, stepping | d) e) Step on left foot Step on right foot |

Walking, stepping right then left, can be written as Ex. 79a. This notation states an action ending with weight on the right foot, then the same for the left foot. As it is such a common action, an abbreviation is used. The general sign for walking, 79b or 79c, is abbreviated to 79d and 79e, the placement of the truncated support sign showing visually whether the step is on the right or on the left foot.

We combine these indications with direction symbols to state the direction in which a step occurs. Ex. 79f shows four fast steps starting with the left foot; in 79g two steps forward occur.

| 79f | Four quick steps starting left | g) | Two for- ward steps, left, right | h) | One slow step on the right foot | i) | One slow step to the right side on the right foot |

The length of the action stroke or of the direction symbol indicates the duration of the transference of weight. Ex. 79h shows one slow step on the right foot; in 79i a sideward step is designated.

Statement of Walking for Travelling, Turning

Walking, 'stepping' actions may occur for several reasons, the most obvious one being to travel. We will deal with this first to see how to indicate variations.

Ex. 80a is the basic sign for travelling on a straight path. If we want to cover ground walking or running will most likely take place, but this path sign does not itself stipulate this. If rolling is to be the mode of travelling, this can be stated as in 80b, the indication for any kind of rolling being placed within the path sign. Similarly, if need be, walking can be specified as in 80c.

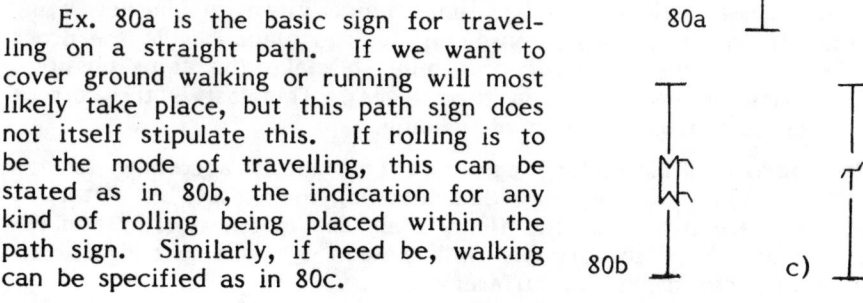

80a

80b   c)

Walking on the knees, Ex. 80d, or on the hands, 80e, can be stated as the means of travelling. The number of steps or whether one starts on the right or left is not stated.

Concentration in stepping may be on the transference of weight. For this purpose the action is usually slower, as in Ex. 79i on the previous page. Transferences of weight may be accompanied by other actions.

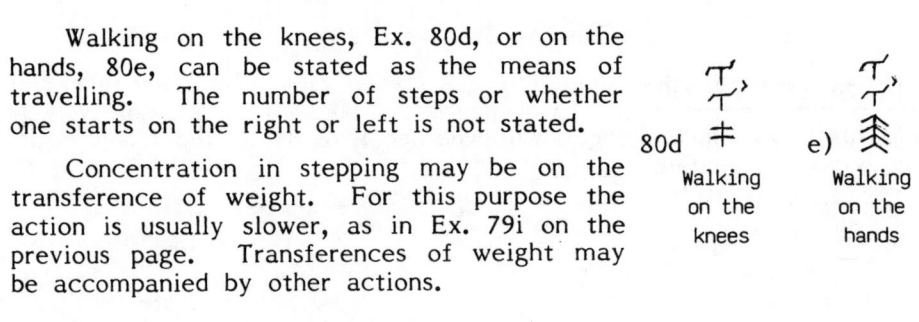

Ex. 80f indicates turning which is accomplished through stepping. Ex. 80g states that the turn includes steps; when and how many is left open. The vertical inclusion bow, 80h, was given earlier. Ex. 80i states just when two steps occur during the turn, a step on the right foot, and later a step on the left, both quite quick transferences of weight. In 80j the same two steps occur, but each is a slow transference with no break between.

Steps may also occur for rhythmic purposes. We are not dealing yet with any specific rhythms, only general timing; however a simple indication can be given for very fast or relatively slower steps by using the vertical wavy line of 80k. This sign is related to the ad lib. sign and means 'continue freely the movement indicated'. In Ex. 80 l very fast steps are shown; in 80m they are slower. These indications can be combined with other actions, as for example, in 80n which states rapid stepping and includes some turning, to right or left. The faster the movement, the smaller the waves in the line become until it represents a vibrating movement comparable to a vibrato or a tremolo in singing.

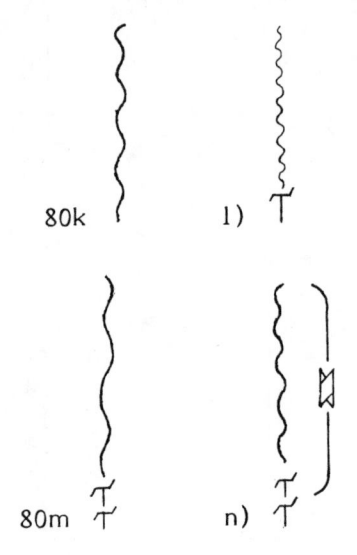

Reading Study No. 20

CHANGE OF SUPPORT

This study starts lying down; whether lying is on the front, back, etc. is not designated.

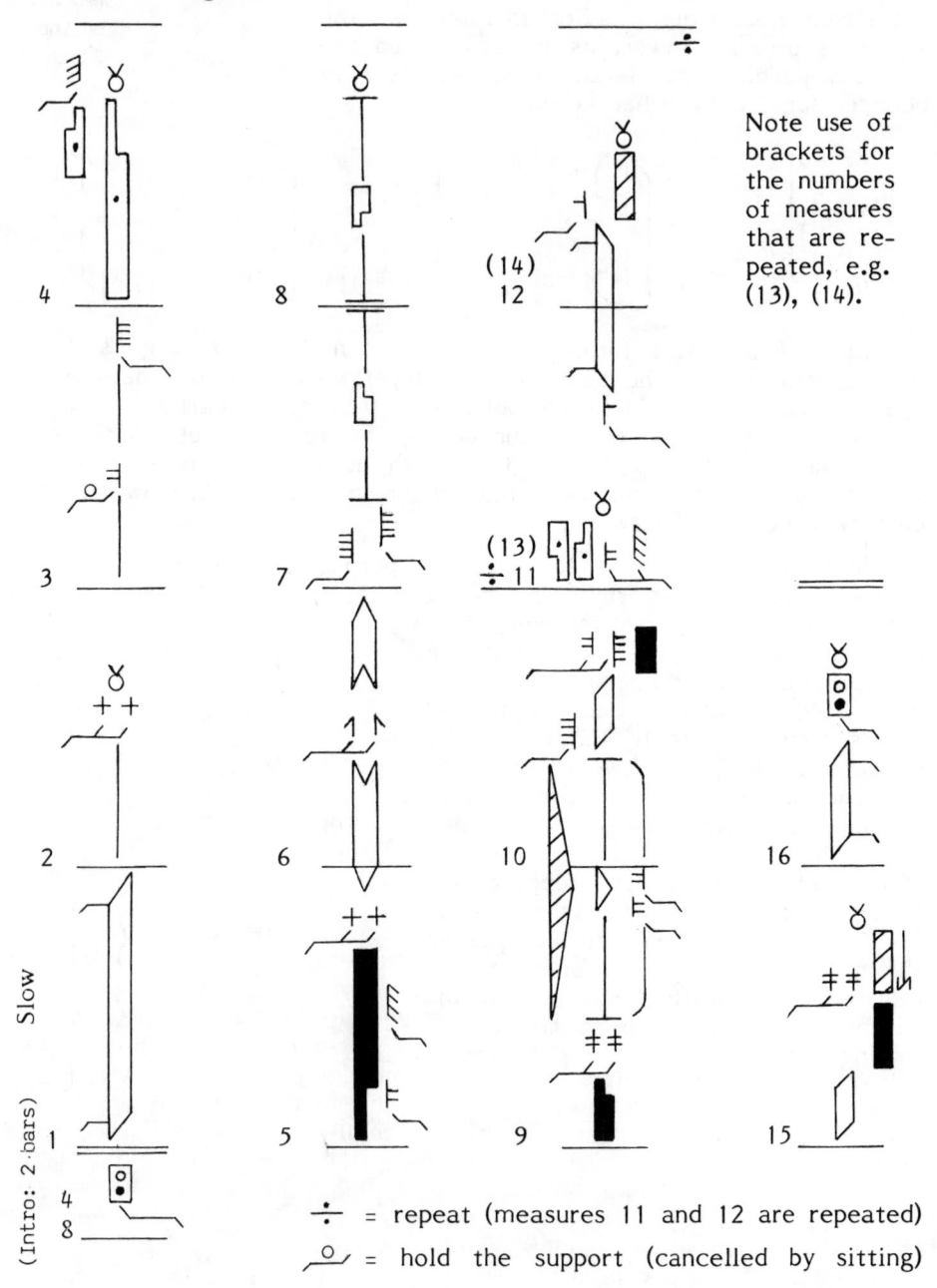

Note use of brackets for the numbers of measures that are repeated, e.g. (13), (14).

÷ = repeat (measures 11 and 12 are repeated)

⌒○⌒ = hold the support (cancelled by sitting)

Chapter Nine
BALANCE, EQUILIBRIUM

Maintaining equilibrium is not an activity which normally occupies our attention. In early childhood we learned to balance on two feet and only under special circumstances do we find ourselves concerned with balance in everyday life. An uneven surface or a narrow plank over a brook may cause us to be aware of balance; otherwise it is only little accidents which cause us to trip that bring home to us what a small surface the foot provides as a base for the weight of the body. It is in the performing arts of gymnastics, acrobatics, dance and skating that extraordinary movements center on equilibrium. We marvel at the ballerina balancing on the tip of her pointe shoe, Ex. 81a, or the tight-rope walker who performs fancy steps and even acrobatic tricks on a swaying wire, 81b.

81a   b)   c)

A SENSE OF BALANCE

Balance is an inherited gift for some performers; others must work hard to achieve it. Indeed, the more we strive the less success may result, for it is a sensation and co-ordination in the body to be mastered through the right kinetic feeling rather than by concentration on the mechanics. Just as an object needs to be rigid to balance on a small surface, so there needs to be adequate tension, tautness, in the body. This tension is achieved through extension, energizing upward through the spine, an inner uplift. In balancing on half toe, the performer's concentration should not be on the foot itself, but on the upward flow of energy. The image should be that of the top of the head lifting toward the ceiling, carrying with it the weight of the body. Invisible strings attached to imaginary balloons lift each inner muscle fibre; the performer does not 'do the work', Ex. 81c. If the limbs are extended, the sense of reaching out in space can assist balance. In a held position the lines in space linking the limb extremities can act as

109

A Sense of Balance (continued)

'electrical connectors' creating spatial tension between the points of this imaginary shape suspended in the air, 82. If there is movement of the
limbs, such movement can also extend energy out
into space, thus creating spatial tension. Concentration on projecting out into space, in contrast to concern with muscles in the body, has
helped many performers to achieve serene and en-
joyable periods of balance. The word 'poise' re-  82
lates to an inner sense of balance. Many body designs (positions) which
are to be suspended in stillness require poise, that is, equilibrium both
in the physical sense and as an inner feeling and awareness. Balance
requires concentration, but too often this produces an introverted, bound
flow state, whereas energy should be flowing outward as though balance
is taken care of by the air around. But sensation alone will not solve
all balance problems; we need to know a few facts, and also how the
center of balance can be used practically as well as expressively.

In Balance; Weight Centered

To explore balance, to achieve a better understanding of it, we must first find the correct
placement of weight, the line of balance in the
body, starting with ordinary standing, Ex. 83a.
How does it feel to have the line of balance, the
plumb line of the center of gravity, correctly
placed? The answer is found through personal experience in mastering control and in anatomical
understanding. For stillness, even on two feet,   83a
awareness of balance is important.

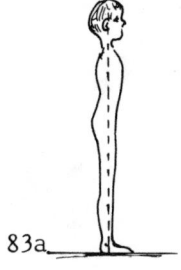

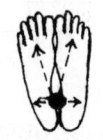
83b

c)
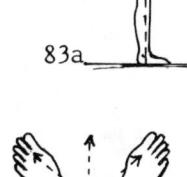
d)

Standing with the feet together, sway from side to side and to and
fro, returning each time to center. Experience the weight shifting in
different directions over the area provided by the soles of the feet until you have found the true point of balance. Experiment with how far
the weight can be shifted when the feet are together, parallel, as in
Ex. 83b, when fully turned out, 83c, or when turned out 45°, as in 83d.
The triangular-shaped base provided by the two feet in 83d is the most
stable of the three positions. The more the center of weight approaches the edge of the supporting base, the less stable the position. Very
little lateral shift is possible when the feet are parallel, and, obviously,
very little sagittal shift for a complete turn out, as in 83c. The correct centered vertical alignment should pass centrally between the two
ears down to just in front of the ankle bone, Ex. 83a.

Automatic Shift of Weight

When the location of an arm or leg is changed, as when the arms are raised, a leg lifted forward or backward, or when the position of the torso and the head are changed, as in a torso tilt, there is automatically a shift in the center of balance in the body. We have all seen an untrained person raising a leg forward and have observed the slight backward lean of the torso which occurs to counterbalance the weight of the lifted leg, Ex. 84a. The trained performer will have developed the necessary muscular control to hold the weight of a raised leg while keeping the rest of the body apparently motionless, Ex. 84b.

84a   b)   c)   d)

A familiar example of weight adjustment occurs when tilting the whole torso forward; there is an automatic shift backward of the pelvis, Ex. 84c. This backward shift can be exaggerated as in 84d so that weight is as far back on the heels as possible. The trained performer can minimize any displacement of the hips but total absence of displacement is impossible for most people.

84e   f)   g)

Ex. 84e illustrates the parlor game of standing heels flat up against a wall and trying to pick up an object on the floor placed near the feet. Inevitably as the weight of the torso moves forward the person falls forward, since no backward compensation is possible and the vertical line of balance passes beyond the base of the support, the feet, 84f. Trained performers have trouble with this action. The circus clown manages to lean at a preposterous angle because his long rigid shoes provided a longer base, 84g.

Images to Aid Equilibrium

Performers are concerned with the line of balance for control and to accomplish difficult movement sequences; in dance balance maintained fleetingly or for more extended periods has an expressive impact. Maintaining balance may be either in stillness or in movement as in multiple turns or in slow changes of level, for example in a sustained transference of weight which includes level change, or a controlled deep knee bend (a grand plié). For each such action finding an appropriate image can be a great help in achieving the right result.

Images to Aid Equilibrium (continued)

85a 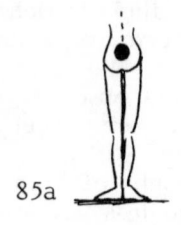 b) 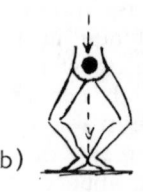 c) 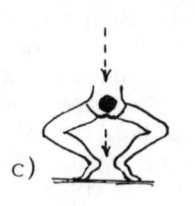 d)

From a centered position, perform a slow full knee bend (a grand plié), Ex. 85a-c. Experience this lowering of the center of gravity as though it were a bead sliding smoothly down a vertical wire, Ex. 85d. The same image is used on the upward movement -- the smooth sliding up the center vertical line until normal standing is reached. Through this image the whole action of lowering and rising concentrates not on the muscular action in the legs, the flexion of the joints, but on controlled and fluent movements of the center. Apart from the technical advantage which this image gives, it concentrates on the sense of being centered, of being coordinated, of being 'in tune'. The resulting serenity is very expressive. Such concentration on balance may be for choreographic reasons to express awareness of what one is doing or to provide a slow control while other expressive gestures take place.

A very slow transference of weight from one foot to another is a good setting for experiencing controlled balance while progressing, particularly if rising and lowering occurs within one step as in the slow steps of a Pavane. While control and smoothness are achieved through correct use of the foot, it may be fatal to place movement concentration there. The image to bear in mind is the undulating line in space, the 85e path of the center of the body as a whole, of the center of gravity. With this in mind the performer will achieve the smooth flowing motion. Such undulating weight transferences should be taken backward as well as forward, and also to the side.

Line of center
of gravity in an
undulating step

Indication of Center of Gravity, Balance

Every object has its center of balance. In the case of bodies with movable parts the location of the center of gravity (C of G) changes according to the configuration of the body, the placement of the parts. Thus we see that the C of G is a movable point within the body. In normal standing it is located near the upper rim of the pelvis. For our purposes we do not need to be exact. The C of G sign is: ●. When in balance, the C of G is on the vertical line, the up/down dimension, Ex. 86a. Balance occurs when the C of G is above, at, or below the point of support. Here we

Sign for
● = center of
gravity

Center of
= gravity in
86a ●   balance

112

are concerned mainly with balance above the point of support, the support usually being the floor, though it may be an object or a partner.

As a contrast to awareness of balance in standing or in a sustained transference of weight, try to find the point of balance at the end of a movement sequence. Take three quick steps running forward leading into a quick high step which is then held, suspended in balance, Ex. 86b. While you are suspending, the free leg may be in one of several positions. Choose one, for balance is more easily mastered when the free limb has a definite placement. In 86b centering of the C of G has been stated to stress that this awareness is important. Because the following stillness is sufficiently long it will demand that balance be kept and so this statement for the C of G could be omitted. However, the positive instruction of awareness of centered balance would be missing. An indication for the C of G is needed when such awareness is required at the start of a sequence, during a transition, or at the end.

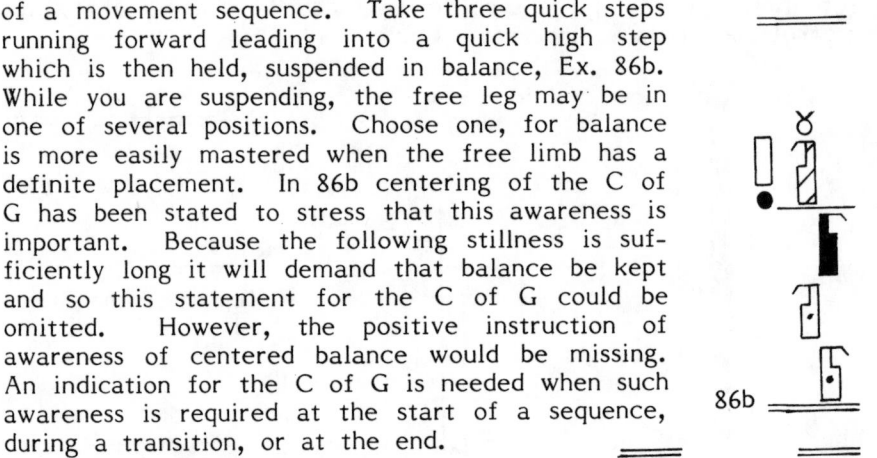

86b

Balance is not a new idea in that it is met and practised from the early stages of movement training. But awareness of being vertically centered, particularly when one is not obviously 'balancing', requires thought and a developed kinetic realization.

The indication of the C of G on the vertical line has two functions. As we shall soon see, when falling occurs the vertical line shows the moment balance is regained. When an in-balance state is understood, the indication calls for awareness of center. How long is that awareness to last? In Ex. 86c there is awareness on the rising but not on the travelling forward or on the forward action; it is again present during the half turn. In Ex. 86d the awareness of center is there at the start and is to be maintained (as indicated by the retention sign: ○) until the end of the turn where the cancellation sign: ⋏ states the retained state ceases to be in effect.

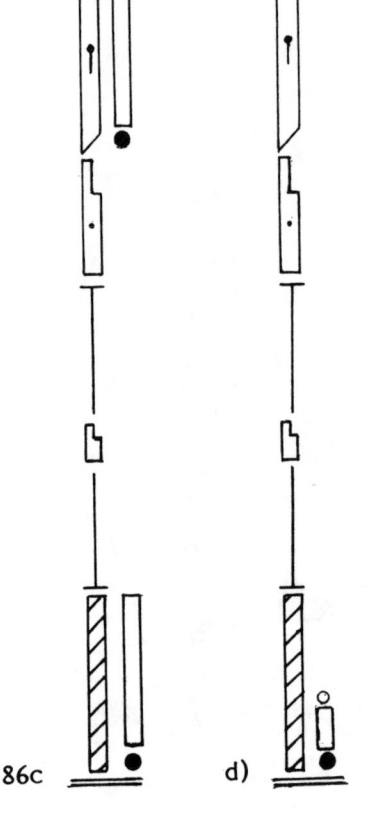

86c   d)

113

Reading Study No. 21

BALANCE

Concentration here is on the vertical line of balance. Note that the retention sign: ○ gives specific instruction to maintain a state. The sign: ∧ cancels a retained state (indication).

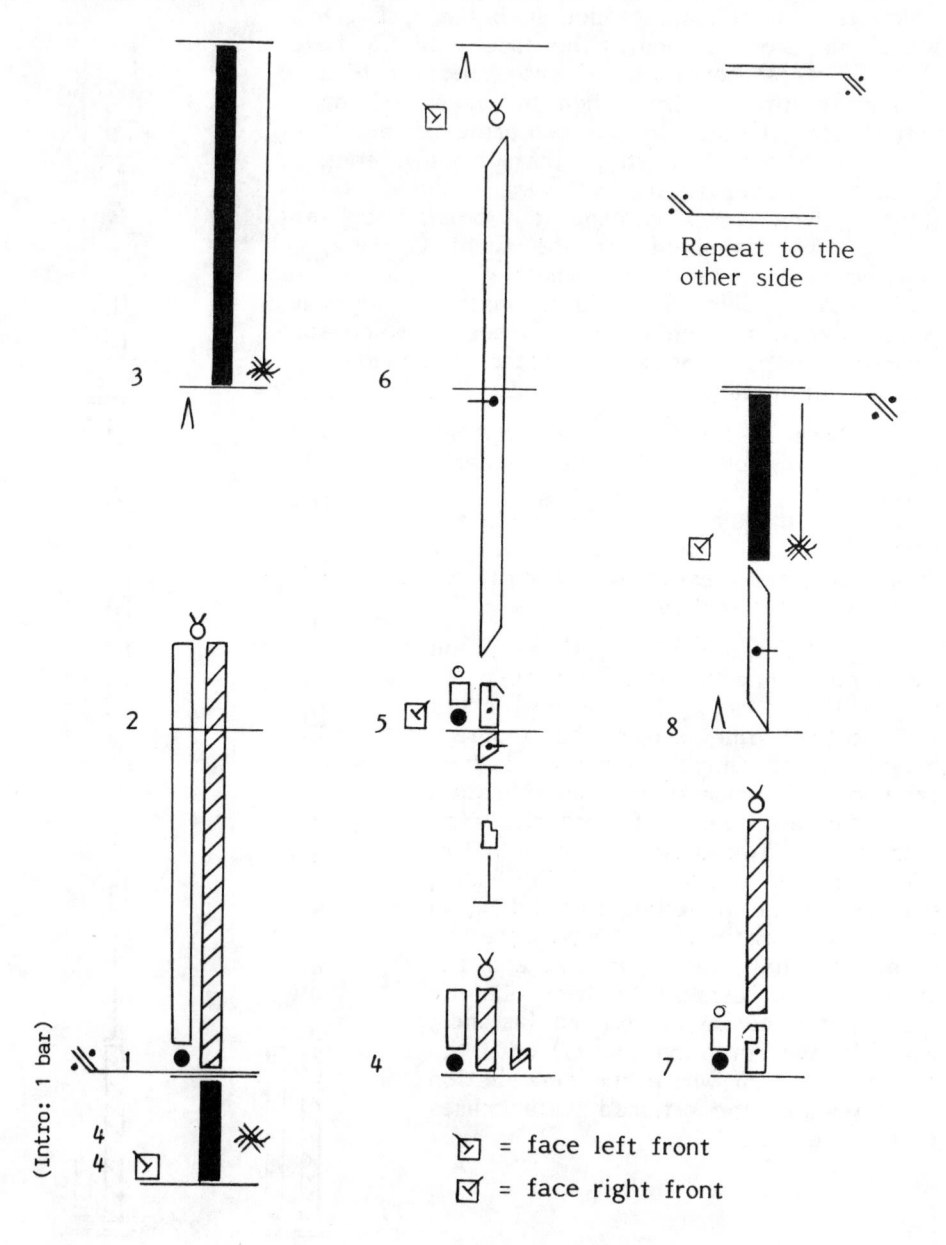

Repeat to the other side

⊠ = face left front

☑ = face right front

Indication of Specific Shift of Weight

Minor spatial displacements are shown with pins, the point of the pin indicating the direction, the head of the pin indicating the level. Small horizontal displacements are indicated by flat pins ('tacks'). In Ex. 87a the C of G is shown to shift forward, then backward, then to return to center (–||–); it then shifts to the right and then left before again returning to center.

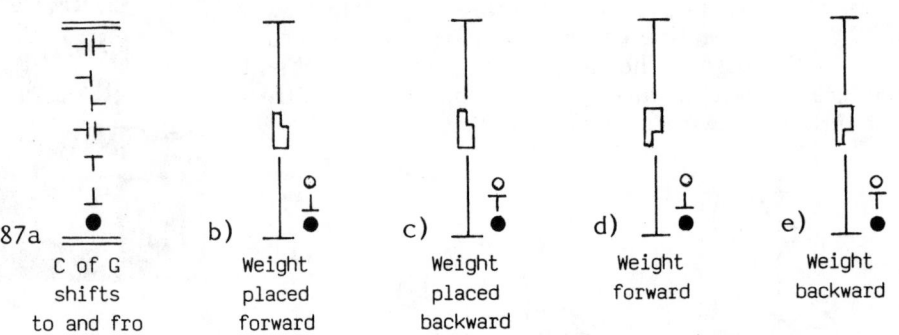

87a — C of G shifts to and fro

b) Weight placed forward

c) Weight placed backward

d) Weight forward

e) Weight backward

A shifted placement of the C of G can affect the expression of a simple walk. Try walking forward with the weight shifted forward, as in 87b, then the same walk with the weight back on the heels, 87c. Be sure that it is a displacement of the center of weight and not a slight forward or backward tilt of the torso, which is quite a different movement idea. In Ex. 87d walking backward with the weight forward is stated, while in 87e the weight is back while travelling backward. Below are movement sequences incorporating C of G shifts.

In Ex. 87f a backward shift of the C of G accompanies a general forward action; there is then a re-turn to center both for the C of G and the general movement. This is followed by a backward action during which the C of G is shifted forward. Level for the forward and backward actions has been left open to choice.

In Ex. 87g a forward, backward, forward swaying leads into travel-ling forward. As travelling finishes the weight is again centered.

Center of gravity shifts may be small movements but they may have a marked effect on the expression of other actions or they may contri-bute to achieving a body placement which aids technique.

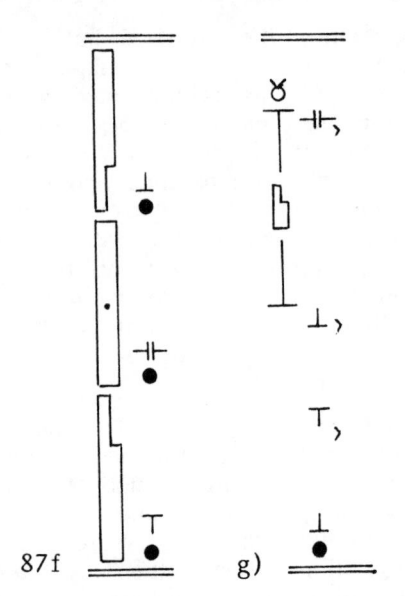

87f   g)

FALLING: SLIGHT LOSS OF BALANCE

Though the center of gravity moves when the weight is shifted, balance is still maintained. The C of G is still under control; it has not taken over the movement in progress, 'running away with it', so to speak. When is balance lost? One has only to think of the Leaning Tower of Pisa, Ex. 88a. At what point, if the leaning increases, will the tower fall? When the line of gravity in the building falls outside the base. The larger the base of an object, the greater the distance weight can shift in different directions without loss of balance.

88a

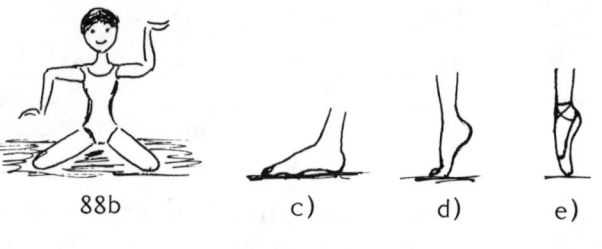

88b   c)   d)   e)

In 88b the dancer is kneeling with knees apart. Between the feet and knees is a large triangular area of support. This allows a range of displacement of the C of G. It is possible to lean in every direction without loss of balance. But on a single foot, 88c, thought must be given to balance, and even more so on half toe, 88d, where the base is so small only a slight shift of weight will produce falling. On full toe as in 88e balance is even more precarious.

Once the C of G has shifted beyond the outer margin of the supporting base, falling occurs. This falling may be slight and easily controlled, or it may be marked, or even hopelessly out of control. We have all seen a person badly lose balance and despite attempts to regain it, end up 'strewn' on the floor, 88g. In dance one must be able to produce such an action intentionally when the choreography demands it. Therefore we must learn to control falling (if one can put it that way) and have it as a servant at our command to be used when needed.

88f

88g

As we have seen, in the process of walking, the C of G moves a little ahead into the next step. The transition is smooth and there is no sense of falling since the foot for the new support is ready to take the weight. The same is true of running; after a moment of weightlessness in the air, the foot contacts the ground and, when no further travelling follows, the C of G becomes centered on the new support. If the running continues, the weight passes across the length of the

116

foot as preparation for the take-off into the next running step. In walking and running no falling as such occurs and therefore as a rule no statement regarding the C of G need be made.

Slight Falling: 'Tombé'

The first stage of falling, when it is still slight, occurs when the C of G leads into the direction of the new step. This C of G in motion, a pleasant experience, is called 'tombé' in ballet terminology. In a rise on two feet, allow the weight gradually to leave center carrying you into the direction of your next step.
The result will be an overcurve into a cushioned support, Ex. 89. As an exaggerated version try a falling step in which the preparatory gesture is missing and the leg moves out only at the last moment to prevent a major fall. The normal smooth transference as in walking is absent; instead there is interrupted flow. The greater the amount the C of G is in motion, the longer the step needed to catch the weight.

89

Indication of 'Tombé'

Center of gravity leading is indicated by the sign for C of G being placed within a vertical bow, Ex. 90a. The length of the bow shows the length of time during which the C of G is in motion. This duration can be brief, a preparation for a single step, or it may continue over a sequence of steps in the same direction. This is a 'passing state' bow in that the movement it indicates - C of G in motion in this case - is over, completed, after the end of the bow.

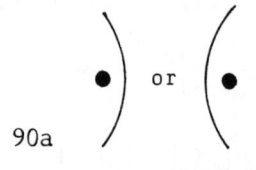

90a

Center of gravity in
motion (leading)

In Ex. 90b there is a slight falling (leading of the C of G) into the path forward. This travelling may be a run since loss of balance, even slight, produces the momentum needed to travel swiftly. On the other hand, such slight falling could lead into a walk or leisurely gallop or skip; the manner of travelling is not stated. In 90c a movement up is followed by a low backward step. Ex. 90d states specifically that the C of G leads into a sideward step on the right foot. In 90e the end of a turn to the right is linked with a step to the left by a slight falling. The direction of the C of G leading is always the direction of the step or path which follows.

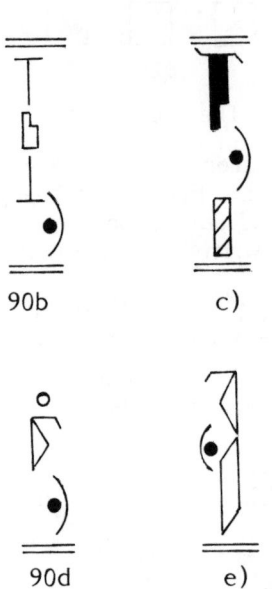

117

Off-Balance Turns

Multiple turns (pirouettes) require centered balance. At the beginning of a turn, in the middle, or at the end, loss of balance can temporarily occur. The weight is briefly off center resulting in a labile turn, in contrast to a stable, centered turn. A swinging motion may be the impetus for a turn and for the momentary off-center balance. Or a sudden swoop may occur during a stable turn, the lean of the torso

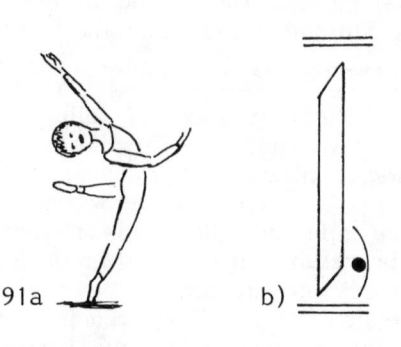

91a   b)

taking the weight off center. Ex. 91a illustrates a labile turn, 91b being the indication of temporary loss of balance at the start of a turn. It is assumed that balance is regained and the turn continues centered.

FRONT SIGNS

Where you are facing in the room is important for you as the performer and for the observer. This aspect of spatial orientation is investigated in detail in Chapter Thirteen; for now we introduce the main signs to provide a more definite statement concerning paths travelled and directions faced. Once the front of the room or of the performing area has been established, the 'compass' of constant directions is set. The performer is at the center of these directions. In Ex. 92a the letter P represents the performer.

92a

The front signs

The appropriate front sign is placed at the left of the movement notation. When a new front is established, the sign for this new front is written and this front is maintained until another is indicated. For minor changes of front the slight turn which produces the new front is not important and so for a general Motif description is not written. The eight front signs are named below.

⊥	=	Facing front	⊠	= Facing right front diagonal
⊢	=	Facing right side	⊠	= Facing right back diagonal
⊤	=	Facing back	⊠	= Facing left back diagonal
⊣	=	Facing left side	⊠	= Facing left front diagonal

TOMBÉ, CENTER OF GRAVITY IN MOTION

Note slight changes in facing direction shown by the front signs.

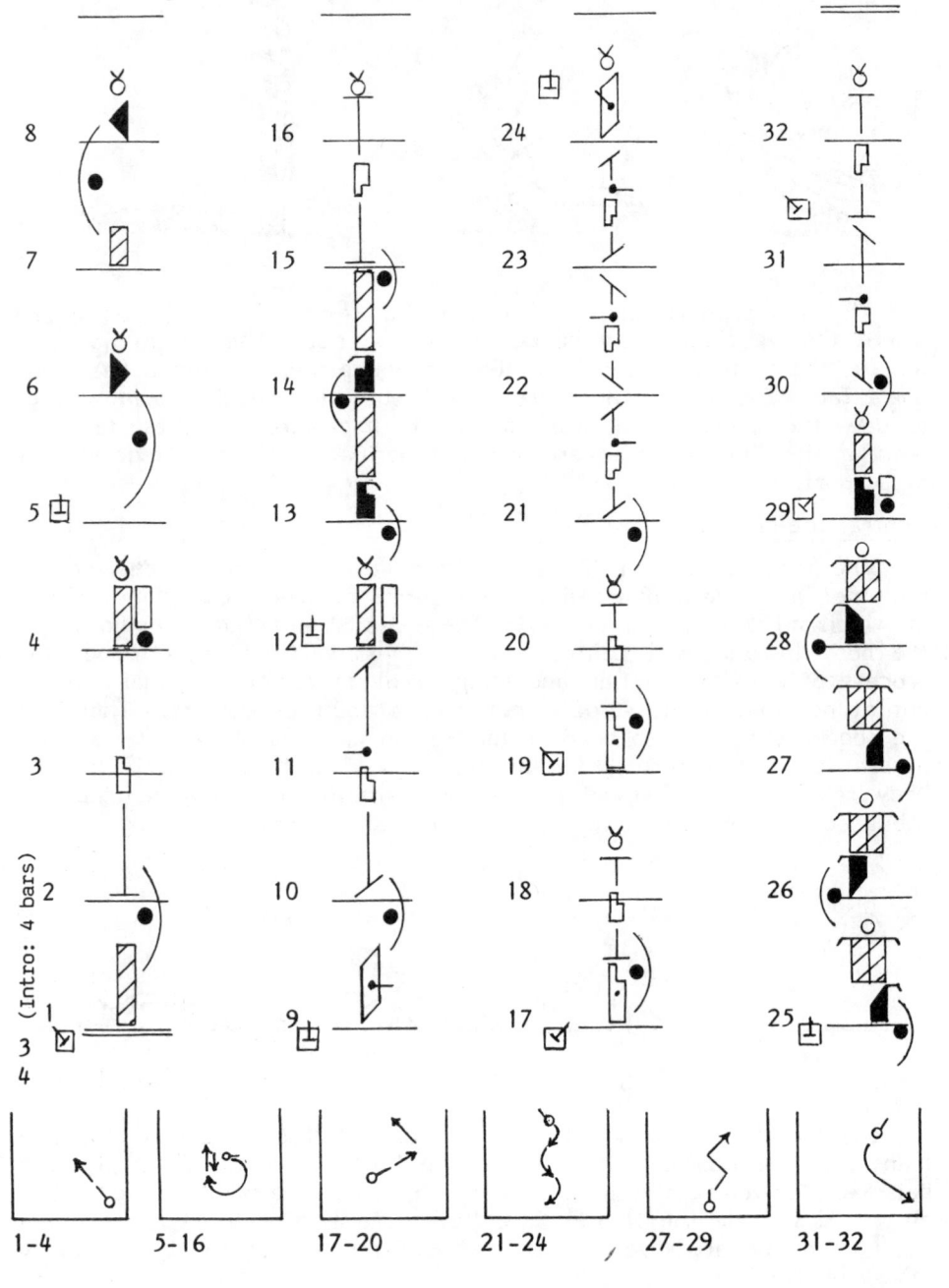

119

FALLING: FULL LOSS OF BALANCE

A true fall occurs when control of balance is lost and the C of G moves far beyond the supporting base, Ex. 93a. A new support must quickly be placed under the moving C of G.

93a   b)   c)

The new support is usually a foot, the result of a lunge, as in 93b where the right foot has darted forward to catch the weight and terminate the state of falling. Falling in one piece, 'flat as a board' on one's face, Ex. 93c, is an extreme version which requires some nerve, as does the same kind of fall sideward or backward. In these falls the path of the C of G is an arc which is peripheral to the previous point of support.

Central 'Falls'

The term 'a fall' or 'falling' is given to certain movement sequences, met in modern dance and other forms of free flowing movement, in which no actual fall occurs. These 'falls' are sequences in which the body lowers on a central, more or less vertical line, through the process of kneeling, sitting and lying. The movement is usually swift, but at no time is the C of G not over a point of support. Therefore the sequence could also be done (and often is) in slow motion. When a person falls as a result of fainting, he seldom hurts himself for the body relaxes and moves downward sequentially, lowering centrally as the knees weaken and give way, the rest of the body following.

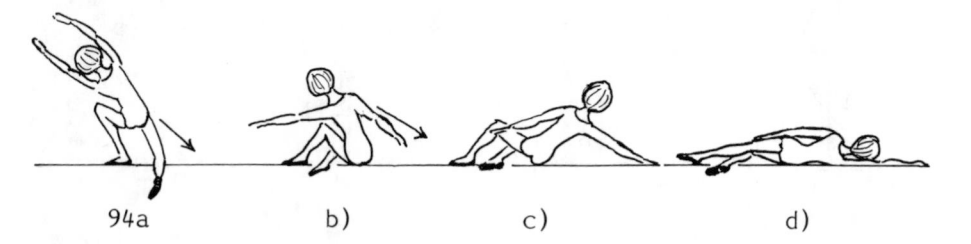

94a   b)   c)   d)

Ex. 94a-d illustrates a typical sideward 'fall'. Note how the body leans into the opposite direction to the 'fall', thus helping to preserve balance. Lowering the torso is aided by the hand taking some weight as it slides along the floor. Such 'falls' are also performed in a backward or a forward direction through greater use of the hands sliding along the floor.

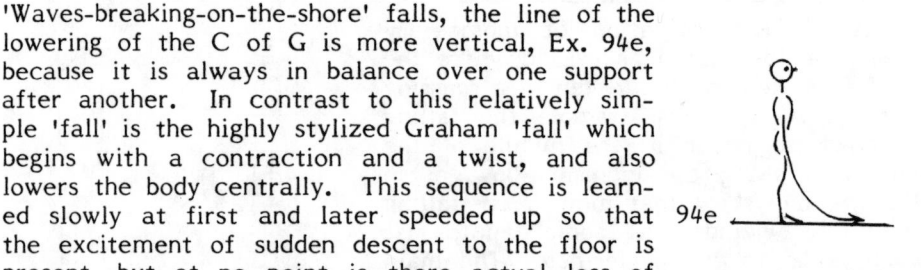

In these central 'falls' which have been called 'Waves-breaking-on-the-shore' falls, the line of the lowering of the C of G is more vertical, Ex. 94e, because it is always in balance over one support after another. In contrast to this relatively simple 'fall' is the highly stylized Graham 'fall' which begins with a contraction and a twist, and also lowers the body centrally. This sequence is learned slowly at first and later speeded up so that 94e the excitement of sudden descent to the floor is present, but at no point is there actual loss of balance. This fall contrasts with the peripheral Graham fall, a true fall, which commences with a sliding separation of the feet and a torso tilt. In understanding movement it is important that we are clear on when a true fall, i.e. loss of balance, occurs.

A Falling Run

In a falling run the C of G is constantly ahead of the point of support so that no centering of balance can take place. Performing such a run requires nerve; it is like continuous stumbling without the security of regaining balance. Try improvisations using such runs and observe just when falling actually begins and where it ends; balance may be regained before you intended it to do so. Observe how the 'brakes' can be applied to halt the falling. Timing for loss of balance may be relatively slow or it may be sudden. Similarly, regaining balance may be gradual or sudden. The most sudden, of course, is arriving flat on the floor, or being 'caught' by a partner. Once the C of G is off balance it may be difficult to control it and contact with another person or a wall can prevent a fall.

Indication of True Falling

Because falling is a major action of the C of G it is indicated by a main direction symbol. For a general description such as we are using here, degree of lowering toward the floor is not needed; thus the symbol is left blank. Length of the direction symbol indicates how long it takes to achieve loss of balance. The duration of falling once it takes place is usually brief; indication of a new support cancels the state of falling. If falling is to be maintained the retention sign: O is used. Cessation of falling can then be indicated by the cancellation: or by indication of centered balance if awareness of center is important. In Ex. 95a balance is slowly lost as you travel forward. In 95b balance is lost at the start of travelling and continues until near the end. Ex. 95c shows continuous falling while travelling but regaining centered balance at the end.

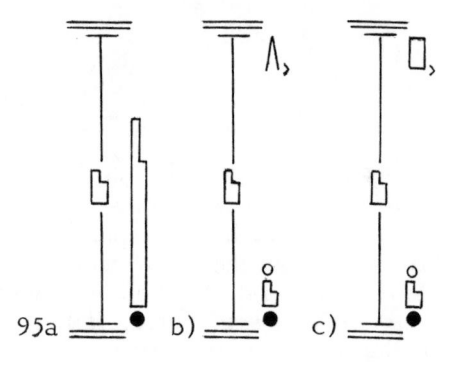

Indication of True Falling (continued)

A general indication of momentary falling can be stated as in 95d where the C of G statement is written in a 'passing state' bow. In this example the falling is shown to occur in the middle of the path. By using the inclusion bow, as in 95e, we can show that momentary falling should be included at some point; just when is up to the performer. The main activity is the travelling of the body as a whole; the extra activity is a temporary loss of balance to be added at some point during the path.

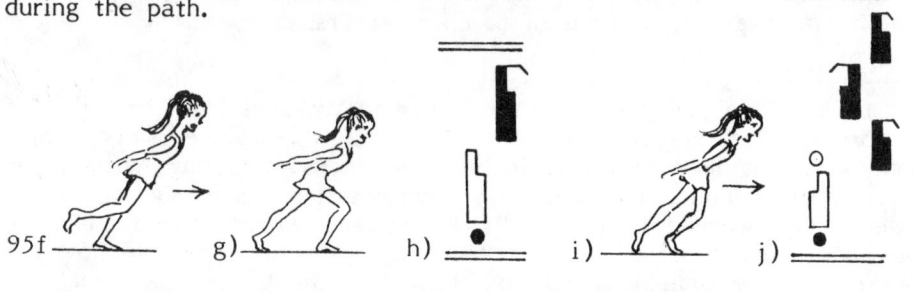

Loss of balance which occurs while supporting on the feet is most comfortably rectified by sudden placement of a foot under the C of G. Ex. 95f shows a person falling. In 95g the right foot has darted forward to take the weight under the C of G. This action is written in 95h. If the step is not long enough, as in 95i, the foot will not be placed under the C of G and the person will still be falling. A series of such inadequate steps will produce a series of off-balance steps as in 95j in which the off-balance continues; it is not cancelled.

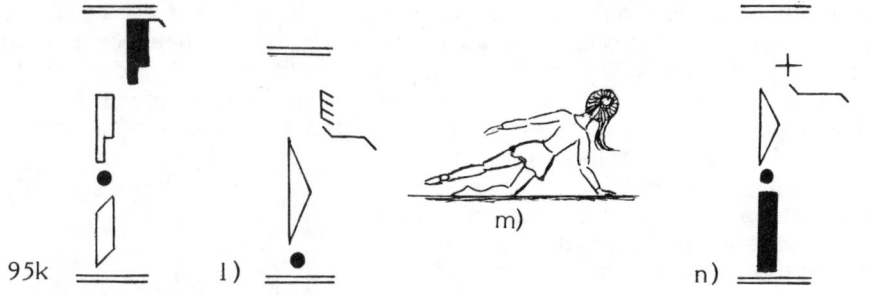

Falling may occur into any direction and onto various parts of the body. Ex. 95k illustrates a turn followed by falling backward and ending with a centered support on the right foot. In 95 l a sideward fall is caught on the right hand, 95m. The lowering action of 95n is followed by a fall to the right which ends on the right hip. Once weight is on the hips or torso, falling has ceased. This is understood so cancellation is not necessary.

FALLING

Find images for this study, perhaps wind or waves causing you to lose balance. Note the significant differences between the moment when falling occurs and when balance is regained.

Note use of the caret: ⟨ meaning 'the same' to obviate having to repeat the center of gravity pre-sign all the time.

REVIEW FOR CHAPTERS EIGHT AND NINE

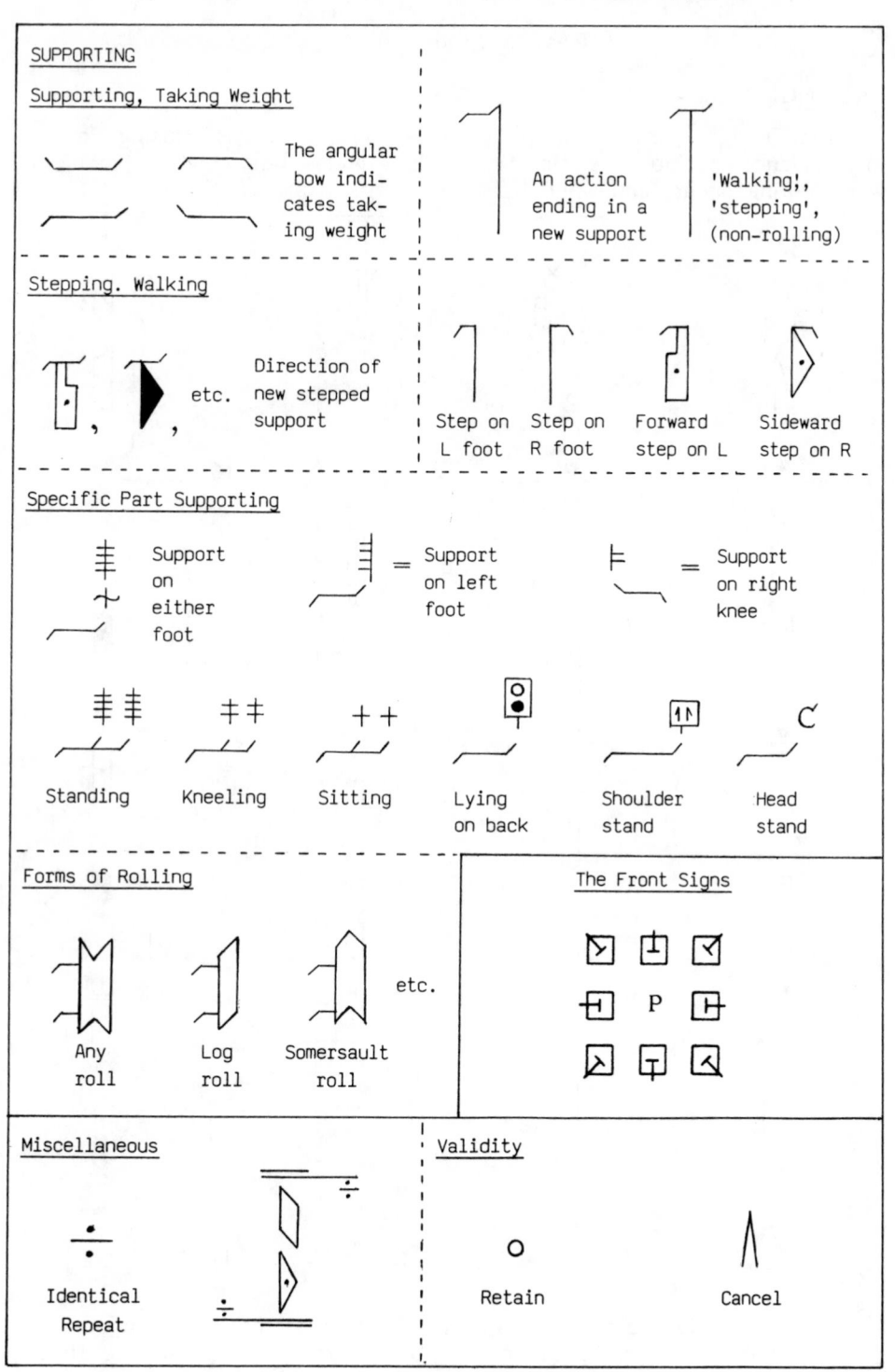

PARTS OF THE BODY

C = head

$\boxed{O}$ = chest

$\boxtimes$ = waist

$\boxed{\bullet}$ = pelvis

$\boxed{\Uparrow}$ = shoulder section

= whole torso

SURFACES OF TORSO

= Front

= Back

= Left

= Right

Limbs

$\mathcal{1}$ = left arm

$\mathcal{1}$ = right arm

$\Uparrow$ = both arms

= left leg

= right leg

= both legs

Joints

Both		L	R	Either side
$+$	hips	$\dashv$	$\vdash$	$+$
$\ddagger$	knees			$\ddagger$
	ankles			
	feet			etc.
	toes			
$\curlywedge$	shoulders			
	elbows			$+$
	wrists			etc.
	hands			
	fingers			

BALANCE - FALLING

$\bullet$ = Center of gravity

= Center of gravity on the vertical, i.e., in balance

Shifting the C of G

$\top$ backward $\dashv$ side to

$\perp$ forward $\vdash$ side

C of G in motion slight falling, 'tombe'

Loss of balance, true falling

Momentary falling

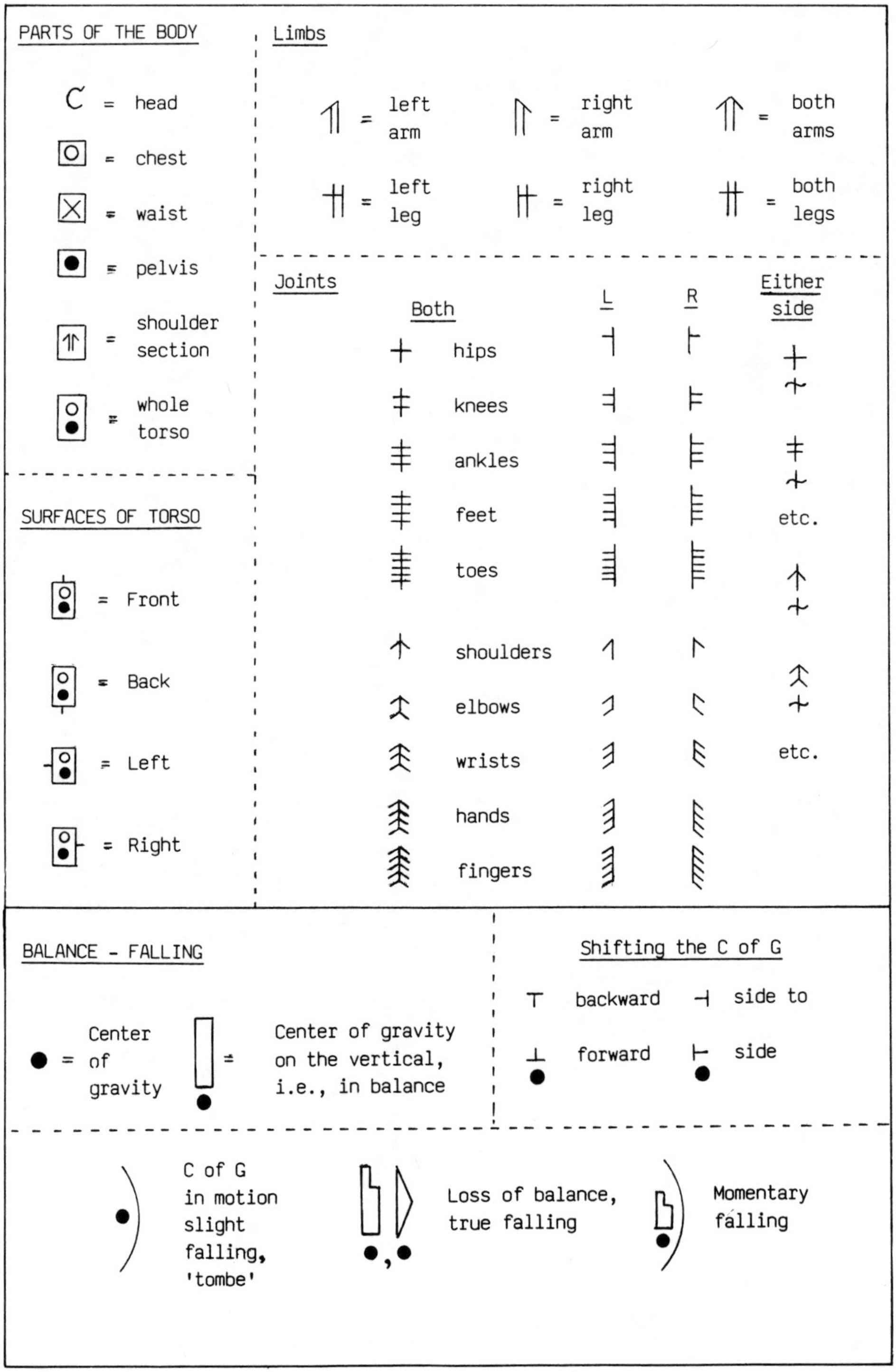

Chapter Ten
RELATIONSHIPS

Relating to the environment begins right after birth. Around us are people, objects, the room. Gradually 'the room' extends to be the house, the village, the country, the world. How physically do we relate to all these? The baby is aware of someone there; he sees the person, he reaches out, touches, grasps. A baby's early movements are based on flexing, extending, rotating in the process of becoming aware, of discovering himself and his surroundings. Before long actions become functionally directed with a reason, a motivation behind them.

96a   b)   c)

Progression in becoming aware develops from self, to other people, to moving objects, to stationary objects, to the surroundings. In our exploration of movement our concern so far has been with basic actions. Now we need to consider both the purpose and the result of such actions.

FORMS OF RELATING

The aim of an action may be far more important than the type of movement used to achieve it. To reach out and touch an object we may use extension. If the object is too far, travelling will have to occur. To touch an object on the ground, lowering will need to take place, and so on. The actual movement used to produce contact will depend on placement of the object; the direction and distance in relation to the performer — in front, behind, at the left, near, far, etc. The form of the movement is often of no importance to the mover; he is often quite unaware of what he does to reach his objective. Only the purpose, the aim, the end result matters. For stylized theatrical dance, actions used may be specifically choreographed, importance being given both to the end result and to how it is achieved. Because the aim of an action is so often of prime importance, specific terms and signs have been evolved to represent the possibilities. The following presentation starts with the slightest degree of relating.

Awareness, Sensed Relating

You are sitting reading. Suddenly you are aware that someone has entered the room behind you. Before you even turn to look, your body is expressing awareness, usually marked by a heightening of tension (very slight) in the body. The attitude is one of 'attention'. Your concentration has shifted from reading to awareness of another person. Such awareness, for which the fine nerve cells send signals, is like radar; energy impulses can almost be seen to emanate from the performer to the other person. Radar is an apt image, since a comparable inborn sense of awareness exists, more highly developed in some than in others. Consider two people working in a small kitchen. With 'radar' tuned in, person A will sense from a slight motion made by B the need to move slightly to one side so that B can reach a needed utensil. If A lacks such developed awareness B must verbally ask A to move over before action can be taken.

How does 'awareness' occur in performing? It may be in relation to another person as happens in a play, a dramatic situation. Or there may be an awareness within one's own body as when both hands are aware of one another despite being spatially far apart. A good example is when the arms move in a parallel fashion, and awareness of the one to the other needs to be maintained. In the balletic attitude position, the hand of the arm which is up (the extremity) should relate to the foot of the raised leg, Ex. 97, thus completing the arc, the circular line of energy. There is no overt action of the extremities toward each other but a distinct awareness, a kinesthetic sense resulting from using kinesthetic imagery. In many dance poses the relationship of the limbs is not just a matter of spatial placement; the limbs are aware of each other, as dancers are aware of one another on stage (or should be). Such awareness

97

heightens dance and lifts it above an ordinary everyday event.

Awareness is the basic form of relating in that it is the first degree, the least 'active' of the many possibilities. In all states of relating it is the aim, the idea, we are concerned with here, not the actual movement which occurs to produce the state of relating.

Indication of Awareness

The sign for awareness, Ex. 98a or 98b, indicates a relating, usually at a distance, of an indirect nature, the performer making no overt action in relation to the point of interest. The term 'point of interest' refers to a person, object or part of the room to which the performer relates. Ex. 98c illustrates mutual awareness which can occur between two people, two parts of the body, etc. Note that signs with dotted lines rep-

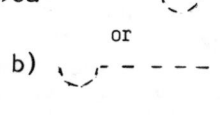

98a

or

b)

c)

Signs of awareness

resent weaker states. Solid lines indicate 'stronger', active relating.

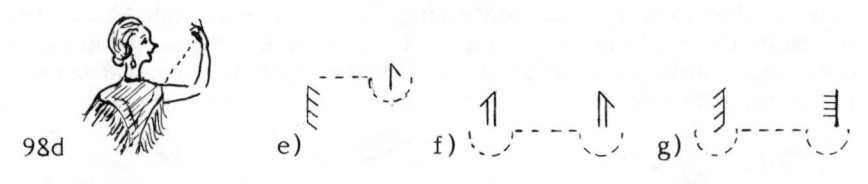

98d e) f) g)

Ex. 98d illustrates a position in which the right hand relates to the right shoulder; 98e is the notation of such relating. Ex. 98f shows mutual relating, awareness, between the right and left arms, and 98g between the left hand and the left foot.

Addressing, Active Relating

Active relating occurs when a visible movement of some kind is made with the aim of relating to someone or something. The general term 'addressing' is used to specify this form. Many everyday actions produce addressing. "What was that?" you think as you glance out of the window. "Put it over there," you say, pointing to a desk without looking. "He went that way," you indicate by a backward diagonal tilt of the head.

The most obvious forms of addressing are looking at, gesturing toward or pointing to the point of interest. Looking may mean directing the whole front of the body to the person or object, or only turning the head, or perhaps only looking with the eyes. The term 'addressing' suggests that looking is the main activity; in fact looking may not be present at all. A gesture toward the point of interest may be made with the arm, the hand, and, in stylized movement, with a foot, knee, hip, elbow, etc. The gesture is such that it clearly expresses relating. The action which produces or results in addressing may be one of turning, leaning, extending, contracting, shifting, etc. If looking accompanies an addressing action, the addressing has greater impact.

Indication of Addressing

When an overt action is made toward or in relation to a person, object, etc. the sign of 99a or 99b is used. If there is mutual addressing, i.e. two active parts, the sign is drawn as 99c.

99a

b)

c)

The timing of a movement which produces a relating is indicated by an action stroke. Relating may occur at the beginning, in the middle or at the end of a movement. The moment when relating occurs may depend on whether the point of interest is stationary or is moving. Ex. 99d shows an action which ends addressing. In 99e addressing is achieved suddenly; in 99f a slow action starts with addressing.

d)

99e f)

129

Person or Object Being Addressed

The active part of the addressing sign is the straight line; this is drawn from the staff of the person who is active, the one who is doing the relating. Inside the 'cup' is placed the indication of the person or object being addressed.

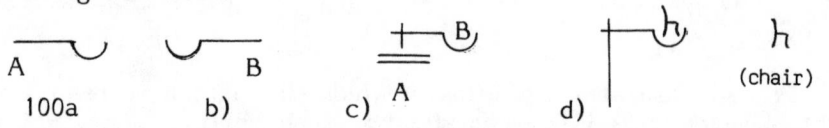

In Ex. 100a person A is active; in 100b it is person B. The addressing sign may extend either to the right or left, whichever best fits the organization of the information. In 100c A is addressing B. Ex. 100d shows an action which ends addressing a chair. The object is drawn as pictorially as possible.

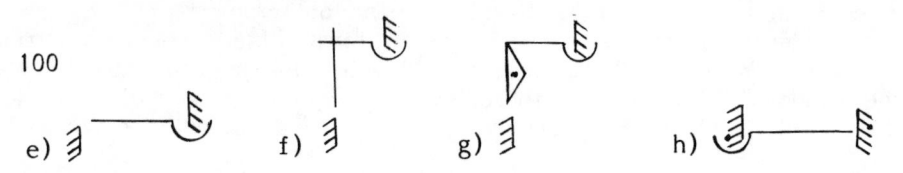

Ex. 100e indicates that the left hand addresses the right hand. Ex. 100f gives timing for this result but nothing indicates what specific movement is used; this is still left open to the performer. Ex. 100g stipulates that it is a sideward gesture for the left hand. In classical mime the gesture for 'marry' involves the right index finger pointing to the left ring finger, as written in 100h. Fingers are written with a five-stroke sign, a dot being added to the appropriate stroke to show the thumb as in 100i, or the little finger, as in 100j. In 100h the addressing sign is drawn to the left since it is the right hand (finger) which is active in relation to the left.

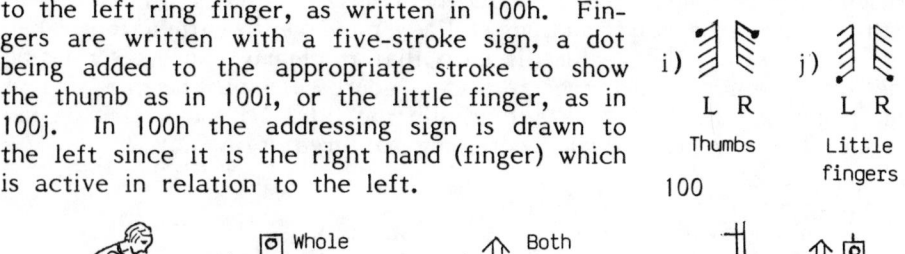

Ex. 100k shows a familiar movement of the torso inclining over (relating to) the extended leg while the arms relate to the leg by taking a line parallel with it. Ex. 100l is the sign for the torso. By adding a tiny stroke to the front of this sign we indicate the front surface of the torso, 100m. Ex. 100n is the sign for both arms while 100o indicates the left leg. Ex. 100p is the notation for the idea behind 100k. If in 100k the relating was intended to be for the extremities, that is, the hands addressing the foot, it would have been written as 100q.

Mutual Addressing

When two people or two parts of the body address one another, the double sign is used.

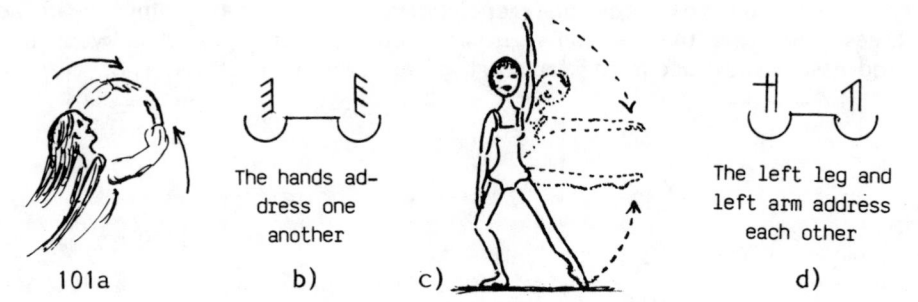

101a	b)	c)	d)
	The hands ad- dress one another		The left leg and left arm address each other

In Ex. 101a as the arms move the hands relate to each other. This can happen even when they are fairly far apart. In 101c the left arm and left leg address one another, this being the intention of the spatial change in location.

ADDRESSING

This study explores different types of movement which may address. Imagine that person A is situated on your right, B on your left. Addressing may occur at the start of an action or at the end.

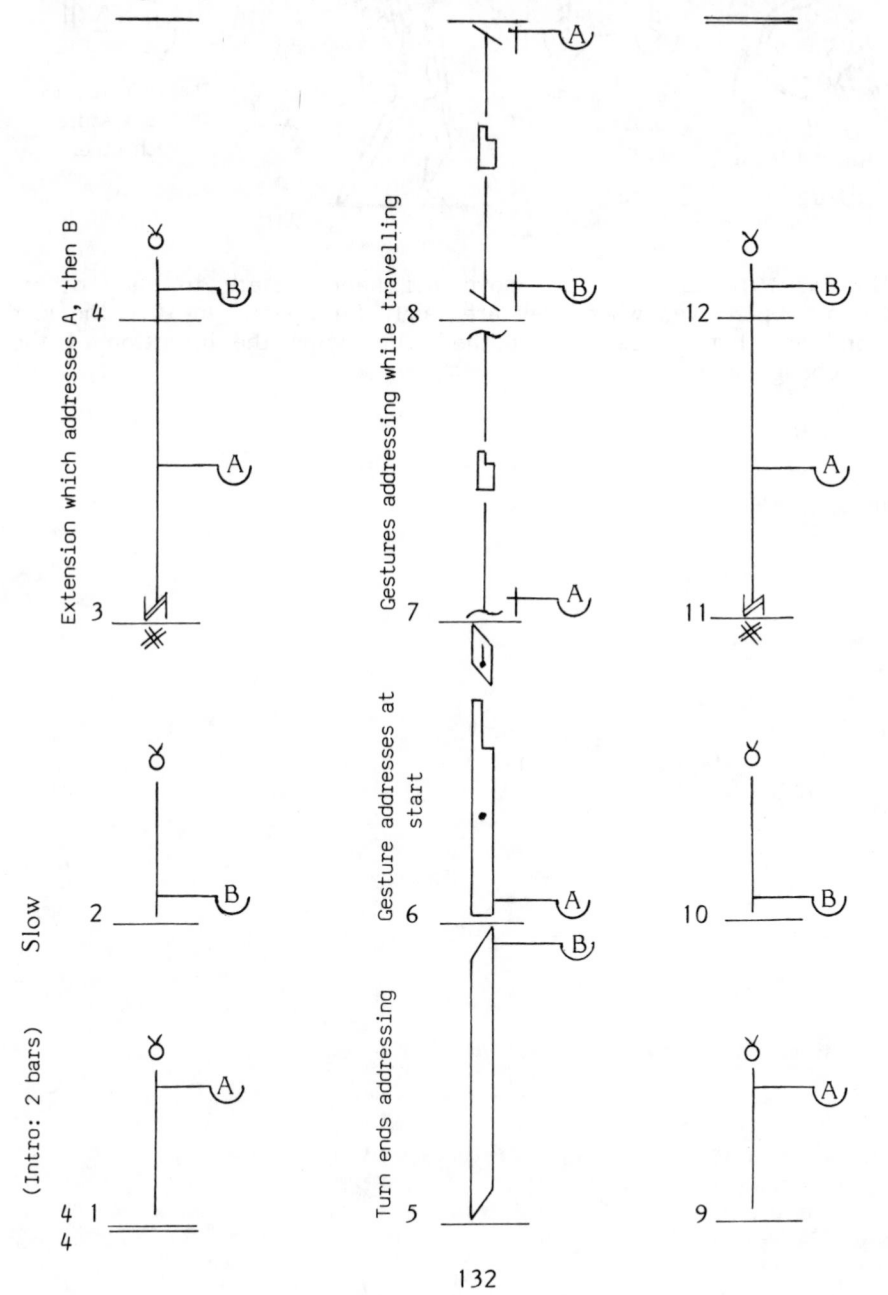

Motion Toward; Motion Away

In relating to the environment, we progress from the slightest form of relating to the closest. The next stage after addressing is motion 'toward'. Addressing can occur at some distance and the action which produced the addressing, turning the head for example, need not involve a gesture which spatially displaces toward the person or object concerned. But very often addressing does take the form of a gesture toward the point of interest. Such a gesture may be one of inclining the head, of leaning the torso, or a gesture of an arm or hand. It might be a gesture of the leg, for instance if one is angry and wishes to indicate kicking the person or object away. For comedy a hip, elbow or heel may be used. We are giving importance to gestures <u>toward</u> since they are moving closer to the point of interest, but gestures away can also be indicated. The fact that they move away may suggest some degree of negative reaction or relationship such as raising one's hand (in reality the arm) backward to strike a person. However, one may draw back in surprise and pleasure at seeing a loved one, a movement which may be a preparation to move toward him.

Indication of Motion Toward and Away

Motion toward is written by placing the indication of the point of interest within an elongated 'V' sign, Ex. 102a. The length of the sign shows duration, Ex. 102b being a quick gesture of some kind toward P, (P being your partner); 102c is a much slower gesture toward a chair.

102

a) V Motion toward

b) V̌ (P)

c) V

d) ∧ Motion away

e) ∧ (P)

f) ∧ (C)

g) ∧ (h)

Motion away is written by placing the sign for the point of interest within an inverted v sign, 102d. Ex. 102e shows a movement away from your partner; in 102f the head makes a motion away from P. In 102g the right arm makes a slow gesture away from a chair.

Note that the basic sign for 'away': ∧ is used alone as a general cancellation when something which was retained is no longer to be in effect, that is, one has "gone away from that state", it has "disappeared", one should "forget about it", no particular state taking its place.

Approaching, Path Toward; Retreating, Path Away

Approaching, i.e. travelling toward a person, object or part of the room, may occur for a variety of reasons, and the timing, the mode of approach and any accompanying gestures may vary considerably, but the main action, progressing closer, is the same. Approaching may be based on a dramatic motivation, a strong reason for getting nearer, or it may simply occur for a practical reason or for choreographic design

133

Approaching, Path Toward; Retreating, Path Away (continued)

as in a folk dance where couples approach one another and then move away. Approaching may occur on a direct path or on a circuitous one; in the latter case the aim, the focal point to be approached, is less obvious or even hidden. Moving away, retreating, need not express desertion; leaving, backward travelling away, may occur in order to get a better view, as in approaching a statue or building. A photographer moves away to get a better composition, and so on.

Indication of Approaching

Approaching is basically an action of travelling; therefore the appropriate path sign is used combined with the indication of what or who is being approached. Ex. 103a states that any path may be used in approaching person P, that the type of path may be varied during the approaching. Ex. 103b indicates an approach to P on a straight path. If approaching is on a circular path, as in 103c, the performer gradually curves in closer to P, approaching through spiralling in, as illustrated in 103d, where Y is the performer.

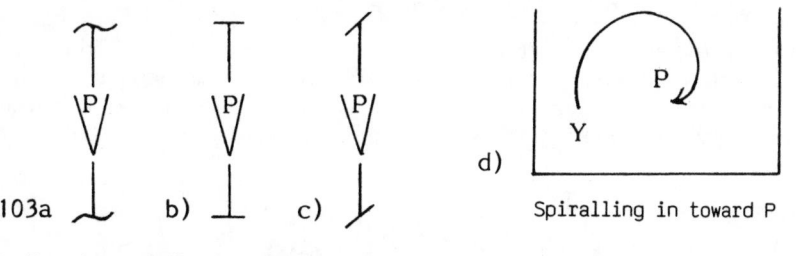

103a   b)   c)   d)   Spiralling in toward P

Indication of Retreating

Travelling away, departing from a person, place or object, is shown by combining the 'away' sign with an appropriate path. Ex. 104a states any path away from P; in 104b a straight path is indicated, while in 104c the performer moves away on a counterclockwise circular path, thus gradually spiralling outward, away from P, as illustrated in 104d.

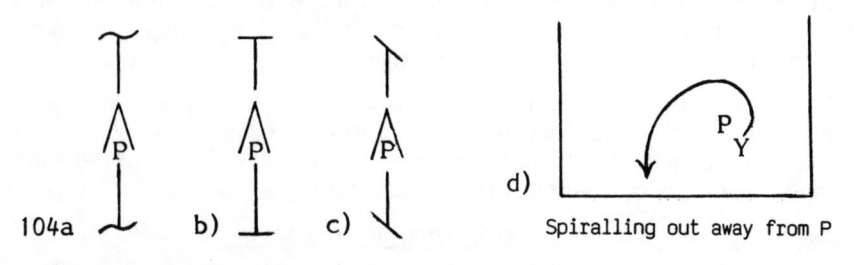

104a   b)   c)   d)   Spiralling out away from P

Arrival, Destination of Path

The final stage in approaching a point of interest is arrival at that point, that is, reaching the person, object or part of the room. Paths to a destination may vary from very indirect, meandering around as if hiding the ultimate aim, to a direct bee-line to the selected spot. A

straight path with a destination may be travelled slowly - fate is call-
ing, there is no turning away. A meandering approach might be casual, might be teasing, or it could be threatening if the idea is one of
stalking a person (the person being approached could be moving at the
same time). Or the path may be purely decorative, choreographed, as
in a gracious ballroom scene for which direct paths might seem inele-
gant and so curved paths are used, the lady waltzing sweepingly across
the floor to arrive at a new partner.

Indication of Destination

The concept of an action with a particular destination, an aim or
an arrival at a particular state, is expressed as Ex. 105a below. At
the end of the action stroke is written the aim; total freedom in choice
of an aim is shown by the ad lib. sign which is connected to the action stroke with a bow to indicate the end result of the action.

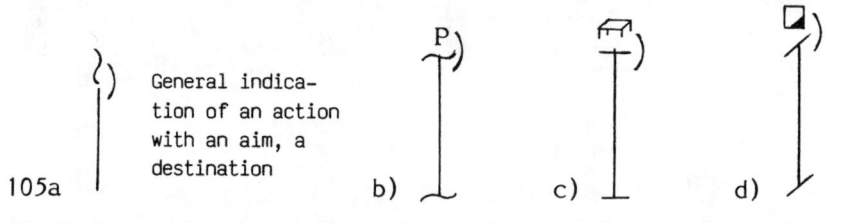

105a — General indica-
tion of an action
with an aim, a
destination

b)   c)   d)

To indicate the destination of a path, we write at the end of the
path sign the indication for the person, object or part of the room,
and tie it to the path sign to show that this is the aim. In Ex. 105b
any path leads to joining (arriving at) your partner. In 105c a straight
path ends at a table, while in 105d circling clockwise is destined to
conclude in the right back corner of the room or stage (see below for
area of the room signs).

Areas of the Room (Stage)

It is important to be able to state the performer's location in the
performing area, usually a room or stage for which nine main areas
are given here as sufficient for our present needs.

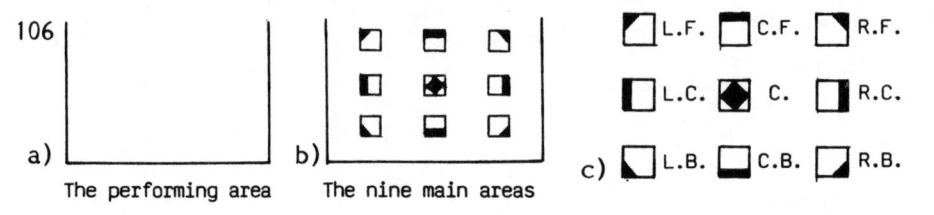

106

a) The performing area   b) The nine main areas

c)   L.F.   C.F.   R.F.
     L.C.   C.   R.C.
     L.B.   C.B.   R.B.

Ex. 106a illustrates the room or stage; 106b shows the nine main
divisions, the specific areas. In the identification of these in Ex. 106c,
C = center, L = left, R = right, F = front and B = back. These signs
are used to indicate the location of the performer. As a destination
for a path, the appropriate sign is placed at the end of the path sign,
as in 105d.

Reading Study No. 25

PARTNERS RELATING (Ending Apart)

Note that 𝟙 B means circle around B, that is, B is the focal point of the circling, the center of the circle.

V and 𝔸 alongside the path are gestures which occur in addition to the path.

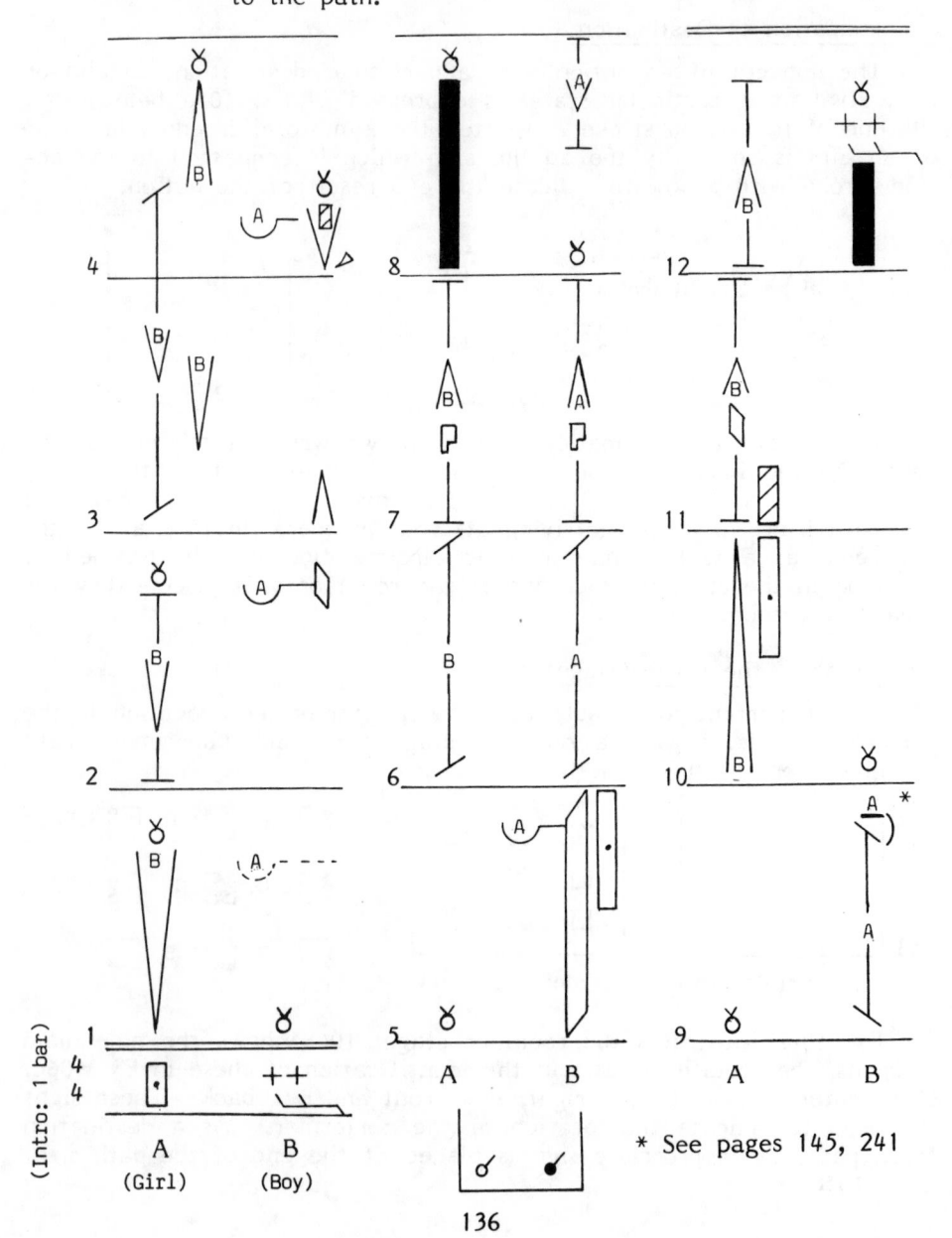

(Intro: 1 bar)

4/4
4/4

A
(Girl)

B
(Boy)

5. A   B

9. A   B

* See pages 145, 241

Proximity, Nearness

Proximity to a person or an object may be for a practical need, as in starting near an apparatus or object soon to be used, or it may have dramatic significance - think of Tosca with her hand near the knife with which she is soon to stab Scarpia. Choreographically, nearness is often used to produce a stylized version of an everyday action, thus removing it one step from reality. A hand near another person's shoulder without actually touching can be more full of meaning than if an actual touch occurred. Palms near each other express a formalized version of prayer. Stopping short of actually touching another person can express great tenderness, delicacy of feeling; it can also be restrained anger - "Wait till I get my hands on you", a threat not yet carried out. Some form of hesitation is often present.

Indication of Near

The sign for near, close to, is a dotted horizontal bow, which may be swung upward or downward, Ex. 107a. This bow connects the indications of the two parts involved.

Near, close to

107a

Ex. 107b shows the hands near each other; in 107c A's right hand is near B's left shoulder. The closeness of A's right foot to B's right foot, 107d, can be important in ballroom dance and in other partnering sequences. Ex. 107e illustrates the hands near the opposite shoulders, 107f.

107e   f)

Except for motions toward or away, for which timing is shown by the length of the 'V' sign, the signs for relating show only the moment when a particular relationship occurs or is achieved. Timing is shown in the usual way for the action which leads into an addressing, nearness, etc. This action may be quite swift or very sustained.

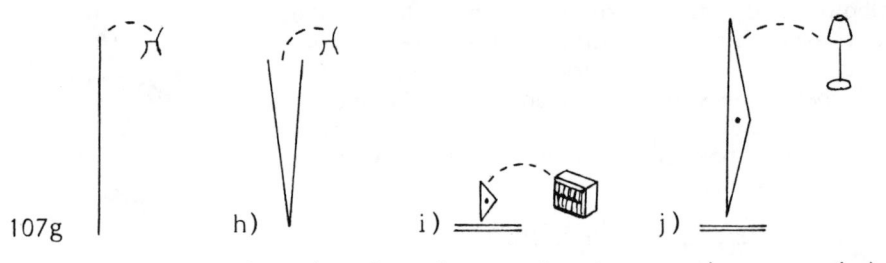

107g   h)   i)   j)

Ex. 107g states that the aim of an action is to end near a chair. In 107h an approaching gesture ends near a chair; this may be a more appropriate statement. In 107i a quick sideward gesture ends near the corner of a bookcase; in 107j a slower similar gesture ends near a lamp.

F

Enclosing Nearness

A butterfly is on the table; you put your hand over it to hide it without touching it. Your hand closes up slightly (becomes curved) as it suspends just above the butterfly. Such enclosing without touching suggests a special relationship with the object, a protectiveness, a tenderness. It is a stylized form of enclosing without actual contact.

Indication of Enclosing Nearness

The dotted bow for near is combined with the X for flexion, closing in, to express enclosing without touching, Ex. 108a.

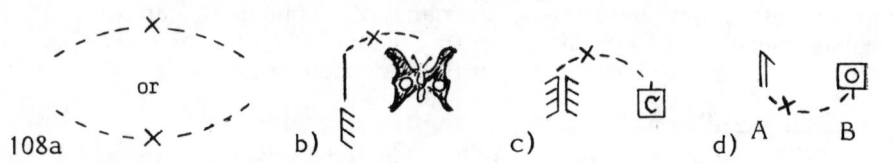

108a or b) c) d) A B

Ex. 108b shows the hand around but not touching the butterfly. In 108c both hands are 'enclosing' your face; this is like 'burying' your face in your hands without actual contact. Note the sign for face: the front surface of the area of the head. In 108d A's right arm is enclosing B's back, a sympathetic gesture which has not produced an actual hug. Note the sign for the back surface of the chest: . The limb, hand, arm, etc. will curve according to the shape of the object.

Touch, Contact

Whereas nearness may register as a suggestion, touching is an actuality; tactile contact takes place. All the examples illustrating nearness can occur with touching. The reason for touching may be practical, functional, decorative or expressive. The manner in which a touch occurs, the use of speed and energy, may range from a careful, delicate contact with a fragile object to the sudden energy of a clap or slap. Repeated contacts, as in tapping, may express rhythmic patterns, or, as in the Bavarian Schuhplattler dance, clapping and slapping various parts of the body - thigh, ankle, etc. - in a rhythmic sequence. Touching naturally involves the hands, but other parts come into play - foot touching the floor, elbow on the table, knee or hip pushing an object away, etc. Contact of the legs, beats as in cabrioles, often occurs while jumping. When two performers are involved, touch is one step closer to being involved with the other person in either a positive or negative way by caressing or punching.

Indication of Touch, Contact

The sign for contact, touch, is a horizontal bow, Ex. 109a. This bow is drawn connecting the parts which touch. It may be swung upward or downward.

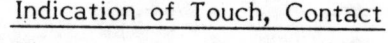

or

109a

Here are some typical examples of contact.

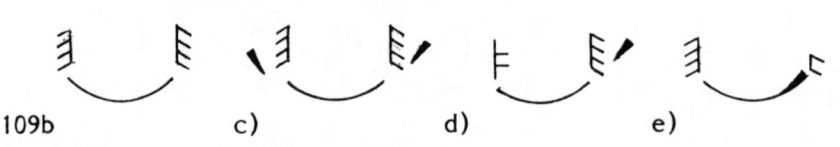

109b   c)   d)   e)

Ex. 109b shows contact between both hands. In 109c strong accents have been added to produce sound, i.e. a clap. In 109d the hand slaps the knee. By thickening the right side of the contact bow, as in 109e, we show that it is the elbow which is active, and not, as would be ex-

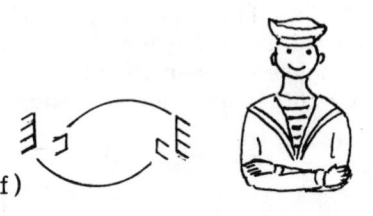

f)

pected, that the hand moves to the elbow. The position of 109f with the right hand touching the left elbow and the left hand touching the right elbow is familiar from the Sailor's Hornpipe.

Grasping

When a contact is accompanied by enclosing it produces a grasp. Whereas a touch may be momentary, a passing occurrence, grasping (clasping, encircling, enclosing) an object, a part of oneself or another person, denotes a greater degree of involvement in that grasping usually has some duration.

110a

The hands are commonly the instrument for grasping, but other parts also serve - as when elbows are linked in a folk dance, a knee grasps a barre, or the arms encircle an object or embrace a person. A leg or both legs may also 'embrace' though with less facility. A contact with enclosing should not include weight-bearing which is a further degree of involvement in relating. How a grasp occurs can vary greatly in expression depending on the purpose or reason: snatching an object, grasping a person's arm to give him help, a warm reassuring grasp, or an arresting grip, and so on. A finger in the mouth may be a form of grasping, as is hugging. Often we 'hold' an object when assisting another person, grasping the object to steady it.

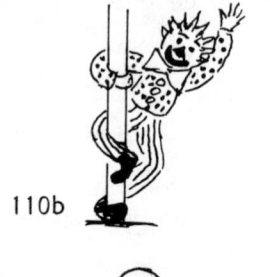

110b

110c

Indication of Grasping

Enclosing contact, grasping, is written by combining an X for flexion with the contact bow, Ex. 111a. This X is placed closer to the part which is doing the grasping.

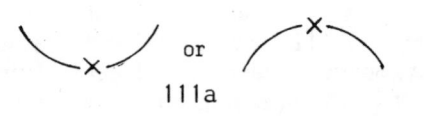

111a

Indication of Grasping (continued)

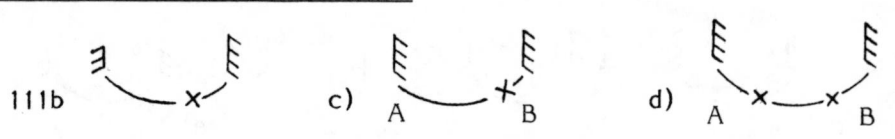

111b   c) A   B   d) A   B

Ex. 111b shows your right hand grasping your left wrist; in 111c B's right hand grasps A's right hand. Both hands grasp equally in 111d, as happens when people shake hands. Each of these occur in daily life as well as in choreography. The following are met in folk dances.

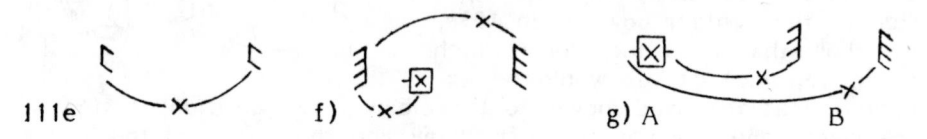

111e   f)   g) A   B

Linking elbows, as in a square dance, is shown in 111e. Ex. 111f states that while the left hand grasps the left side of the waist, the right hand is grasping the left hand, a position sometimes taken by a man while waiting. Ex. 111g shows B's hands grasping A's waist, a position often used in folk dances when turning, the girl's hands usually being placed on the man's shoulders.

Fingers Grasping, Interlacing

All examples given so far in the use of the hand for grasping and carrying have represented the natural action of the thumb closing in opposition to the fingers. Occasionally only the fingers grasp, or it may be only one finger. The signs for the fingers are:

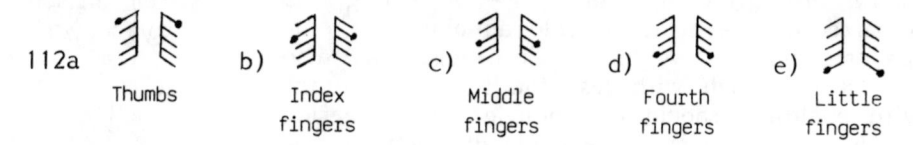

112a Thumbs   b) Index fingers   c) Middle fingers   d) Fourth fingers   e) Little fingers

Here are some familiar examples of grasping with the fingers:

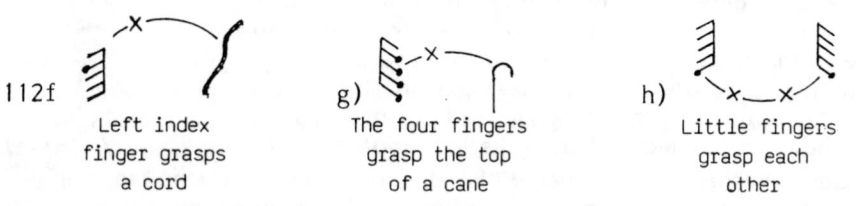

112f Left index finger grasps a cord   g) The four fingers grasp the top of a cane   h) Little fingers grasp each other

In an ordinary hand clasp one hand grasps the center portion of the other hand, its thumb being inside the thumb of the other hand. In Ex. 112j the right hand grasps the left. A more symmetrical grasping occurs when the fingers interlace, 112k. Interlacing, entwining, penetrating is indicated by a double X. This usage is a convention to show this different kind of enclosing.

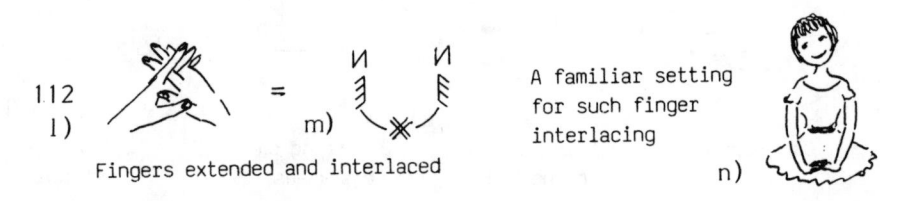

112j Usual form of hands grasping each
other. Here the left thumb is on
the outside.

k) Hands clasped with fingers
intertwining.

Ex. 112k is written as an action of the hand as a whole since the bulk of the hand, the palm, is involved. If, as in 112l and m) entwining of the fingers involves only the fingers it is written as such.

112
l)

m)

Fingers extended and interlaced

A familiar setting
for such finger
interlacing

n)

These are only general indications for some of the basic possibilities for such hand relationships. Obviously much more must be stated to produce specific configurations.

Carrying

In general, carrying is comparable to touching but the contact includes the important fact of taking weight, of supporting the object or person. Carrying can be of the simplest kind where the object or person rests on the surface of the body, as when a waitress carries a tray or a jar is carried on the head, or it may be a person sitting on someone else's knee, as illustrated below.

113
a)

b)

c)

d)

Grasping an object may lead to picking it up to carry it; we now bear the weight of the object or person, but through an enclosing and not just supporting on a body surface. Carrying a partner may involve both arms, one arm, or both hands depending on the position established and whether the partner is helping or others are contributing to the support. With most objects carrying includes grasping because it produces a more secure hold. The degree of closing the hand, of folding the arm, etc. depends on the shape of the object. In carrying a pencil the hand may close around it almost into a fist, whereas carrying a large beach ball will require a more open hand. The part of the body doing the carrying-with-grasp will automatically adjust to the size and shape of the object.

Indication of Carrying

The sign for taking weight is already familiar from our exploration of supporting and change of support (Chapter Eight). Now we are concerned not just with supports on the floor but with supporting an object or a partner.

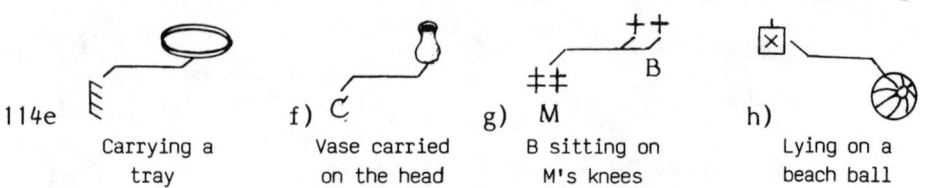

114a   b)   c)   d)

The angular bows of 114a and 114b can be used when no doubt exists as to which is carrying and which is being carried, e.g. a feather in the hand. The bow of 114c or 114d shows at the top what is being carried and below the part or object doing the carrying, the supporting.

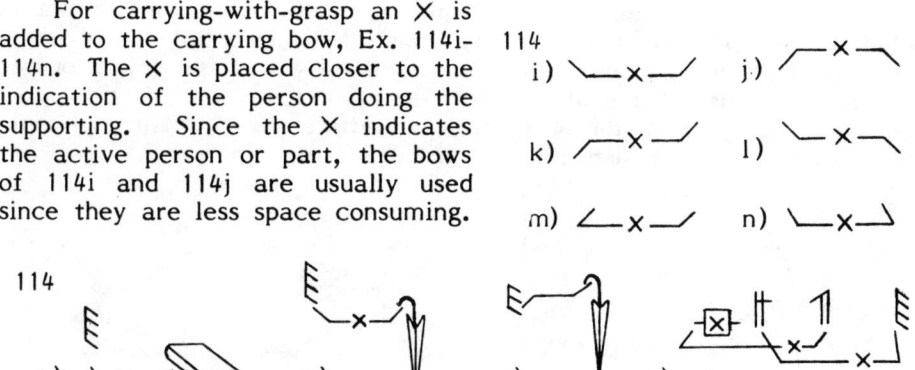

114e   f)   g)   h)

| Carrying a | Vase carried | B sitting on | Lying on a |
| tray | on the head | M's knees | beach ball |

The above show the notation for the carrying aspects of the figure illustrations of 113a-d; 114e = right hand carrying a tray; 114f = vase supported on the head; 114g = baby (B) being carried (hips supporting, sitting) on man's (M's) knees; and 114h = lying on the front of the waist on a large beach ball.

For carrying-with-grasp an X is added to the carrying bow, Ex. 114i-114n. The X is placed closer to the indication of the person doing the supporting. Since the X indicates the active person or part, the bows of 114i and 114j are usually used since they are less space consuming.

114

i) ⟍—x—╱   j) ╱—x—⟍

k) ╱—x—╱   l) ⟍—x—⟍

m) ∠—x—╱   n) ⟍—x—⟍

114

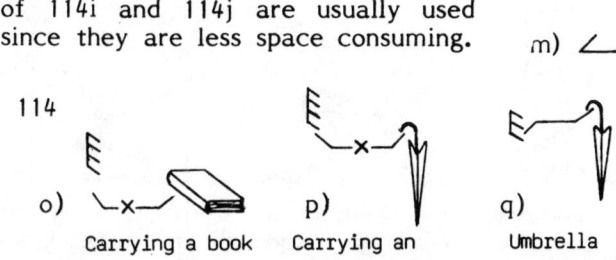

o)   p)   q)   r) A   B

| Carrying a book | Carrying an | Umbrella | B lifts A by grasping |
| (with grasp) | umbrella | on wrist | waist and right leg |

Ex. 114o shows carrying (with grasp) a book in the right hand. In 114p an umbrella is carried by the handle, but in 114q it is resting on the wrist, no grasping occurs. Ex. 114r shows a boy carrying a girl with his left arm around her waist and his right hand grasping her right leg. This information gives only the basic facts of carrying; how the performers got into that situation, details on exact placement of the arm and hand, and what happens during the lift all need to be spelled out for a specific performance.

SUPPORTING WITH A PARTNER

Below are some familiar supports which occur when working with a partner. Only the supporting, the focus of the activity, is written in the notation. In each case the feet are also supporting on the floor; this is not given in the notation except for 118b.

Mutual Support: Leaning Toward

Note the addition of a small stroke to the chest sign to indicate the back of the chest.

115a 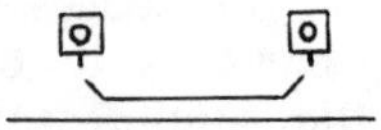   =   b) A   B

Mutual Support: Leaning Away

Here each person also supports the other, but by grasping.

116a 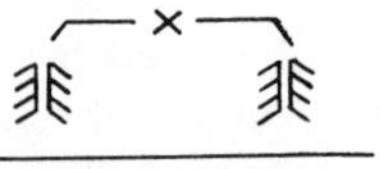   =   b) A   B

Partner Taking Partial Weight

Person A leans toward B who prevents her from falling by a grasping support. In fact grasping need not occur; it could be plain supporting.

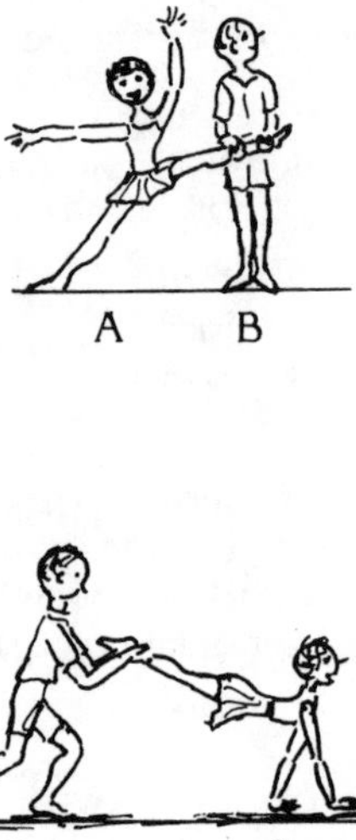

117a   A B   =   b) A   B

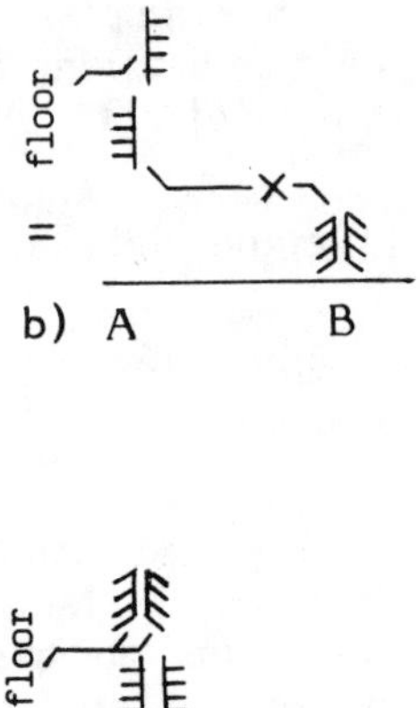

Horizontal Partial Supporting

Here is the familiar wheelbarrow position in which the girl's hands are supporting on the floor while the boy is supporting her feet.

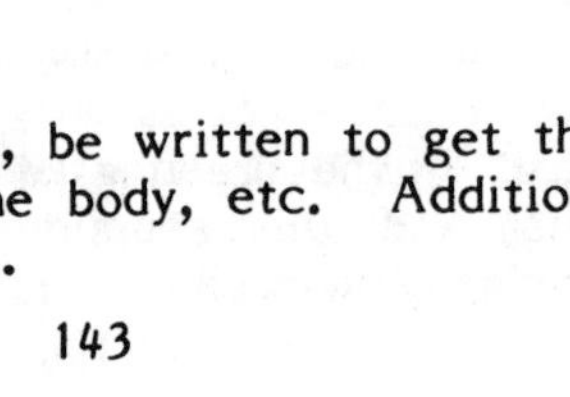

118a   B   A   =   b) A   B

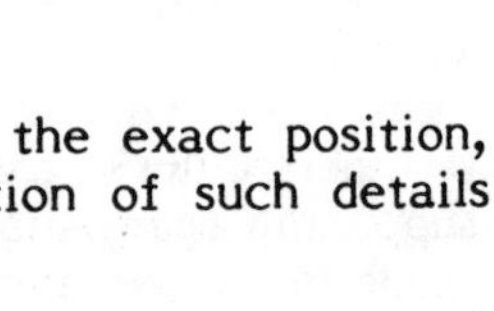

More detail must, of course, be written to get the exact position, the direction faced, angle of the body, etc. Addition of such details leads into Structured Description.

143

Indication of Active Part in Relating

In many instances it is quite clear from the context as to which part is active in relating and which part is passive.

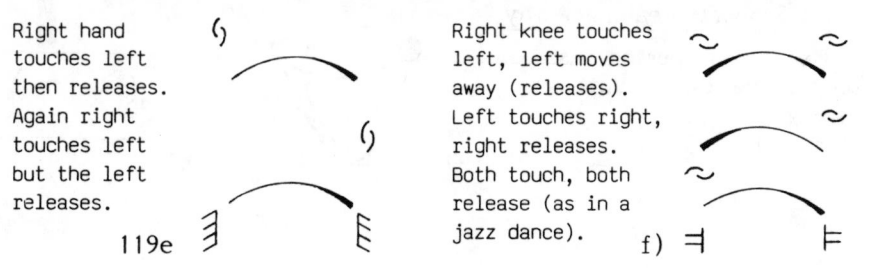

119
a) Left hand addresses. b) Both hands near. c) Right hand active. d) Right hand active.

In addressing, the active part is that from which the straight line extends. In Ex. 119a the left hand addresses the right. In Ex. 119b the simple statement is made that the hands are near each other. No indication is given as to which hand moved near to the other. We indicate the active side by thickening the appropriate end of the bow. Thus in 119c the right hand is active. This same device is applied to contact, touch. Note that a release means a slight moving away.

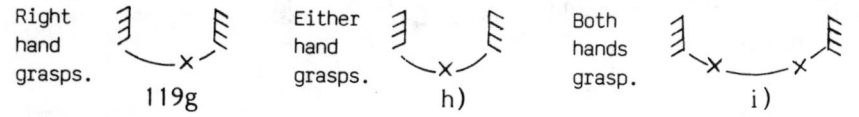

Right hand touches left then releases. Again right touches left but the left releases.

119e

Right knee touches left, left moves away (releases). Left touches right, right releases. Both touch, both release (as in a jazz dance).

f)

In examples such as 119e and f) we assume that subsequent movement indications are for the same body part, that the same pre-sign is still in effect.

For grasping, placement of the X indicates the active part. In 119g the right hand grasps; in h) it is either hand; in i) it is both.

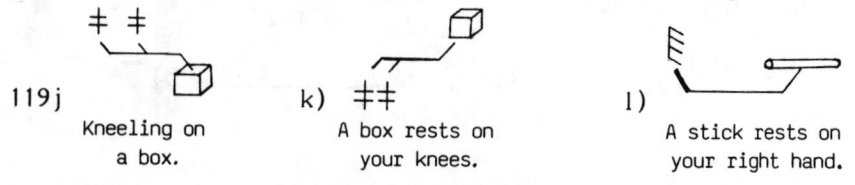

Right hand grasps. 119g

Either hand grasps. h)

Both hands grasp. i)

For indications of support the angular bow is modified to show what part is taking weight and what part is being supported. The end that slants down shows where weight is placed. For symmetrical bows the active end (the part supporting) is shown by thickening that end.

119j
Kneeling on a box.

k) A box rests on your knees.

l) A stick rests on your right hand.

In Ex. 119j and k) the drawing of the supporting bow indicates the supporting part. In 119l the left side of the bow is thickened since a stick might be taking your weight - it depends on the context.

144

Reading Practice

NEARNESS, TOUCHING, GRASPING, CARRYING

A duet for two people - not too serious.

-⊠- = sides of waist   ∿ = release, let go   ∧ = delete, cancel, move away

C̄ = face   ▷ = accent   Ā = A is behind you   B̲ = B is in front of you

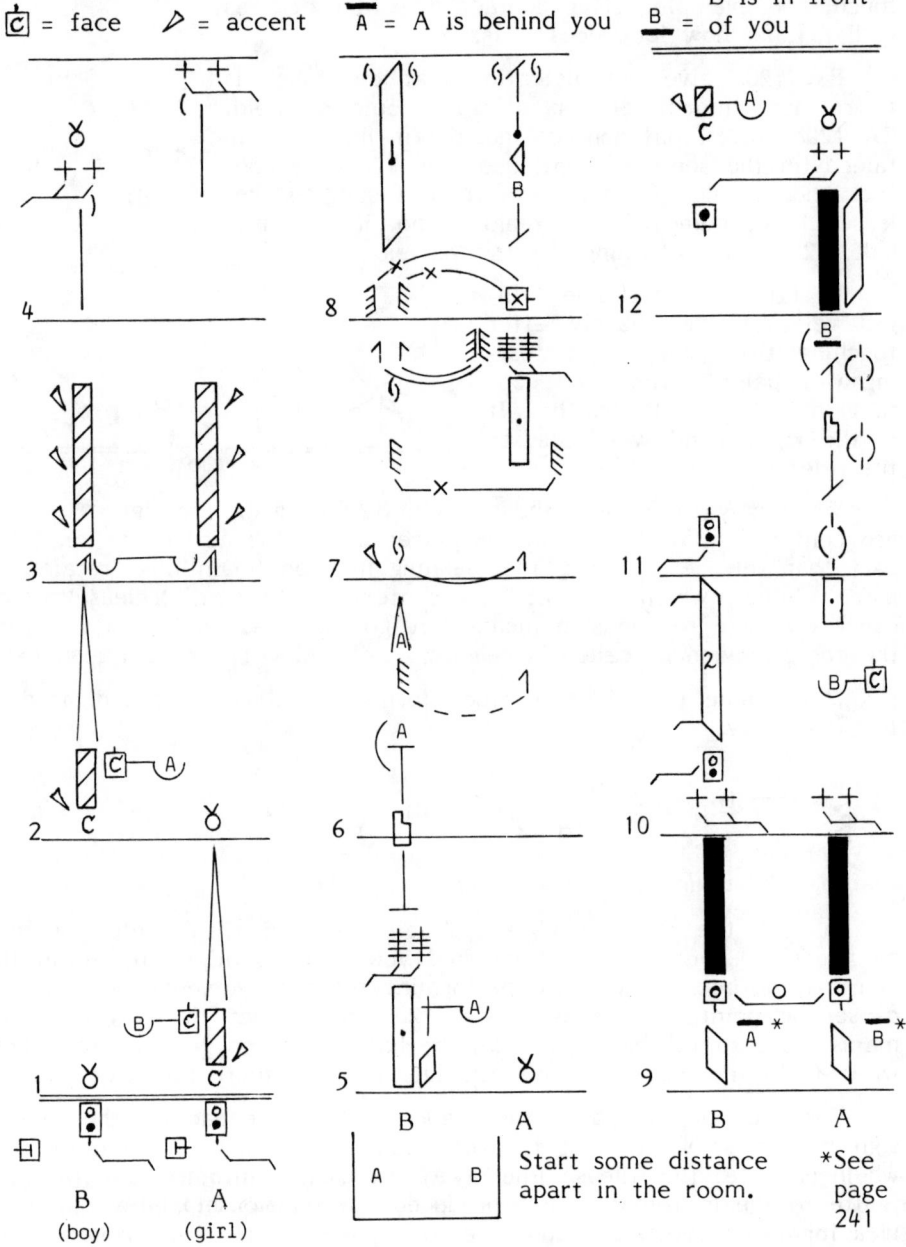

B   A
(boy)   (girl)

Start some distance apart in the room.

*See page 241

DURATION OF RELATING

In Motif Description the result of an action is understood to be over (automatic cancellation) when something else happens. In itself an indication of relating does not state either that it should remain or that it should be cancelled (disappear). Take a touch, for example, after contact is established, as in Ex. 120a; how long does it last?

120a

b)

c)

d) or e)

Ex. 120a gives no indication that the touch is to release immediately or that it should be held. Ex. 120b states that contact should remain, be maintained (in the sense of continued). In 120c the contact should release immediately. The sign for release, 120d, comes from breaking the hold sign in half, 120e, and entwining the two halves.

In 120f the left index finger releases immediately after touching the chair, as if testing wet paint. The hand contact in 120g is held briefly. It is the right hand which causes the release.

120

f) g)

When only the bow is shown, as in 120b and c), the signs o and 𝔖 are centered. For ∿ the sign is placed above the active part, i.e. the part that releases. For o the meaning may be 'maintain', 'retain', or 'keep', 'hold', whichever suits the context. The term 'release' which cancels a held relationship means 'let go' and has no connection with the torso movement called 'a release' in the Martha Graham technique.

Maintaining or releasing other forms of relating are indicated in the same way:

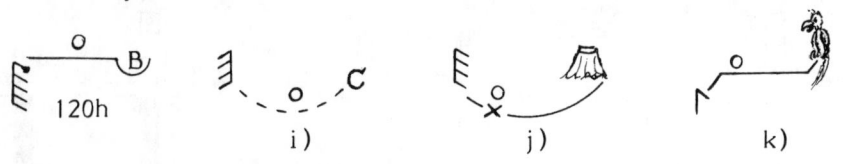

120h   i)   j)   k)

In 120h the right thumb keeps pointing at B. This retention may be needed because B is moving and you have to adjust to retain the pointing, or because you are performing other movements which might cause the pointing to cease. Ex. 120i states that the left hand remains close to the head. In 120j the hand keeps on grasping the skirt, while in k) the parrot on your shoulder remains there for some time.

For each of the above the reader will look ahead for the release sign to see at what point the retention is cancelled. The movement which produces the release, the 'away', is usually into the direction opposite to the movement which produced the relationship. For example, if a forward movement produces a touch, the release will be backward.

Duration of a Passing (Sliding) Relationship

Movement in a limb which is involved with relating may result in a 'passing' or 'sliding' relationship. Such a relationship is most easily understood in touching. If the touching limb moves and touching is retained, it becomes a sliding, brushing. A single contact becomes a moving contact, which is shown by doubling the sign.

121a   b)   c)

Ex. 121a is the indication of a moving contact. Such momentary sliding could occur when flicking ash off the table. In 121b the right hand briefly brushes the left arm. Ex. 121c shows the right foot briefly sliding on the floor (as nothing is written the floor is understood).

121d   e)   f)   g)

This same doubling of the sign is applied to a passing nearness, Ex. 121d; to a passing addressing, 121e; a sliding grasp, 121f; and a sliding support, as in slipping, skidding, 121g, as illustrated below.

121h   i)   j)   k)

In 121h the left hand passes near the head; 121i shows glancing at a partner, the sign: representing the eyes. A passing addressing can be through looking (glancing at a shop window), or with a gesture (waving at a group of people). In 121j the right hand briefly rubs the left arm (grasping is included). A hat is sliding off the head in 121k.

If the above 'sliding' relationships continue for more than a moment, further duration is shown by adding the sign: O with the meaning of 'keep on', 'maintain' this state. For a static state, such as a touch a hold sign means 'keep', 'hold'; for a passing 'sliding' relationship, it means "Carry on!", i.e. continue with what you are doing. In Ex. 121l-o) the stated relationship is to continue.

121 l   m)   n)   o)

Passing relationships occur with movement; the particular movement may continue and the relating may cease sooner, or it may last. In 121p sliding continues during the action; in 121q sliding is brief.

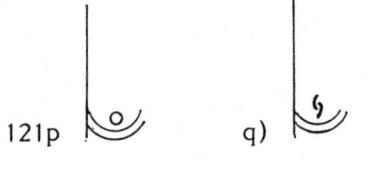

121p   q)

Reading Study No. 26

PARTNERS RELATING (Ending Together)

A duet for boy and girl telling a little story.

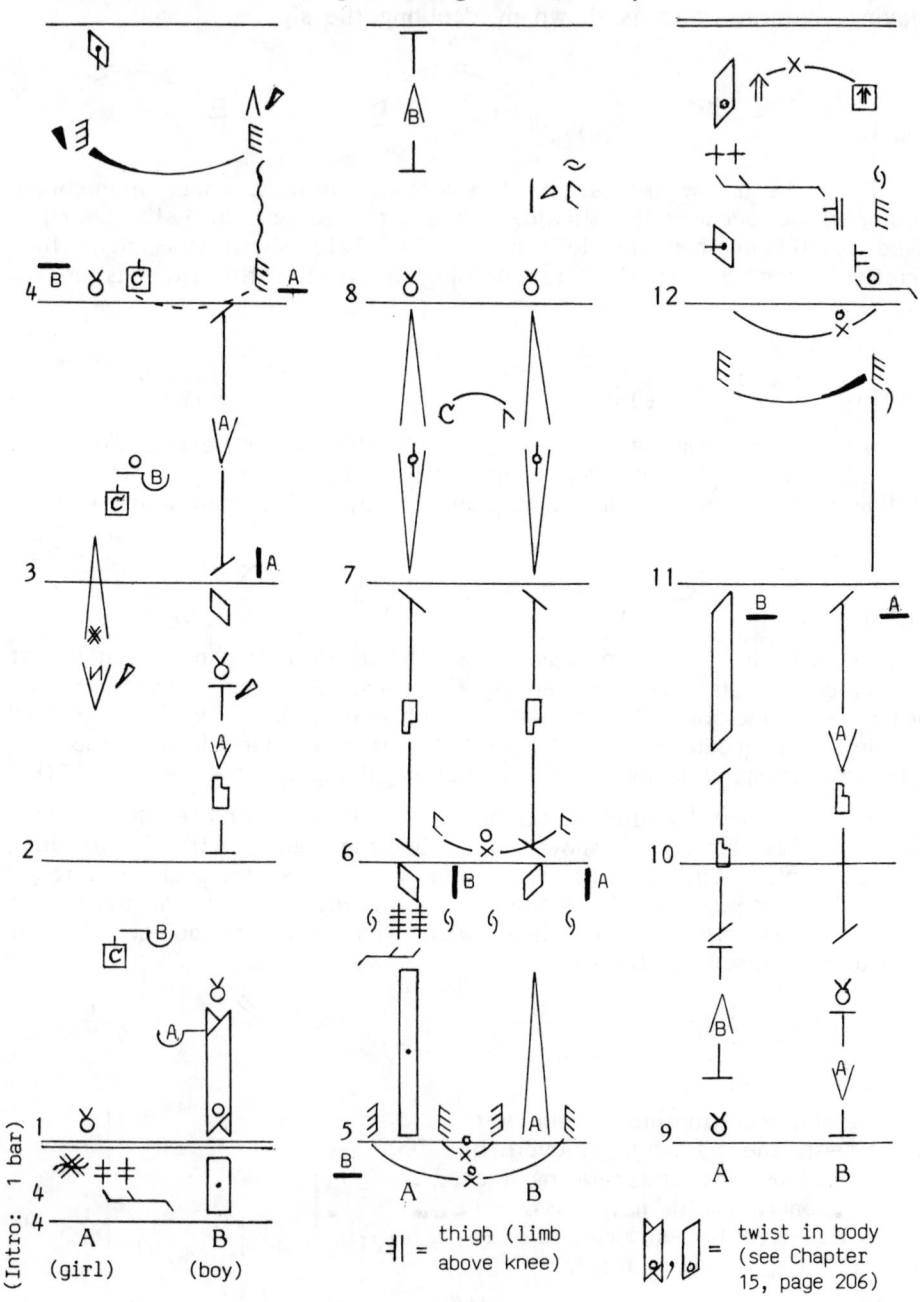

	thigh (limb above knee)

	twist in body (see Chapter 15, page 206)

148

Relationships

Reading Practice

THE STORY OF A BONBON

This little mime sequence is to be explored and performed without music.

BB = Bonbon   = index finger   = thumb   = mouth

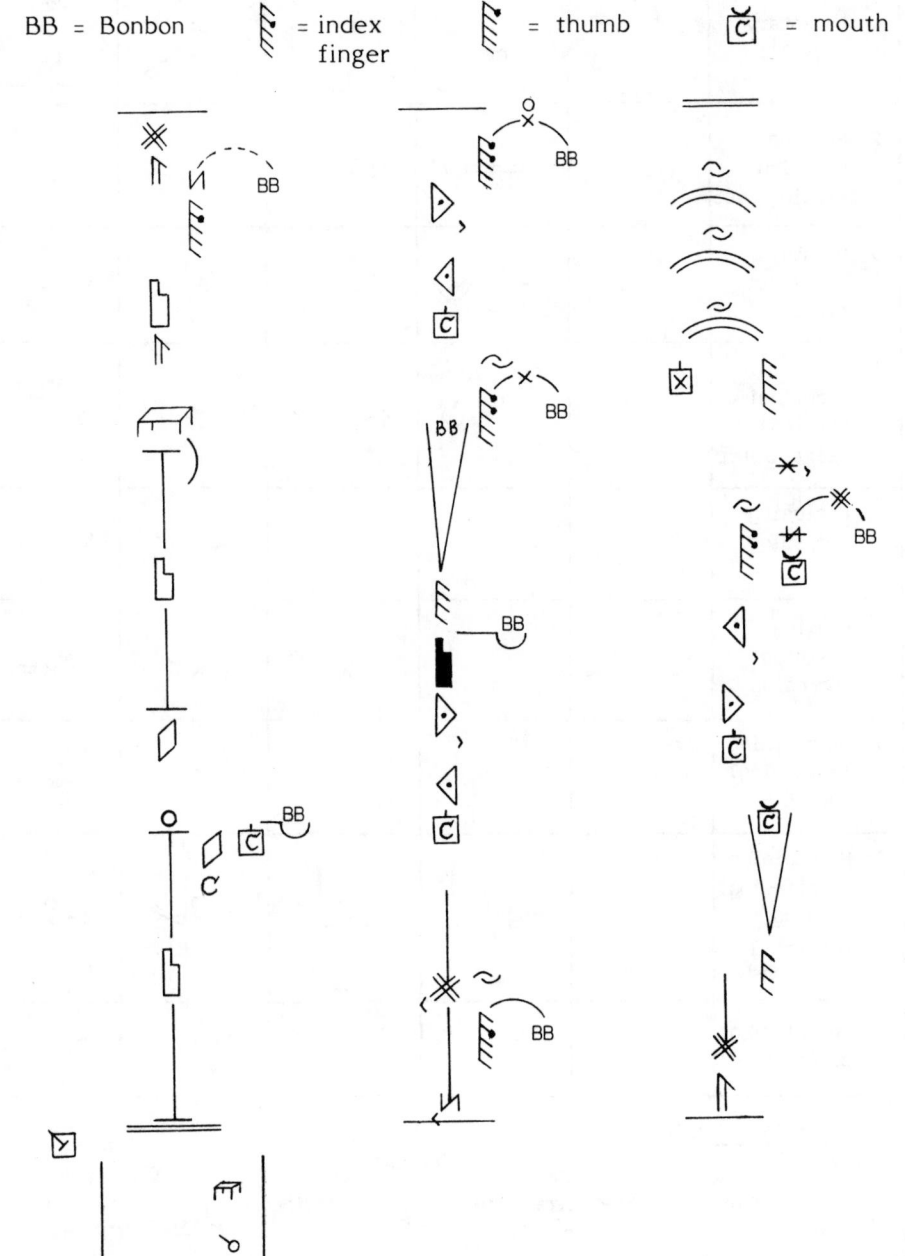

REVIEW FOR CHAPTER TEN

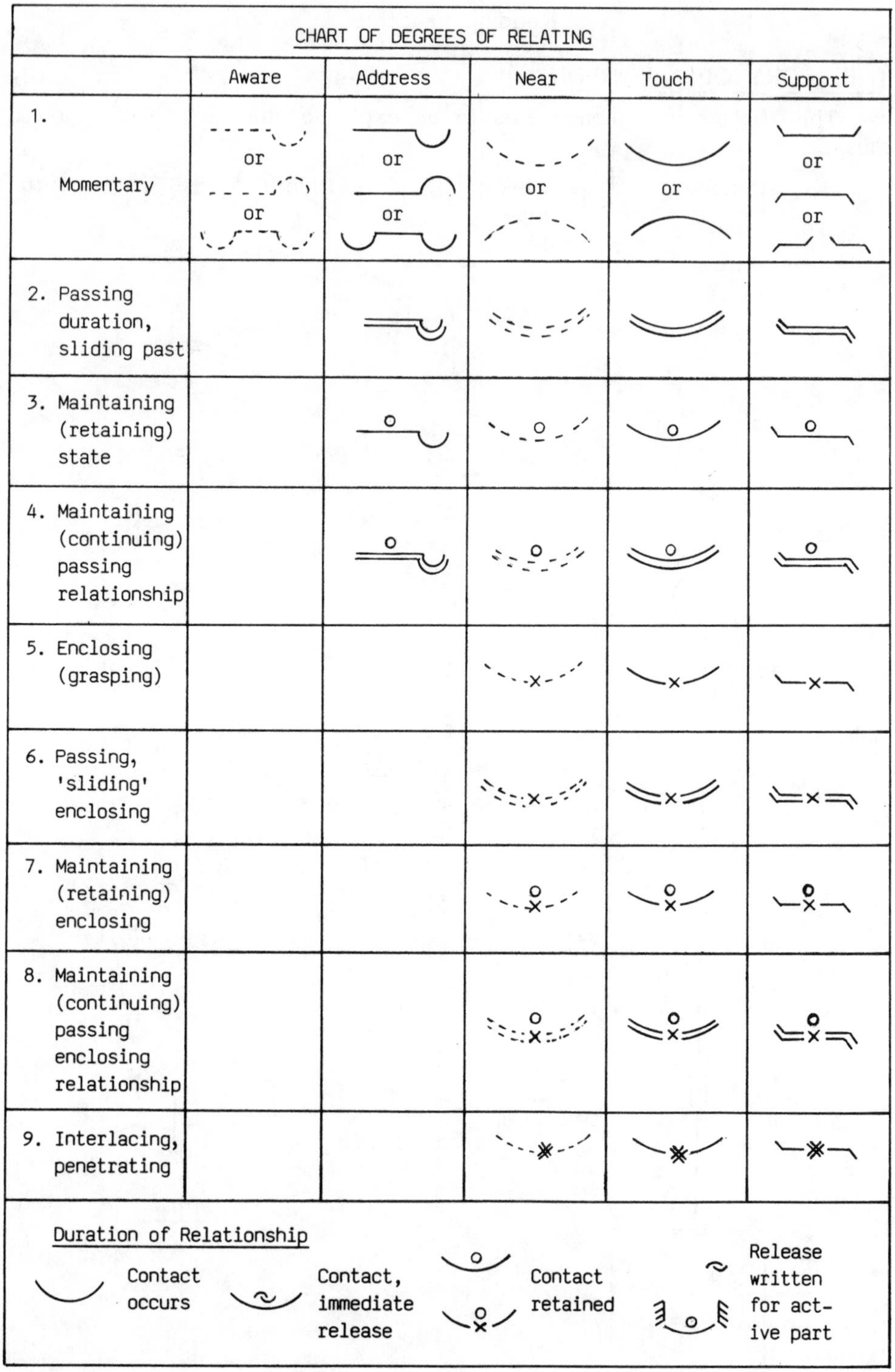

CHART OF DEGREES OF RELATING					
	Aware	Address	Near	Touch	Support
1. Momentary	or / or	or / or	or	or	or / or
2. Passing duration, sliding past					
3. Maintaining (retaining) state					
4. Maintaining (continuing) passing relationship					
5. Enclosing (grasping)					
6. Passing, 'sliding' enclosing					
7. Maintaining (retaining) enclosing					
8. Maintaining (continuing) passing enclosing relationship					
9. Interlacing, penetrating					

Duration of Relationship

Contact occurs   Contact, immediate release   Contact retained   Release written for active part

150

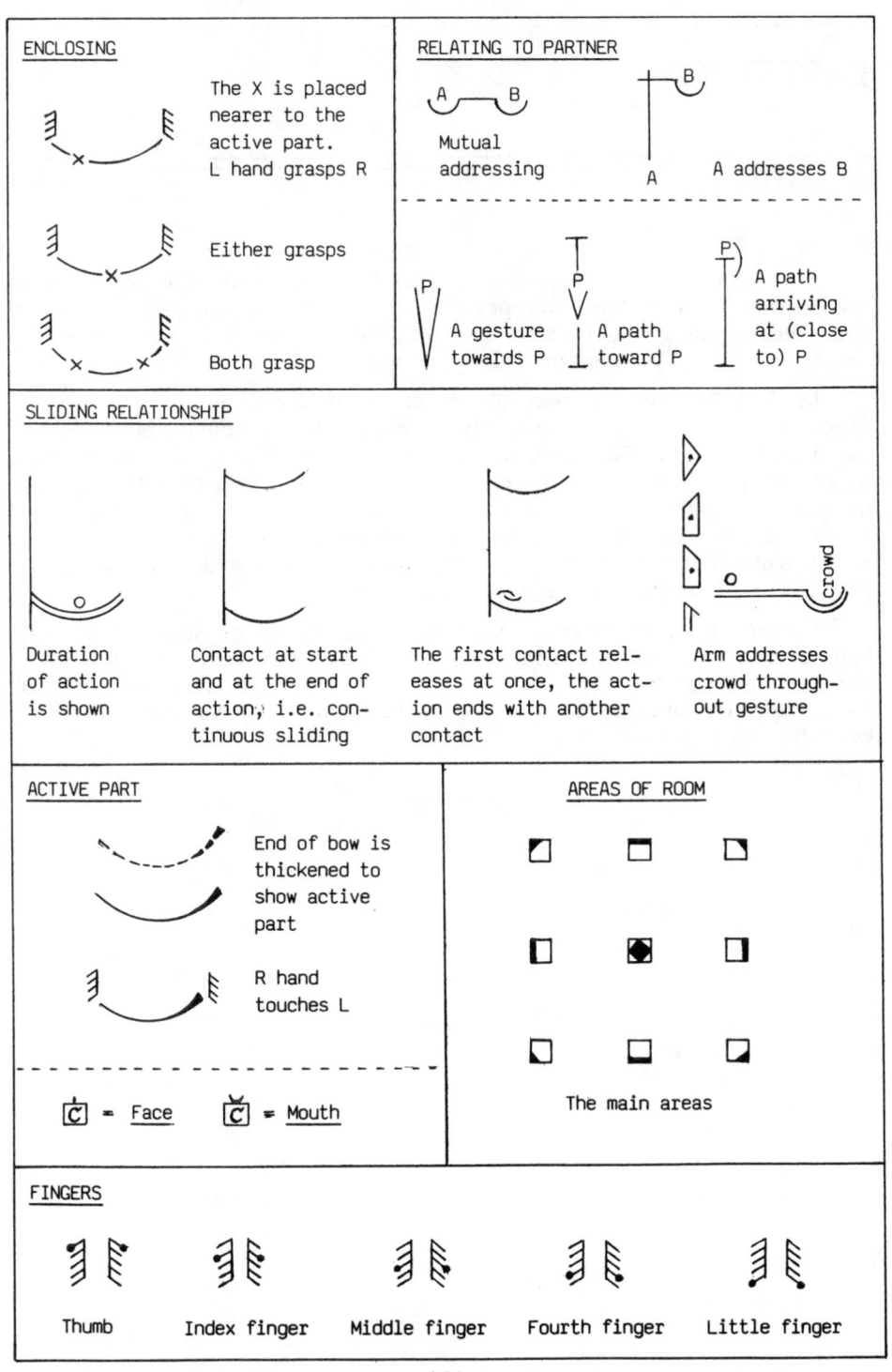

ENCLOSING

The X is placed nearer to the active part.
L hand grasps R

Either grasps

Both grasp

RELATING TO PARTNER

Mutual addressing

A addresses B

A gesture towards P

A path toward P

A path arriving at (close to) P

SLIDING RELATIONSHIP

Duration of action is shown

Contact at start and at the end of action, i.e. continuous sliding

The first contact releases at once, the action ends with another contact

Arm addresses crowd throughout gesture

ACTIVE PART

End of bow is thickened to show active part

R hand touches L

C = Face   C = Mouth

AREAS OF ROOM

The main areas

FINGERS

Thumb   Index finger   Middle finger   Fourth finger   Little finger

PART TWO

Part One of this book dealt with the first general exploration of the Prime Actions given on page xxiii. Much leeway in performance and freedom in interpretation was allowed as long as the basic movement concept was understood and portrayed.

In Part Two exploration covers much of the same ground but the focus is on becoming increasingly specific, thus leading toward Structured Description. Although many specific details are introduced, such as use of parts of the body and variations in interpreting direction, the movement exploration continues to be comparatively free and is still presented and described on paper through Motif Description. The transition from Motif to Structured Description in which details are specifically stated is given in Appendix B.

Reference to the Family Tree of Verbs, given in Appendix D, will help in relating new material to that already covered. As details on the various 'families' of movement are further explored the chart of Verbs helps to provide perspective on how the new material relates to what has gone before.

Chapter Eleven
PART LEADING, GUIDANCE

The manner in which a basic action is performed can affect the expression and add color and interest to a movement. The more specific details added to a basic form, the more it will take on a particular style. This style may be highly individual or it may combine details which produce a recognizable type with a known origin and name.

Initiation of an action, its source in the body, how it flows out of the body - all greatly color the expression and meaning of a movement. Our concern in this chapter is with the effect of one part leading a movement and of the guidance of actions. Initiation of an action may be from a central part such as a hip, or shoulder, i.e. some part of the torso, or the movement flow may be led by an extremity, the hand, foot, head, or the mid-joint of a limb, the elbow or knee. Guiding, a form of leading, may be performed with a surface or an edge of a limb.

PART LEADING

The direction and level of a movement may dictate what part of the body will be leading. Let us take the simple action of lowering and rising. Lowering of the body may be led by the knees, as in 122a.

 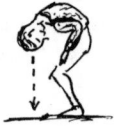 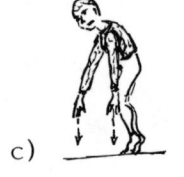

122a   b)   c)

Such lowering may produce very little lowering in the rest of the body; the spine could remain vertical, yet a lowering of the whole has taken place. If, however, lowering is led by the head, 122b, the head will bow first, the rest of the body following. The result will be a curved spine, a much more closed conclusion. If lowering is led by the hands, 122c, the expression of reaching for the safety of the floor can result. The spine will be curved but the head may still remain upright. Leading with the hips, which suggests a desire to sit, will produce a folded leg position. Use of the front of the chest in leading downward may suggest compassion toward something on the floor (a small animal perhaps?), while leading with the face stresses focussing on a point of interest on the floor nearby.

153

Part Leading (continued)

In a somewhat similar way the manner of rising is affected by which part
is leading.   By exploring the possibilities
of leading with the face, 123a, with the
top of the head, with a hand, 123b, the
elbows, the back, the front of the chest,
a shoulder, and so on, one can uncover a
range of different meanings, moods and
emphases.

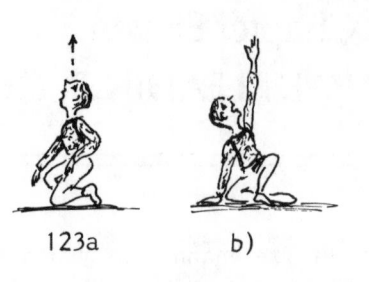

123a   b)

A simple exploration can be based on a simple walk.   Travelling
may be led by a hand, perhaps by the finger tips or the palm.   The
head could lead.   Very different expressions may be achieved by leading with the top of the head, the face, or - to be even more specific
- the chin.   The chest or the hips may initiate the travelling.   Many
people walk leading with the knees.   The stylized balletic walk has
each step led by the foot, the tip of the toes when the leg is straight,
the instep if the leg unfolds.

Observe the different feeling and expression which result when
leading with an extremity as opposed to a central part of the body.
Smaller surfaces such as finger tips or the tip of a foot seem to pene-
trate space, to explore, to search.   The edges of limbs, particularly the
edges of the hand and lower arm, cut through the space around.   We
see such cutting in the karate chop in which a wooden board is sliced
with the little finger edge of the hand.   The elbow and knee are like
extremities but limited in scope, their leading actions being arc-like,
that is, following curved lines.

Parts which are at the center of the body, i.e. parts of the trunk,
relate to space more in the sense of pressing against it or pushing it
aside, as though space were a tangible foam cloud.   A movement which
is led by a central part usually flows out to other parts.   Central
parts of the body are limited spatially, whereas a peripheral part such
as the fingertips has the whole range of the kinesphere to explore in
its role of part leading.

Indication of Parts Leading

A part of the body which is to
lead an action is placed in a
curved vertical bow adjacent to the
movement it qualifies.   Thus Ex.
124a indicates a lowering led by
the right hand such as might occur
in picking up an object.   In 124b
rising and extending are led first
by the elbows and then by the
hands, such as might happen in a
yawning stretch.   In 124c the left

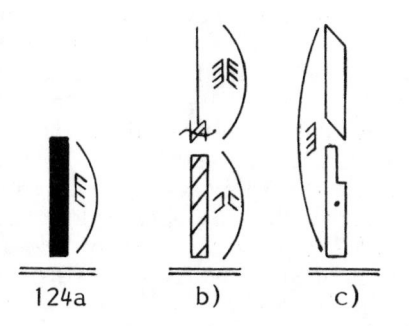

124a   b)   c)

hand leads an advancing movement and also the turn which follows. One interpretation of this notation could be exploring in the dark, reaching out to feel what might be there.

Surfaces and Edges for Part Leading

Indication of the hand in general allows considerable freedom in exactly how the hand is used; the interpretation most appropriate to movement it qualifies will be given. Use of particular surfaces and edges of the hand can be most expressive in conjunction with specific actions. Below are the signs for the surfaces and edges of the hand.

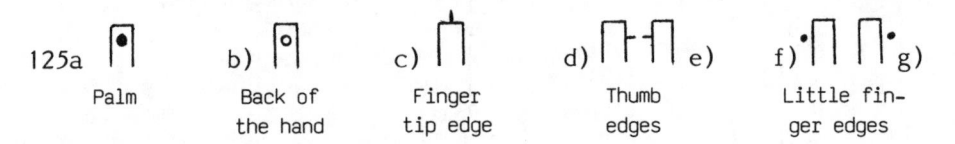

125a	b)	c)	d)	e)	f)	g)
Palm	Back of the hand	Finger tip edge	Thumb edges		Little finger edges	

The signs of Ex. 125a-c are placed on the right side when they refer to the right hand and on the left when they refer to the left hand. Ex. 125d shows thumb side for the left hand, 125e thumb side for the right. In the same way the little finger signs indicate left, 125f, and right, 125g. Where need be, hands or feet can be designated, 125h-k.

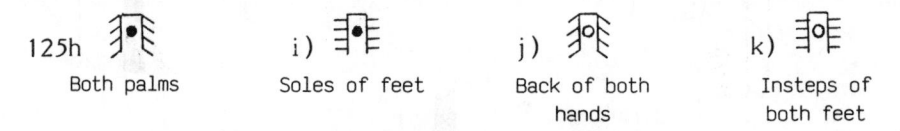

125h	i)	j)	k)
Both palms	Soles of feet	Back of both hands	Insteps of both feet

Surfaces of the parts of the torso are indicated by placement of a short stroke on the appropriate side or corner of the basic sign:

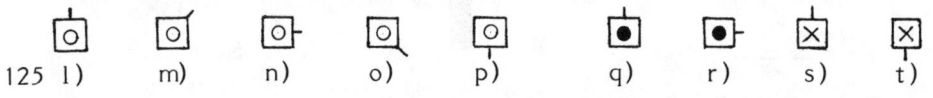

125 l)	m)	n)	o)	p)	q)	r)	s)	t)

Ex. 125l shows the front of the chest, 125m the right front diagonal surface of the chest, 125n the right side of the chest, and so on. The same device is applied to the pelvis (125q being the front surface, 125r the right side), and also to the waist (125s being the front of the waist, 125t the back of the waist).

Timing for Part Leading

A leading activity may occur all through a movement or may occur only at the start or only toward the end. As the curved vertical bow has time significance such differences are easy to show. In Ex. 124a, page 154, the bow started and ended with the movement it qualified, thus the hand led the movement from beginning to end. In Ex. 126a the left shoulder leads at the start of an action; in 126b palm leading occurs only at the end.

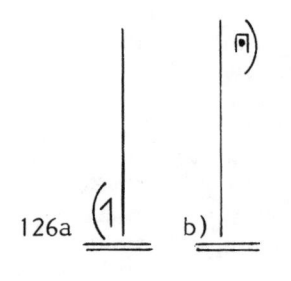

126a   b)

PART LEADING

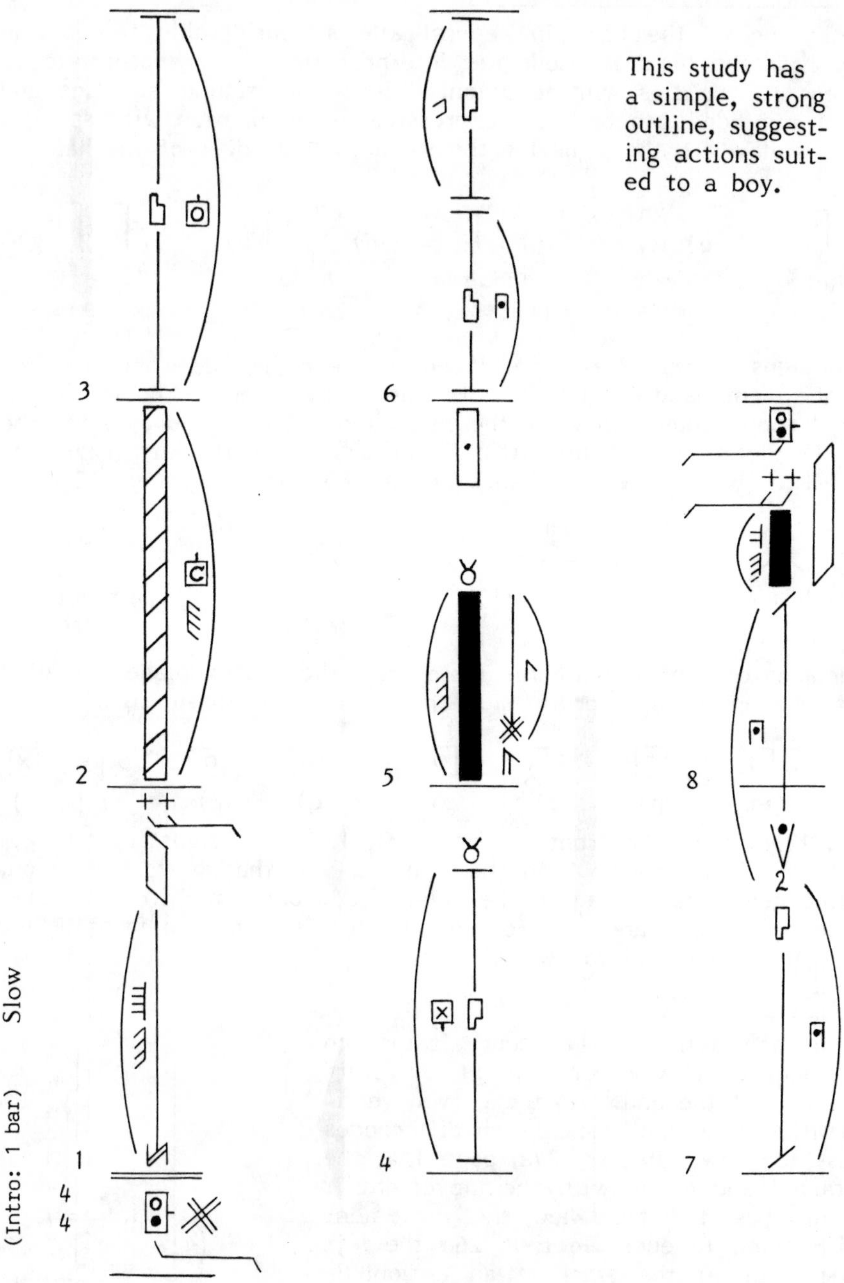

This study has
a simple, strong
outline, suggest-
ing actions suit-
ed to a boy.

Slow

(Intro: 1 bar)

3

2

++

1

4
4

6

5

4

8

2

7

156

PART LEADING IN LYRIC STYLE

A flowing, swaying study in slow waltz time.

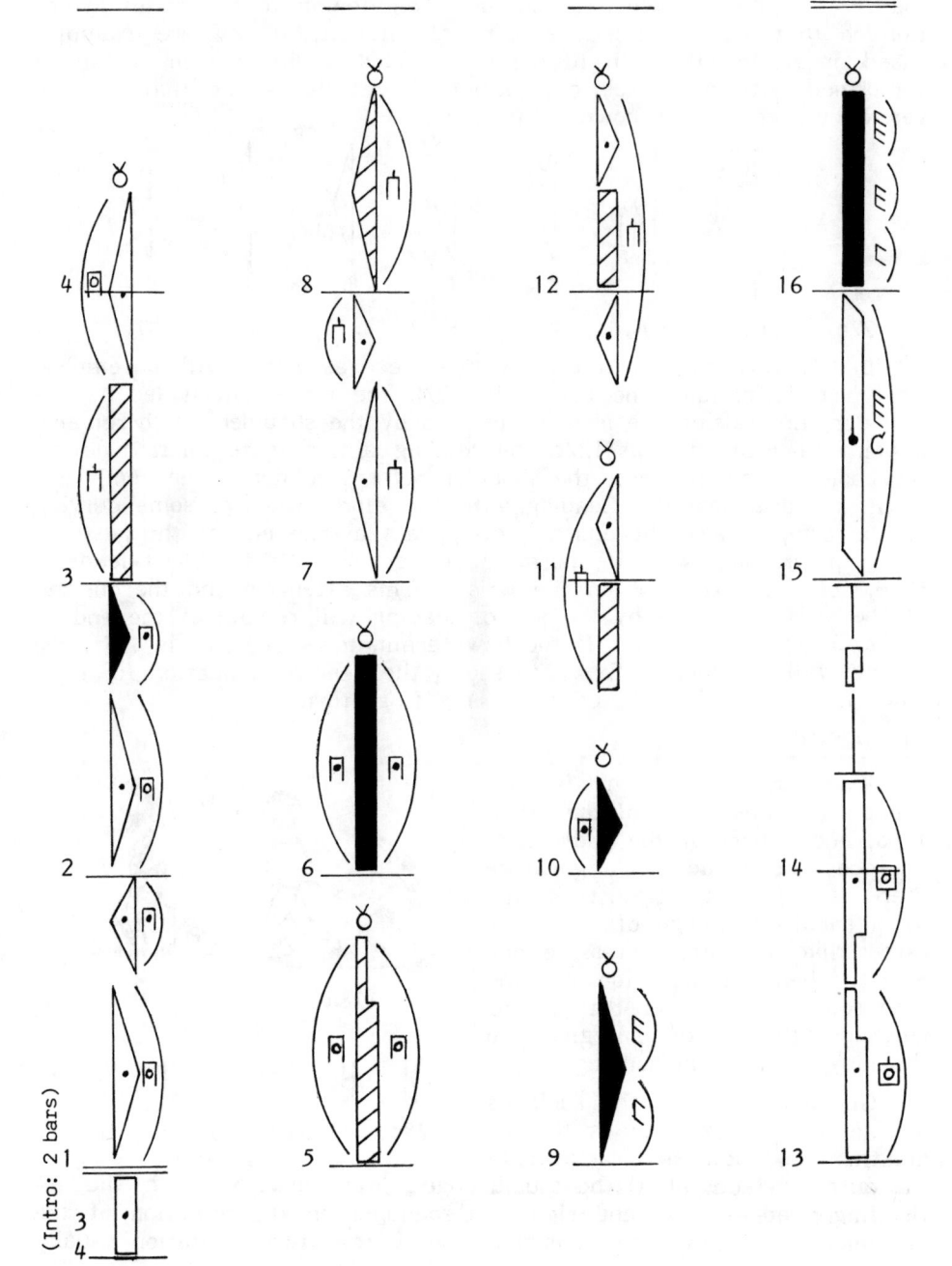

(Intro: 2 bars)

Point of Interest

Initiation of a movement may be hidden, unseen, or it may purposely be made visible, perhaps only through a slight change in the configuration of the limb or body part, or a slight tension in a part of the limb, a tension which produces a heightening that focusses attention on that part making it a point of interest.   Below are examples based on raising the arm to the side.   This simple movement can be performed with many subtle variations.   Let us assume that in each version the arm starts down.

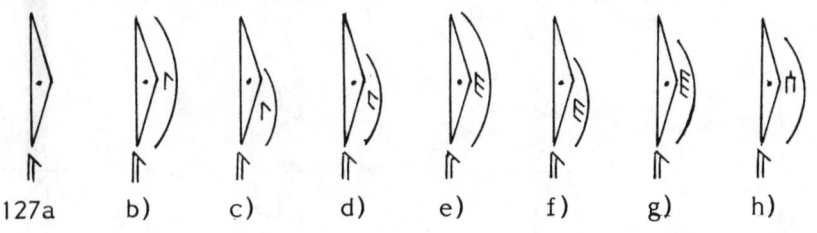

127a	b)	c)	d)	e)	f)	g)	h)

In Ex. 127a the arm moves in one piece as a unit with no emphasis or stress on any one part.   In 127b the movement is led by the shoulder, i.e. raising the arm is initiated by the shoulder which remains a point of interest.   In 127c the leading action is terminated before the basic movement ends; the shoulder returns to normal and emphasis on it has disappeared.   Leading with the elbow requires some curving of the arm; usually this curving disappears at the end of the gesture, the arm finishing with its normal carriage, Ex. 127d.   Wrist leading, 127e, focusses attention on the wrist.   This attention and the curving of the wrist produced by the act of leading will remain at the end of the arm gesture in 127e.   If the bow terminates sooner, as in 127f, the leading will disappear.   Ex. 127g shows the general indication for hand leading, while 127h specifies use of the fingertips.

GUIDANCES

Whereas leading suggests that one person goes ahead of the other, 128a, and a part of the body leading does 'go ahead', in a guidance there is a pressure against the air by a surface or edge of the limb, rather like the slight pressure one exerts when walking side by side with someone, 128b, or the kind of guidance the gentleman gives to the lady in ballroom dancing.

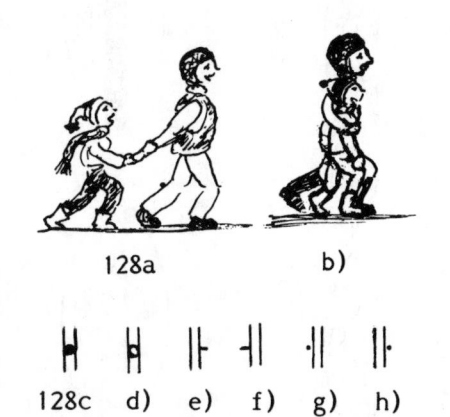

128a   b)

Guidances involve the surfaces of the limbs.   Ex. 128c is the indication for the inner surface; d)

128c   d)   e)   f)   g)   h)

the outer surface; e), f) the thumb edges, left and right; g), h) the little finger edges, left and right.   Depending on the direction of the movement, a slight, unemphasized inward or outward rotation usually precedes a specific guidance. An outer surface guidance, as in 128i, concludes with palm facing down. The inner surface guidance of 128j requires an outward preparatory rotation of the arm and will conclude with palm facing up. In 128k the thumb guidance brings the thumb immediately into the line of the

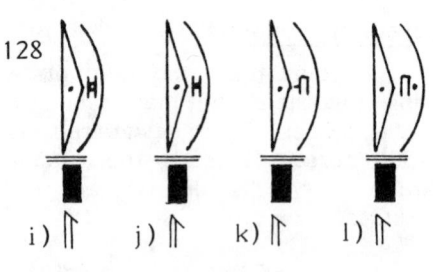

128

i) ⇑   j) ⇑   k) ⇑   l) ⇑

movement so that the palm faces forward from the start. But this palm facing is incidental; the emphasis is on the thumb edge cutting through the air. Inward rotation is needed to start the little finger guidance of 128l. Find the different feeling and expression for each of these guidances in this spatial setting, then experiment with each guidance for different directional movements of the arms. Explore variations in guidance for leg gestures. The signs of 128c-h also apply to the legs (big toe edge, little toe edge, etc.). Though less flexible than the arms, the legs can perform many interesting variations.

Variations in Walking

In the simple activity of walking one can observe a great number of variations among people in the street, let alone among trained performers. Let us disregard differences in timing, in size of the step, in how the foot is placed on the ground, and be concerned only with initiation: specifically how the leg is brought forward to take the next step. Starting at the top of the leg we see examples of hip leading, Ex. 129a, initiation from the groin. Hip initiation can involve a very slight or a marked pelvic rotation, the most exaggerated being when the outer side of the hip initiates each step, 129b. The top (outside) surface of the thigh, 129c, or the knee, 129d, may lead the leg. The foot in general or the instep may start the leg swinging forward, 129e, 129f. In the stylized balletic walk the tip of the toes leads, Ex. 129g. Other parts may initiate travelling: the pelvis as a whole (which usually happens when the chest is sunk and displaced backward) or the waist (as in men with beer-bloated waistlines). Leading with the chest may express a desire to travel, or may, when the chest continuously leads step after step, induce a feeling (usually) of lightness. A rhythmic inner impulse results when a new initiation comes with each step. These are only some of the possibilities which can be indicated through the use of appropriate symbols.

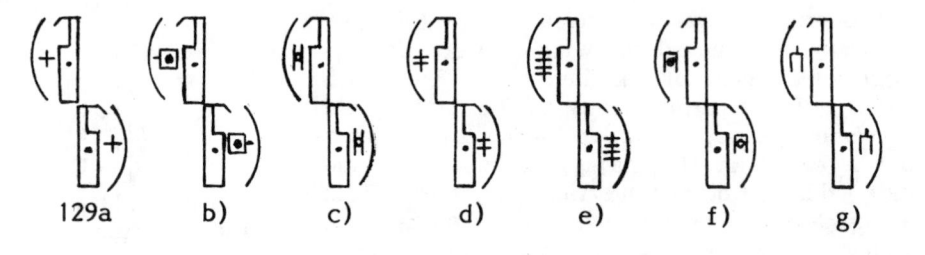

129a   b)   c)   d)   e)   f)   g)

Leading, Following

Leading may also take place when two or more people are travelling together; one may take the lead and the others follow. In Ex.
130a person A is designated as the leader for the straight path; in
130b person D leads the circular path.   Identification of the person,
usually by a letter, is tied to the start of the path sign by a short
vertical bow.

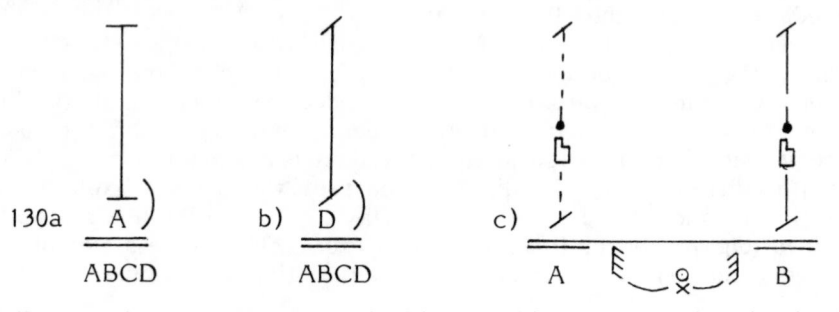

130a   A   b)   D   c)

ABCD   ABCD   A   B

Two performers may travel side by side, yet one be the leader.
Ex. 130c shows A and B holding hands.   B then leads A in a clockwise
circle.   A is shown to be passive by her path sign, which is written as
a dotted vertical line.   Dotted vertical lines mean 'resultant', 'passive'
in contrast to solid vertical lines which mean 'active', as in the basic
action stroke.   In 130d below, B, who is holding A's hand, is shown to
be turning on the spot to the right while A passively travels on a circular path being led by B.   Quite the reverse is stated in 130e.   Starting with elbows linked, A circles around B causing B to pivot on the
spot.   Dotted passive lines used for the turn sign indicate the resultant
nature of the action.

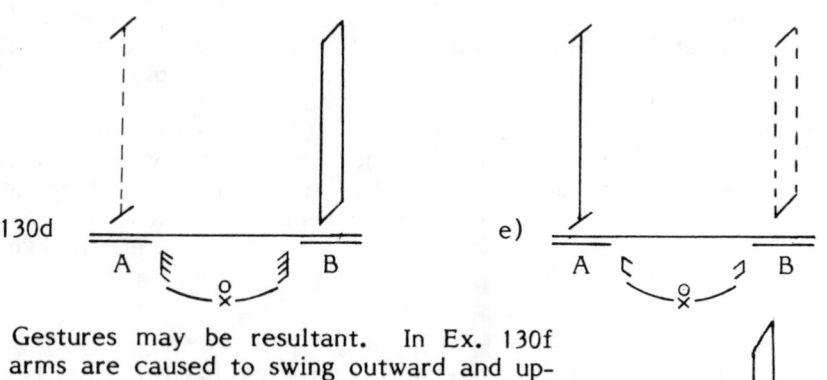

130d   A   B   e)   A   B

Gestures may be resultant.   In Ex. 130f
the arms are caused to swing outward and upward as a result of the fast turn.   The destination of the arms needs to be stated; the
movement is not an active raising of the arms
but a result of the turning action.   To indicate this a dotted vertical line is placed
alongside the direction symbol to indicate the   130f
manner of performance for this movement.

160

RESULTANT, PASSIVE MOVEMENTS

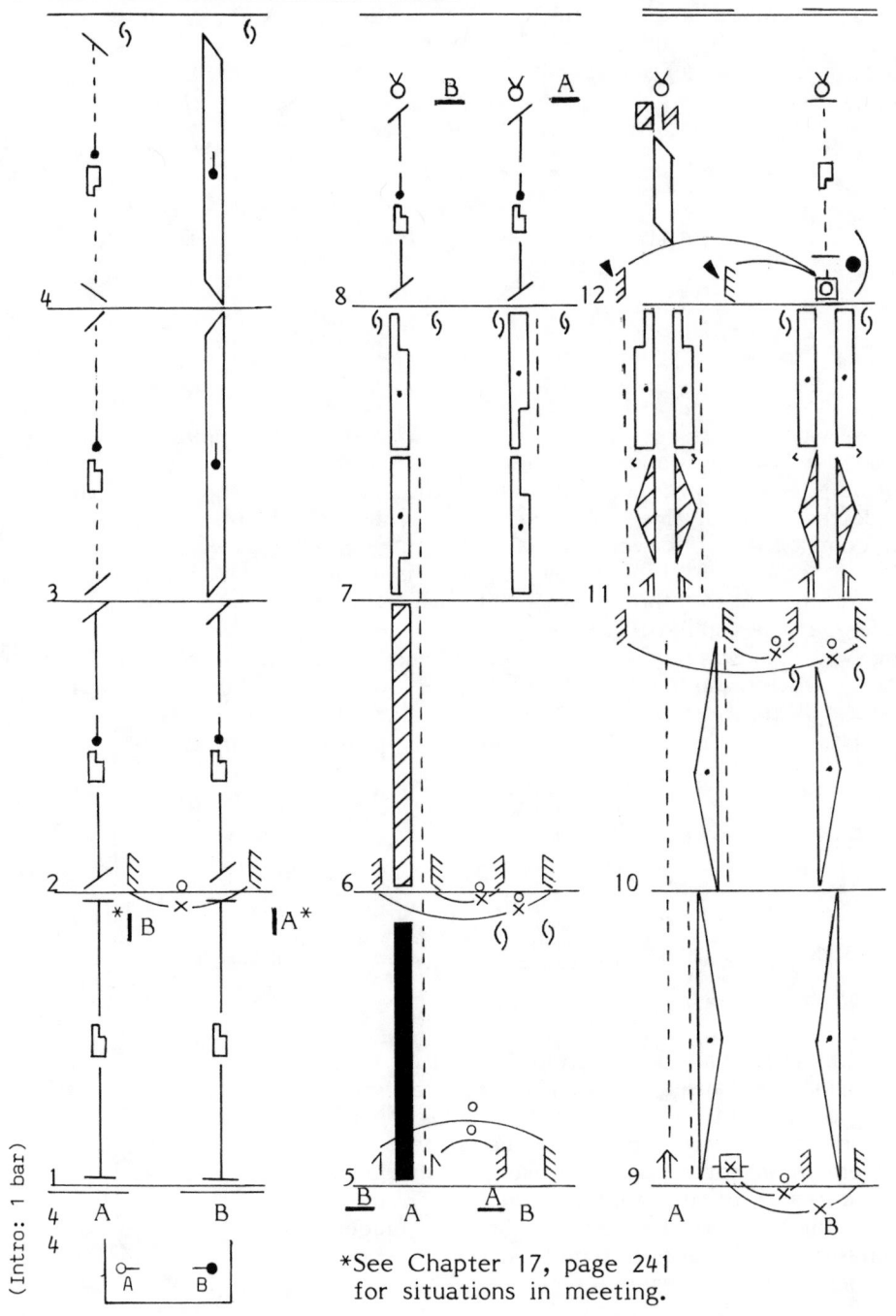

(Intro: 1 bar)

*See Chapter 17, page 241
for situations in meeting.

Chapter Twelve
ONE-SIDED GESTURES; SHAPES AND PATTERNS FOR GESTURES

This chapter investigates further details in the manner of performing gestures, their intention and expression.

ONE-SIDED GESTURES

The instruction of Ex. 131a can be performed in many ways. Gestures forward low may be symmetrical or there may be an intentional lack of symmetry with emphasis on one side of the body. One-sided actions have a focus or an impact different from two-sided, symmetrical actions. The expression of Ex. 131b is significantly different from that of 131c.

When only one arm or leg gestures into a sagittal direction, inclusion of one side of the body can augment the action and hence the expressiveness. In 131b the left arm gesture forward low is accompanied by a postural inclination into that direction. This inclusion of the upper torso involves both inclining and twisting, but these actions are not important in themselves. The tilt forward and the twist to the right are resultant, by-products of the main movement. Note that in these drawings F (forward) represents the established front, the previous direction faced. This previously established front is called Stance, since usually it is the feet (stance) which retain that front.

In 131d a backward tilt and a twist to the right enlarge the backward low arm gesture and make it more comfortable to perform. Because the feet have maintained the original front, the movement is seen as one away from that front, i.e. backward. This idea of Stance forward and backward can be seen in archery, in which a definite twist in the body occurs but does not affect the sense of the forward-backward directions. Bowling or pitching a ball also involves maintaining Stance despite tilting and twisting.

One-Sided Gestures (continued)

In Ex. 131e a step backward has been added to the movement of 131d, but the head remains looking forward and thus is a strong factor in maintaining that direction. If the head joins the direction of the arms, as in 131f, only the left leg retains Stance and this may not be enough to prevent the impression of a sideward movement following an unstressed quarter turn to the right. If, after performing 131f, the dancer returns to the Stance front, as in 131g, the relation of the action of 131f to that front is clear. Any turning that occured was resultant, taking place only to augment the main backward downward gesture; therefore in the context of the event there has been no change of front, no facing a new room direction.

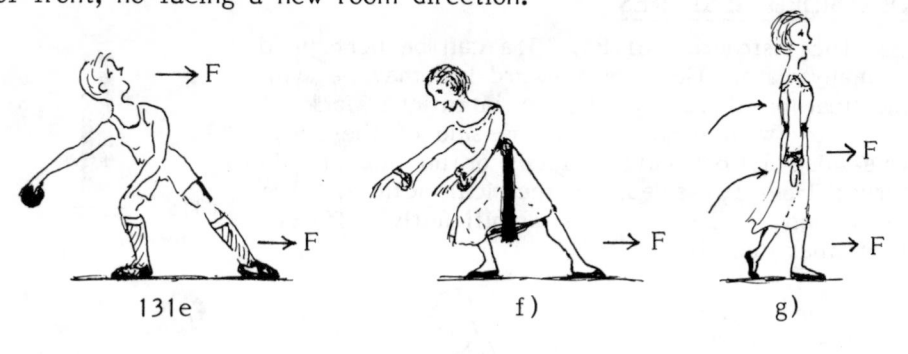

| 131e | f) | g) |

Indication of Right or Left Side

Until now we have been concerned with general actions of the body as a whole. When nothing is specified, general indications are usually interpreted as general body actions; therefore the sign for 'body as-a-whole', Ex. 132a, has not been needed. In the progression toward a more specific description, we arrive at the need to localize an action to the right or left half of the body. For example, an action may feature or be concerned with the right arm, right leg, the right shoulder, right hip, or the right side of the torso.

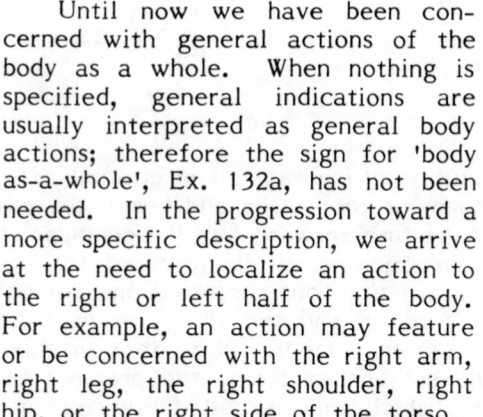

132a   Body as a whole

132b

c)

We indicate right or left sides by using the sign: and extending the center line to represent the center line in the body which divides right and left, Ex. 132b. Thus indications placed on the right of this center line are to be performed by the right side of the body, those on the left, by the left side. In 132c an action backward for the right side of the body is followed by an action up for the left side. As the center line indication then terminates, the action forward is one of the body-as-a-whole. The sign of 132a is derived from the three-line vertical staff used to represent the body in the full Structured Description of movement.

In the following examples the area of the left sideward direction is used first by the left side of the body, the 'open' side, Ex. 132d, which is illustrated in 132e, and then by the right side of the body, the 'crossed' or 'closed' side, Ex. 132f, which is illustrated in 132g.

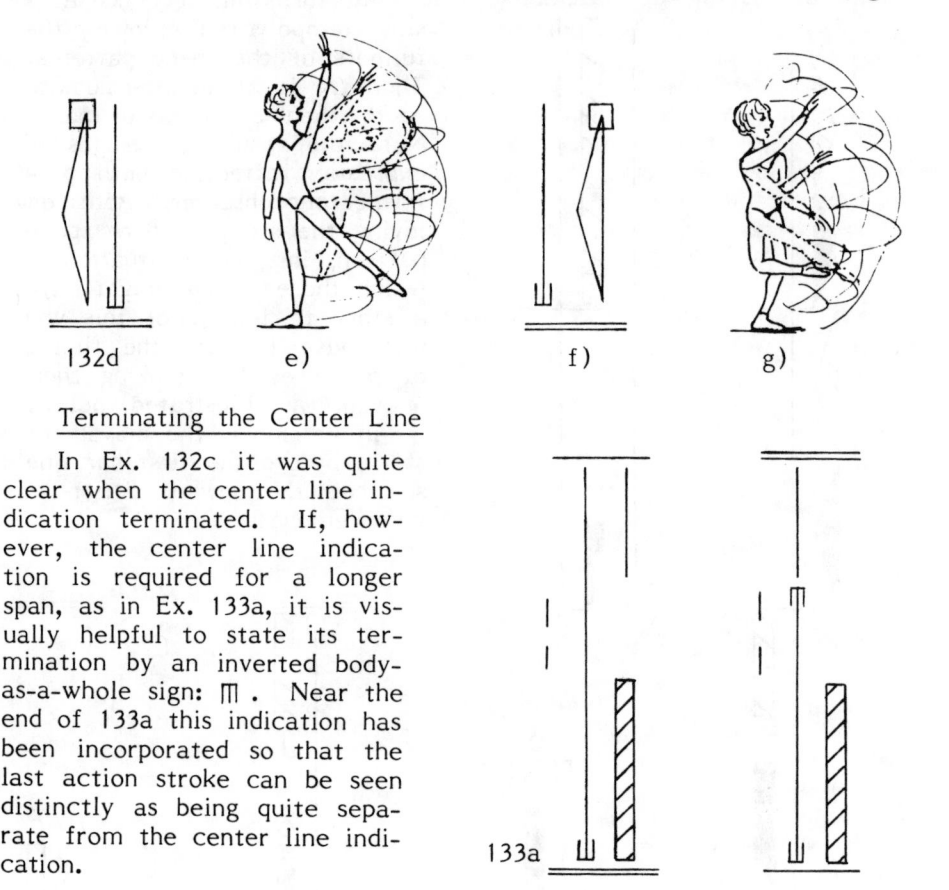

132d　　　　　　e)　　　　　　　　f)　　　　　　g)

Terminating the Center Line

In Ex. 132c it was quite clear when the center line indication terminated. If, however, the center line indication is required for a longer span, as in Ex. 133a, it is visually helpful to state its termination by an inverted body-as-a-whole sign: ⊓ . Near the end of 133a this indication has been incorporated so that the last action stroke can be seen distinctly as being quite separate from the center line indication.

133a

Reading Study No. 30

ONE-SIDED ACTIONS

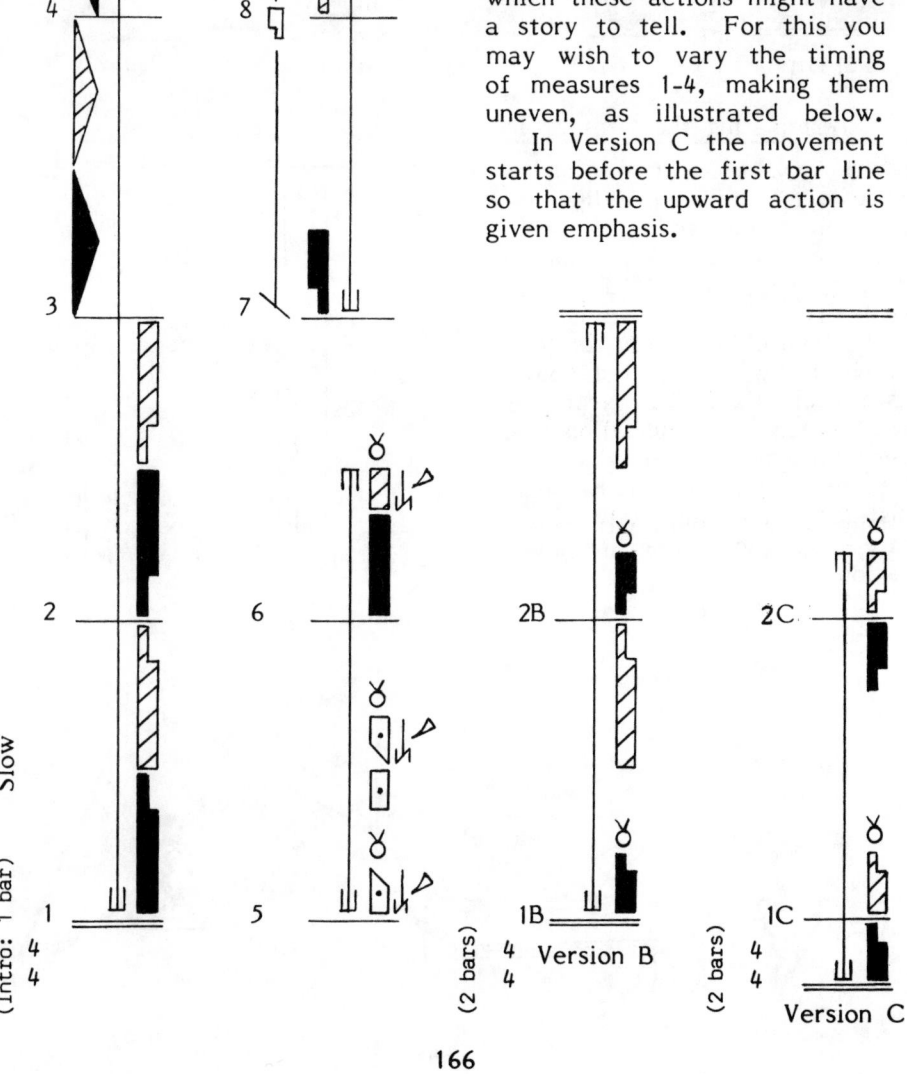

Perform this sequence at a slow tempo first, enjoying the fullness of the space patterns. Then try it at an intermediate pace, then at a faster pace. Note the resulting changes in expression affecting both performer and observer. After enjoying the study as pure space pattern, imagine a situation in which these actions might have a story to tell. For this you may wish to vary the timing of measures 1-4, making them uneven, as illustrated below.

In Version C the movement starts before the first bar line so that the upward action is given emphasis.

Version B

Version C

PATHS FOR GESTURES

This book started with exploration of travelling, of paths for the whole body. Let us now look at other kinds of paths. When a limb moves through space the intention or expression of the movement may be that of describing a path in the air with an extremity. These paths may be designs, tracings in the air of many kinds. All forms are composed basically of straight or curved lines. The curves may be arcs, complete circles, or wavy, undulating 'S' curves, loops, etc. Straight lines, if they are short, may produce zigzag patterns. In dance the concept of paths is behind many actions: for example, the straight path for the sideward shifting head movement, the Sundari in East Indian dance; the horizontal figure-eight path of the hips in the Tahitian pelvic gyrations, or the somersault paths for the rib cage met in certain African dances. These are all subtle and generally unfamiliar to western dance; let us therefore begin with simple obvious actions.

Straight Paths

Gestures in which the extremity follows a straight path may be functional, may mimic functional actions (as in pantomime) or may be purely decorative. A good example of straight path gestures in mime is that of Marcel Marceau believing himself to be trapped in a room and nervously feeling with his hands along the non-existent walls for an opening.

A good example of a functional straight path action is Ex. 134a which illustrates a punch in boxing. This same path from the center out can occur for many other reasons and also for pure spatial design. Ex. 134b is comparable to 134a, being a kick forward, the foot following a straight path. Contact with a flat surface automatically governs the path of a gesture as when the edge of a table is dusted, Ex. 134c, or a vertical line is drawn on a blackboard, 134d. Each of these movements requires a degree of flexion and extension in order to achieve the straight path, as does 134e in which a zipper on a tent is being pulled up.

134a

b)

c)

d)

e)

Curved, Circular Paths

With the help of flexibility in the upper spine the arms can perform a great number of interesting and enjoyable circular paths around the body. A simple lateral (a cartwheel-like path) is illustrated in Ex. 135a; 135b shows a backward sagittal circle (like a backward somersault path), and 135c shows a clockwise horizontal circle. Smaller replicas of these dimensionally based circles can occur all around the body. In Ex. 135d a figure eight is described in front of the body using cartwheel paths, right and left. In 135e a small forward somersault path is described with the arm out to the side, while in 135f a small horizontal circle is being outlined overhead. The extremity of the torso, the head, can also describe circular paths as in the clockwise arc produced by the tilted torso in Ex. 135g.

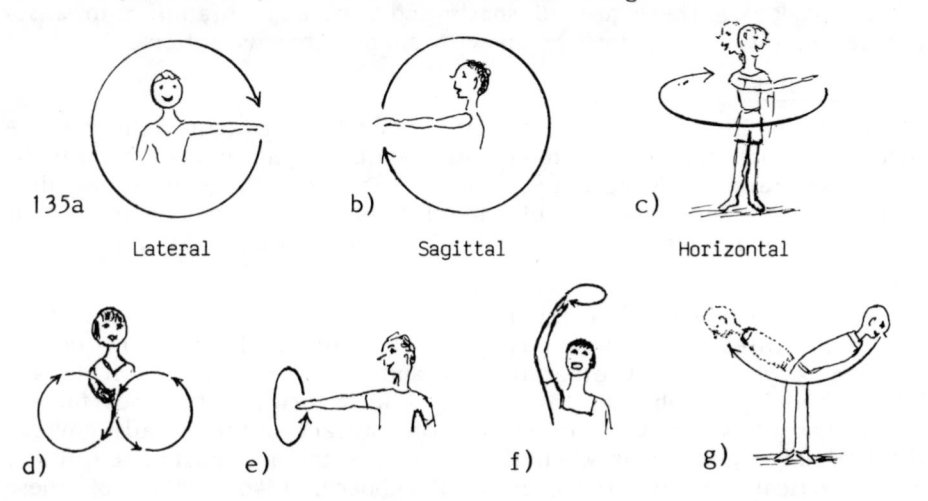

135a   b)   c)

Lateral   Sagittal   Horizontal

d)   e)   f)   g)

Combinations of the above forms used freely can produce a variety of curved paths as illustrated below in 135h and 135i.

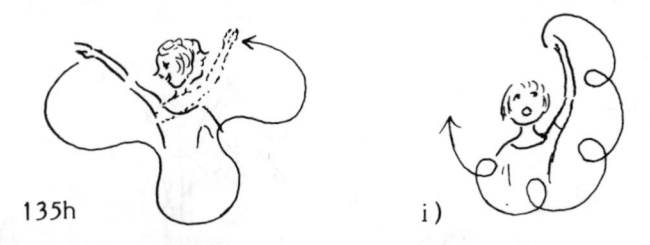

135h   i)

Use of rotation helps to produce three-dimensional designs. All paths are augmented visually and the air design expanded by use of objects such as ribbons, soft flowing silk, etc. Choreographers such as Alwin Nikolais have made effective use of a variety of props to extend air designs made by the limbs, in both angular and curved paths. Free flowing movement may naturally take the form of circular designs. As noted earlier, circular patterns (curved paths) allow for long, unbroken movement phrases.

Indication of Paths for Limbs

The path signs we have used so far describe travelling of the whole body. When a limb describes a path, the base of the limb (the point of attachment) makes no path; we are aware of the path made by the extremity travelling through space. The same path indications are used but with an addition for Motif Description to state that it is a gestural path.

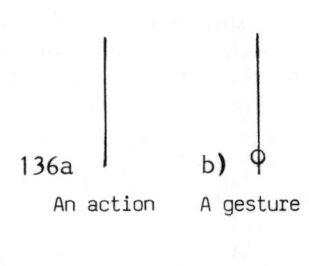

136a

An action

b)

A gesture

As explained earlier, Ex. 136a indicates an action, a general movement, usually for the body as a whole. When the retention sign: O is added to the action stroke the indication becomes an action of a limb, a part of the body which is attached (hence the retention sign at the base of the movement indication). Thus 136b expresses a gesture of a limb. By placing the hold sign at the base of a path sign we show that one end of the limb is held, i.e. attached.

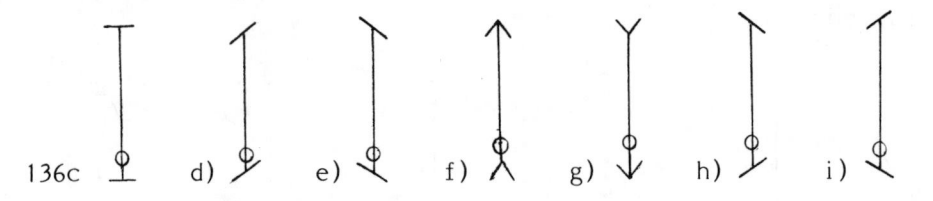

136c   d)   e)   f)   g)   h)   i)

Ex. 136c indicates a straight path gesture, no particular direction being indicated; 136d and 136e indicate horizontal circular paths, clockwise and anticlockwise. Ex. 136f and 136g illustrate sagittal circles - a forward somersault path and a backward somersault path. In the lateral plane the cartwheel path signs are usually simplified to 136h for a cartwheel path to the right and 136i for a cartwheel path to the left. Ex. 136j and 136k are the full signs for cartwheel paths right and left.

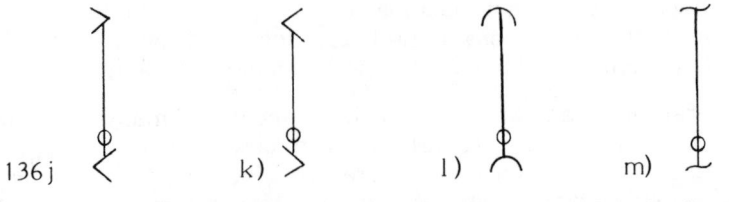

136j   k)   l)   m)

If the nature of a circular path need not be specified, the general sign for 'a curved path', 136l is used. The sign of 136m allows total freedom for improvisation on gestural paths. In the above signs no statement is made concerning size, distance or degree of circling. Small circles may be performed close to the body or out at the periphery. Patterns may include circles on planes, arcs and cone shapes of many sizes placed to the right or left, in front or behind or above the body. Below the body is more limited but can be indicated.

G

Indication of Specific Limb

Stating which limb performs a gestural path is the
next step in progressing from general to specific. Ex.
137a, the sign for 'a limb', is modified to show a specific limb.   The arm is the limb below the shoulder;
the leg is the limb below the hip, as indicated below:

||

137a

137b	c)	d)	e)	f)	g)
Left arm	Right arm	Both arms	Left leg	Right leg	Both legs

For both legs to make gestural paths one would need to be sitting,
lying or in a shoulder stand, or perhaps held by a partner.   One leg
and both arms may be creating spatial paths while the performer is
standing.   Similar or dissimilar patterns may occur at the same time
or in sequence.   The variety of possibilities provides a rewarding movement exploration.   As each limb is stated and the kind of path used is
defined we move closer to a Structured Description.   Try the following
possibilities:

137h	i)	j)	k)	l)
The right arm circles hori- zontally on a clockwise path	The left arm circles sag- ittally forward	The right leg circles CCW	Both arms circle lat- erally to the right	The left arm makes a straight path forward

For these simple indications it is expected that the rest of the
body will participate in producing a fluent, comfortable action.   For example, in 137h the torso will probably bend and twist passively to allow
the arm to continue the circular path behind the body.

Lateral and sagittal arm circles appear in many movement techniques, for example, in cricket overarm bowling employs a sagittal circular path.   Swinging an object often involves multiple circles as in the
Chinese Ribbon Dance.   A three-quarter lateral or sagittal circle takes
place in many dance forms; multiple circles are more rare.   Windmill-
like sagittal circles occur in George Balanchine's *Serenade*, the effect
is of two circles for each arm, one following the other, though in fact
the amount is less.   The purpose, manner of performance and the emphasis can all vary; the importance of the circular pattern in space for
a limb remains.

Reading Study No. 31

PATHS FOR GESTURES

Note the indication of the directional destination of a path at the end of measure 4 where the meandering path is to end up. In measure 8 the lateral cartwheel path has a side horizontal destination.

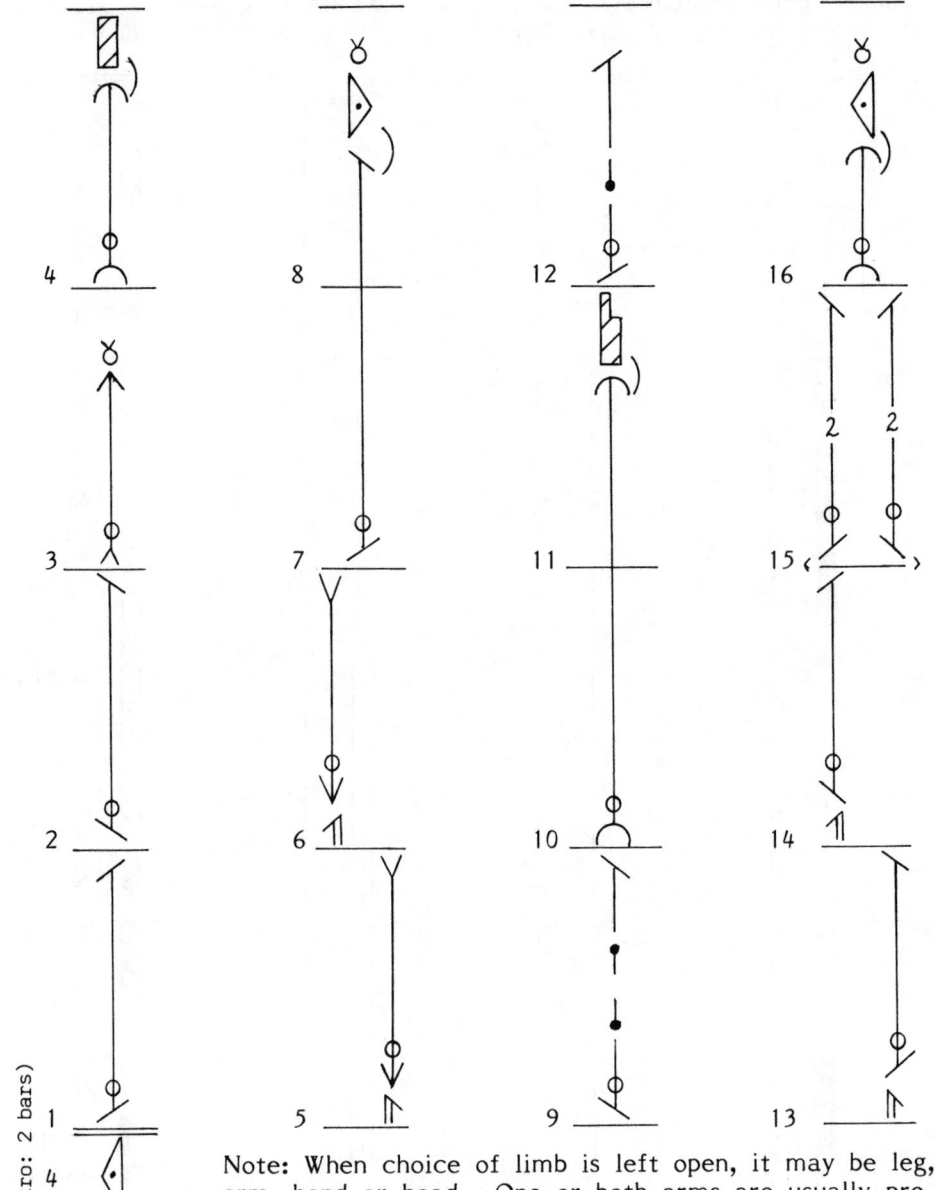

(Intro: 2 bars)

Note: When choice of limb is left open, it may be leg, arm, hand or head. One or both arms are usually preferred because of the greater range of movement.

171

Reading Study No. 32

GESTURAL PATHS WITH DIRECTION AND TRAVELLING

In this study direction for straight gestural paths has been added by placing the appropriate direction symbol in the path sign. The number of circles to be described is indicated by placing the appropriate number within the circular path. Note that while ⇑ suggests unison in use of the arms, ⇑⇑ suggests both arms in action but independent.

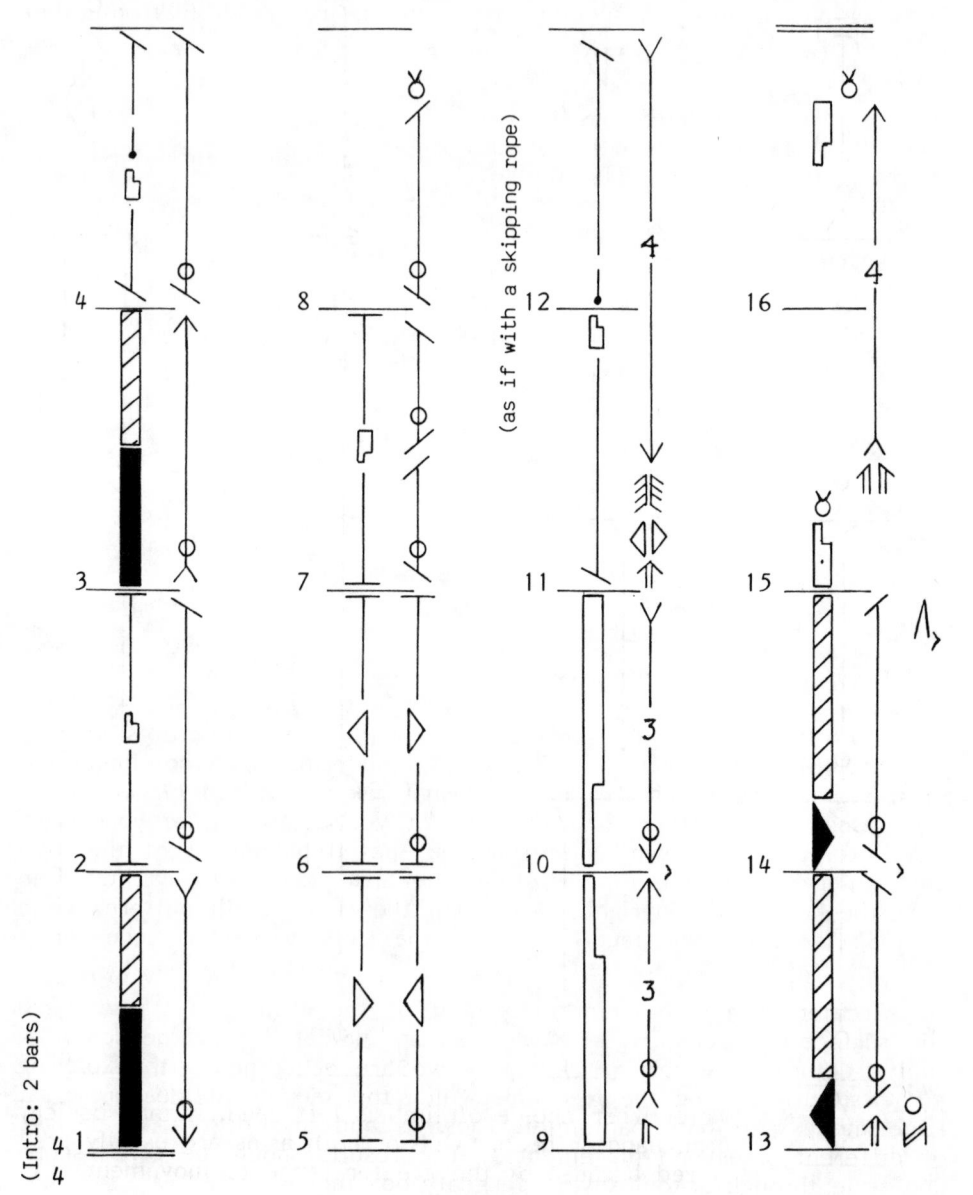

(as if with a skipping rope)

(Intro: 2 bars)

$\frac{4}{4}$

DESIGN DRAWING

Paths for gestures may take many forms. In pantomimic gestures the aim may be to describe an object or to perform an activity which is familiar in daily life without the actual tools in hand. Some designs in the air are tracings as though writing or drawing on an imaginary wall. The shape, the pattern which these tracings make is the focus of the movement, therefore these patterns are represented on paper as they appear in the air. This form of gestural paths is called Design Drawing and is given a special path sign to distinguish it from other forms of paths.

Ex. 138a shows the sign for 'a shape'; 138b is the path sign derived from this sign to show a travelling 'shape', i.e. a design. The desired design is drawn in the center of the path, a black dot indicating where the design begins.

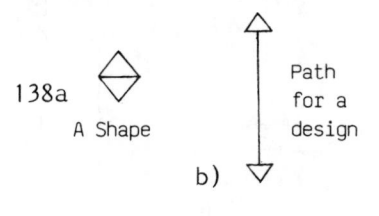

138a — A Shape

Path for a design

b)

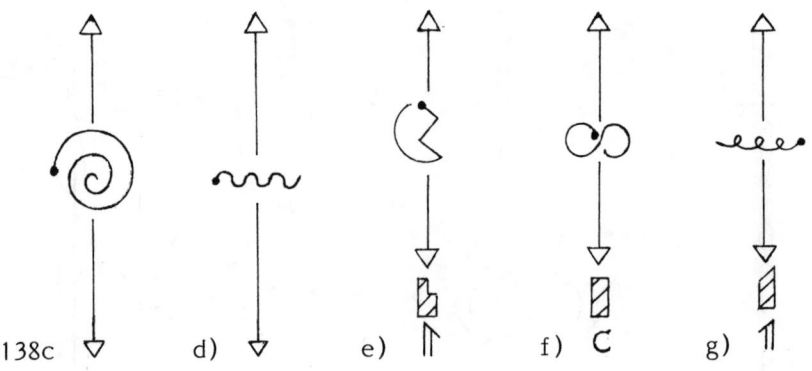

138c   d)   e)   f) C   g)

Ex. 138c describes a spiral pattern, while 138d illustrates a wavy line travelling from left to right. Exact performance is not important at this stage, the 'message' is the design itself. Spatial placement of the design, i.e. whether it is in front of you, overhead, at your right side, etc. can be shown by stating the spatial placement of the limb performing the design. In Ex. 138e the arm starts forward high. In 138f the head starts upright to perform the figure eight pattern, while in 138g the left arm starts across to the right to perform the series of loops travelling to the left.

Greater details in exact placement of the design, of its size and the surface on which it is drawn can be indicated when needed in a full structured description. For now we are concerned with exploring all possibilities, using the freedoms which this movement idea presents. Experiment with both pantomimic designs and also decorative designs of different sizes and placements. The results should be given scope and style through accompanying general body movements.

173

Reading Practice

DESIGN DRAWING

Length of the design path indicates the length of time available in which to draw the design. Experiment freely with the following ideas.

= draw the design as though it is on the floor.

= draw the design as though it is on the wall at your left.

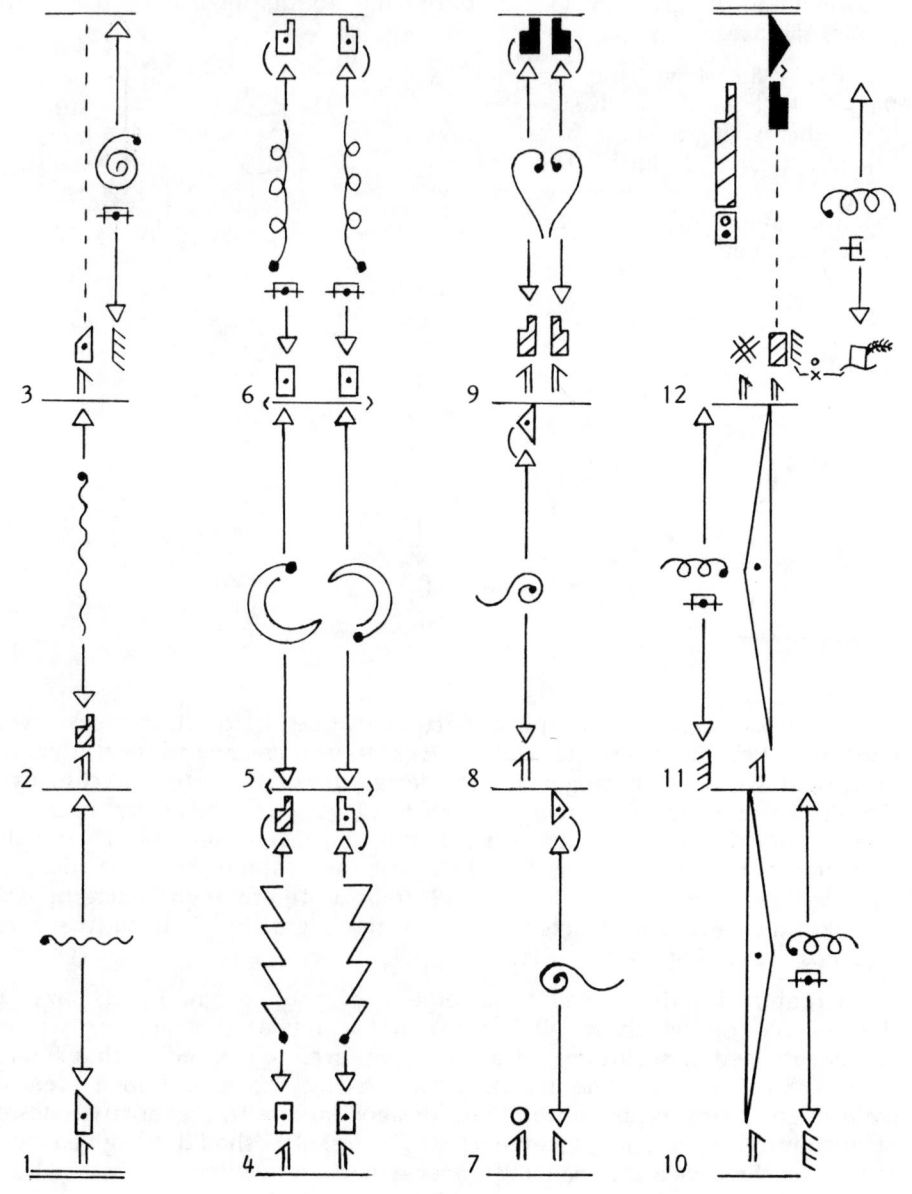

GATHERING AND SCATTERING

Two very expressive movements which incorporate curved paths with movement 'toward' and 'away' are the actions of gathering and scattering. Dictionary definitions are not very helpful when it comes to determining what must happen in movement to make a gathering action or a scattering action. Let us start with investigating gathering, since scattering is its reverse in idea and spatial action.

Gathering

"Draw limbs together", "bring closely to-gether", "take into possession", "contraction, accumulations, assemblage": these dictionary words for the meaning of 'gathering' provide no direct image of the desired movement pattern. Yet gathering to you a dozen fluf-fy chicks, Ex. 139a, or collecting a pile of autumn leaves into your arms gives the basis of the action very clearly. How does the simple act of taking, Ex. 139b and 139c, dif-fer from gathering?

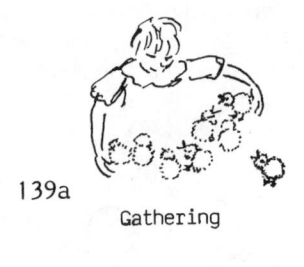

139a

Gathering

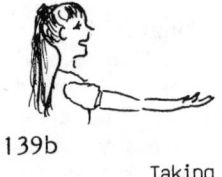

139b

Taking

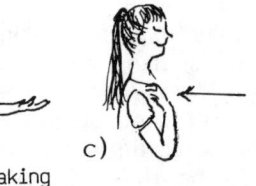

c)

d)

Gathering

Taking is a straight line action. The arm starts extended, then draws in to the body on a straight line. It is a simple, direct move-ment. In gathering, the arm starts more open, often as wide as pos-sible to allow for a greater degree of gathering. It then moves in to-ward the body on a curved path, an inward spiral ending near the tor-so, 139d (bird's-eye view). This relation of the movement to the torso is important; there is a strong sense of 'to me', 'mine', in the expres-sion of the movement. An accompanying outward arm rotation is often present. In theory one would expect an inward rotation to accompany an inwardly directed action, however, outward rotation (outward arm twist) places the palm in a more functional position. Inward rotation produces a stylized movement, one which might occur in gathering if the palm were sticky and the back of the hand had to be used — a use of the hand seen in the Sailor's Hornpipe in which hitching up the pants is done with the back of the hand, as palms and fingers are tarry.

The pathway in gathering may be horizontal or may curve upward or downward. Another term for gathering is 'scooping', which suggests a definite downward motion on the way, an undercurve.

175

Scattering

The simple action of giving (the opposite of taking) also usually makes use of a straight line, Ex. 140a.   But scattering is quite another idea; it is spatially a 'generous' action in that it sweeps out from near the body on a curved arc which may end diagonally backward.   Ex. 140b illustrates the familiar sowing of seed.   The line of

140a   Giving

the movement is an outward spiral, 140c. Another term for this action is 'strewing'.   One can imagine a person searching a basket for the right pair of tights and throwing out garment after garment, strewing them all over the room, 140d.

 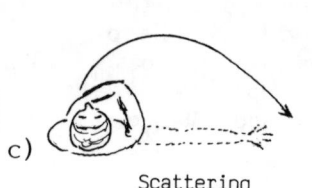 

140b   c)   d)

Scattering

Gathering and scattering actions may express sharing feelings with other people, sharing in an activity or sharing space.   "Come, all of you, gather around to share these ideas!" may be expressed by double-sided scattering followed by gathering.   A wide opening of the arms at start or finish expresses generosity and warmth; the expression of these feelings is heightened by opening or closing the arms on a curve.

In dance gathering and scattering may occur purely as design and often in a highly stylized manner.   Waltzing steps are often accompanied by gathering or scattering arm gestures; only one arm may be featured or both may move in a symmetrical or parallel manner.   A forward or backward balancé is often performed with a slightly stylized scattering on the forward sway and gathering on the backward. In certain lyric forms of modern dance gathering and scattering are used abstractly as movement design and usually incorporate an ebb and flow in energy.   Use is made of the falling action toward gravity by tracing a figure eight-like pattern which comes toward the body on the gathering before swinging out and away on the scattering, 140e.   Note in this diagram the dotted lines which show unemphasized transitions.

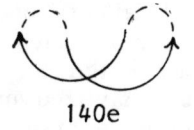

140e

The larger movements of gathering and scattering performed by the arms for functional or expressive purposes can be localized in the hands alone.   Such movements occur in Spanish dance where they are augmented by rotation of the lower arm and sequential use of the fingers.   Usually the little finger leads the action, the other fingers following in sequence.

176

One-sided Gestures; Shapes and Patterns for Gestures

Expressive use of gathering can center on the concept of inwardness, of bringing the energy and the line of movement or 'a volume of space' to the self. Similarly, expressive use of scattering can be concerned with sending the energy or the line of movement away from the self, of pushing 'a volume of space' outward and away from one's center. In these actions, as in many others, space can be experienced as something tangible. This tangibility of space can best be experienced if one imagines oneself to be in a thick fog or in air which is heavily laden with smoke - at which times one can actually see the result of sweeping body movements. Smoke swirls when one waves one's arms; the sensation of an airplane cutting through low lying clouds provides an awareness of the existence of air and space around. Another useful image is to think of space as a huge mass of foam; then actions such as gathering it up, dispelling it, containing it, pushing it away can be better understood. All such actions could be performed with quite a different focus or intention, in which case they would have different expressions. Abstract movement can be given a particular expression if space is regarded as an entity with which to deal. Space is more than just a practical fact of life.

Indication of Gathering and Scattering

As the ideas of gathering and scattering are simple and fundamental, simple signs have been chosen to represent these composite actions.

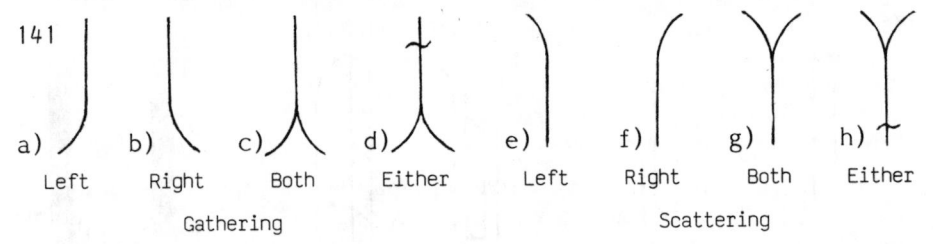

141

a) Left b) Right c) Both d) Either e) Left f) Right g) Both h) Either

Gathering   Scattering

Ex. 141a is gathering for the left side of the body, 141b for the right. The two signs combined, 141c, indicate both sides gathering. To show either side, leaving the choice open, the sign for 'either side': ⊬ is added to 141c, as in 141d. Scattering is the reverse sign handled in the same way: 141e shows scattering for the left side of the body, 141f for the right, and 141g for both at once. Ex. 141h leaves the choice of side open.

From the movements already explored it is possible to spell out the component parts which produce a gathering action. These are: relationship to the center line of the body, Ex. 141i; for the right arm, anti-clockwise circling, 141j; approaching the body, 141k; approaching the torso may be specifically stated as in 141l (or the chest could be indicated when more appropriate);

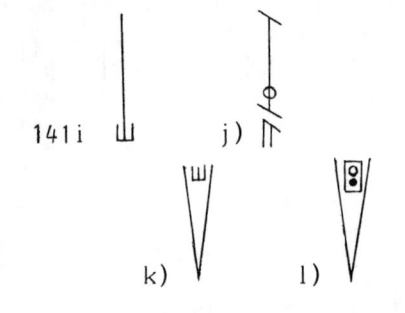

141i   j)

k)   l)

177

Indication of Gathering and Scattering (continued)

outward rotation (or twist),* Ex. 141m, and some degree of flexion, 141n.

Thus the simple sign of 141o for the action of gathering represents the composite information of 141p. For scattering the simple sign of Ex. 141q represents the motions of 141r.

Gathering and Scattering Combined with Other Actions

Any of the basic movements which we have explored so far may be accompanied by gathering or scattering actions. Below are some examples, each of which can be interpreted in several ways still adhering to the instructions given. Many more can be explored and interesting sequences developed. Note that two-sided scattering may be written as 142c or 142d. The same choice is open to gathering, 142e, 142f).

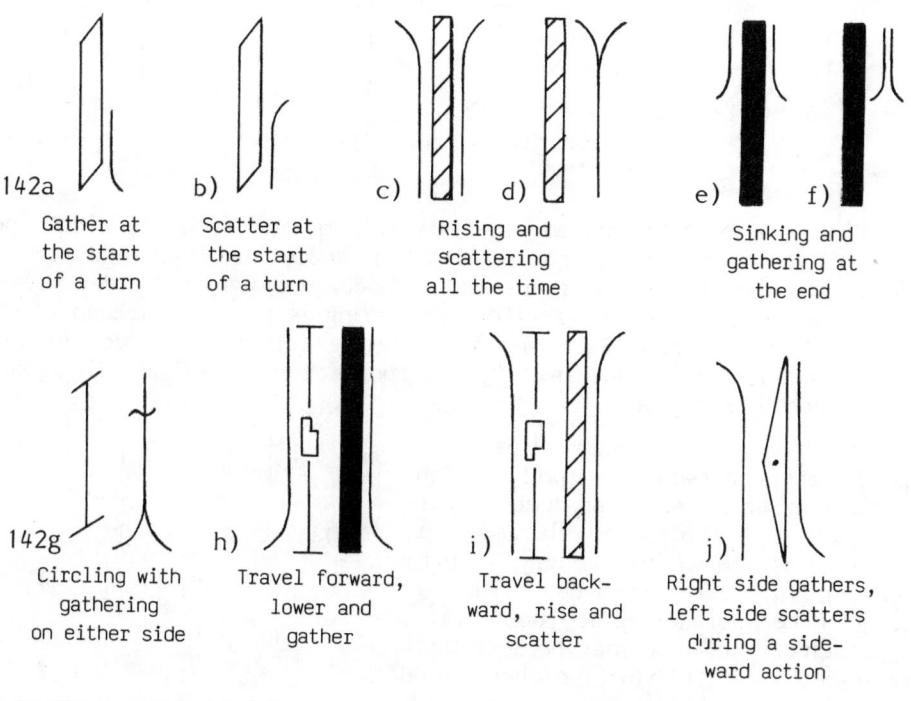

142a Gather at the start of a turn

b) Scatter at the start of a turn

c) d) Rising and scattering all the time

e) f) Sinking and gathering at the end

142g Circling with gathering on either side

h) Travel forward, lower and gather

i) Travel backward, rise and scatter

j) Right side gathers, left side scatters during a sideward action

* See Chapter 15 for twists.

GATHERING, SCATTERING

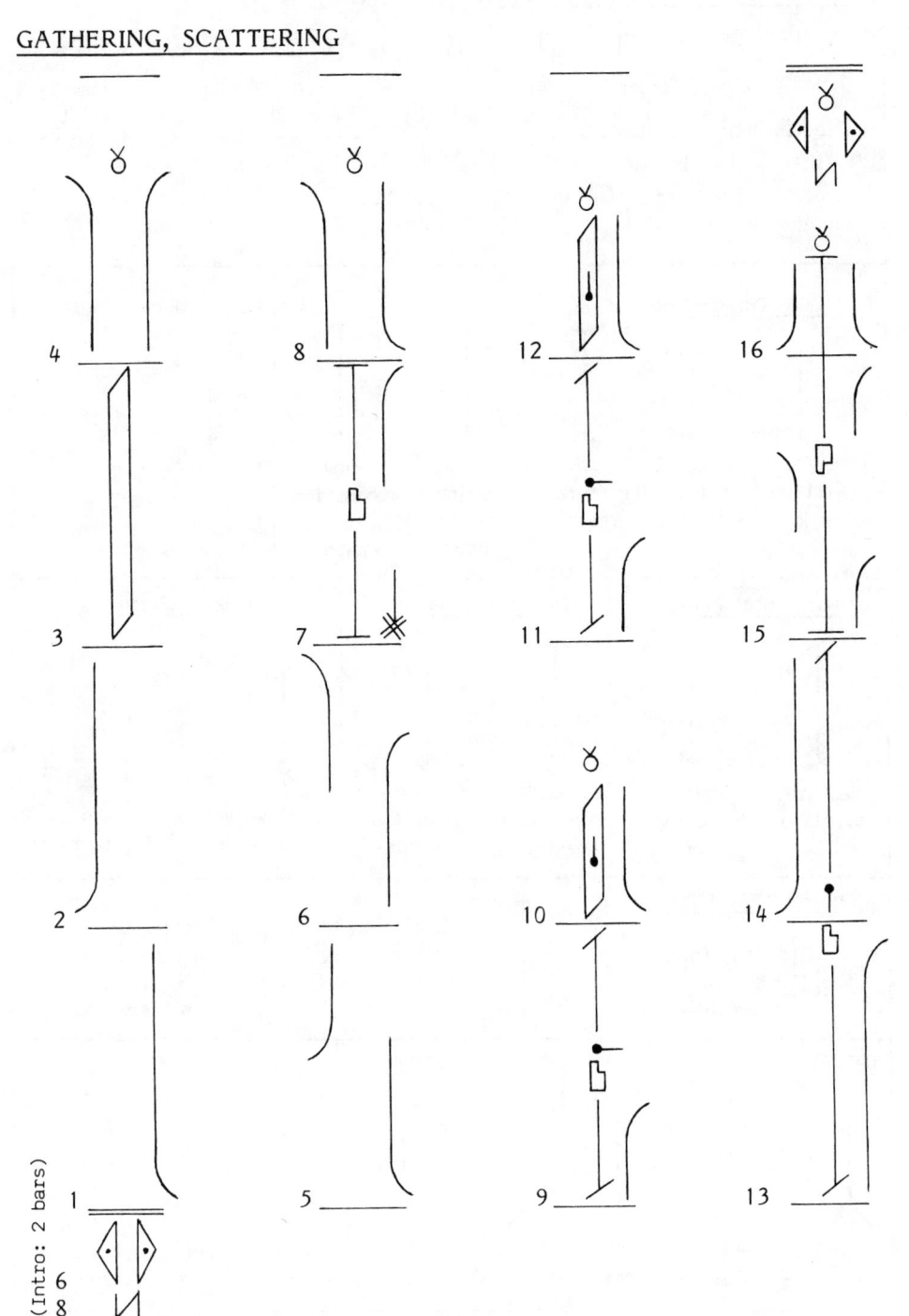

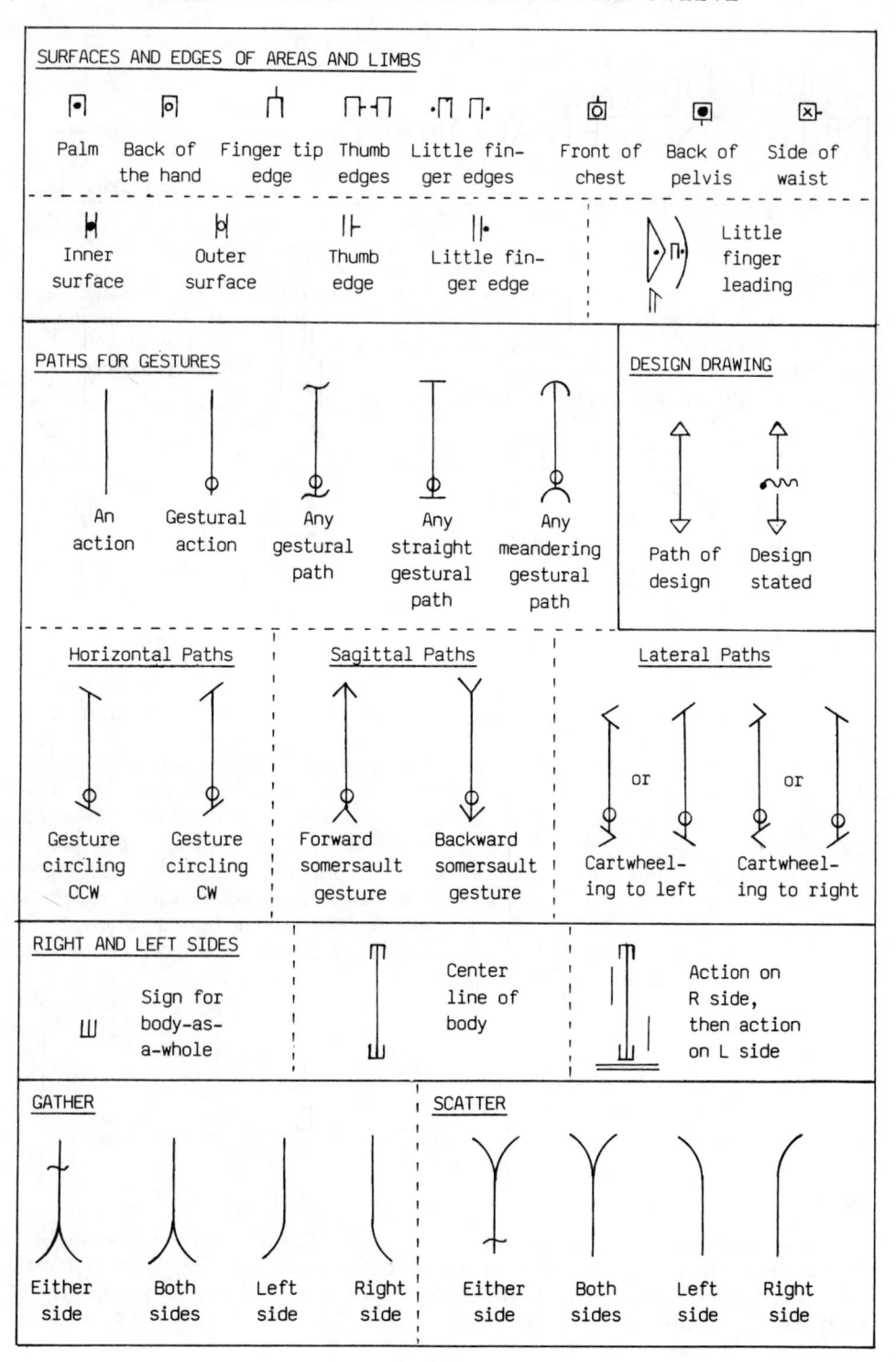

SURFACES AND EDGES OF AREAS AND LIMBS

Palm	Back of the hand	Finger tip edge	Thumb edges	Little finger edges	Front of chest	Back of pelvis	Side of waist

Inner surface	Outer surface	Thumb edge	Little finger edge		Little finger leading

PATHS FOR GESTURES

An action	Gestural action	Any gestural path	Any straight gestural path	Any meandering gestural path

DESIGN DRAWING

Path of design	Design stated

Horizontal Paths

Gesture circling CCW	Gesture circling CW

Sagittal Paths

Forward somersault gesture	Backward somersault gesture

Lateral Paths

or	or
Cartwheeling to left	Cartwheeling to right

RIGHT AND LEFT SIDES

Sign for body-as-a-whole

Center line of body

Action on R side, then action on L side

GATHER

Either side	Both sides	Left side	Right side

SCATTER

Either side	Both sides	Left side	Right side

Chapter Thirteen
DIRECTION: THE DIAGONALS

Between the sagittal and lateral direction, Ex. 143a, lie the four diagonal directions, Ex. 143b. The term 'diagonal' is used by some people to mean a line slanting upward or downward. In the analysis of movement presented here the word is used only in connection with the directions illustrated below in 143b.

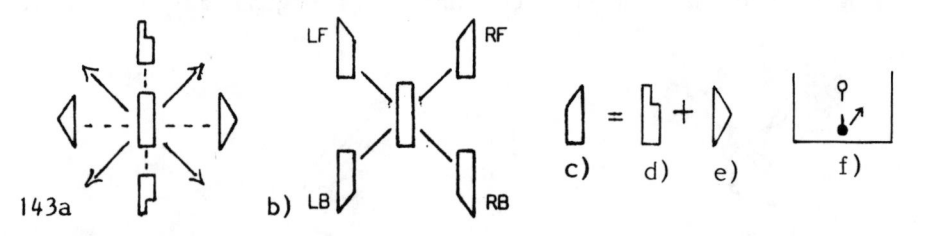

143a   b) LB   RB   c)   d)   e)   f)

Open Diagonals: Steps, Gestures

The expression of actions in the diagonal directions is a blend of forward and sideward, or backward and sideward. The right-front diagonal of 143c used by the right side of the body contains both approaching and opening in one action; it is therefore in certain respects richer and subtler than pure forward or pure sideward movement. The expression may be just that — advancing toward someone but keeping to one's own side. Such a diagonal progression may happen for a practical reason such as passing a person in front of you, 143f. A right arm gesture into the right front diagonal direction relates less directly to a person in front of you; the meaning is strengthened when both arms are used symmetrically. To express "Welcome!" which would you choose, 144a, 144b, or 144c?

144a   b)   c)

The forward action of 144a relates more directly to the person being addressed; it is narrower in that it focusses only on that person. The more open gesture of 144b could express welcoming a group; it is expansive and hence less personal. Ex. 144c combines the personal with the open welcome.

Crossed Diagonals: Steps, Gestures

Crossed diagonal directions for both gestures and steps may be expressive or functional. Any step which crosses the center line of the body has a narrowness, a feeling of being enclosed, of being spatially 'tight'. Although this feeling is most marked in crossed sideward steps, it is also a component of crossed diagonal steps. (Details on analysis and performance of diagonal steps are given later in this chapter.) Both arms in the crossed diagonals express self-enclosing, especially if the arms are rounded. In folk dances crossing the arms when holding hands in a small circle is not uncommon, Ex. 145a. Because each arm balances the other, there is no tendency to turn the body as can easily happen when only one arm is used. Ex. 145c is the incorrect performance of 145b. If such turning occurs the movement becomes a forward gesture (forward from the chest from where direction of arm gestures is judged), and the expression contained in a diagonal gesture is lost.

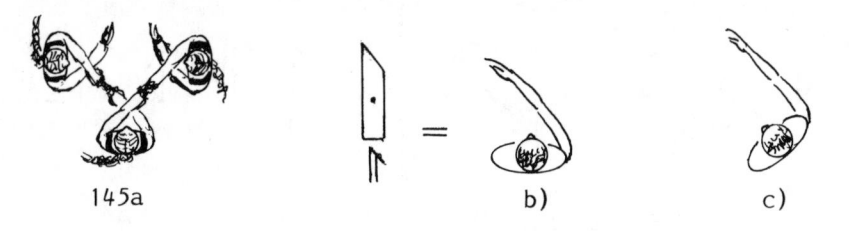

145a   b)   c)

Diagonal Steps: Directional Reference

Taking diagonal steps brings us face to face with how to interpret 'diagonal' when it is applied to transference of weight and to travelling. We discover that three different references exist. Since specific names have not universally been applied to each, the ideas as well as the verbal instructions are often confusing. The performer knows what to do more from following the motions of the instructor than from the actual words used.

On a standard proscenium stage, used so much in western dance in recent centuries (and still today despite theatre-in-the-round and other special shaped areas), the sides and corners of the stage provide directions to which frequent reference is made - see Ex. 146a, the audience being front, the right side being stage right, and so on. During rehearsals many directional instructions are interpreted as relating to stage directions rather than to the personal direction of the performer, i.e. to his front, his right side, etc. A good example of this possible confusion arose during a rehearsal of Jerome Robbins' ballet *Fanfare*. He instructed three male dancers to "take three steps forward, three steps to the right and three steps backward." As the dancers were facing the audience, the

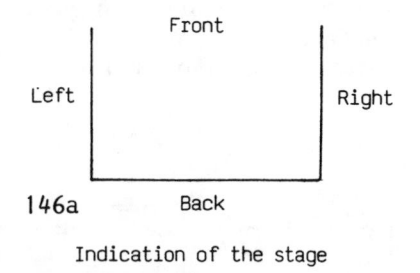

146a

Indication of the stage

182

first three steps were forward both from the stage directions and from the dancer's body, Ex. 146b. (Note that ♦ represents a male performer.) But what of the 'three steps to the right'? How was that instruction to be interpreted? Robbins wanted them to turn to face stage right and to take three steps into that stage direction, as in 146c. From his words the dancers could have taken steps sideward from the hips while still facing front, as in 146d. 'Three steps backward' were to be interpreted as forward steps facing upstage (the back of the stage), 146e, and not steps backward from the hips while still facing front, 146f.

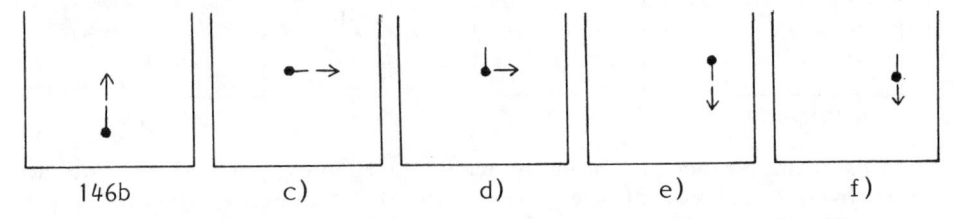

| 146b | c) | d) | e) | f) |

Robbins had said nothing about turning to face another direction but since he demonstrated as he spoke, the dancers took their cue from what he did. Had they been blindfolded very probably they would have performed 146d and 146f.

Performance of Diagonal Steps

When no key or other instruction is given, directions are judged from the body's front, i.e. from where the performer is facing. Direction for steps is judged from the front of the pelvis. In the following illustrations a black pin represents the performer who is shown facing into three different directions to illustrate the analysis, interpretation and performance of diagonal steps.

147a b) c) d) e) f) g) h)

i) j) k) l) m) n) o) p)

A movement diagonally right-forward, Ex. 147a, will produce the movement illustrated in 147b, c), or d). Facing into a different stage direction does not change the diagonal direction in relation to the performer's front. A left-front diagonal movement, 147e, is performed as 147f, g), or h). Similarly a right-back diagonal movement, 147i, would produce 147j, k), or l). A left-back diagonal movement, 147m, would result in 147n, o), or p). Only three of the eight possible main facing directions are shown here; the same analysis of movement applies to them all.

Travelling Diagonally

When a performer is facing front, steps written right-front diagonal will be diagonal from the body line as well as in relation to a diagonal line in the room, Ex. 148a. But if he faces the front corner of
the room and travels in that direction, 148b, his steps will not be diagonal but forward from his body. It is important to separate these two
interpretations of 'diagonal' — the personal diagonal of the performer
and a diagonal in the room.

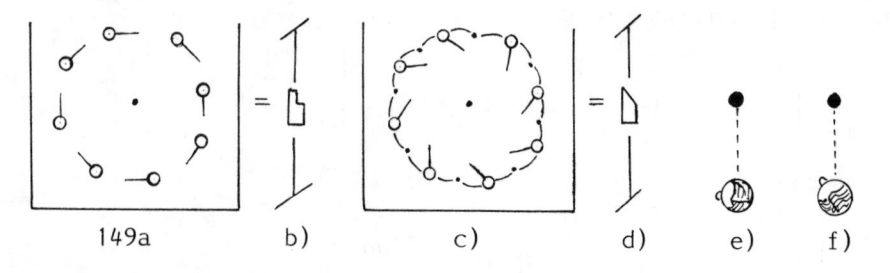

148a   b)   c)   d)

For transference of weight, walking, running, etc. directions are
taken from the front of the pelvis. Ex. 148c indicates a path travel-
ing diagonally right-forward. This path will be interpreted as in Ex.
148d by three performers each having a different front.

Walking 'Forward' on a Circle

In folk and historical circular dances, when performers hold hands
and are instructed to walk 'forward' in the line of the circle, they will
walk into the direction of the circling, but the steps will not be true
forward from the hips. Because they are holding hands the dancers do
not turn the whole body to face the circling direction; thus the steps
are not true forward but a more comfortable in-between direction, a
diagonal line to the body.

149a   b)   c)   d)   e)   f)

Ex. 149a shows a circle of performers not holding hands travelling
forward on a clockwise circular path. In 149c, because they are holding hands (indicated by ⌣•⌣ on the floor plan) they will be performing
diagonal steps, as illustrated in 149c and 149d. Ex. 149e and 149f illustrate (bird's-eye view) the dancer's relationship to the center of the
circle (the focal point, indicated by •). Relationship to this point is a
help in determining orientation. In 149a the right side is toward the
focal point; in 149c the focal point is on the right-forward diagonal
line. When you travel on a circular path the line of relationship to
the focal point is always at right angles to the direction of the steps.

Direction: The Diagonals

The Room or Stage Diagonals

The lines connecting the corners of the room or stage provide diagonals along which locomotor sequences frequently travel both in technique classes and in choreography. The diagonal is used because it is the longest straight line in rectangular areas. But note how these diagonal lines vary in angle according to the shape of the room, Ex. 150a -150d. Ex. 150a illustrates a square area; 150b shows the more usual

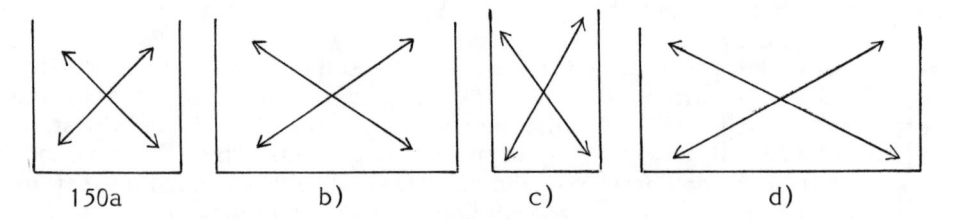

| 150a | b) | c) | d) |

proportions for a stage; 150c is a very deep stage (a few of which actually exist), and 150d a very wide room or stage. It can be seen that in relation to the axis of direction established in the center of each of these stage areas, the angle of the room diagonal lines varies significantly. Are these variable diagonal lines the ones to which we relate? Yes, sometimes, but there is a set of constant spatial diagonals to which we relate more frequently.

The Constant Directions

While the term 'Constant Directions' may be new to many people, the idea is not. It is based on the concept of a square stage in which the performer is standing in the center. From this point all room directions (corners and walls) are at their correct 45° relationship to each other. Ex. 151a illustrates such a square stage with the main directions indicated.

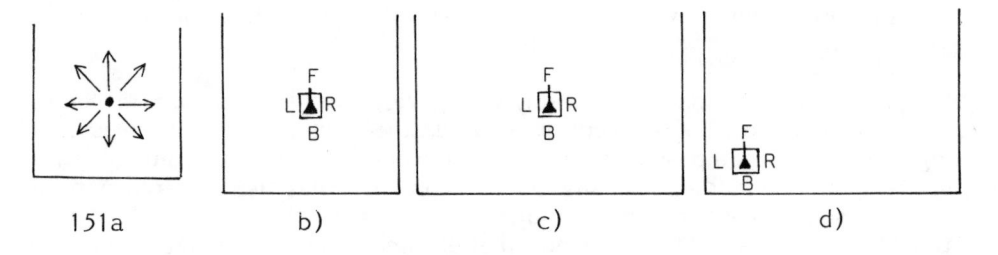

| 151a | b) | c) | d) |

The performer visualizes and experiences this 'square' as a small square around himself, as in 151b in which the black pin ▲ represents a man facing front. No matter the shape of a stage or performing area, this square is still square, Ex. 151c. As it is centered in the performer it travels with him. In Ex. 151d he is located in the left back (upstage) corner of the stage but the square and its directions remain the same. Though the square travels with the performer, it does not turn.

The Constant Directions (continued)

In 151e the person is facing stage right but the Constant Directions of the square have remained un- changed (constant) — front is still toward the audience and so on. Thus the per- former's own front and the Constant front, which were

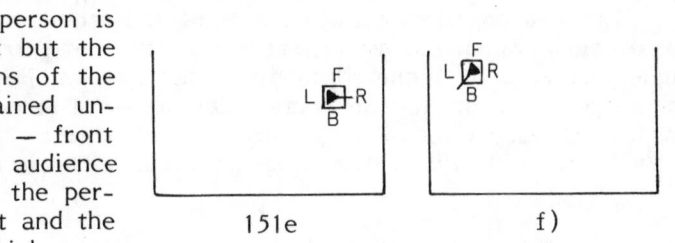

151e   f)

the same in Ex. 151b-d, are no longer the same. Ex. 151f illustrates another stage location and another facing direction. Situated in the left front (downstage) area the performer is now facing the Constant left-back diagonal direction. For performing areas which have no ob- vious front, the 'compass' for the Constant Directions must be set by choosing one wall or a horizontal line between two objects as 'front'. With this done, all performers have a common set of Constant Direc- tions with which to synchronize directions faced.

Key for Constant Directions

The sign for 'an area': □ is combined with the sign for a cross of directions: + to make the key for the Constant Direc- tions: ⊞. This key is used with a direc- tion sign to indicate that a gesture or tra- velling should be performed into a Constant Direction rather than in relation to a

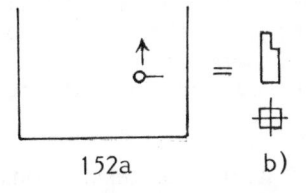

152a   b)

standard body direction. In Ex. 152a the performer who is facing stage right is to make a movement in the direction Constant forward. This will result in a sideward left action judged from her body. Aware- ness of the audience and of movement toward it will dictate use of such a description, or a practical need arising from simultaneous turn- ing and travelling may require a Constant Direction description.

The Front Signs

The key for Constant Directions provides us with the Front Signs, indications as to which direction in a defined area a performer is fac- ing. In most composed movement sequences it is important to know where you are facing at any given moment, that is, the relation of your personal front to the established Constant Directions. Note that this reference is different from the physical room or stage areas — center stage, downstage center, stage left, etc. These show location as well as aim or destination for travelling. When we say "Face the corner" we do not mean the actual physical corner of the stage, the boards or curtains. Usage and signs for stage areas will be dealt with later. Ex. 153a shows the eight main front signs. Particular direc- tions to be faced apply no matter where on stage

153a

186

a performer is located. Thus facing front (the audience) is always the same, as illustrated in Ex. 153b. In 153c all performers are facing the left-front corner: ◩ . Although they are spread across the stage their facing directions are all parallel.

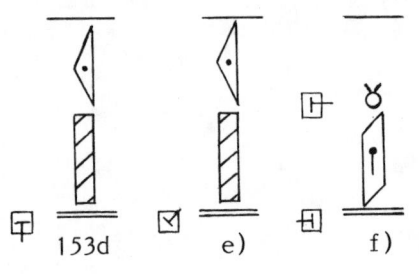

153b

c)

The front signs are not movement indications; they are orientation signs which are placed at the start of a score on the left and restated subsequently whenever there is a change of front to help the reader keep track of where he is facing. In 153d the movement sequence starts facing back, while in 153e the same sequence starts facing the right front corner. In 153f another sequence starts facing stage left (constant left). As this example contains a turn the new front is stated when the turn is finished.

153d

e)

f)

Diagonal Travelling

In taking diagonal steps there is a natural tendency on the part of the performer to make a slight turn and walk forward or backward.

Ex. 154a is a sequence on diagonal travelling in which the performer faces front all the time and takes steps which are diagonal from the hips (pelvis). Ex. 154b is spatially similar but all the steps are forward or backward from the hips while the travelling progresses into the Constant diagonal directions. The first sequence, 154a, provides an interesting alternation between open and crossed steps such as might occur in a Tango or in a Spanish dance. If there is a change of front as in 154b, the tension of the crossed steps is lost.

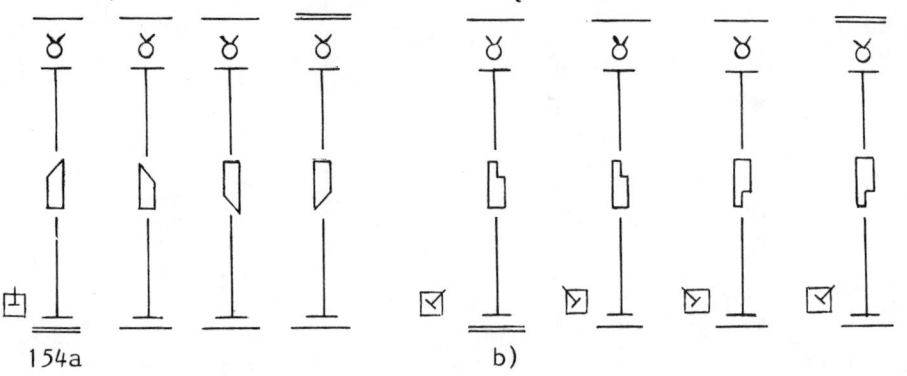

154a

b)

187

DIAGONAL TRAVELLING

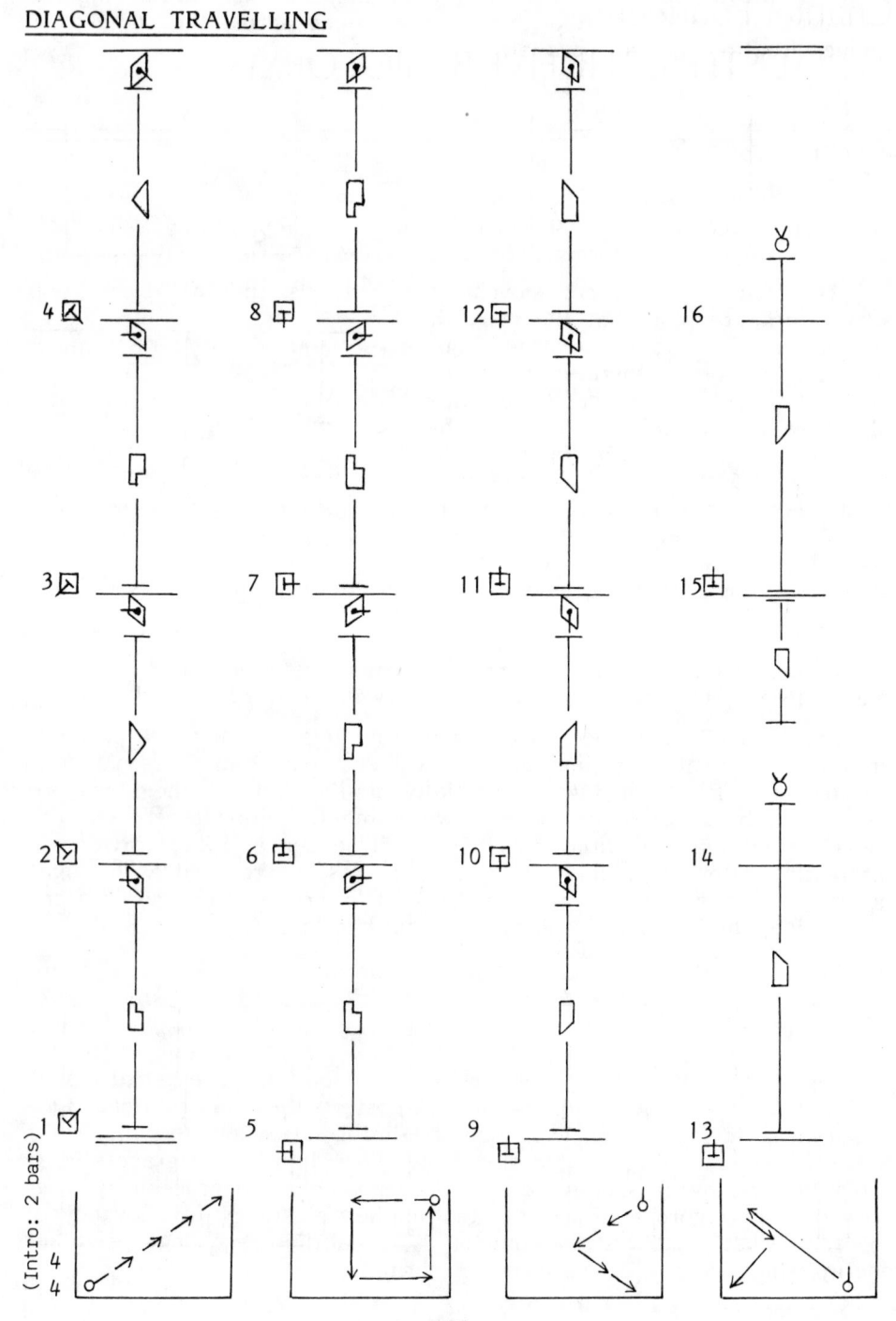

188

Chapter Fourteen
AERIAL STEPS: THE FIVE BASIC FORMS

Despite the seemingly enormous variety of jumping steps which one witnesses in different forms of dance, there are in fact only five basic possibilities for leaving the ground and returning to it when only the legs are used. They are:

		Ordinary Name	Balletic Name
1.	From one foot to the other	Leap	Jeté
2.	From one foot to the same	Hop	Temps levé*
3.	From two feet to two feet	Jump	Soubresaut
4.	From one foot to two feet	(closing spring)	Assemblé
5.	From two feet to one foot	(opening spring)	Sissonne

Many people expect skips and galops to be included in the five basic forms: they are, in fact, a hop or leap form combined with a step, i.e. 'hop - step, hop - step', or 'leap - step, leap - step'.

Terminology: Everyday Names

Have we something to learn from the words used in everyday language? Dictionaries use the words 'jump', 'leap', 'hop', 'spring', 'bound' interchangeably. It is generally agreed that the word hop refers to a spring from one foot to the same, and a leap is sometimes recognized as being from one foot to the other. It is amusing to realize that 'going to a hop' is (or was) slang for going to a dance. A 'short hop in an airplane' is a common phrase. When we 'hop on a bus' no doubt a leap form is used. The command 'hop to it' will doubtless produce speed, rather than an aerial step, just as 'to jump the queue' does not involve springing. 'Skip from stone to stone' gives a definite movement impression though it is doubtful that an actual skip step would be practical for such travelling. Another word for jumping, to 'vault', suggests springing over something, especially with the help of the hands or of a pole. Webster's New International Dictionary provides the following specific information on the difference between skips and bounds: "to skip is to move lightly and gracefully; it often implies joy or sportiveness. To bound means to proceed by longer and more vigorous leaps; it often implies elasticity or buoyancy of spirit." What each has in common is an action requiring speed and energy which is true of all forms of springs.

* in most schools

Terminology: Language of Dance Names

Because there are no ordinary names for Nos. 4 and 5 in our bas-ic list, the balletic terms are frequently used. It must be stressed, though, that reference is made only to the basic forms of the step and not to the specific use of leg gestures familiar in ballet technique. Sissonne and assemblé forms appear in national dances and also in modern and jazz dance, but as they usually look quite unballetic they are not recognized by the ballet eye as being sissonnes and assemblés.

In Language of Dance terminology 'hop', 'leap', 'jump', 'assemblé' and 'sissonne' refer specifically to these basic forms, thus providing quick and direct communication. The word 'spring' is used as a gener-al term which does not specify any one form — a useful and often needed ambiguity. The words 'elevation' and 'aerial steps' or 'aerial movements' are also used without divulging which form is being used. The term 'a jump' (in the singular) is given to the form which leaves the ground from both feet and returns to both. This must not be con-fused with use of the word 'jumping' for the activity in general.

A rather charming, amusing and not altogether irrational solution was proposed by a group of young children to the question of everyday terms for 'assemblé' and 'sissonne' which they saw as mixtures of a 'jump' and a 'leap'. When a spring starts like a leap but ends like a jump (assemblé) they called it a 'lump', while the form which starts as a jump but ends as a leap (sissonne) they called a 'jeap'.

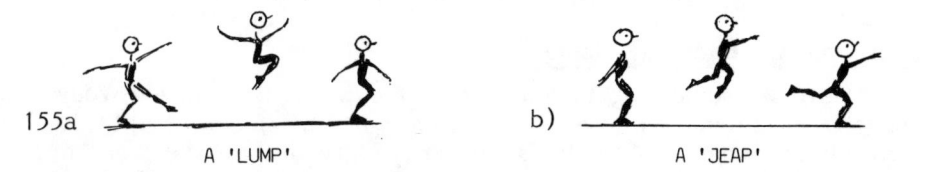

155a   A 'LUMP'   b)   A 'JEAP'

Indication of the Five Basic Forms

By adding which foot is supporting to the basic sign for a spring we can state which of the five basic forms is being used.

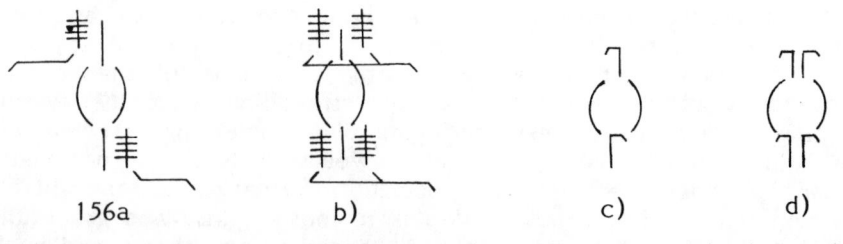

156a   b)   c)   d)

Ex. 156a spells out a spring from the right foot to the left, while 156b states a spring from both feet to both feet. This logical applica-tion of the signs for supporting and the signs for the feet can be ab-breviated to 156c and 156d. However, an even simpler device is avail-able to state which support is being used. Ex. 156e shows the general sign for a spring, while 156f indicates that it is from two feet to two feet. Ex. 156g shows a sissonne from two feet to one while 156h shows one foot to two. Neither of these specifies whether the single support is on the right or left foot.

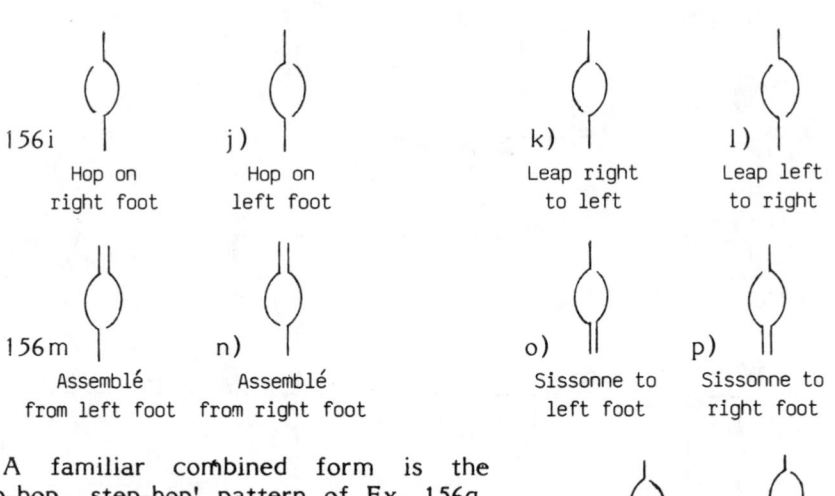

156e — A Spring

f) — A Jump

g) — A Sissonne

h) — An Assemblé

Attachment of one or other of the curved bows to the support indications shows visually how a spring involves the same or another foot. In 156i the spring is from the right foot to the right foot -- a hop. Ex. 156j states a hop on the left foot. In 156k a leap occurs from the right foot to the left, while in 156l a leap from left foot to the right is shown. Ex. 156m shows an assemblé taking off from the left foot and landing on both, while in 156n the take-off is from the right foot. Ex. 156o states a sissonne onto the left foot, while 156p shows a sissonne onto the right foot.

156i — Hop on right foot

j) — Hop on left foot

k) — Leap right to left

l) — Leap left to right

156m — Assemblé from left foot

n) — Assemblé from right foot

o) — Sissonne to left foot

p) — Sissonne to right foot

A familiar combined form is the 'step-hop , step-hop' pattern of Ex. 156q. Compare this with the 'step-leap, step-leap' pattern of 156r. Ex. 156q is the basis of a skip and may start as above or with the hop (hop-step, hop-step). Ex. 156r is the basis of a galop. These basic foot patterns will not be true skips or galops unless the appropriate uneven binary or ternary rhythm is used. These rhythms are explored in the Structured Description of movement, as are all variations in use of direction, flexion, extension, etc. in the various forms of aerial steps.

156q — Step hop, step hop

r) — Step leap, step leap

Reading Study No. 35

AERIAL STEPS - THE FIVE BASIC FORMS

The sign: ⊥ means 'either side' of the body, i.e. either foot, etc. e.g. ⟨ means hop on either foot. Note the indication of slight turns before a new measure to face a new direction.

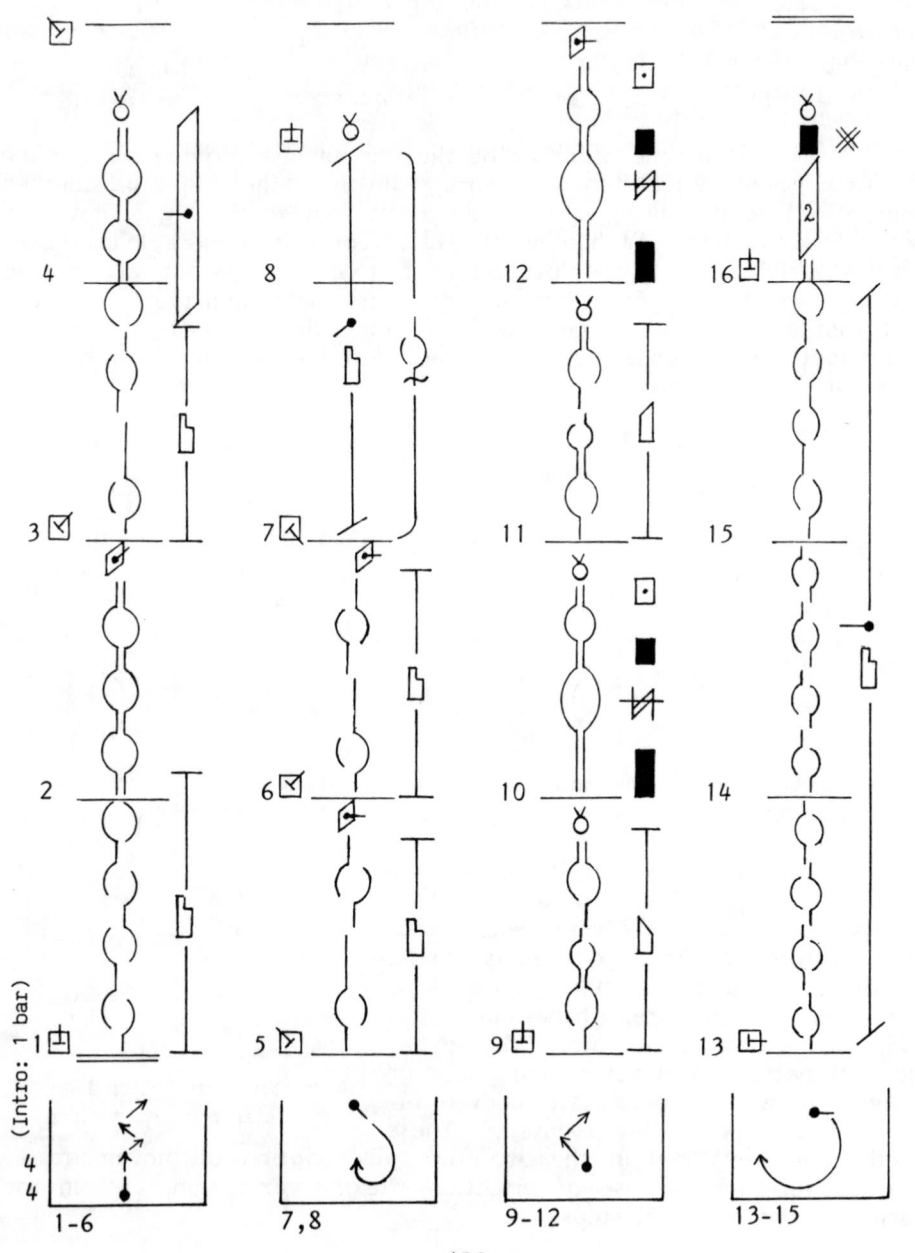

Aerial Steps: The Five Basic Forms

The Five Basic Forms in Ballet

The following survey is presented here for any readers who may not be familiar with allegro steps in the ballet vocabulary which are variations of the five basic forms. Ballet students who can perform these steps with ease often have not actually considered to which basic form each belongs. Rapid leg work such as beats, ronds de jambe (leg circles), etc. featured while in the air can almost disguise the basic form. It is important to realize that, even if a particular aerial step may be preceded by both feet on the ground, the actual take-off, the spring itself, may be from one foot only. Similarly a spring may end on one foot, the other closing so rapidly that the unwary person is given the impression that landing on two feet occurred, which, of course, it did not. It is the moment of take-off and the moment of landing that determine the basic form. In the following drawings preparations and conclusions are not indicated, only the actual take-off and landing for each form.

HOP FORM

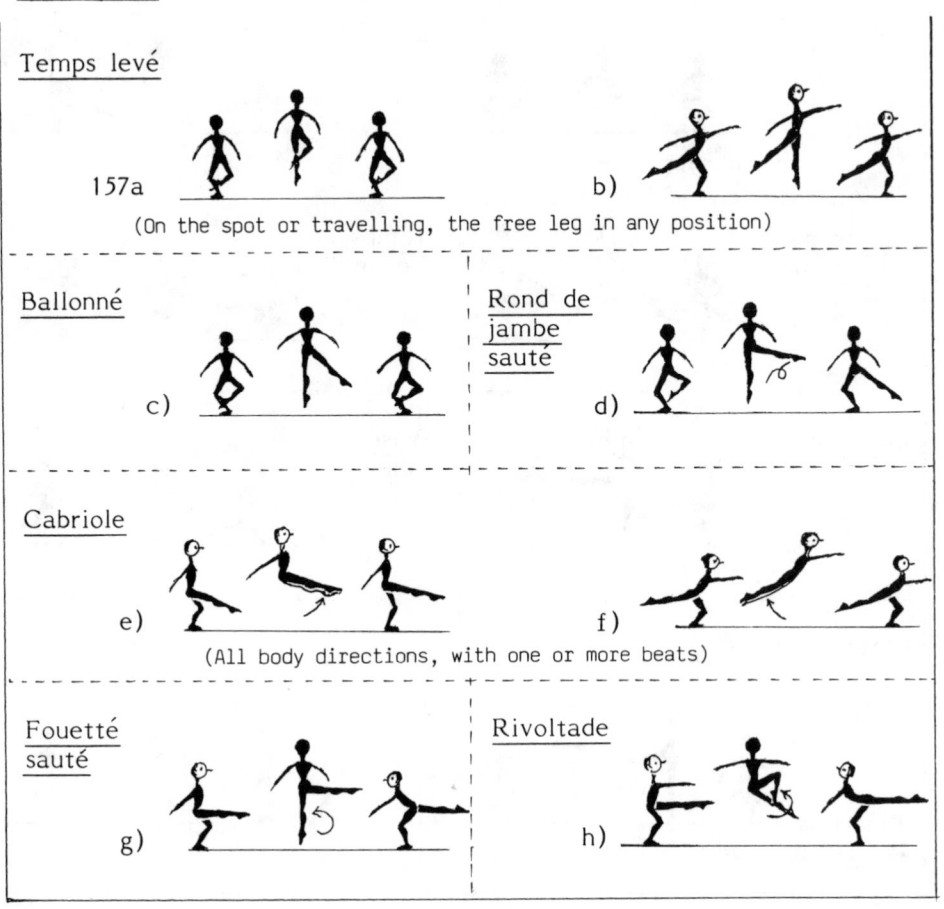

Temps levé

157a

b)

(On the spot or travelling, the free leg in any position)

Ballonné

c)

Rond de jambe sauté

d)

Cabriole

e)

f)

(All body directions, with one or more beats)

Fouetté sauté

g)

Rivoltade

h)

The Five Basic Forms in Ballet (continued)

LEAP FORM

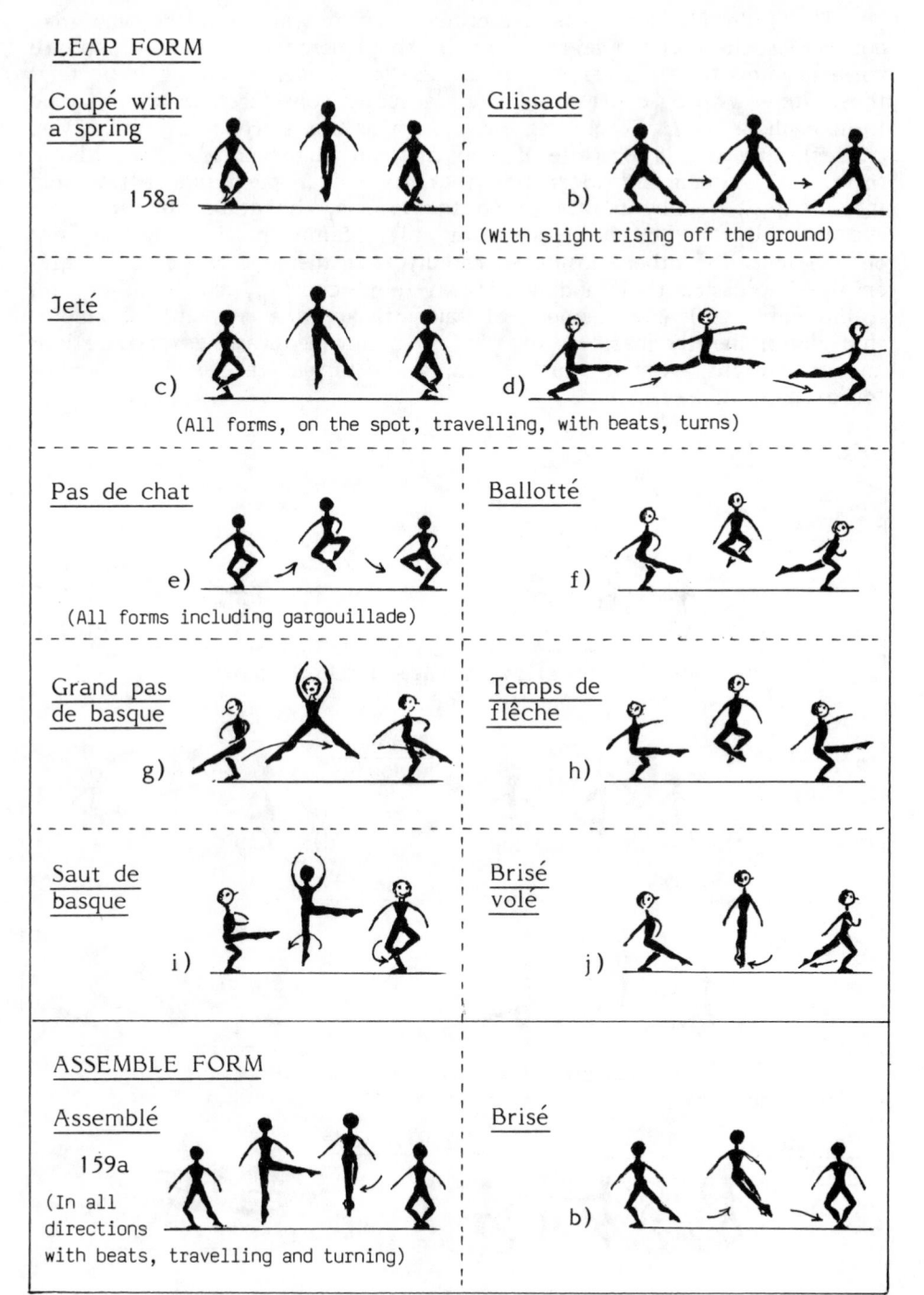

Coupé with a spring

158a

Glissade

b)

(With slight rising off the ground)

Jeté

c)

d)

(All forms, on the spot, travelling, with beats, turns)

Pas de chat

e)

(All forms including gargouillade)

Ballotté

f)

Grand pas de basque

g)

Temps de flêche

h)

Saut de basque

i)

Brisé volé

j)

ASSEMBLE FORM

Assemblé

159a

(In all directions with beats, travelling and turning)

Brisé

b)

Aerial Steps: The Five Basic Forms

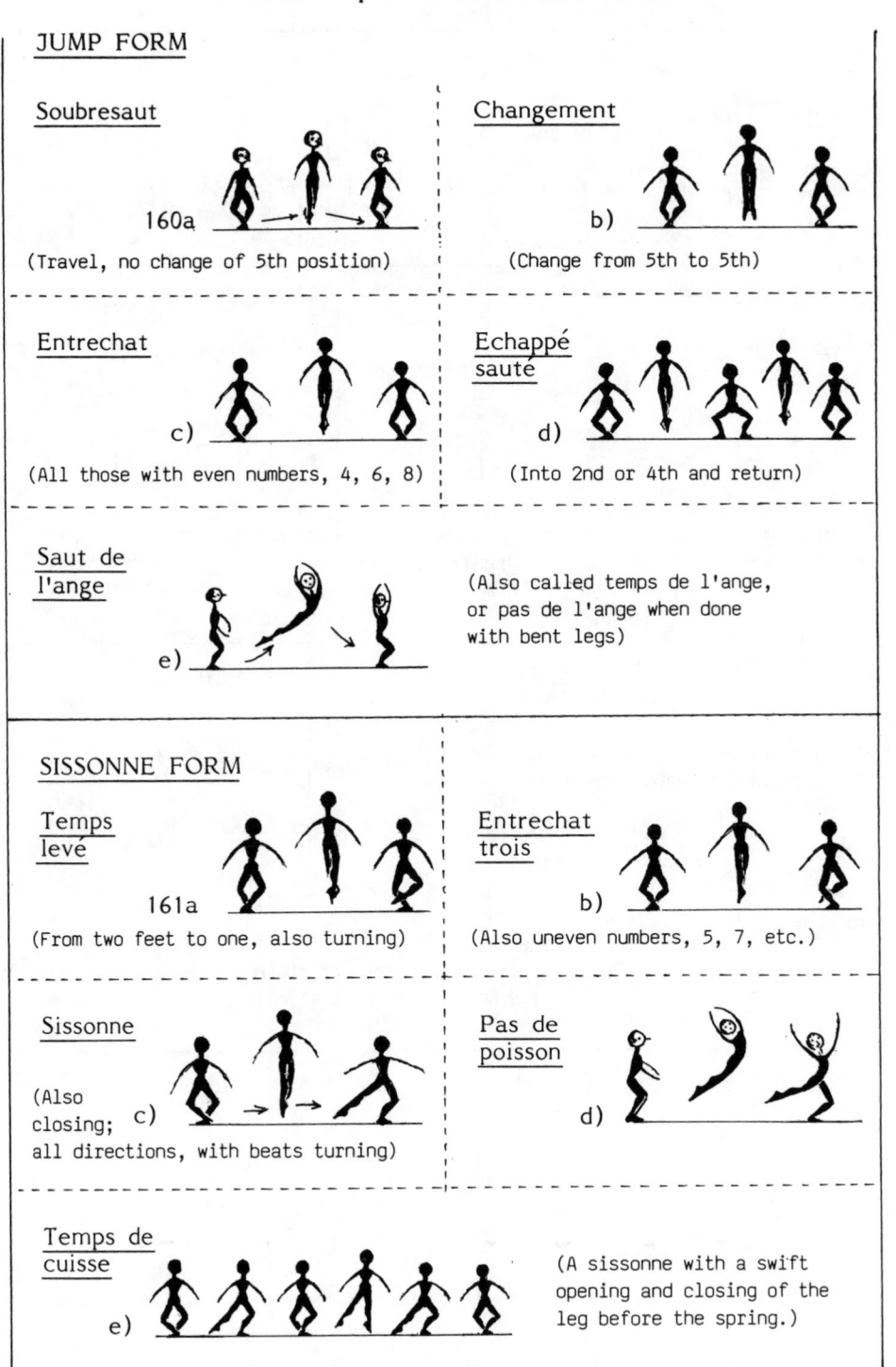

JUMP FORM

Soubresaut

160a

(Travel, no change of 5th position)

Changement

b)

(Change from 5th to 5th)

Entrechat

c)

(All those with even numbers, 4, 6, 8)

Echappé sauté

d)

(Into 2nd or 4th and return)

Saut de l'ange

e)

(Also called temps de l'ange, or pas de l'ange when done with bent legs)

SISSONNE FORM

Temps levé

161a

(From two feet to one, also turning)

Entrechat trois

b)

(Also uneven numbers, 5, 7, etc.)

Sissonne

(Also closing; c) all directions, with beats turning)

Pas de poisson

d)

Temps de cuisse

e)

(A sissonne with a swift opening and closing of the leg before the spring.)

REVIEW FOR CHAPTERS THIRTEEN AND FOURTEEN

DIAGONAL DIRECTIONS
Diagonal directions judged from the front established by the body
Gesture to diagonal direction from body
Travelling diagonally (body direction)
CONSTANT DIRECTIONS (established in the performing area)
= Key
Constant Forward general body movement
General body movement to Constant right-front diagonal
Arm gesture Constant right-front diagonal
Travel in Constant right-front diagonal direction
Room Area
Travel toward the right down-stage corner of the room (stage)
THE FRONT SIGNS - Performer's facing direction in relation to the Constant Directions
The audience (Constant forward)
Stage right (Constant R)
Upstage (Constant back)
Stage left (Constant L)
Right Front Corner
Left Front Corner
Right Back Corner
Left Back Corner
Placement of front sign at start of score
Indication of new front after a turn
AERIAL STEPS - THE FIVE BASIC FORMS
Jump
Hop
Leap
Sissonne
Assemblé
Hop either side

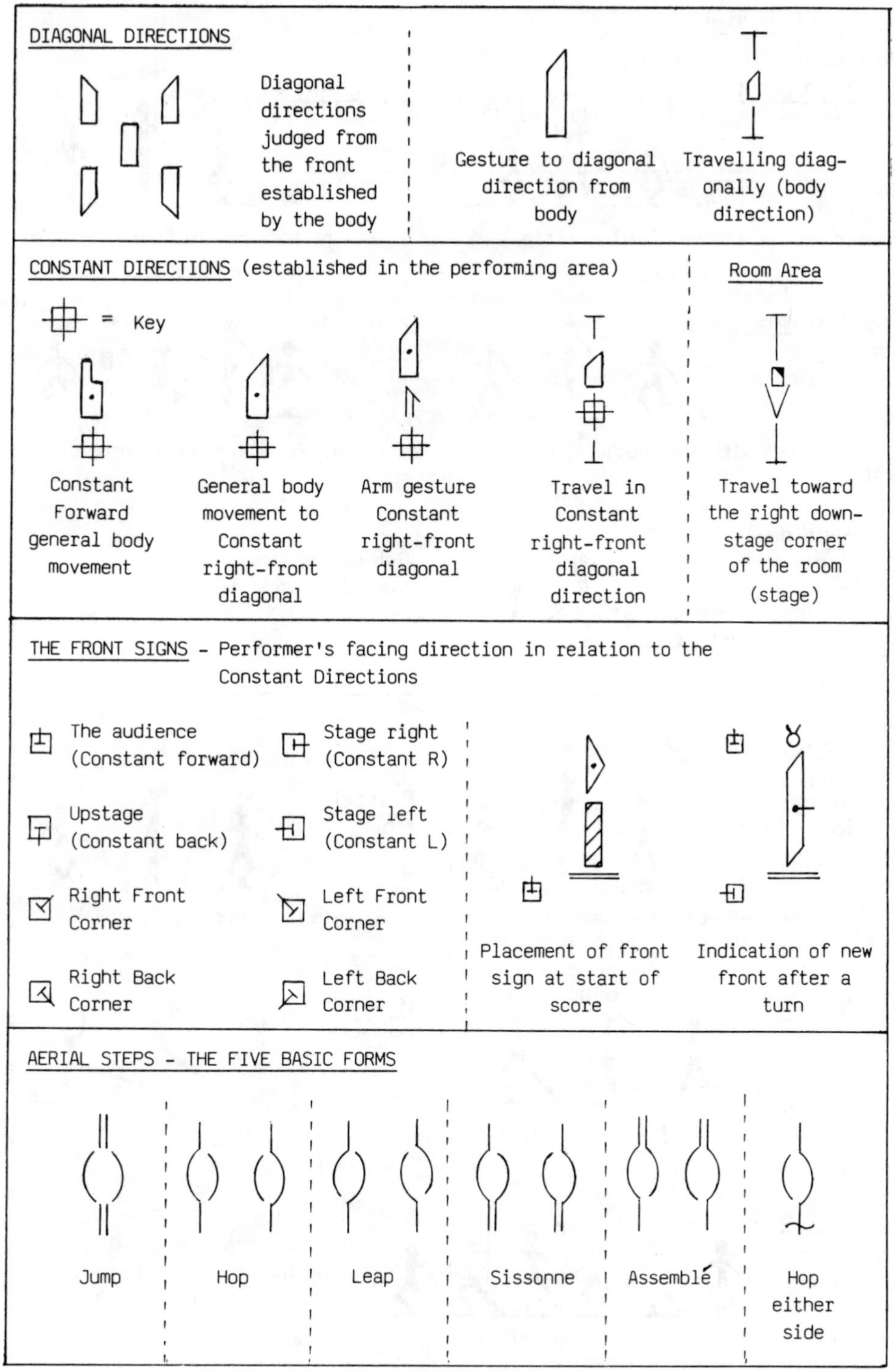

Chapter Fifteen
TURNING OF BODY PARTS: ROTATION, TWIST

The basic action of rotating as a unit may be modified into a twist. Twisting, a familiar movement pattern, takes various forms in the world around us. How do these forms relate to movement? What have we to learn from these forms that can enrich our understanding of similar patterns in the body? First let us see what nature provides.

Rapid rotary motion around a central axis occurs in whirlpools, water spots, whirlwinds, maelstroms, vortices, cyclones and tornadoes. Often covering a wide area a tornado whirls inward to a narrow center. The spiralling action may move across miles, the rotary action continuing all the time. In dance we see a spiral action starting in the body, progressing into turning and whirling through space, the effect of the action being especially marked when a flowing costume is worn. In a group dance the same pattern can emerge, the spiralling out into space being seen in the rotating and spreading out of many performers. Conversely, they may be spiralling in; in both cases an interesting and often exciting movement is produced. Smaller but equally interesting are the patterns made by twirling objects held in the hands and manipulated through twisting, circular motions of the wrists and lower arms.

162a

Elizabethan chimney

In a gentler vein we see tendrils coiling, entwining, winding, a loose enclosing which ends with a tighter twisting around an object. Helical shapes, twisted spiral designs in furniture and architecture are often functional as well as decorative. The winding of fibres into a rope produces greater strength than the same number of straight strands. This form also produces resiliency as in coils of wire.

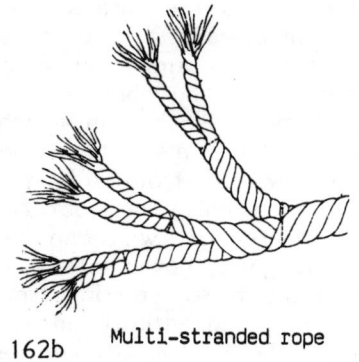

162b   Multi-stranded rope

197

Coils may be two or three dimensional. A helix is a coil in which the diameter does not diminish, thus we see that in fact a spiral staircase is actually helical rather than spiral.

A three-dimensional
spiral (a coil,
like a chair
spring)   162c

A helix (the
diameter does
not diminish)   d)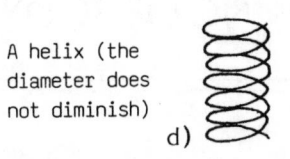

Twists in the body have functional as well as expressive use in movement. The concept may be of a twist in the same spatial volume or of closing in to a center or of opening out from a center as the twisting occurs. Motivation for twisting movements may vary considerably; the following words may evoke an image of what is wanted: gyrate, writhe, wring, contort, wind, intertwine, wreathe. Each contains particular elements which gives it its identifying character. Counterparts of everyday meanings exist in gymnastics, swimming, and skating as well as in dance.

TWISTING ACTIONS: FUNCTION AND EXPRESSION

A twist in the torso may be functional in that it may be preparation for a turn of the whole body as, for example, in skating where a torso twist leading into a slight lift of weight produces the smooth change from travelling forward to travelling backward. In diving half twists and full twists are familiar forms. Throwing an object usually involves a preparatory torso twist in one direction, the follow-through being into the other. Such twists in the body as a whole are illustrated clearly in a golf drive, the preparation being a twist to the right and the follow-through to the left. Change of weight from right foot to left allows a greater range of twist than would be possible on just one foot or if both feet were stationary on the ground. Total twist allows for a smooth transition at the moment of impact with the ball.

In dance every pirouette or aerial turn starts with some degree of twist. In ballet the twist preparation in the opposite direction to the turn is usually hidden as much as possible, occurring in the muscles of the torso. As the turn starts, it begins as a twisting action, though soon it becomes a turn of the body as a whole. The movement is so fast and the twisting part so brief that only in slow motion films can the twist itself be observed. A familiar form of twist is that in which the feet are apart, the arms outstretched and the body is twisted from side to side, Ex. 163a. With only one foot supporting a greater degree of twist can be achieved, the twist going down into the foot. A twist in the torso, starting from the base and moving sequentially up is a central figure of the Martha Graham technique.

163a

198

There it is called a 'spiral', and one trains to be able to extend the range of this spiralling as much as possible for both its expressiveness as well as its functional use. Torso twists occur in many forms of contemporary dance as well as in jazz and African dance. The Twist, made famous by Chubby Checkers, featured twisting in every part of the body — the more the better.

163b   c)   d)   e)

How do twists affect the expressiveness of an action? An increased degree of twist produces a torsion with an inevitable accompanying tension. Relax the muscles and the twist will disappear, the limb will return to its normal alignment, the untwisted state. Tension accompanying a twist can be exaggerated by bringing the antagonist muscles into play, i.e. resisting the twist but at the same time allowing it to continue or to be maintained.

ANALYSIS OF ROTATION, TWIST

In the category of rotation (revolution, turning) two main forms exist. As a <u>turn of</u> a body part is expressively and functionally different from a turning action <u>within</u> a body part, specific terminology and notation have been selected to differentiate between the two.

Turn: the general term.

<u>Rotation</u> - each part turns an equal amount, i.e. the limb or torso turns in one piece, Ex. 164a.

164a

Rotation

<u>Twist</u> - the free end turns more than the base thereby producing torsion in the limb or trunk, Ex. 164b. A torsion may also result from opposite twists occurring simultaneously at both ends of the limb or trunk.

164b

Twist

Somersaults and cartwheels are examples of rotations (revolutions) of the body-as-a-whole moving in one piece. In a spinning turn such as a pirouette, the whole body can turn as a unit, Ex. 164c. In log-rolling (turning while lying on the floor) the body also usually turns in one piece, 164d.

c)   d)

199

Analysis of Rotation, Twist (continued)

In our further investigation into the function of and the expression in twisting actions we will consider the main parts of the body separately and also observe whether the part is rotating in one piece or whether a twist occurs within that part.

The Whole Torso

Twists in the torso, slight or marked, may express strong feelings, positive or negative. The latter may be based on fear, conflict, antagonism, aversion, disdain, suspicion or secrecy. Spatially a twist often occurs to enlarge the range of movement around the body, extending the scope of gestures by bringing into use space behind the body and facilitating performance of gestures across the torso, as in 165a, 165b. A twist may start at the extremity and successively move to the base, or vice versa. A return to normal carriage may also start at the base or the extremity and move part by part through the spine, particularly when the movement is slow. Such a successive progression is less observable at speed.

165a

b)

Explore such use of the torso by itself and also combined with other forms of movement. After exploration to discover expressive possibilities find out how specific actions occur. Compare twisting with rotating the torso as a unit. Ex. 165c shows a rotation of the whole torso; 165d shows a twist within the torso. Each of these actions involves a twist in the leg(s). It is this twist in the leg(s) which makes a rotation of the torso as a unit possible. Degree of such rotation is limited to how far the pelvis can rotate; after that further turning involves twisting in the upper part of the torso, the chest and shoulder section. The following illustrations analyze twisting with the base (the feet) as the static part and also the extremity (the head) as the static part.

165c   d)

If from the untwisted state, Ex. 165e, a pivot turn was attempted with one foot glued to the floor, the result would be a twist in the body, 165f. The head would turn the most, shoulders less, and so on. Or it could be that the head is the fixed end and the rest of the body turns away, the feet achieving the greatest degree of turning, as in Ex. 165g.

165e   f)   g)

The Head

Turning the head is such a familiar everyday action that we may not be aware of how many different expressions this simple anatomical action can produce. We turn the head to look, to focus our attention on something or someone, or the reverse - to look away. We 'shake' the head to say no, to express dismay, sadness, etc. and, again, it is a rotary action. Or the head turns to test freedom in the neck muscles, perhaps while one is recovering from a stiff neck. By combining head rotations with tilting and shifting actions we are able to express many different thoughts and emotions.

Though the muscles on the face may twist, the head itself is a solid mass which rotates through a twisting action in the neck, Ex. 166. Though it is essentially a neck movement, the focus of the action is on the head and so it is usually described and written as a turn of the head. The neck can only twist.

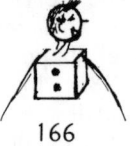

166

The Chest

Rotating or twisting the upper part of the torso is a movement that jazz would hate to be without. Reacting to a basic beat in the music may take the form of isolated chest twists which may be spatially quite small or may grow to become thrusting actions. Often chest twists initiate other movements. Energy within the body may be focussed on the rib cage (thorax). Or, as mentioned before, a chest twist may occur to augment the range of movement for arm gestures. It may also happen in sitting when a change of front takes place for the upper part of the body without affecting the lower.

Rotation of the chest in one piece occurs through a twist in the waist area, Ex. 167a. The amount of turn possible for the chest in one piece depends on the length and flexibility of the waist area of the spine. The degree is small; a large amount produces a twist in the chest itself (i.e. the thoracic spine), the shoulder line achieving the greatest amount of turn. A small degree may involve just the upper body, the shoulder section of the spine as in a balletic épaulement, 167b. Epaulements may also be slight chest twists.

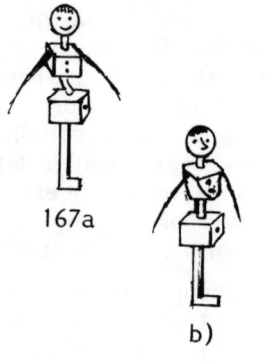

167a

b)

The Pelvis

Pelvic rotations as a high art have been mastered by more than one culture around the world. The rapid figure eight twisting patterns of the Tahiti dancers is augmented by the resulting swirl of the grass skirt. North African belly dancers wear a costume which spatially augments their hip rotations and it is astounding to see such activity in the lower half of the body while the top remains so calm that a vase otherwise unsupported is carried on the head.

201

H

The Pelvis (continued)

These movements require training; what range is there for western dancers? Hip rotation can give an ordinary walk an aggressive or a coy look depending on the direction of the rotation in relation to the stepping leg. A sagittal leg gesture pulled out from the body will take the hip with it thus causing a rotation of the pelvis. Balanchine's use of hip thrusts does not usually include lateral rotation; such rotation is more typical of jazz with its overtone of sex. Many people use slight rotation in their ordinary walk. As with the chest, pelvic rotations may mark the pulse or beat of the music. Hands on hips will make one more aware of the direction and degree of pelvic rotations.

The pelvis is a solid body mass and so can only rotate, this rotation being produced through a twist in the supporting leg(s) plus a twist in the waist, Ex. 168. In a pelvic rotation the chest should be kept still, that is, it should remain uninvolved, but for greater degree of pelvic rotation the lower part of the chest must join in the twist at the waist.

168

The Legs

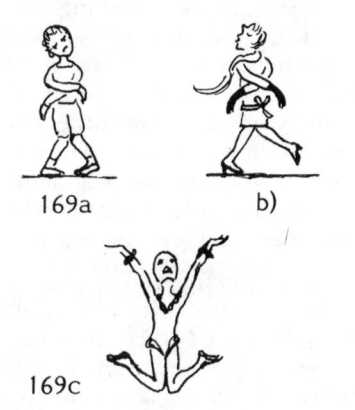

169a   b)

169c

Leg rotations, particularly when the limb is bent, provide expressive distortion which may serve comedy or pathos. The baleful stance of 169a is basically the same as the tongue-in-cheek Charleston which, of all dances, probably features leg rotations more than most. Leg rotations appear in many jazz steps both for the supporting leg and for the gesturing leg. Russian and Chinese dances feature smooth travelling which is accomplished by symmetrical or parallel leg rotations with change of weight from ball of the foot to the heel. Classical ballet appears to use constant outward rotation of the legs, but in fact the degree varies with certain steps and parallel (untwisted) legs are used for swift forward running steps.

Changes in degree and direction of leg rotation occur frequently in many step and locomotor patterns. When we walk in a circle, that is, on a circular path, an unemphasized rotation of the legs into the direction of the circling occurs on each step. The fewer the steps for a full circle, the more evident is this action. As each step is completed the body 'catches up' with the degree of rotation by 'untwisting' from the ankle up. In many European folk dances the feet are parallel in a closed position but turn out slightly for steps which follow. A slight change in the rotational state of the legs will make any known style of dance look wrong; thus the rotational state of the legs is an important factor in dance style.

Turning of Body Parts: Rotation, Twist

To avoid injury, teachers of physical education and dancing stress rotation of the leg as a unit (i.e. in one piece), the action taking place only in the hip socket, Ex. 169d. All too easily a twist in the legs will occur, 169e, particularly if the foot is forced outward (or inward) to a degree the thigh cannot match. When the knee is bent some twisting action in the lower leg is possible, 169f. From below the ankle the foot can 'roll' through flexibility in the ankle. Such foot rotation produces a support on the outside edge of the foot (inversion), 169g, or on the inside edge (eversion), 169h. In addition to this rotary action the foot itself can twist, but let us not get too detailed at this point.

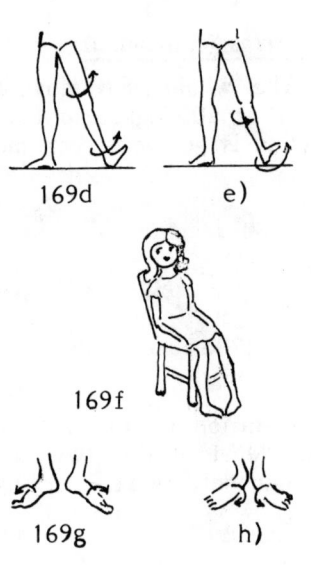

169d   e)

169f

169g   h)

The Arms

What of rotations, twists, in the arms? Some degree of rotation or twist is such an everyday occurence that we are usually unaware that it is taking place. Often rotary actions are thought of and described in other terms. We check whether it is raining with an upward facing palm, Ex. 170a, or touch something with palm facing down, 170b, without realizing that twisting of the lower arm made such palm facings possible. Arms akimbo, 170c, requires inward rotation of the upper arm, while outward arm rotation is needed to express bewilderment or lack of knowledge as in Ex. 170d, which gesture could accompany "I don't know" or "Where did it go?" or "Who cares?"

170a   b)   c)   d)

Many hidden rotations occur in simple circular patterns of the arms, particularly full circles. Such unemphasized rotations during arm circles are discussed fully later. The sinuous arm ripple of East Indian dance requires rotations in the center of the arm. Some rotations/twists are more obvious, as, for instance, the hand circles in Spanish dance and in many Asian dance forms. Practical use of rotation/twist occurs in using a screwdriver, in turning a radiator cap on or off and in changing a light bulb, all of which make use of twisting movements in the lower arm. Functionally important arm rotations/twists occur in gymnastics and are vital to the accomplishment of certain feats. In a simple cartwheel placement of the hands (produced by the degree of arm twist) affects the line of travel.

The Arms (continued)

The whole arm moving in one piece (i.e. as a unit) can achieve only a small degree of rotation around its own axis, Ex. 170e-f). The rotation is augmented if the shoulder takes part.

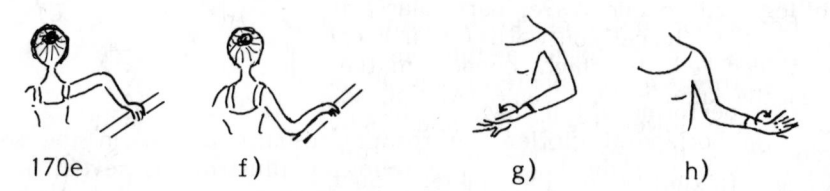

| 170e | f) | g) | h) |

Rotation of the arm as a unit is less usual than a twist in the arm. Most of this twist occurs in the lower arm. By itself the lower arm can only twist, carrying the hand with it, Ex. 170g, h).

The Hands

Rotation of the hand functions like a rotation of the head in that we are aware of the part turning, the hand, rather than of the adjacent part, the twist in the lower arm, which produces the movement. Because emphasis is on the hand, the movement is described and written as a hand rotation.

A twist can occur within the hand through the action of the thumb and fingers (the metacarpals and phalanges), Ex. 171. The wrist joint itself does not allow for any rotary movement, being built quite differently from such joints as the hip and shoulder which allow much freedom for rotary actions of the leg and arm.

171

Arm Rotations during Circular Gestures

Circular paths of the limbs involve rotations/twists which may be observed and experienced to a greater or lesser degree. Many performers are unaware that one full arm circle involves one full arm rotation. This rotation may occur gradually throughout the circle so that it is 'absorbed' and not generally evident, or the full rotation may occur during a small section of the circle in the form of 'getting over the hump'. The following examples are for the right arm. In a forward sagittal (somersault) circle, Ex. 172a, a full outward rotation occurs; for a backward sagittal circle an inward rotation takes place. In sagittal circles the rotation usually occurs between the directions up and backward horizontal. For a lateral circle (cartwheel) to the right, 172b, a full inward rotation is needed; for a lateral

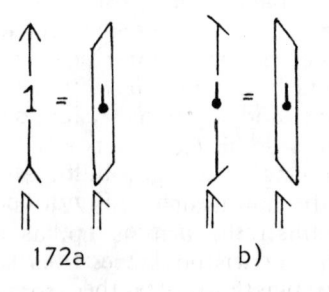

172a   b)

circle to the left a full outward rotation is needed. In lateral circles the
rotation is usually spread out evenly
so that many performers are unaware
that a rotation is occurring.

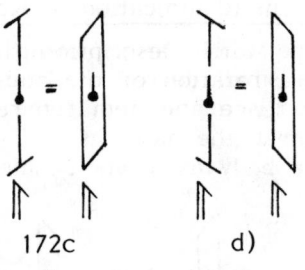

For a horizontal clockwise path,
172c, the arm performs a full outward rotation; for a counterclockwise
circle it performs a full inward rota-
tion. In horizontal circles the rotation usually occurs in the section
which lies behind the body. The following illustrations reveal how the
rotation occurs in a lateral circle and what happens if no rotation at
all takes place.

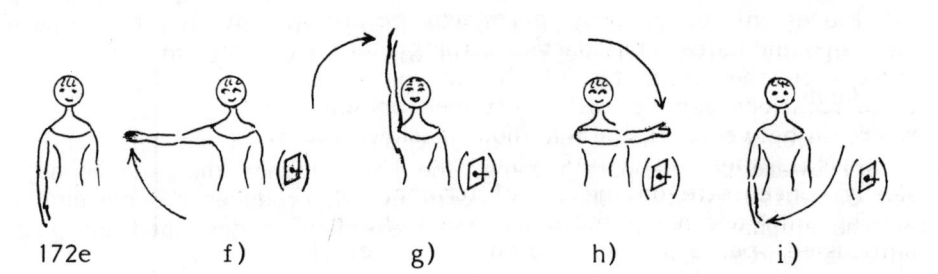

Ex. 172e-i) illustrate a familiar lateral circle which starts with the
arm down and the palm facing in (the standard rotational state). As
the arm lifts to the side the 'hidden' rotation brings the palm to face
front; as the arm rises to overhead, the hidden rotation brings the
palm to face 'in' again. When the arm arrives across to the other
side, the palm is facing back; on the arm's return to the down position the palm again faces in toward the body. Some people feel that
it is more 'natural' to 'leave the palm facing' as the arm is raised so
that when the arm arrives side horizontal the palm is facing down, Ex.
172j. Palms down when the arms are out to the side is common to
several movement disciplines but, as can be seen, it cannot be taken
as the standard carriage for the arms in that direction.

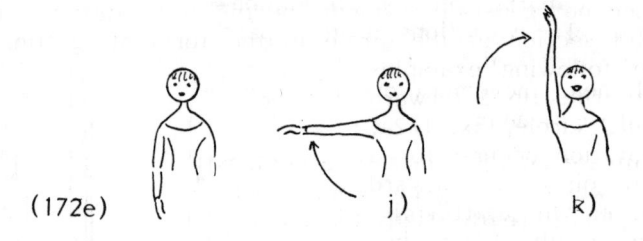

If the usage of 172j is carried further, the palm will end facing
out when the arm is up, as in 172k. This carriage can clearly be seen
to be a twisted state. As soon as the arm muscles are allowed to relax the palm will return to facing in, as in Ex. 172g.

General Indication of Rotation, Twist

In Motif Description the signs of Ex. 173a and 173b indicate a turn, a rotation of the body as a whole. In a twist one extremity is held, hence the sign for retention, hold: ○ is placed within the turn sign near the base, as in Ex. 173c,d). This indication refers to a twist in the body as a whole unless a specific part of the body is indicated.

173a   b)   c) = Twist to the left   d) = Twist to the right

Statement of Part Rotating, Twisting

C = head

Placement of a body part sign before a turn sign indicates what part is turning. Let us start with the head, for which the sign is C. Head rotations can be swift, sustained or some-where in-between. Ex. 174a shows a slow rota-tion right, then left. As you turn the head slowly concentrate on the act of turning, not of looking into another direction. Keep the eyes unfocussed, perhaps even closed, and feel the turning action, the rotation around the axis of the spinal column. As mentioned before, this action is correctly analyzed as a twist in the neck, so try the movement again this time with concentration on the neck. When might such an action occur in everyday life? In dance? What motivation might there be for it? A dramatic situation? Would such actions occur just for the enjoyment of moving? As a decorative ef-fect?

174a

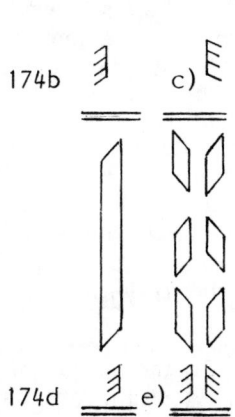

174b

c)

174d

e)

Having rotated the head alone, by itself, make it now the central movement in a 'clus-ter', that is, support this main action with mi-nor actions in other parts, perhaps an inclina-tion of the body. Try variations in the speed of the movement (not indicated in the nota-tion). Can such head movement occur as pure movement, devoid of meaning?

Next, concentrate on the hands, two centres of expression for which turning plays an impor-tant part. Ex. 174b,c) are the signs for the left and right hands. First try a very slow rotation of the right hand only, 174d, then put it into a movement context. What other movements might support this main action? Then rotate both hands symmetrically, 174e, at a moderate speed.

How can such movements be set into a dance form? Symmetrical hand rotations occur in certain Russian folk dances, the arm gesturing forward and outward to the audience while the feet repeatedly perform a fast push-off step. The expression is very gay, vivacious and lighthearted. No Lady Macbeth looking at her bloodstained hands, turning them, palms up, in disgust. At a very fast tempo, Ex. 174f, this rotary action of the hands can become a shaking, vibrato movement producing a very different expression.

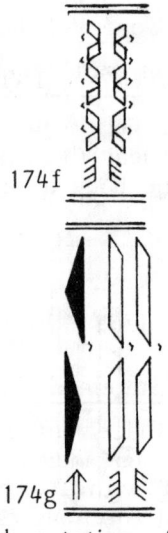

174f

Quite another effect is produced by parallel hand rotations, as in Ex. 174g. This relationship may seem unusual, yet at a slower tempo it is used with low side-to-side arm gestures in a lilting balancé waltz step, the rotation going into the direction of the path of the arms.

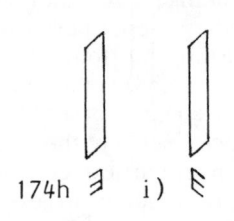

174g

Although a change in palm facing occurs through rotation of the hand (lower arm twist), if direction of palm facing is the intention or emphasis of the movement the notation is written with palm indications (see page 246). When emphasis is on lower arm turning, the hand remains passive; it does not catch the eye of the observer since it is not featured. A common action of this kind is turning the wrist to look at one's watch, an inward twist, Ex. 174h; or it may be the reverse for the purpose of inspecting the inner surface of the lower arm. Ex. 174i indicates such an action for the right wrist.

174h   i)

Parallel or symmetrical leg rotations can occur while standing through swivelling the feet on the floor or when lying on the back when both legs are free to gesture together. Ex. 174j shows two outward symmetrical leg rotations followed by inward rotations, first slower, then faster. In 174k the rotations are parallel, each leg moving in turn and then both in unison. In the Charleston symmetrical rotations involve a mixture of one leg supporting while the other gestures. In the above examples each additional movement indication which follows the body part pre-sign is understood to refer to that same part of the body. If a gap occurs, as in Ex. 174k, a caret, < or > can be used to make clear that reference is to the same part of the body. The caret has the meaning of 'the same'. Some writers prefer to use carets as a matter of course as a constant reminder.

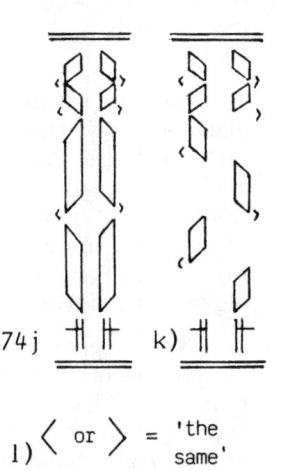

174j   k)

l) ⟨ or ⟩ = 'the same'

carets

Reading Study No. 36

ROTATIONS, TWISTS

Study A uses general indications; Study B deals with rotation of specific parts.

$\boxed{\bullet}$ = pelvis $\boxed{⇑}$ = shoulder section of the spine $\big\}$ = swift continuation of indicated action

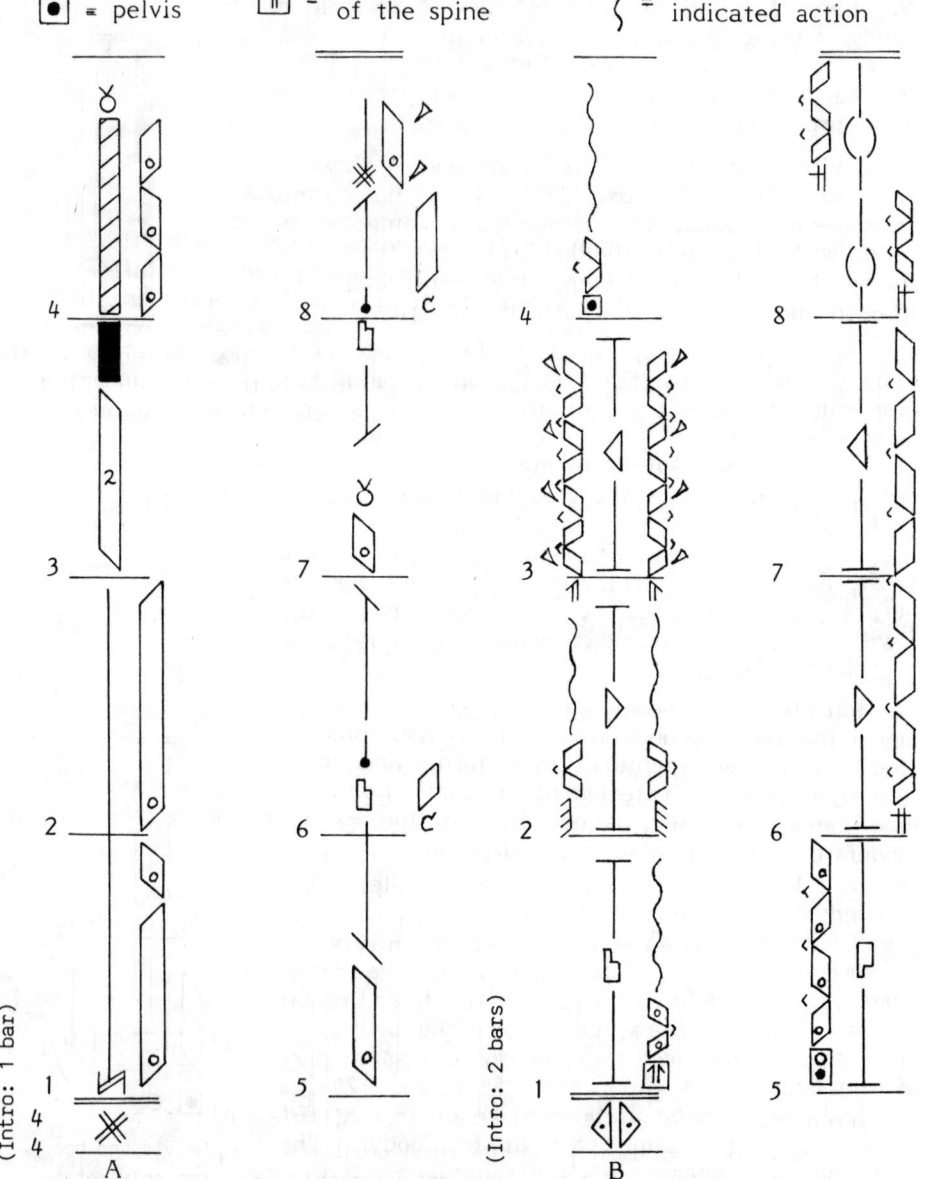

(Intro: 1 bar)

A

(Intro: 2 bars)

B

Remember that automatic cancellation is the general rule;   one action has its moment and is then replaced by another.

Twisting Combined with Flexion, Extension

Many arm gestures combine a flexion or extension with a rotation. The examples below all illustrate movements for the right arm.

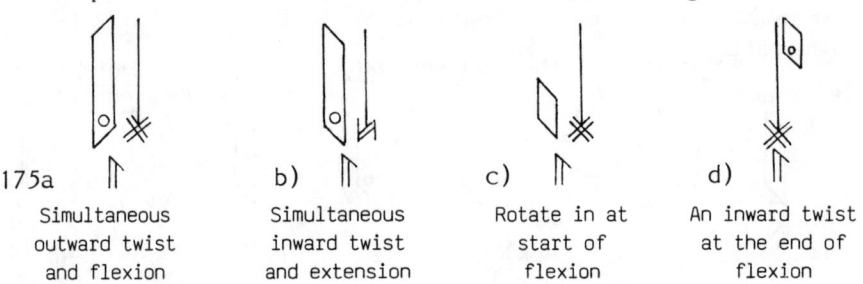

175a	b)	c)	d)
Simultaneous outward twist and flexion	Simultaneous inward twist and extension	Rotate in at start of flexion	An inward twist at the end of flexion

The simple material of Ex. 175a (twist combined with flexion) can be varied in timing and in degree to produce a range of difference in expression as in 175c and 175d. Such actions also occur in the legs, though the range is more restricted. The torso may also combine flexion and extension with rotating or twisting. Note the centering of the arm sign in the examples above to state that both movement indications refer to the arm. Ex. 175b illustrates twist with elongation.

Indication of Rotation Versus Twist

In the examples of reading material given for rotations, twists of parts of the body, it may have been observed that in some cases the unmodified turn sign, Ex. 176a, was used and in others the specific indication for a twist, 176b, was stated. Because certain parts of the body can only perform one form of turning the general sign of 176a is used when the form is understood. However, some body parts are capable of both forms and so the sign for equal rotation of all parts, i.e. in one piece, Ex. 176c, is needed. In the examples below the natural, understood form is placed in parenthesis.

176a = General sign for turning

b) Twist c) Rotate in one piece

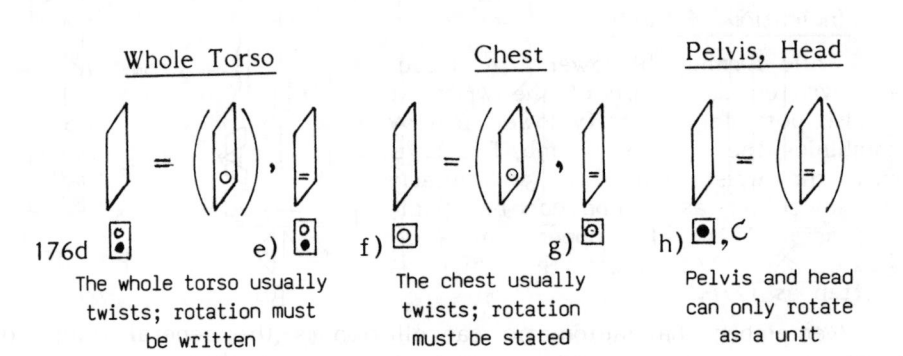

Whole Torso	Chest	Pelvis, Head
176d e)	f) g)	h)
The whole torso usually twists; rotation must be written	The chest usually twists; rotation must be stated	Pelvis and head can only rotate as a unit

Indication of Rotation Versus Twist (continued)

The following examples feature limbs of the right side of the body; each statement applies equally to the left side.

Whole Arm	Lower Arm	Hand

176i   j)   k)   l)   m)

The whole arm usually twists; rotation as a unit must be stated

The lower arm can only twist

The hand rotates as a unit (through lower arm twist)

Twist in the hand

Whole Leg	Lower Leg	Foot

176n   o)   p)   q)   r)   s)   (or)

The whole leg rotates as a unit; twist must be stated

The lower leg can only twist

The foot can rotate or twist

Note that we say the whole leg rotates as a unit. This is true in intention though not always in fact. When a leg twist is wanted it can be stated. The possibilities for foot rotation or twist depend on factors such as whether the foot is supporting or not and the state of flexion or extension at the ankle.

Indication of Limb

While turning the lower arm is usually written as a turn of the wrist, it is also possible to specify lower arm by combining the sign for a limb, Ex. 177a, with the wrist sign, 177b. Similarly the lower leg as a limb can be specified as in 177c. The upper arm is indicated as 177d, while the thigh is written as 177e.

177a ‖ = a limb

177b ⪢ = ⫶⪢   c) ⪢ = ‖⪢

177d ⪡ = ⫶⪡   e) ⪢ = ‖⪢

Full details on degrees for rotation/twist for various parts of the body are covered in the Structured Description of movement.

ROTATION, TWISTS OF SPECIFIC PARTS

◇ = means the face remains looking into the same direction despite
Ⓒ   the accompanying chest twist.   (◇ is the sign for retention of
     a spatial direction.)

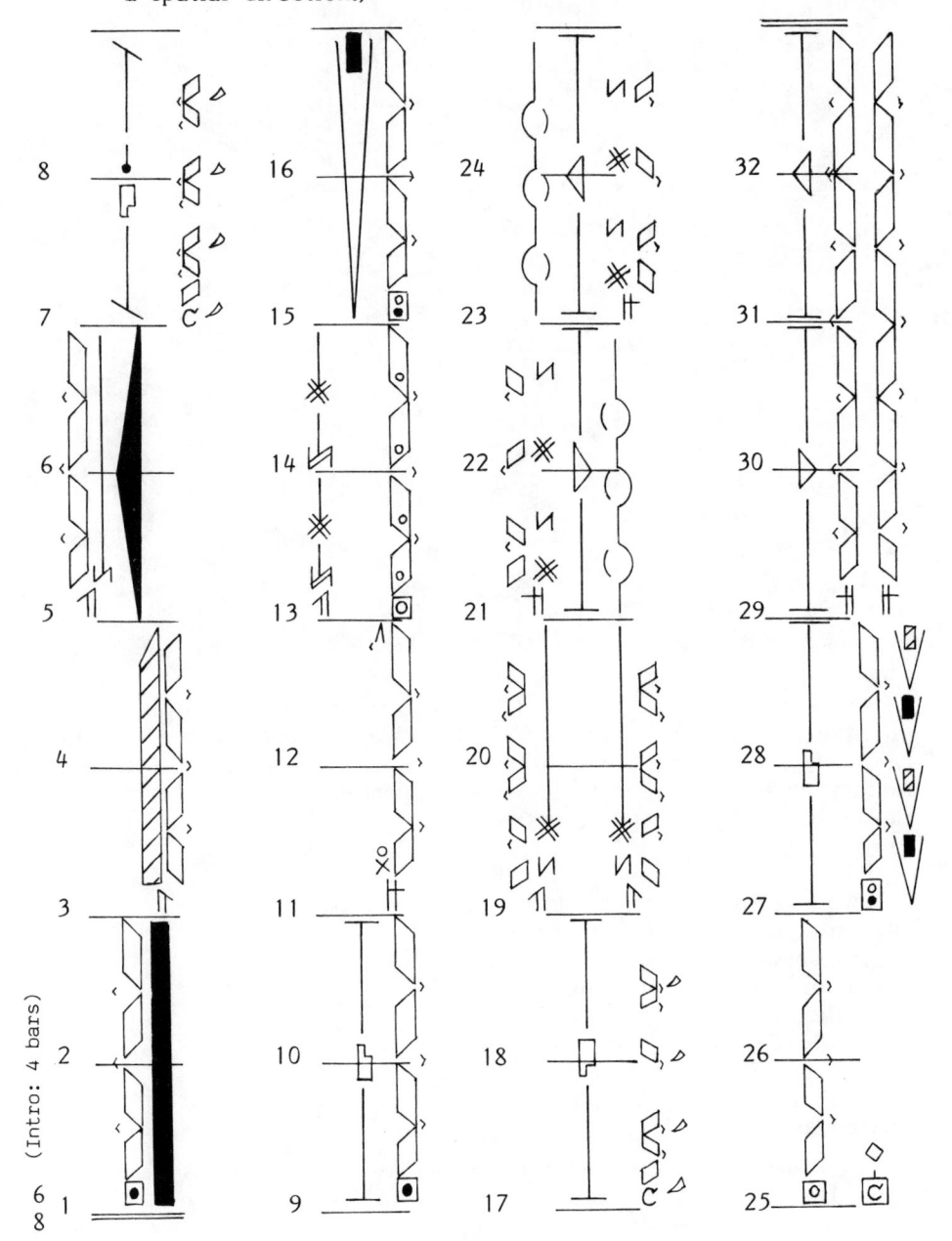

(Intro: 4 bars)

6/8

211

Chapter Sixteen
FLEXION AND EXTENSION: SPECIFIC FORMS

In our previous exploration of flexion and extension several words were found to describe the various possible actions which come under these general headings. Now we will investigate and identify the specific forms, giving consideration to how they function and also to their expressive use.

THE THREE FORMS OF FLEXION

Three distinct forms of flexion are defined by special terminology and signs. Bearing in mind other disciplines and terminology in movement analysis, the Language of Dance has chosen those terms which have generally proved to be most appropriate. The three forms are:

1. Contract*   2. Fold   3. Join

For each of these terms synonyms exist. Contracting may also be called shortening, pulling in, retracting, shrinking. Folding may also be experienced as curling, curving, arching, wrapping, or furling. Joining, closing in, may also be lapping or overlapping in the lateral or sagittal dimensions, that is, closing in in relation to the 'width' (breadth) or the 'depth' of the body part. Adduction is lateral closing.

Our earlier exploration of general flexion made use of all three foms as the movement idea required. Flexion occurs naturally when one is reacting to fear, to a threat. The body pulls in, closes up for self-protection. One is not aware of exactly how the action occurs, what form it is taking; it is a reflex action. Similarly, reacting to cold causes the body to contract, to fold up. Or there may be a practical need for folding/contracting such as crouching to pass through a small space, or closely inspecting one's toenails. Many tumbling tricks require making the body as small as possible.

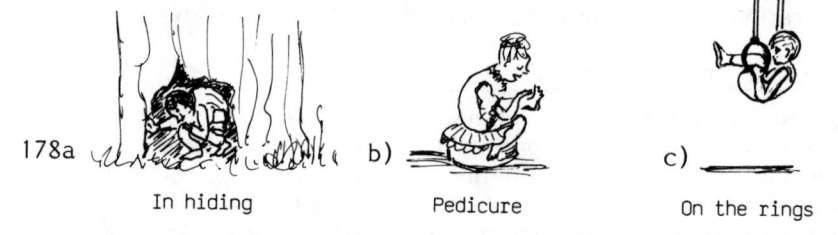

178a   b)   c) _____

In hiding   Pedicure   On the rings

---

* The terms 'contract', 'contraction', 'contracting' are here used in their general sense and are not to be confused with the specialized use met in the Martha Graham contemporary dance technique.

THE THREE FORMS OF EXTENSION

The specific forms of extension relate directly to those of flexion. They are:

1. Elongate   2. Unfold   3. Separate

Elongate involves lengthening, stretching, reaching out. The term 'protract', which usually refers to drawing out, lengthening in time, according to Webster's International Dictionary, can also be used in relation to space and is anatomically used for a muscle which extends a part (the opposite of retract). 'Protract' might seem to be the obvious opposite of the term 'contract', but since it is unfamiliar in this context it is replaced by 'elongate' as the more familiar term. The usual term for the counterpart of 'fold' is 'unfold', though 'unwrap', 'unfurl', etc. may be appropriate and descriptive in certain instances. Separating, spreading out, occurs in the width or breadth of a part of the body, i.e. in its lateral or sagittal dimension. Abducting is lateral opening.

Emotions which produce expansion in the body - great joy, exhilaration, exuberance - will make use of general extension with no awareness of how the different forms are being used in different parts of the body. Extension may occur for practical reasons such as in holding outstretched a roll of wallpaper, extending to cast a line when fishing, or in a predicament we hope never to encounter, Ex. 179a-c.

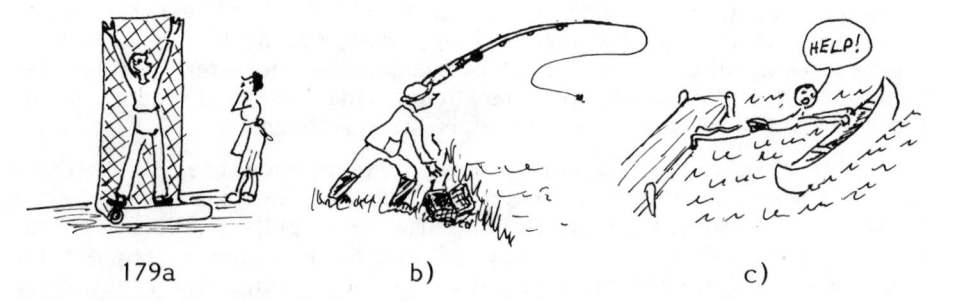

179a   b)   c)

By 'contracting' and 'elongating' we do not mean literally that the body itself shrinks and grows but that it makes use of (occupies) less or more space. The following technical exploration of what happens spatially when contraction and elongation occur will be followed by consideration of how these actions are used expressively.

CONTRACTION AND ELONGATION

Contraction means shortening, drawing nearer, and this shortening occurs on an established spatial line. Elongation means drawing out, lengthening on the established line. An inchworm provides a handy example. By bringing its back legs in, it contracts its length (shortens the distance between its extremities); then, to progress, the front legs move forward into the direction already established, travelling being accomplished by lengthening on the same spatial line.

Analysis of Contraction and Elongation

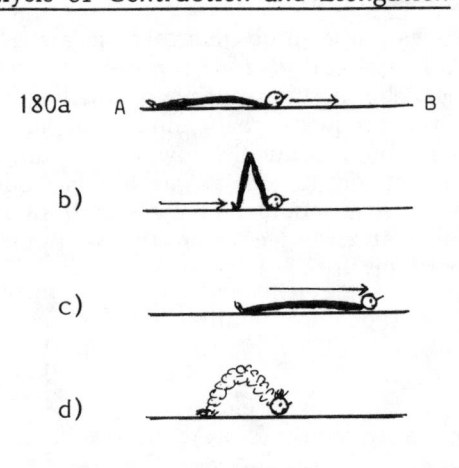

180a A   B

b)

c)

d)

The established direction, A-B is kept all the time. Here it is the direction forward horizontal. The line between the extremities does not change, even though the middle is displaced upward. The inchworm behaves as though it has only one center joint in its length, the result being similar to contraction of an arm or leg, each of which has only one center joint.

In contrast to the angle produced by the single hinge of the inchworm, a caterpillar, Ex. 180d, contracts with a rounded hump since it has a multi-jointed 'spine'. For us such rounded contractions occur in the torso and in the hand. The diagrams below illustrate the spatial result of such contractions. Ex. 180e shows the result for a limb with a single central joint; 180f the result for a multi-jointed part.

One central joint: Multi-jointed:

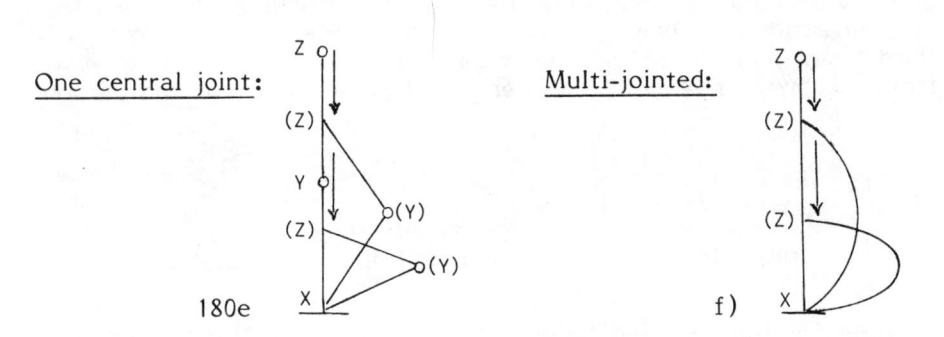

180e   f)

Note the following facts:

Path:	Straight path. The extremity of the body part, 'z', draws in toward the base 'x' on a straight line.
Line of Direction:	The extremity 'z' maintains the same directional relation with the base 'x'.
Displacement:	The center joint 'y' is displaced out of the original line of direction.
Involvement of Joints:	For the arms as a whole to contract there must be articulation in both shoulder and elbow joints (i.e. in 'x' and 'y').

215

Analysis of Contraction and Elongation (continued)

Elongation is the reverse process, the limb lengthening along the same line. Everyday examples of elongation and contraction include pushing and pulling a door or other object, contraction of the legs in a deep knee bend (a squat) and the subsequent rising and straightening. In sports the leg and arm actions which occur in rowing a scull, Ex. 180g, h), are basically contraction and elongation, as are the actions of lifting a weight with the legs while in a shoulder-elbow stand, 180i, j). The path of the movement in this last example is on the vertical line because of balance and the force of gravity.

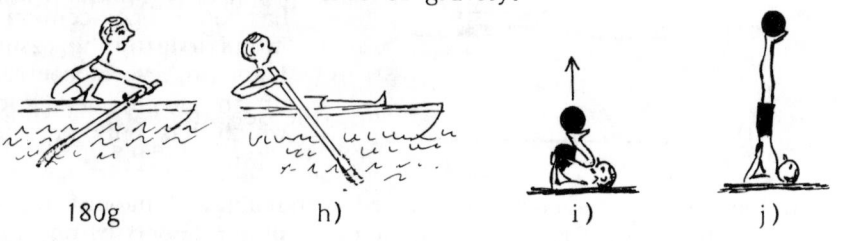

180g   h)   i)   j)

Specific Signs for Contraction

The general signs for flexion (any form of flexion) are: ✕ for a slight degree and ✳ for a greater degree. Without ∼ , the signs ✕, ✳ represent contraction, two-dimensional closing in along the longitudinal axis of the limb or torso, Ex. 181a,b. Shrinking, three-dimensional contraction, is shown by adding a horizontal line representing the third dimension, Ex. 181c,d. Only certain parts of the body (as distinct from the body-as-a-whole) can perform three-dimensional contraction.

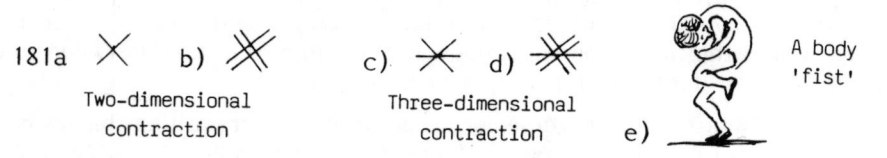

181a ✕   b) ✳   c) ✶ d) ✸   A body 'fist'

Two-dimensional   Three-dimensional
contraction   contraction   e)

Specific Signs for Elongation

The general signs for extension (any form of extension) are: ⊬ for a slight degree and ⊭ for a greater degree. Without ∼ the signs ⊬, ⊭ mean elongation, two-dimensional lengthening along the longitudinal axis of the limb or torso, Ex. 182a,b. Three-dimensional extension, expansion, is indicated by adding a horizontal line to represent the third dimension, Ex. 182c,d.

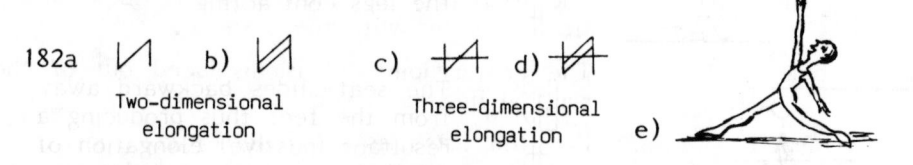

182a ⋈   b) ⋈   c) ⊬ d) ⊭

Two-dimensional   Three-dimensional
elongation   elongation   e)

Contraction, Elongation of the Legs

Bending the legs happens in a variety of circumstances and the form used and the basic direction involved are not always immediately evident. Therefore an exploration into many of the possibilities may be helpful. In the following examples the notation states the leg direction and state of contraction or elongation for each figure.

In a way similar to the inchworm moving forward or backward, we can 'inch' along while sitting on the floor by contracting and elongating the legs. The movements of Ex. 183a-c produce travelling forward.

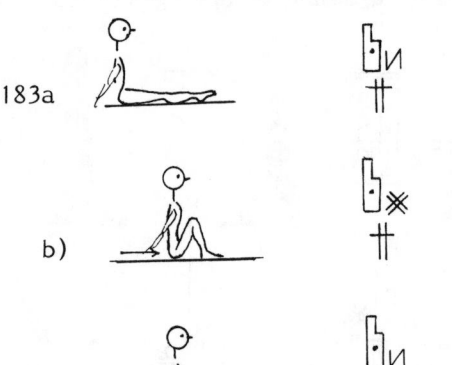

183a

Start sitting with the legs outstretched forward horizontal.

b)

Shift the seat forward by sliding toward the feet; as a result the legs become contracted. A dotted vertical line means a passive, resultant movement.

c)

The feet move away from the hips thus lengthening the legs which end extended forward.

The action of Ex. 183a-c) is the same as 180a-c); the basic direction for the legs has not changed. The legs contract as the hips move toward the feet; they then lengthen as the feet move away from the hips. By repeating this action the performer gradually inches forward along the floor. The fact that the knees 'bulge' out into another direction when the legs contract does not change the line between the extremities, the feet and hips; it is still forward.

In Ex. 184a-c) the reverse process produces travelling backward. The basic direction for the legs remains forward middle.

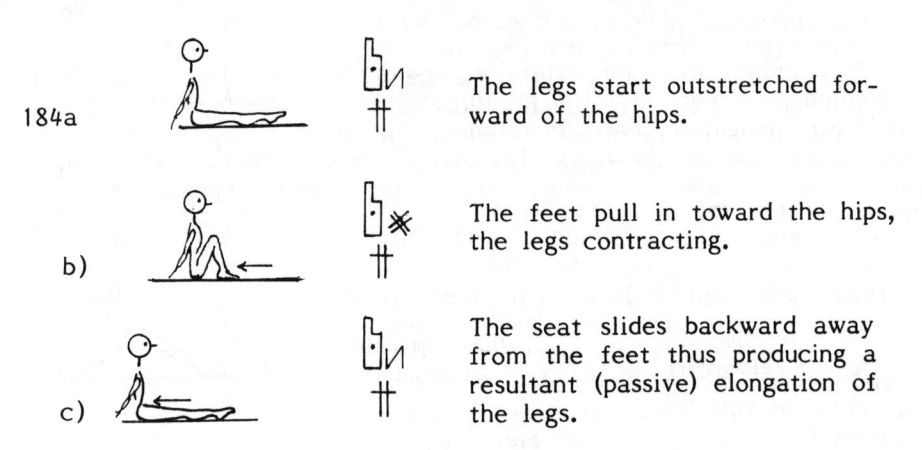

184a

The legs start outstretched forward of the hips.

b)

The feet pull in toward the hips, the legs contracting.

c)

The seat slides backward away from the feet thus producing a resultant (passive) elongation of the legs.

217

Contraction, Elongation of the Legs (continued)

A change in the rotational state of the legs produces a different look to the movement. In every leg contraction the center joint, the knee, must flex and therefore be displaced spatially. If the legs are parallel as they have been in both 183b and 184b, the knees will point toward the ceiling. If outward rotation is used the knees will point sideways, as in 184d. This difference in knee placement does not affect the basic direction established for the leg as a whole.

184d

185a

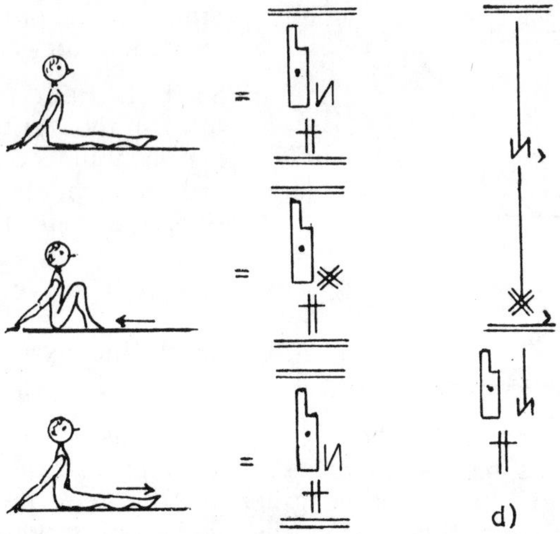

b)

c)

d)

Ex. 185 shows a familiar exercise in contracting and elongating the legs, the hips remaining where they are. Next to each figure illustration is written the position reached. Ex. 185d shows the exercise written as a movement sequence.

Let us now take a similar movement in the forward middle direction, but with one leg in the air while you are standing on the other. We get exactly the same spatial pattern, but without the floor under the limb to facilitate retention of the basic forward horizontal direction.

186a

The sequence of 186 is as follows: the leg starts forward middle of the hip. Leg contraction causes the knee to lift but the foot is still forward in line with the hip. Elongation straightens the leg; the knee returns to the forward middle line, i.e. in line with the foot and hip. If outward rotation is used this line between foot and hip is still retained.

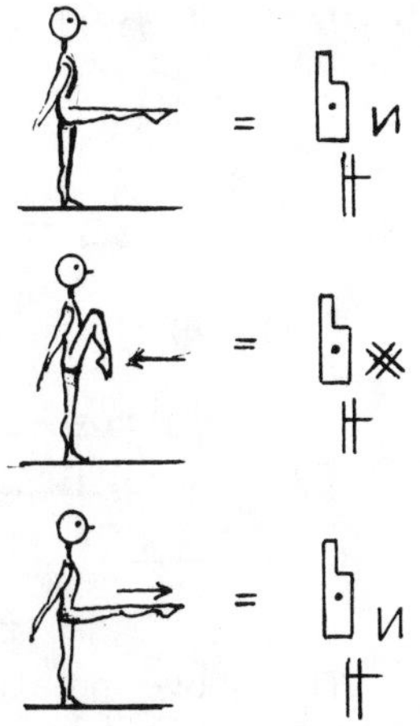

b)

c)

218

Now let us examine this same contraction - elongation movement when the leg is placed sideward horizontal.

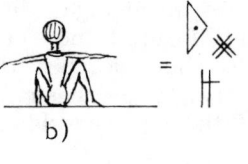

187a

Ex. 187: the right leg is side horizontal, resting on the floor.

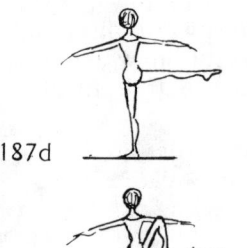

187d

b)

As the foot draws in to the hip, 187b, the leg contracts; the foot re- mains to the side of the hip.

e)

c)

The leg elongates in the side middle direction in- creasing the distance be- tween foot and hip, 187c.

f)

Ex. 187d-f illustrate exactly the same leg pattern performed with one leg in the air while the other is standing.

In certain barre exercises a similar basic action occurs but with the hip approaching the foot.

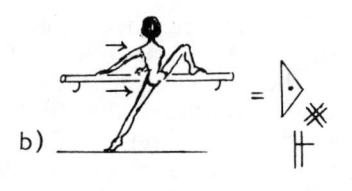

188a

The right leg is on the barre, the foot is side middle from the hip, Ex. 188a.

b)

The foot remains where it is, it does not move from the spot. As the leg contracts, the hips move toward the foot and the knee is displaced upward, Ex. 188b.

c)

As the leg extends, the hips return to where they started. The basic leg di- rection remains side middle, 188c.

The above notations describe just the main activity, not the total picture as would be spelled out in Structured Description.

Contraction, Elongation of the Legs (continued)

Next we explore contraction and elongation of the legs in the downward direction. A very good example occurs in *Petrouchka*, the ballet in which the dolls are supported by a bar under the armpits and so are free to move both legs without needing them as supports.

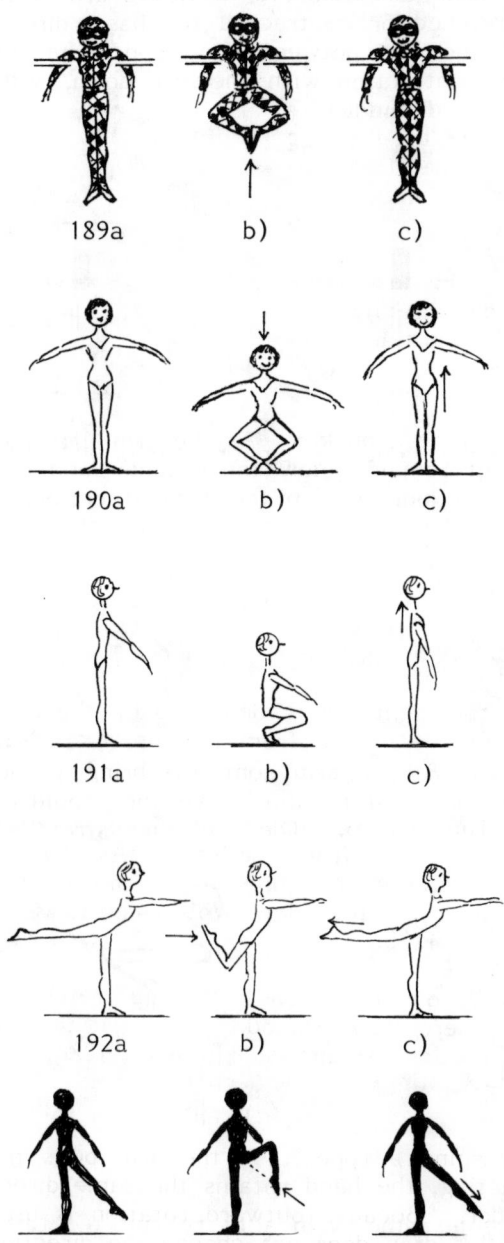

189a   b)   c)

190a   b)   c)

191a   b)   c)

192a   b)   c)

193a   b)   c)

The legs start straight down, under the hips. As the legs contract, the feet approach the hips on a straight line. As turn-out is used the knees displace to the side, but this does not change the basic direction of the leg as a whole.

This same basic action occurs in a deep knee bend (a grand plié) but because the feet are supporting, the leg contraction brings the hips toward the feet. Again, because outward leg rotation is used the knees open out to the sides as the legs contract.

Here the same knee bend is performed with parallel legs, resulting in the knees displacing forward as the legs contract.   Feet and hips keep the same spatial relationship as in 189 and 190; the look and the feel of the movements are different.

With legs parallel, the free leg is backward horizontal. As the leg contracts the knee drops down and the foot approaches the hip.   The line from hip to foot is still back middle. Outward rotation will bring the knee out toward the side, similar to an attitude.

Low or high level gestures follow the same logic, the line of direction between base and extremity is maintained. The right leg is shown contracting and elongating in the side low direction.

220

Flexion and Extension: Specific Forms

Contraction, Elongation of the Arms

The greater rotational scope for the arm and greater freedom in the shoulder joint provide a wider range of directional possibilities as well as variations in how contracted arm gestures look and feel. However, the same understanding of basic directions for a flexed arm still applies. Whether an arm is stretched or contracted the basic direction for the arm as a whole is the line between hand and shoulder. The following examples illustrate contraction with the arm down, with the arm up, and with the arm forward middle.

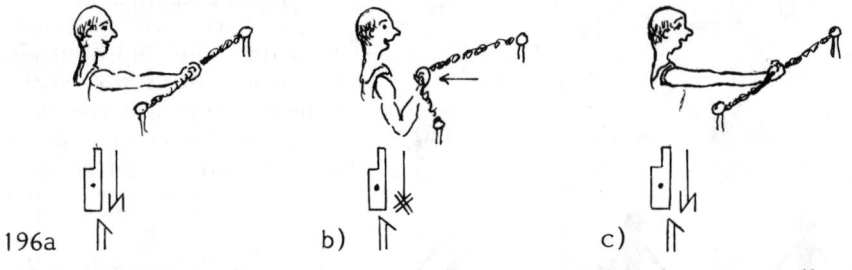

194a   b)   c)

The arm is down, the hand holding a bucket. As the arm lifts the bucket (contracts) hand and bucket remain below the shoulder and the elbow displaces backward. The arm lengthens in the same direction.

195a   b)   c)

The arm is up, holding a ball. As the arm contracts bringing the ball closer to the shoulder, hand and ball remain above the shoulder. The basic direction for the arm remains up. The arm then stretches into the same direction.

196a   b)   c)

The arm starts forward, grasping a rope. As the arm pulls the rope toward the body by contracting, the hand retains the same directional relationship to the shoulder. Because outward rotation is used the elbow drops downward, but this drop does not change the direction for the arm as a whole. The arm then extends on the same line.

221

Contraction, Elongation of the Arms (continued)

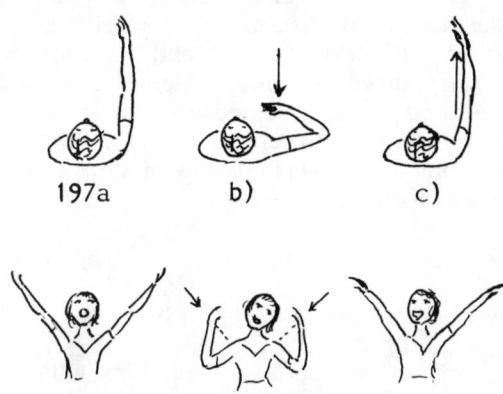

197a   b)   c)

Ex. 197 illustrates a contraction of the arm in the forward direction (seen bird's-eye view) in which the palm is facing to the left at the start. This rotational state results in the elbow being displaced to the side.

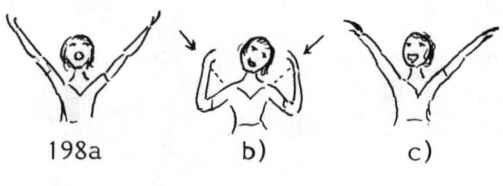

198a   b)   c)

Notice what happens when the arms are in an open side-high position palms facing upward. As the arms contract and the elbows drop the hands move in on a straight line toward the shoulders; the basic line of direction is retained, 198.

Contraction, Elongation of the Hands

Because the hand has additional joints, curves are usually produced rather than angles. Hand movements can be quite complex; we will deal only with a simple contraction and elongation here.

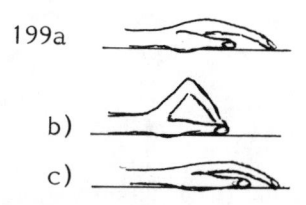

199a

b)

c)

The hand is forward, resting on a table. As the extremity (fingertips) draws in to the base (heel of the hand) the center joint (knuckles) is displaced upward from the original line. As the hand lengthens the fingertips travel on the same line and the knuckles return to that line.

Contraction, Elongation of the Torso

To investigate the action of the torso when it contracts, let us once more look at our friend the caterpillar. Once again we must remember that this is a general, basic movement of contracting, and not the highly stylized version central to the Graham technique.

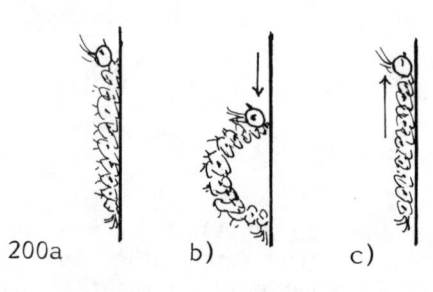

200a   b)   c)

This caterpillar is backing down, the head travelling downward through contraction of the body, i.e. the extremity is approaching the base. It then elongates, the head moving upward to return to the original situation. No matter how much it arches, the basic direction, the vertical line, remains the same.

In a torso contraction the free end (the shoulders) approaches the base (the hips) on the vertical line, Ex. 201a-c).

201a   b)   c)

When the torso contracts*, the free end (shoulders) approaches the base (hips) on a straight line, the shoulders remaining vertically over the hips. To accomplish this contraction the center part (waist) must 'bulge' outward, hunching backward as with the caterpillar. The pelvis (upper rim) changes its line of direction, tipping more and more backward as the contraction increases. In straightening (elongating), the free end lengthens upward, the bulge disappears and the waist returns to the vertical line maintained between the shoulders and hips.

It is important to note that for torso contractions we are concerned with the direction of the extremities of the torso - shoulder line to hip joints. The head is not considered part of the torso; it reacts passively in that it retains its relationship to the torso, continuing the curve established in the rest of the spine without making any special movement of its own.

The most natural contraction of the torso occurs over the front surface as in the examples above. It is possible, however, to contract over the back surface and also over the sides and the diagonals. In each of these contractions the pelvis tilts, that is, it changes its line of direction as did the upper arm in arm contractions.

Signs for Specific Contractions

When the symbol X is used for a body part it is generally understood that the contraction occurs over the inner, volar surface. For the torso this surface is over the front. For specific statement of the direction of a contraction, a short line is added to the contraction sign to indicate which surface (i.e. which direction) is involved.

202a   b)   c)   d)

* Note that the term 'contraction' is used here with its basic meaning and not for the highly specialized Graham 'contraction'.

223

Signs for Specific Contractions (continued)

Diagonal contractions can also be shown by combining two lines:

202e |X Over the right
          front surface   f) |X Over the right
                                          back surface   etc.
      (X plus |X)   (|X plus X)

Contractions of torso or limbs often occur in conjunction with a change of direction for that part. When this change happens, the new direction must be stated and this becomes the line of direction for the extremities.

Expressiveness of Contracting and Elongating

We have investigated the basic facts regarding specific forms of contraction and elongation, i.e. their practical, functional use; but what of their expressive use in dance?

Jabbing actions in jazz sequences express an 'out-in' thrusting penetration of the air around. These actions move in a spoke-like manner out from the center of the body and in again. The limbs shoot out piercing the space around. If the kinesphere were a huge bubble it would have burst as its 'skin' was reached. Expressively, the strength of such actions lies in their directness. The arms usually start with the hands near the shoulders to provide the greatest range in piercing space. The body often accompanies the gesture thus augmenting the reach, or it may 'set off' the movement by a simultaneous motion in the opposite direction. Though sharp, sudden movements are typical for this kind of action, the same patterns may take place with smooth gliding, with sustained pressure, or with an interrupted, jagged progression. Such details add to the expression, change the style, and enrich the basic activity of contraction and elongation.

203

224

CONTRACTION, ELONGATION

FOLDING AND UNFOLDING

What is folding?   The dictionary definition defines it as: "Putting one part of a thing over another, laying one section over another, bending into a fold."   Unfolding is, of course, the reverse process. Let us look at some typical examples from everyday life.

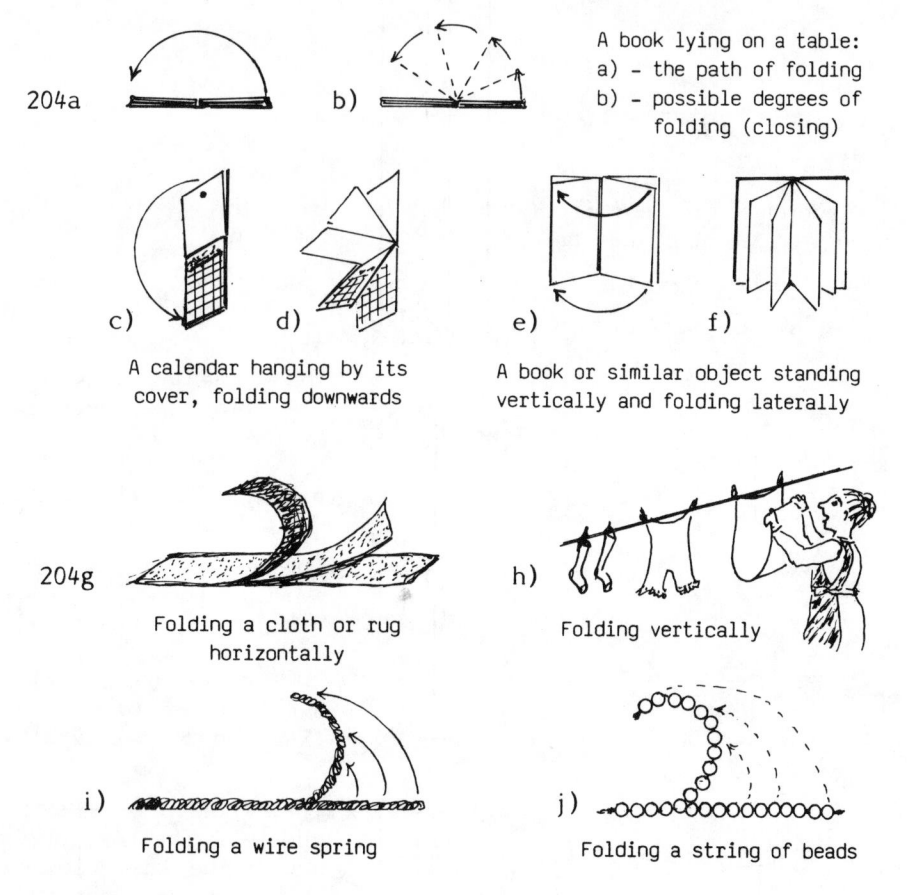

204a   b)

A book lying on a table:
a) - the path of folding
b) - possible degrees of
     folding (closing)

c)   d)   e)   f)

A calendar hanging by its
cover, folding downwards

A book or similar object standing
vertically and folding laterally

204g   h)

Folding a cloth or rug
horizontally

Folding vertically

i)   j)

Folding a wire spring

Folding a string of beads

Analysis of Folding

When an object is folded usually one part is moved and one part stays still.   The part which does not move retains the basic direction established for the object.   This is the 'base' toward which the free part moves.   In the case of a stiff object such as a book, there is only one joint, a hinge at the center.   The free end approaches the base on a curved path.   In Ex. 205a-c, A-B is the fixed part which does not move, and C is the extremity of the moving part, the free end.   Thus C approaches A on a curved path while B (the mid joint) folds.   In a many-jointed object - a wire spring or a string of beads - a curve is produced instead of an angle.   Ex. 205d-f illustrate the extremity C approaching the base A (the last fixed segment) in a many-jointed object.

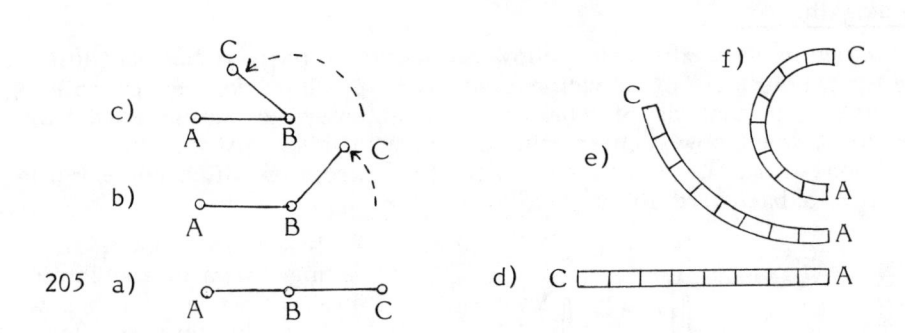

According to the part of the body involved, the words 'curving', 'curling' or 'arching' may be applicable to this action.

Folding the Leg

Let us look first at actions of the leg.

The basic direction for the whole leg is down. The lower leg, hinging at the knee joint, folds backward. There is no movement for the thigh.

206   a)   b)   c)   d)

The whole leg is forward. The lower leg folds at the knee moving closer to the base, i.e. the hip joint. Compare this example with 186a and b), page 218.

207   a)   b)   c)

The whole leg is side middle. The leg folding at the knee causes the foot to approach the supporting leg on a curved path.

208   a)   b)   c)

Folding the Ankle

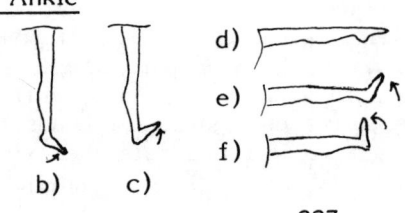

209a   b)   c)

d)
e)
f)

The action of folding the ankle brings the extremity of the foot, the toes, closer to the lower leg. The toes describe a circular path in the air.

Folding the Arm

Examples for the arm follow an identical pattern but, because of the greater range of movement and the possible degrees of rotating and twisting, analysis of what is occurring may not be so easy. Like the knee, the elbow (center joint of the arm) can only fold in one physical direction, i.e. 'forward', with the exception of hyper-extension which is a backward folding, i.e. 'over the back'.

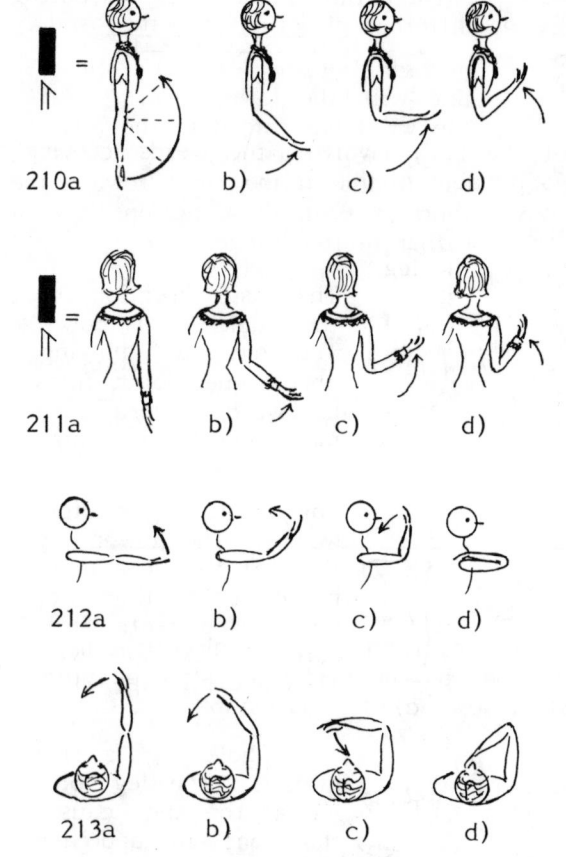

With the arm down, palm facing forward, the lower arm hinges at the elbow and folds forward until the hand is close to the shoulder. The upper arm remains down. The hand describes a semi-circle in the air.

210a   b)   c)   d)

Here the same physical action occurs as in 210, but outward rotation of the arm causes the lower arm to be carried out to the side.

211a   b)   c)   d)

With the whole arm forward at the start, palm facing up, the folding action in the elbow brings the hand on a circular path toward the shoulder.

212a   b)   c)   d)

The arm starts forward, palm facing side (bird's-eye view). Folding the elbow produces a spatial displacement which is different from Ex. 212, but within the arm the action is the same.

213a   b)   c)   d)

As can be seen from Exs. 210-213, the spatial result of a folding action, i.e. where the moving part goes, depends on the rotational state of the limb.

Folding the Wrist

A folding action of the wrist displaces the hand spatially. Unlike the knees and elbow, the wrist has a greater range of flexion, being able to fold forward and backward as well as slightly sideward and diagonally. When the wrist folds, the lower arm, its 'base', does not change direction. The degree of wrist folding varies among performers. Asian dancers train to develop as great a range as possible.

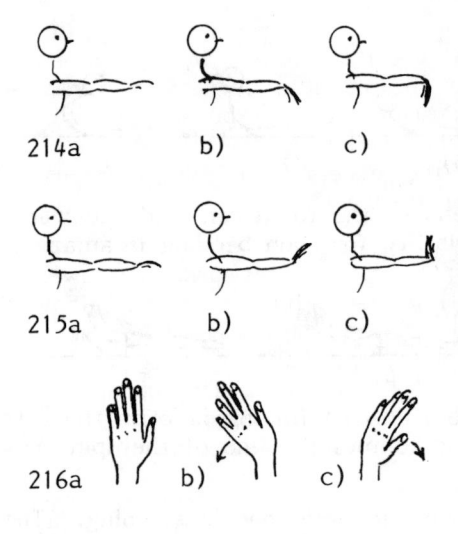

With the arm forward, palm down, a forward wrist folding causes the hand to drop toward the floor, Ex. 214a-c. A backward wrist folding, Ex. 215a-c, brings the hand up to the ceiling. These same physical actions may occur in many different spatial placements producing different directions for the hand.

In Ex. 216a the left hand starts in line with the lower arm. In 216b the wrist has folded to the left toward the little finger; in 216c it has folded to the right toward the thumb. Both these actions have a rather limited range.

Folding the Torso

The torso and hand, being multi-jointed parts, form a curve when folded. The base, no matter how small, still retains the previously established direction. A curving, folding action of the torso occurs naturally from a supine position.

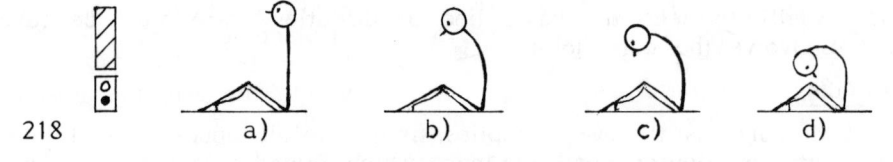

217   a)   b)   c)

In lifting from the ground the free end of the torso folds forward. The hips (line of the pelvis) keep the original line of direction, in this case backward horizontal. As soon as the performer sits up and the line of the pelvis has changed, a new diréction is established, 217c.

218   a)   b)   c)   d)

Folding the torso from a vertical sitting position is exactly the same as in Ex. 217; but here one does not have to battle with gravity, hence it is usually easier to achieve a greater degree. The amount possible will vary according to flexibility in the spine. It is important, however, that the base, the pelvic line, does not change direction, that is, unless a change of direction is stated.

The flexibility of the spine allows the torso to fold over different surfaces, i.e. over the front, the right side, the back, the left side and also the diagonal surfaces between. We will deal with only the simpler examples here.

229

Folding the Torso (continued)

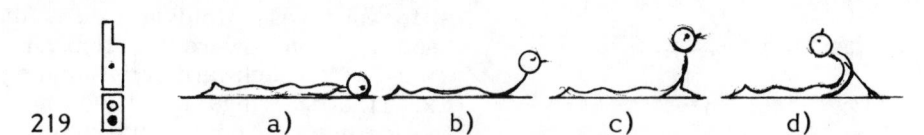

219   a)   b)   c)   d)

If one is lying prone, the free end of the torso can fold backward. In some acrobats the degree of flexibility for such bending is amazing.

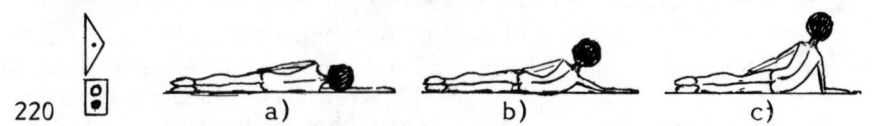

220   a)   b)   c)

When one is lying on the right side sideward folding is over the left side of the body. Note that the head follows the line of the spine unless another direction is stated for it.

These same physical actions can occur while one is standing. The movement (physical change) is the same, but it looks and feels different because of the different relation to the line of gravity and the different 'picture' produced.

Folding the Hand

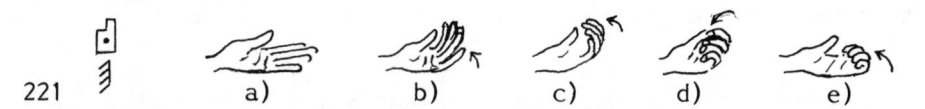

221   a)   b)   c)   d)   e)

The hand is resting on a surface, palm up. The fingers fold toward the base of the hand ending near the center of the palm. The base of the hand, the metacarpals, does not move. This same action can happen for the fingers only, the palm being unaffected, as in 221e. Folding the hand in the upright situation (or indeed in any direction) is the same as Ex. 221a-d. If there is no flat surface to help physically and visually to keep the basic line of direction, care must be taken not to involve the wrist joint.

Unfolding

Unfolding, as the word implies, is the exact opposite of folding; the joint(s) straighten until the part which folded is again in its normal alignment with its base. Exs. 206-221 need only to be read in reverse to see unfolding take place until the unfolded state is reached.

Signs for Folding, Unfolding

The signs for folding are derived from the sign for contracting. In a contraction two joints are affected (marked 'a' and 'b' in Ex. 222) and two segments of the body (marked 1 and 2) are spatially displaced. In folding only one joint (b) moves and only one part (marked 1) is displaced. Note that this analysis is for parts with one central joint; the sign is used also for multi-jointed parts.

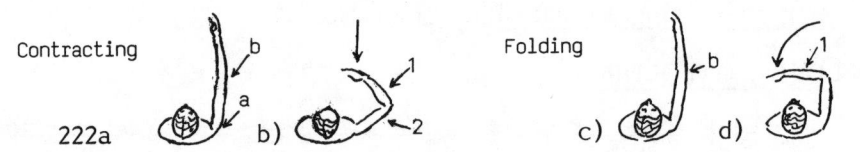

Contracting   b

222a   b)   1   2   Folding   b   c)   d)

The sign for folding is, therefore, half of the sign for contracting. Half of $X = \diagdown$. A greater degree is shown by $\diagdown$.

By selecting the manner of dividing the X sign in half, we indicate the physical direction of the movement, i.e. toward which surface the folding occurs: front = volar or ventral surface; back = dorsal surface.

223a $\diagdown$ b) $\diagup$ c) K d) $\diagdown$

Over the front   Over the back   Over the right   Over the left
(volar, ventral)   (dorsal)   (right side)   (left side)

The sign is turned to indicate
the diagonal possibilities: e) $\diagdown$ f) $\diagup$ g) $\diagup$ h) $\diagdown$

The sign for unfolding is the reverse of folding: Λ. Only one degree of unfolding is used* since the action is understood to mean a return to the normal alignment of the limb in the established direction. The unfolding sign is used for each of the possible directions of folding.

EXPRESSIVENESS OF FOLDING, UNFOLDING

In contrast to the directness of contraction and elongation, folding and unfolding seek to encompass or enclose the space around. A large circular movement of the arm may conclude with a folding in the elbow and perhaps also in the head. This movement will often be followed by an unfolding which develops into a sweeping circular gesture around the body. Many of Isadora Duncan's gestures were of this type. By varying the space patterns and the rotations used, 'rich', 'generous' movement can result. The outer reaches of the dancer's space are not 'punctured' but are stroked, caressed or swept along into curved arcs. The curved nature of the gestures allows for softness and gracefulness. Flowing spatial patterns are much augmented by use of scarves and draperies. In certain Asian dances a folding and unfolding action of hand and wrist is augmented spatially by manipulation of a long sleeve, as in Japanese dances, or light silk scarves hanging from the waist as in Javanese dances.

224
    a)   b)   c)   d)

* The additional signs given in the 1970 Labanotation textbook have been found to be generally unnecesary.

Reading Study No. 39

FOLDING, UNFOLDING

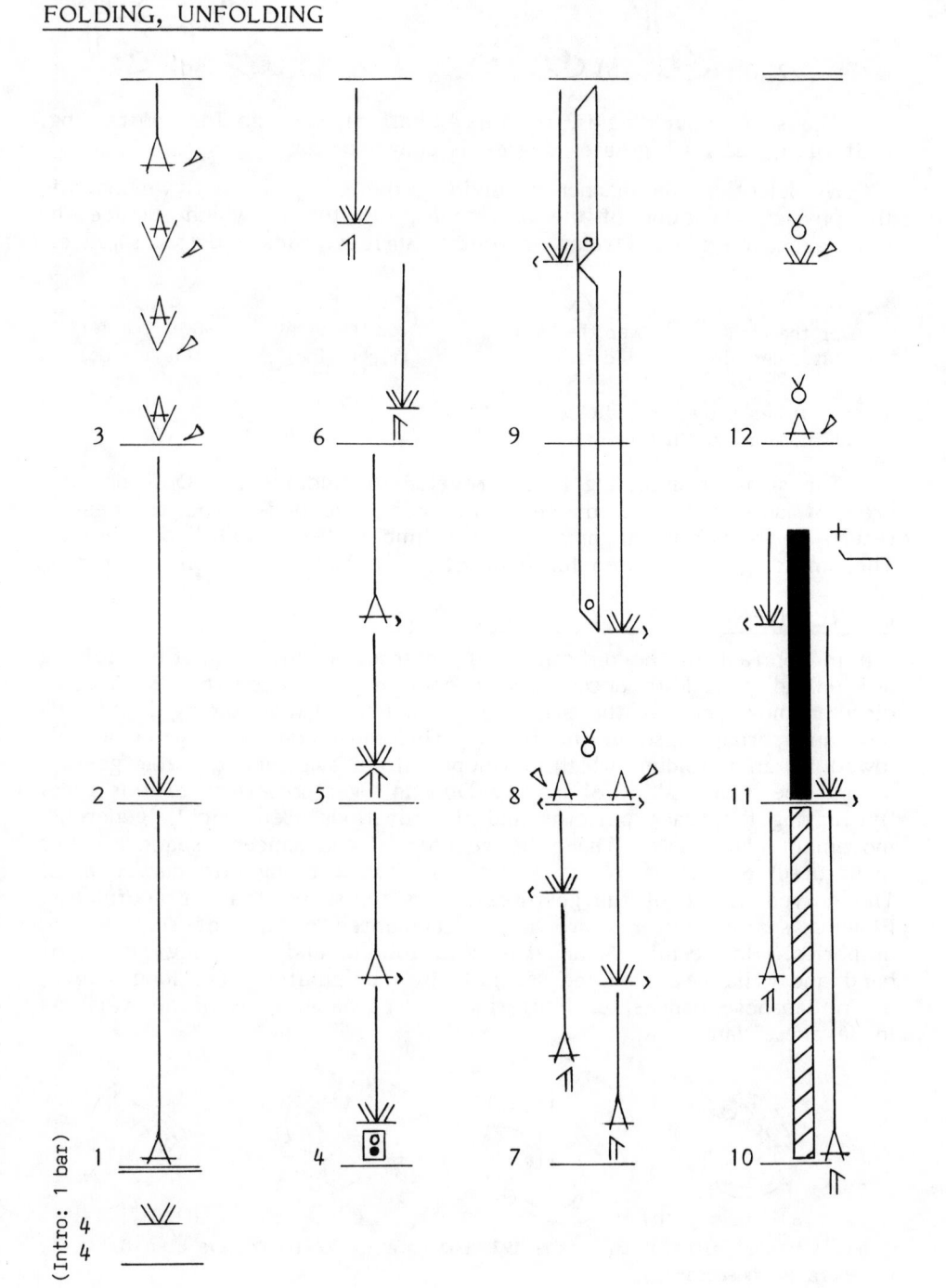

(Intro: 1 bar)

FLEXION, EXTENSION: MIXED FORMS

A contracting action may be followed by unfolding and a folding action may be followed by elongation. Is such a mixture common? What happens spatially? Let us take a simple example in which the arm begins forward middle. These illustrations are seen in a bird's-eye view.

225a   b)   c)

The action of contracting brings the hand closer to the shoulder and displaces the upper arm sideward, 225b. In unfolding, the lower arm moves out into the direction established by the new placement of the upper arm, 225c.

226a   b)   c)

In Ex. 226 the arm starts side middle. The lower arm folds in, 226b. The directional relationship established between the hand and shoulder dictates the line into which the limb elongates, 226c.

Such switching from one form to another may seem strange, but in fact it is not uncommon, particularly where exactness in spatial placement is not important and actions of flexion and extension are. A good example involving the torso occurs in modern dance exercises where the line within the torso is more important than the spatial direction achieved. Here is one version of such a torso exercise.

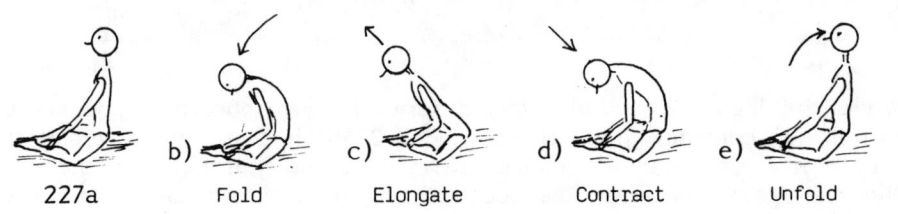

227a   b)   c)   d)   e)

      Fold   Elongate   Contract   Unfold

The torso starts vertically up, elongated. It then folds over forward as much as possible, 227b. The degree of such folding varies according to the build and flexibility of the performer. The torso then elongates lengthening along the line established between the shoulders and hips, 227c. There follows a contraction along this new line, 227d. Finally the torso unfolds to the line established by the base, the pelvis, returning to an upright sitting position, 227e.

J

Flexion, Extension: Mixed Forms (continued)

A series of foldings followed by elongation will gradually completely change the spatial placement of a limb.   The same is true of a series of contractions followed by unfolding; there will be a constant
change in spatial placement of the limb or torso.   The build of the
body imposes limitations on such sequences, unless the degrees are
small.   For spatial precision exact degrees for contraction and folding
would need to be known.   The full scale is not being investigated here.

Développé, Enveloppé

The movements of développé and enveloppé are familiar in ballet,
contemporary dance, jazz, etc., and are usually part of basic western
dance training; yet one must stop to think to realize how differently
the leg functions in doing these movements according to which direction is used - forward, sideward or backward, and whether the leg is
turned out or parallel.   It will be found that sometimes a développé
uses elongation, sometimes unfolding.   Similarly sometimes an enveloppé uses contraction and sometimes folding.   Let us investigate to be
sure this difference is clear.

228a   b)   c)   d)   e)

Ex. 228 illustrates développé and enveloppé in the forward direction
with the legs parallel.   The leg contracts, 228b, before unfolding, 228c.
It then folds, 228d, and then elongates, retracing its path, 228e.   This
same sequence occurs when the leg is turned out and moving to the
side (a sideward développé and enveloppé).

229a   b)   c)   d)   e)

When the leg is turned out and a forward développé-enveloppé occurs,
the initial contraction of the leg, Ex. 229b, is followed by elongation
into a new direction - forward, 229c.   At the start of the enveloppé
the leg again contracts, the foot coming in as close as it can to the
hip, thus causing the knee to move to the side, 229d.   The end of the
enveloppé uses elongation to return to the starting position, 229e.
This same pattern occurs in the backward direction when the legs are
turned out, and also in the sideward direction when the legs are parallel.   A parallel backward développé-enveloppé entails contraction, then
elongation into a completely different direction (the thigh must move
180°).   The thigh is brought forward again on the next contraction and
finally elongation takes place for a return to the starting position.

JOINING, SEPARATING

The third form of flexion and extension is 'joining' (closing in, ad-hering) and 'separating' (opening out, spreading). In anatomical terms these are comparable to adduction and abduction. In group arrange-ments joining and separating are actions which are familiar, as they are even with only two performers. How does one person make use of this form? Essentially it concerns the limbs in relation to each other or to the torso; in the case of the hand it is the relationship of the fingers one to another.

230

In a jump the legs may start apart, then join in the air, separate, and join again before landing feet apart, as illustrated in Ex. 230.

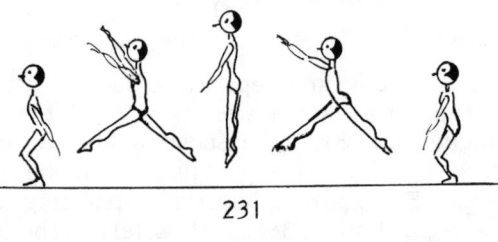

231

Such separating and join-ing can also happen in the sagittal plane, as in 231 where the legs start together, separate and join again in the air, then separate once more before landing feet to-gether again.

Many such possibilities exist for the legs while one is lying or per-forming a shoulder or head stand, not to mention in such special situa-tions as swimming, diving, parachuting, suspending from aerial wires or a high spring from a trampoline - each of which provides opportunity for the legs to move freely without being concerned with weight bear-ing.

The arms can similarly abduct, that is, separate from the torso, and adduct, join it again. In Ex. 232 the right arm abducts, then as it adducts, the left arm abducts. In such actions the degrees of separa-tion and subsequently joining may not be important and the destination of abducting may not matter (the spatial placement).

232   233   234

The arms may join or separate from each other, as in Ex. 233, in which the lower arms join and separate, or as in 234 where they join and separate overhead.

Joining, Separating (continued)

Arms may hug the body or the legs, as in Ex. 235a in which a 1920s flapper reacts to a mouse. The limbs may also cross the body or each other — a greater degree of joining (adducting). Ex. 235b shows a shy simpleton. Note that many of the result-ing positions could be described as direc-tional placement for the limbs, but such

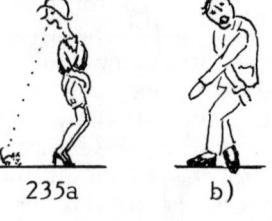

235a   b)

placement is not important and the destination may be indefinite. Em-phasis is on closeness or distance of the limbs to or from each other or the torso.

Signs for Joining, Separating

The indication for joining (closing) and separating (spreading) are pictorial in that they suggest a base with two 'wings' which close and open.

Lateral plane: 236a Join   b) Separate   Sagittal plane: c) Join   d) Separate

These signs indicate two-sided joining and separating such as usual-ly happens with the fingers. If a one-sided action is wanted the ap-propriate side of the sign is thickened. Ex. 236e shows a lateral sepa-rating to the right; in this case the lateral separating would be per-formed by the right arm or leg. Ex. 236f, a sagittal separating for-ward, would be performed by a right limb, 236g with a left. The sign for 'either side' would be used if choice of side is to be left open.

236e   f)   g)   h)   i)   j)   k)   l)

When use of both legs or both arms is stated, as in 236h and 236i double-sided actions will result. If only one limb is stated, 236j and 236k, thickening one side of the symbol is not necessary as only one direction for closing or separating exists. In 236l the left arm and right leg are shown to spread (separate) sagittally. What is not stated here is which limb moves forward, which backward; this is left open to choice. A specific statement can be made by use of an indication such as 236f or 236g for each limb.

Terminology

The terms 'opening' and 'closing' are in common use and can as well be applied to three-dimensional contraction and extension, to fold-ing and unfolding and also to gathering and scattering. For spreading (separating) and joining of the legs, as in Ex. 230, many people would just say 'open' and 'close' the legs. But separating and joining indi-cate an awareness of the other part, a relationship different from gen-eral opening and closing.

236

JOINING, SEPARATING

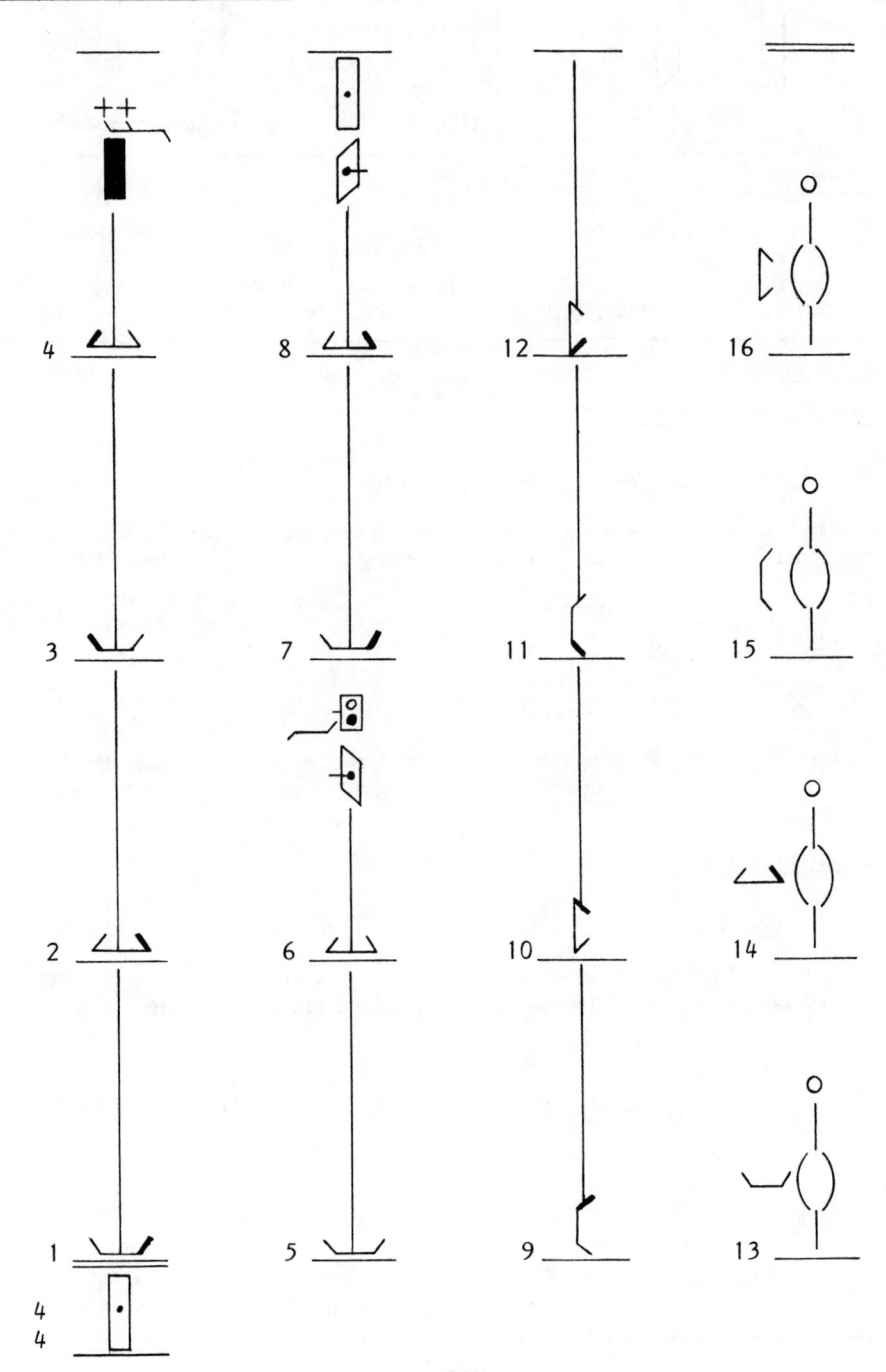

REVIEW FOR CHAPTERS FIFTEEN AND SIXTEEN

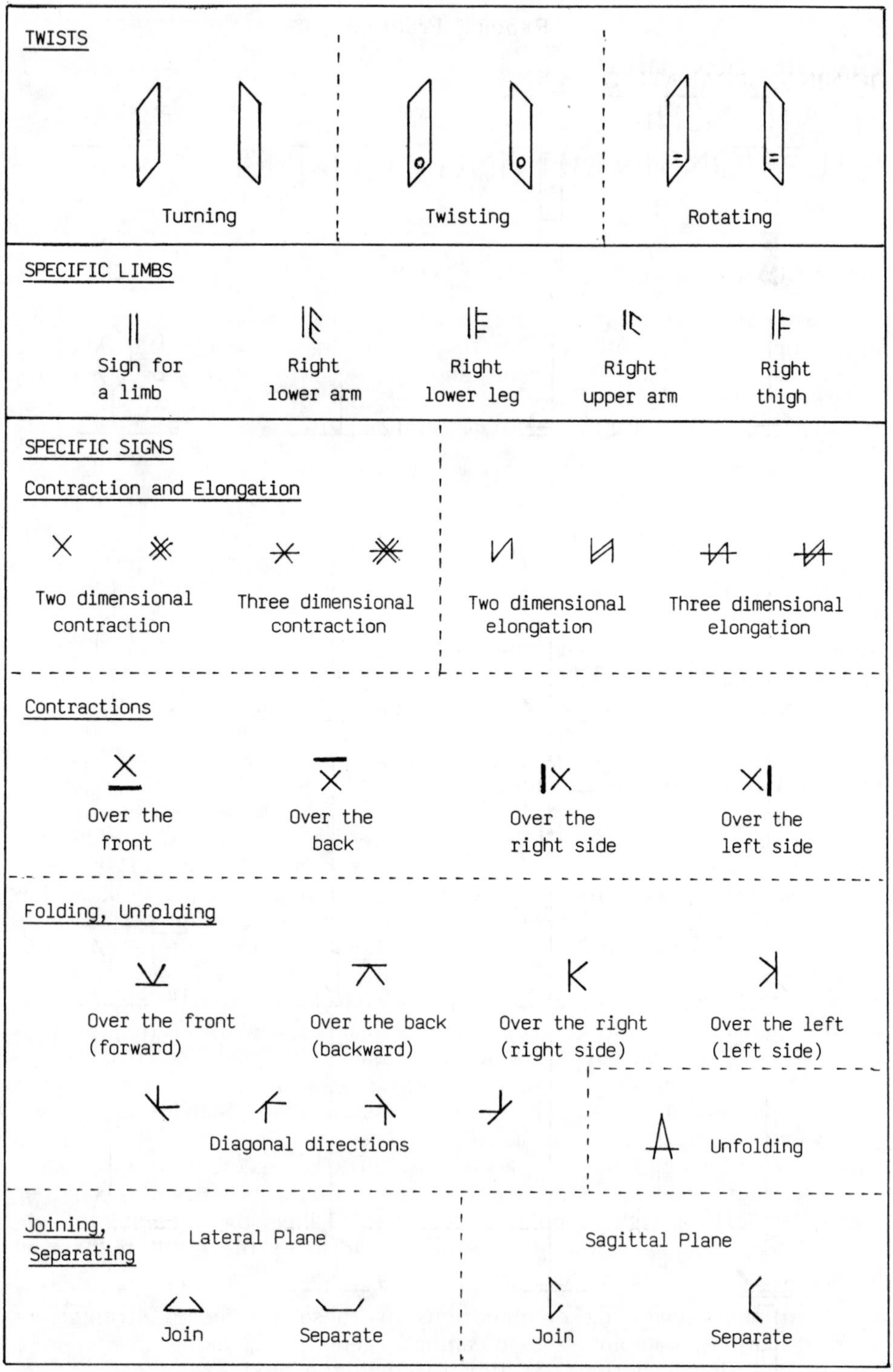

TWISTS

Turning	Twisting	Rotating

SPECIFIC LIMBS

Sign for a limb	Right lower arm	Right lower leg	Right upper arm	Right thigh

SPECIFIC SIGNS

Contraction and Elongation

Two dimensional contraction	Three dimensional contraction	Two dimensional elongation	Three dimensional elongation

Contractions

Over the front	Over the back	Over the right side	Over the left side

Folding, Unfolding

Over the front (forward)	Over the back (backward)	Over the right (right side)	Over the left (left side)

Diagonal directions

Unfolding

Joining, Separating

Lateral Plane		Sagittal Plane	
Join	Separate	Join	Separate

238

Chapter Seventeen
RELATIONSHIP:
SITUATIONS IN MEETING; LOOKING

SITUATIONS IN MEETING

Exploration of relationship must also include how two people stand in relation to one another. In everyday life when two people meet we expect that they will face one another; when walking together they will usually be side by side, and so on. Let us investigate such relationships and the possible meanings each might have.

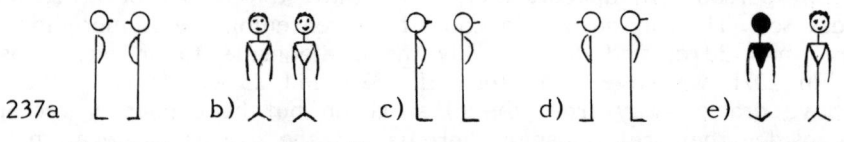

In Ex. 237a two people face one another. They may be deep in conversation as close friends or they may be confronting one another in a head-on dispute. The placement of 237a commonly suggests an equal status, as does 237b in which two people are side by side, a relationship expressing equality or a belonging together, a sharing, a mutual stance in facing the world. Generally speaking it makes no difference on which side each stands, although man and woman relationship in folk dances have traditionally placed the man on the woman's left. Placement one behind the other as in 237c expresses an unequal relationship. It may be a follow-the-leader situation in which the one in front knows the way and therefore is the dominant one. The one in front may be ignoring the other or may be acting as a protector. The one behind may be in a weaker, subservient position, being perhaps less sure, less knowledgeable. However, there is a mutual interest in that they are both facing and perhaps travelling in the same direction. In 237d the back-to-back situation suggests differences of outlook, of non-sharing, possibly of mutual rejection, a dispute, or of mutual protection: keeping a look-out in both directions. In 237e the two people are side by side but facing in opposite directions. This situation has a sense of transience, of a moment in passing, rather than of a relationship which might last for some time. There is no real sense of sharing; they might be two people passing in the street, having a quick word without changing the direction they intend to travel. Whether they pass left or right shoulders does not change the meaning of the relationship, though certain dances have a 'rule of the road' to pass on the right.

Placements involving combinations of these five main straightforward situations combine the meanings, generally making them more casual, less clearly defined, as illustrated in the next examples.

Situations in Meeting (continued)

 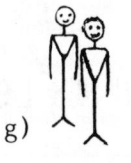 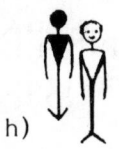

237f   g)   h)

Ex. 237f shows two people facing one another but on a diagonal line, a mixture of 237a and 237e. Such a relationship occurs often at a social gathering where one may wish to converse but also to be open to others and hence able to move away. It may suggest two people assessing each other, perhaps cautiously, leaving the path open to move away if need be. In 237g both are facing the same way, but one is diagonally behind the other. The relationship is unequal, as in 237c, the front person still appears more important, the leader or protector, but less so. The person behind could be threatening; he is more in the picture than 237c, and could easily move alongside to an equal position. In 237h we have a mixture of 237d and 237e. It is as though they have drawn away from the e) situation but have paused, perhaps to reconsider their relationship; there is not the degree of negation inherent in 237d. In each of 237f, g) and h) the positioning could be on the other side with no change in meaning. A summary of these relationships is given below using the standard floor plan pins for people: ○ = girl, ● = boy. The examples here illustrate one sex only to avoid any male-female connotations. Note: 'equal' means equal status.

237 i)	j)	k)	l)	m)	n)	o)	p)
Mutual interest or hostility (equal)	Sharing (equal status)	Dominating or disregarding	Rejection or mutual protection (equal)	Transitory, brief pause (equal)	Assessing (equal status)	Aiding, protecting (to lesser degree)	Reconsidering, withdrawing (equal)

In partner work, if the girl is in front of the boy, she may be in any of eight clear relationships to him, as illustrated below.

237 q)	r)	s)	t)	u)	v)	w)	x)

Note that in Ex. 237i and j), l) and m), n) and p) the two people have the same relationship to one another.

Such relationships also occur between a performer and an object. The dramatic or humorous possibilities may be explored. A story line can be developed, other movements being added to provide color and meaning, or changes may be based on design, developing shapes.

Indication of Situations in Meeting

To understand how these situations are written, imagine yourself inside a black-edged box, the front of the box being where you are facing, i.e. your front, Ex. 238a. The edges (the black lines), 238b, are used individually to represent you, the performer. In the illustrations below, your partner, P, is represented by a faceless circle since where P is facing may vary. P may be turning and yet still remain in front of you.

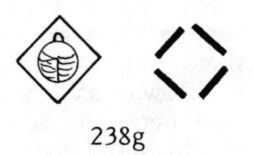

238a   b)

238   c) $\bigcirc$ = P   d) = |P   e) = P̄   f) = P|

In 238c your partner is in front of you; in 238d P is on your right. Ex. 238e shows P to be behind you, while in 238f P is on your left. A separate statement is needed to indicate where P is facing.

The diagonal situations are indicated in a similar way; the box has now become a black-edged diamond, 238g, and the slanting lines represent you, the performer. In Ex. 238h P is on the diagonal line in front and to your right, while in 238i P is diagonally behind and to your right. In 238j and k) the left front diagonal placement and the left back diagonal placement are illustrated.

238g

238   h) = \P   i) = /P   j) = P/   k) = P\

Indication of your partner's relationship to you as well as your relationship to him (his point of view) gives the total picture of where each of you is situated in relation to the other. The meeting lines, as they are called, give no information as to where in the room you are placed, nor do they give the room direction faced. You may turn and yet, while turning, you may be keeping the same relationship to your partner. Because of the many different possibilities these indications are kept separate.

Ex. 238l states travelling for performers A and B with the destination that each ends with the other on the right side. As no other information is given we do not know where they started, whether each travelled with forward steps, etc. We only know what their destination must be in relation to each other. Therefore the room direction faced could be any of the possibilities given on the next page.

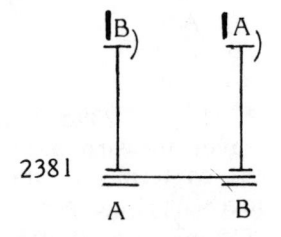

238l

A   B

Indication of Situations in Meeting (continued)

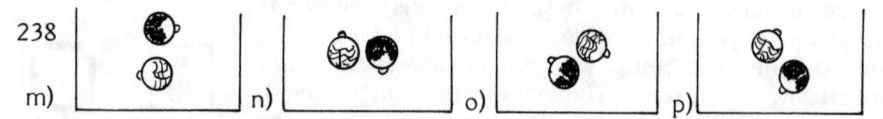

238
m)   n)   o)   p)

Variations in room orientation for partners on the right

Paths Crossing

The meeting line is also used to show on which side people pass one another when crossing. In Ex. 239a two lines called A and B trav-el sideward across the stage, line A passing in front of line B. This is illustrated in the floor plan of 239b. The stage traffic rule established long ago in Russia is for people on stage left to pass in front of those on stage right. This rule is shown on the floor plan here and also next to the path sign at the moment of passing.

239
a)

A   B

Stage left   Stage right

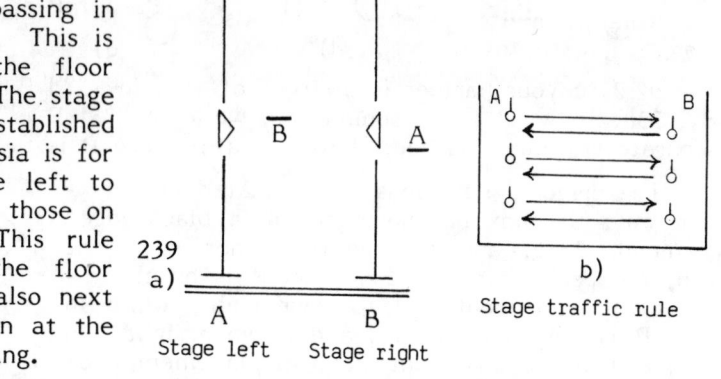

b)

Stage traffic rule

Many instances of passing occur in folk dancing. In the following examples the directions faced at the start are given and also the di-rection of travelling, but other performance details are left out. In each example A starts stage left, B (the boy) stage right.

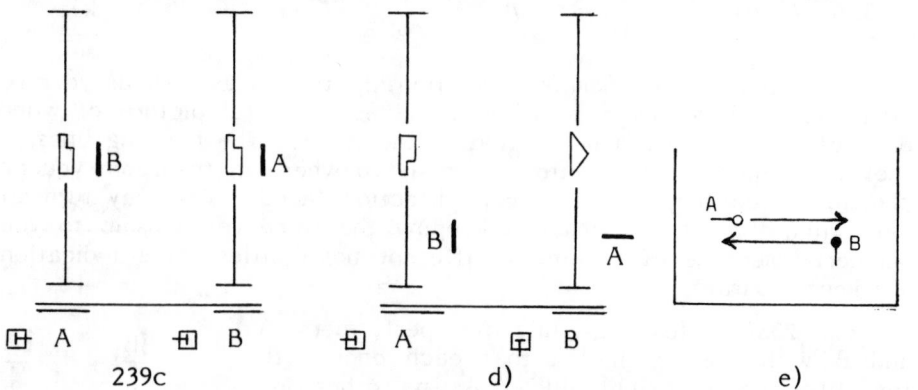

A   B

239c

B   A

d)

A   B

e)

In Ex. 239c B starts facing stage left, A facing stage right. They travel forward passing right shoulders. Ex. 239d shows an asymmetri-cal pattern. A starts facing stage left and travels backward while B faces upstage and travels to his right. A has B on her left as they pass whereas B has A behind him at that moment. Note indication of this on the floor plan, 239e.

When paths literally cross, the arrow on the floor plan is broken for the person who passes behind. In Ex. 239f the boys pass behind the girls as each group travels diagonally across the stage.

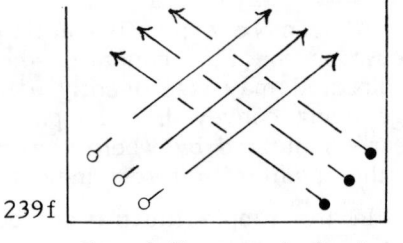

239f

Stage left passes in front

Relating to an Object

Relationship to an object may also need to be indicated. A path may end close to an object or a performer may pass an object or relate to it while travelling. In these examples a chair is the object and floor plans are provided to illustrate one possible interpretation.

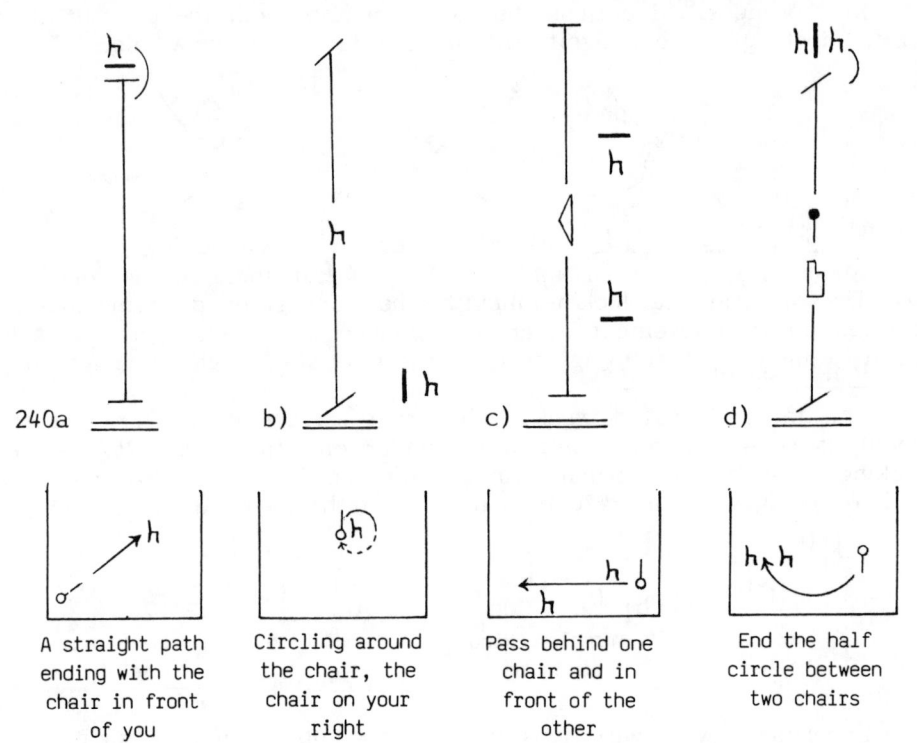

| A straight path ending with the chair in front of you | Circling around the chair, the chair on your right | Pass behind one chair and in front of the other | End the half circle between two chairs |

In many folk and national dances couples weave in and out and exchange places. Usually passing right shoulders is the established rule but in less traditional dances many variations are possible and with any large group it may be important to know who is passing whom at any given moment. The meeting line provides such information in a simple, practical way.

243

LOOKING

What more expressive action is there than looking? A change of focus for the face can alter the meaning of an action. Where a look is directed may significantly affect the expression and hence the message being conveyed. The point of interest in a movement is usually clearly indicated by where the performer looks; however, there may be another point of interest indicated by another part of the body.

In the simple illustrations below only the head is changed (the direction into which the walker is looking).

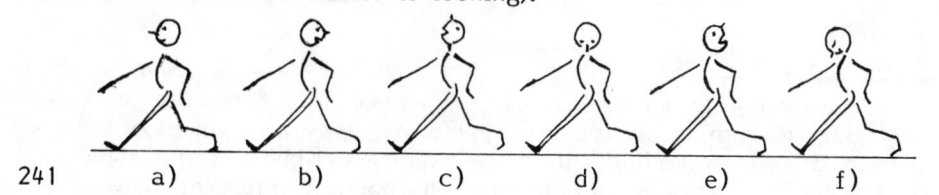

241   a)   b)   c)   d)   e)   f)

In choreographed actions the focus for the face, the concentration of the looking, is very significant in its relation to the whole.

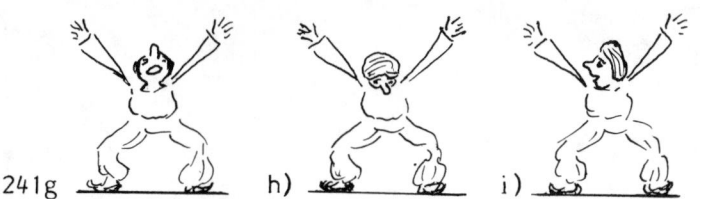

241g   h)   i)

The direction of looking may be harmonious or disharmonious to the rest of the movement.

Indication of Looking

The face, indicated by ⌷ (the front surface of the area of the head), is shown as addressing a particular direction. Ex. 242b states looking forward, the normal situation for the face. In 242c the face is looking up, while in 242d it is looking to the right.

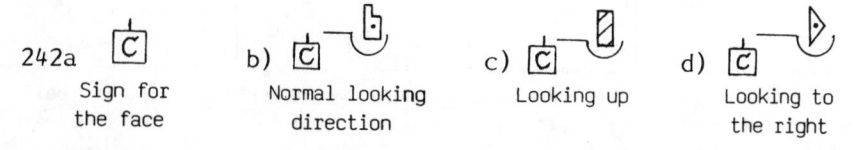

242a   b)   c)   d)

Sign for   Normal looking   Looking up   Looking to
the face   direction   the right

Experiment with variations in looking combined with a simple action. Sense the different feeling and observe the different resulting expression when others improvise on this aspect of movement. Travel in different directions with changes in facial focus. Compare the resulting different expressions when the following movement examples are performed: lowering (sinking) while looking down; lowering while looking up; lowering while looking sideward. Changes of focus while rising will also give very different results to a simple basic action.

Indication of Looking (continued)

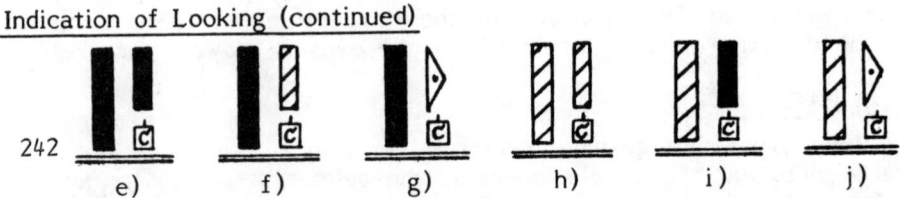

242

| e) | f) | g) | h) | i) | j) |

Note that in the above the 'spelling' has been simplified in that the action of addressing is understood when a direction symbol is written following the sign for the face.

Independent Action for the Eyes; Gazing

We have spoken of looking with the face, the front surface of the head; of course it is the eyes which do the actual looking, the focussing on a person or object. But the eyes can move and focus on a direction, person or object other than that toward which the face is directed. Given the choice we turn the head so that the eyes are in their normal alignment in the face (or nearly so). To distinguish between an ordinary 'face looking' and an independent eye action we use the term 'gazing' for looking involving only the eyes. Observe the differences between the following illustrations.

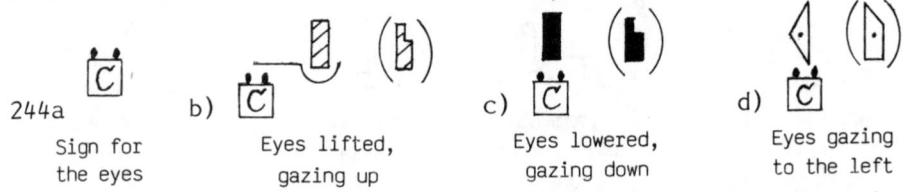

243

| a) | b) | c) | d) | e) | f) |
| Eyes look up | Eyes look down | Eyes look sideward | Face looks up | Face looks down | Face looks sideward |

Looking with the face involves a rotation or a tilt (inclination) of the head, sometimes both, but these actions are the means and not the purpose of the movement.

Indication of Eye Movements; Gazing

The sign for the eyes: ☑ is combined with the addressing sign to show gazing (moving eyes only). As with the face this indication can be abbreviated to the use of a direction symbol only.

244a

| b) | c) | d) |

Sign for the eyes

Eyes lifted, gazing up

Eyes lowered, gazing down

Eyes gazing to the left

In Ex. 244b the eyes are written as addressing (being directed) up. In fact they cannot totally achieve that direction without some change in the head alignment, so forward high (as indicated in brackets) might seem a more appropriate description. However, the effort to look up rather than forward high does produce a slightly different expression and this difference may be important. Therefore we sometimes write what we have in mind, the aim or the intention, rather than a limited

245

achievement.   In Ex. 244c and d) the description has been simplified and the direction actually achieved for the eyes is shown in brackets.

PALM FACING

Many expressive gestures center on or feature a particular spatial placement of the palm.
As Doris Humphrey pointed out, the palm choreographically is the 'face' of the arm and can
be very expressive in a way similar to the face.
She often spoke of the 'greeting' hand, Ex. 245a,
in which the palm addresses the audience. This
same idea was used by Sigurd Leeder for the
two 'pale sisters' who glide colorlessly across stage, palms facing forward, in his ballet *Danse Macabre*, 245b.   Conversely it is with the
palm that we stop people from advancing toward us, 245c.   The priest
supplicates with palms up, 245d, blesses with palms down, 245e.

245a

Greeting

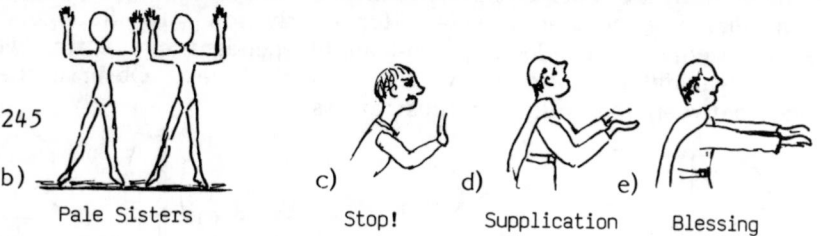

245

b)

Pale Sisters   c) Stop!   d) Supplication   e) Blessing

Many such gestures are understood and accepted as the norm without ever being specifically analyzed.   A change in palm facing may
provide a positive or a negative message.   Without appropriate palm
facing, a gesture may be meaningless.

Indication of Palm Facing

The sign for the palm surface of the hand is ⊡ , Ex. 246a.   This
is followed by an addressing sign plus the appropriate direction, 246b.
As with the face, this statement can be shortened to use of the direction sign only, as in 246c.   The palm sign is a surface sign and surfaces 'face' or 'look at' the direction stated, as in Ex. 246d.

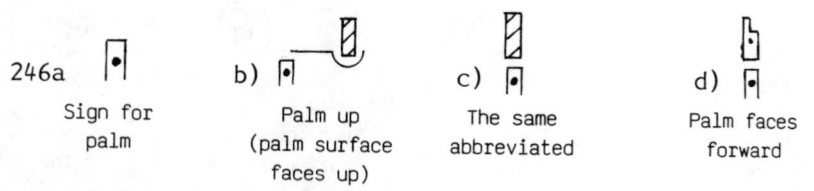

246a

Sign for
palm

b)

Palm up
(palm surface
faces up)

c)

The same
abbreviated

d)

Palm faces
forward

The reading examples which follow describe some everyday movements in which the palm is used expressively.   Below are a few unfamiliar signs used in the next page.

246e   Whole arm,   The right ear   Forehead
                  left & right   f)   (side of head)   g)

Reading Examples for Palm Facing

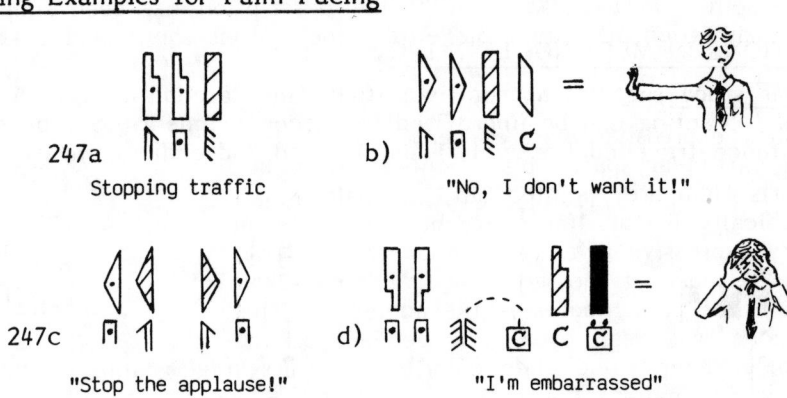

247a   Stopping traffic

b)   "No, I don't want it!"

247c   "Stop the applause!"

d)   "I'm embarrassed"

Ex. 247d contains the following information: palms backward, hands near face, head inclined forward, eyes down. More detail could be added to achieve an exact position, but the main ingredients are there. Below are various pantomimic gestures in a simple form.

247e   "Greeting! Hello!"

f)   "What did you say?"

g)   "There it is!"

247h   "Can't understand it"

i)   "It's finished"

Note the differences in meaning among the three examples below. In each the hand contacts the forehead but each time produces a different message according to the facing direction of the palm.

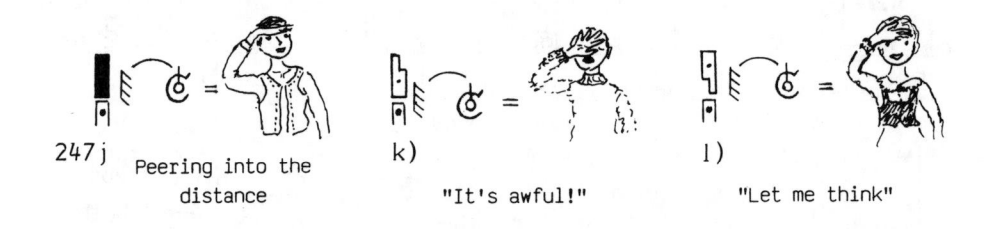

247j   Peering into the distance

k)   "It's awful!"

l)   "Let me think"

Reading Practice

SITUATIONS IN MEETING; LOOKING

This study suggests a primitive ritual dance around a fire. A drum beat and chanting can be improvised for accompaniment. See page 268 for distance travelled (meas. 1,2) and 1st and 2nd endings (meas. 16).

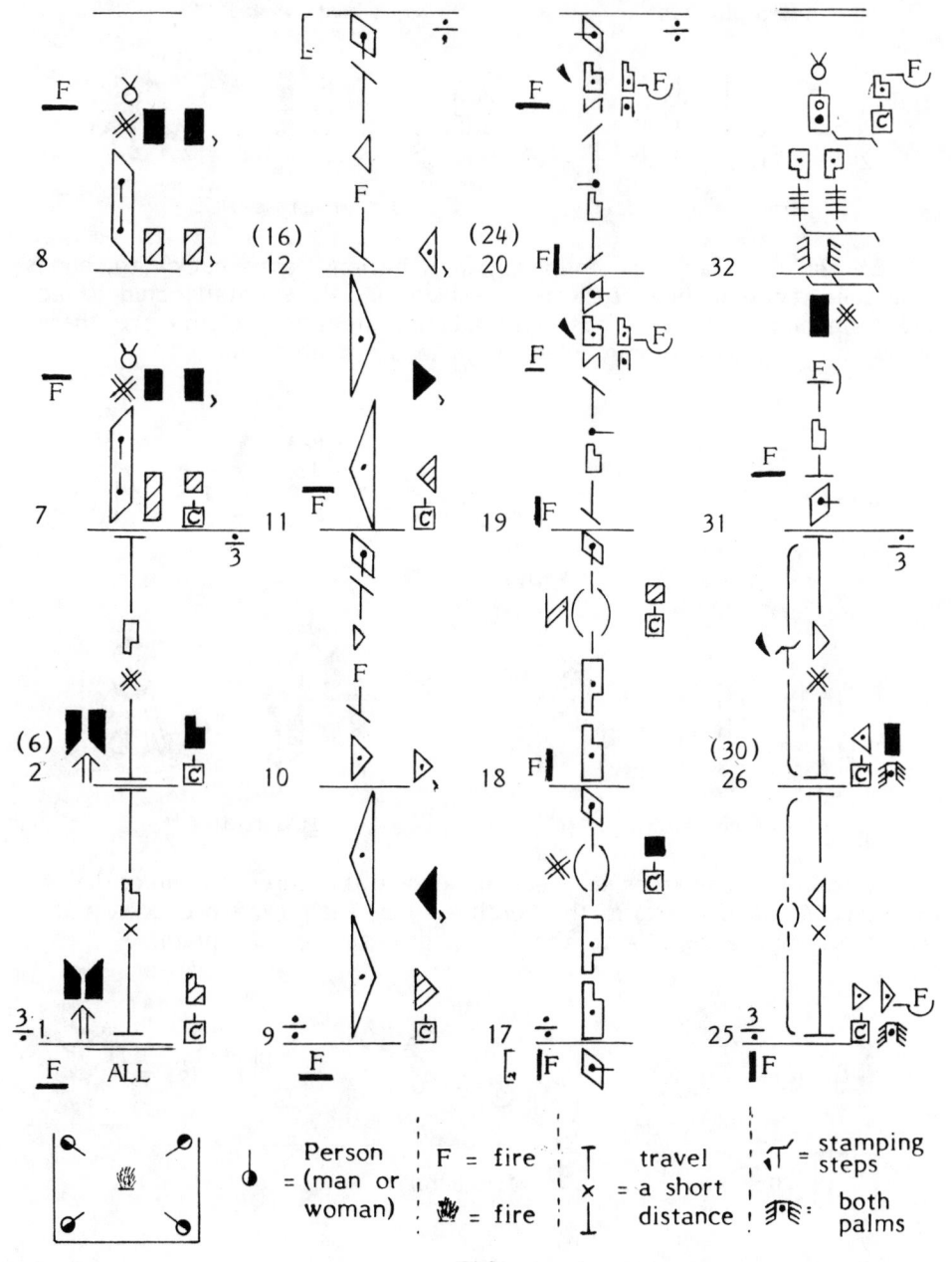

Person = (man or woman)	F = fire	travel	= stamping steps	
	= fire	× = a short distance	= both palms	

RELATING TO OBJECTS

Note use of ribbon with
ends marked A and B.

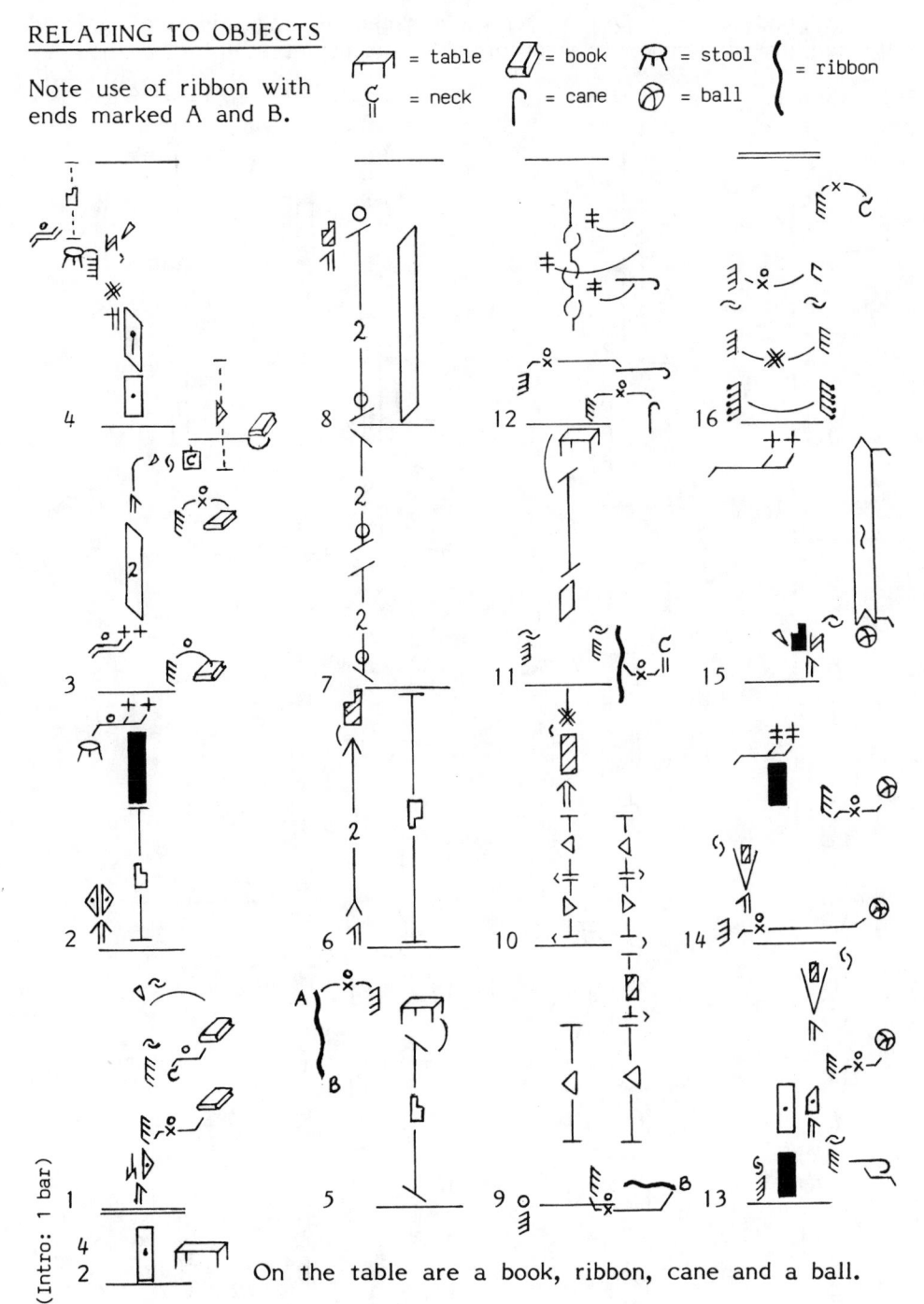

On the table are a book, ribbon, cane and a ball.

PROGRESSION IN RELATING

A good way to explore the whole range of stages in relating is to use a lightweight chair as a prop. There is no music for this study.

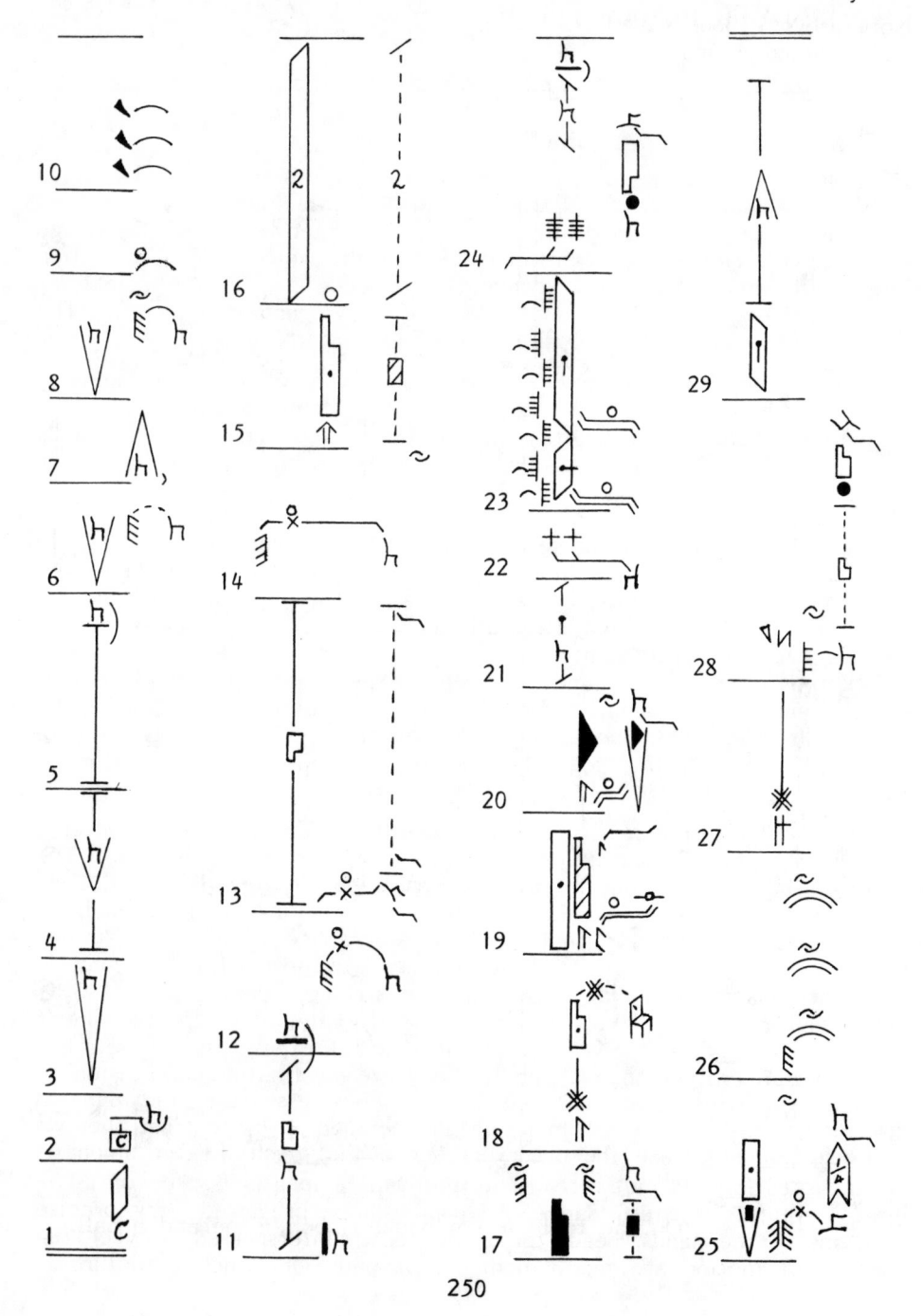

Chapter Eighteen
DESTINATION, MOTION

Are the terms 'destination' and 'motion' familiar as used in relation to physical movement? Does an image come immediately to mind of a movement which is destinational in character? Can you envisage a movement, similar but significantly different, which expresses motion with no destination? These concepts, touched upon in the course of movement analysis and training, are rarely investigated in depth. The following discussions aim to take a fresh look at these movement ideas.

Let us once more start with the child. The earliest movements it makes are pure motion; the baby explores physically what its body can do without conscious thought. In discovering movements of its hands it is not yet thinking of holding a pen or grasping a golf club, for which certain positions are considered the most efficient. In extending its legs the baby does not have in mind the streamline required for diving or an extended dance position such as an arabesque. For a baby the range of movement is limited only by the body build and the surrounding clothing or cot. However, movement soon begins to have an aim: the hand reaches out to grasp an object and the motion of extending has a definite point at which it stops, a destination. But this is an exterior destination, not a physical one, i.e. a chosen placement of the limbs. Depending on the culture, destinational placement of the limbs will gradually come as the child learns to sit cross-legged or to kneel in prayer, palms together, or to assume any of a number of taught body positions.

Motion is spontaneous, often unpremeditated and hence unstructured. Some early stages of learning to dance concentrate on motion. The Laban-based Modern Educational Dance provides movement explorations based on efforts such as slashing, pressing, flicking, gliding, each of which is pure motion, set in no one choreographed form. In a similar way Laban's spatial exploration, which involves destinational points, is concerned principally with the rising and sinking, opening and closing, advancing and retreating of the dimensional scale, and with the fluent changes in the various Space Harmony scales, the progression itself being important rather than a specific physical destination, a position to be achieved by the body. Dance for laymen stresses the enjoyment of the movement, not how it looks to the beholder. In contrast theatrical dance must please the observer; hence the much greater emphasis on the creation of 'pictures'. This pictorial emphasis is true of Eastern as well as Western dance. Temple dances required very precise positions of the hands, head, torso and feet. Interspersed between sequences of motion are many moments of pause in which a picture is

251

created. The observer enjoys these moments of stillness particularly if the form and design made by the body is aesthetically pleasing. Classical ballet is full of movement, but even in jumps and travelling actions the limbs are placed - if only momentarily - so that an attractive picture results.

'Free dance' sought to be free from poses; emphasis certainly was placed much more on motion, with moments of stillness providing an 'ending' significant more for capturing a particular quality or expression than for presenting any architecturally interesting form. Without appropriate dynamic content many such free-dance pauses would be meaningless. Several forms of African dance are based on motion rather than on destination, the range of placement of the limbs and torso varying considerably from one performer to the next, yet the basic impact and expression of the movement remaining the same. Nor is content absent from such highly structured forms as classical ballet. Margaret Craske, the world-famous Cecchetti teacher, once criticized a port de bras as being 'all wrong'. In fact the body/space/time pattern of the arm movements was correct, but the quality, the attack, the flow, the nuances of performance which produce the desired balletic style and expression were not there. Therefore, to her eye, the port de bras was not acceptable.

In the field of sport we see movement having the goal of achieving a particular result, usually that of getting a ball into or over a net. In many games it is not important how one kicks or hits the ball; only the result matters and one works to find an efficient way to produce that result. In other sports, swimming for example, experience and tests have proved that training in specific movement patterns will produce the best results. Swimming may be motion in the sense of continuity, but the movements are channeled into precisely defined paths. In Olympic gymnastics and in skating, style (how the body is held) is extremely important and hence highly trained. Moments of pause must show correct physical destinations.

Before investigating the movement possibilities which come under the heading of 'destination' and 'motion', let us look at some everyday situations to see how these can shed light on our investigation. The statement "After waiting an hour we will start driving north" is relative. The statement "At 4 o'clock we will start driving to Sheffield" is specific. A definite time is given and a definite destination. "After waiting an hour" could be at any time (when does one start counting the hour?) and north is a direction in relation to the starting point but provides no destination. How far north? Specific movement statements employ actions which have clear destinations. But relative descriptions of motion often capture the essence, the initiation or concept of the desired movement.

DESTINATION

The idea of destination is very familiar in everyday life as well as in dance. Before taking concrete examples, let us consider what lies behind destinational actions, what are some typical features, some pre-valent attitudes.

PURPOSE—DETERMINATION—INTENTION—DECISION—AMBITION

Destination is premeditated. Before a movement is started the idea of the destination is set, a choice has been made. This decisiveness shows in the eyes of the performer, in the carriage of the head and in other supporting actions. In dance a destination may be a situation on stage (a chosen point to which to travel), or a destination for a gesture (a point of arrival to be reached in relation to the body, a clearly defined point in the kinesphere).

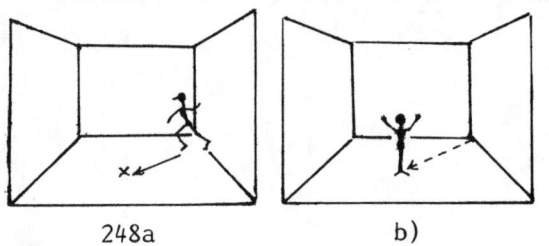

In Ex. 248a the performer has just entered and X marks the spot to which he plans to proceed. In 248b he has arrived at that location. This destination was in mind before he started.

248a   b)

Ex. 248c shows the intended destination for an arm gesture; 248d illustrates the arrival. Intended destination and actual arrival are also illustrated in 248e and f). Manner of performance, a supporting focus of the head and a clear moment of pause will all contribute to the expression of a destinational gesture.

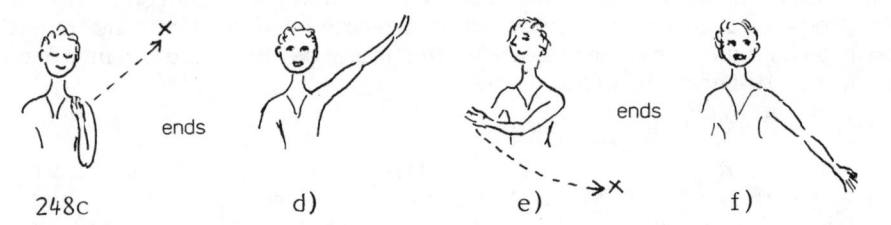

248c   d)   e)   f)

ends   ends

An action which has a definite aim, a destinational movement, is expressed by Ex. 248g. The desired destination is written at the end of the action stroke and is tied to it with a small curved vertical bow. In 248g no specific destination has been given; the ad lib. sign: ⟩ meaning 'any', states that the destination can be anything. In 248h a straight path is shown to have the aim of ending at the center front (downstage) area of the stage.

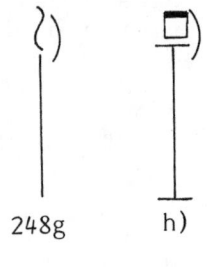

248g   h)

What factors contribute to destinational movement? Which are usually present because of the nature of this kind of movement? We will consider how time, space and dynamics are used.

253

Time in Relation to Destination

Whatever may be the speed of a movement to a destination there is always at least a brief pause once the destination is reached, this pause having the visual effect of informing the observer that this is the intended point of arrival. Destinational movement embodies enjoyment of arrival. In many everyday situations one travels only to reach a destination; the journey is often not enjoyed, and the traveller can't wait to arrive at the desired place. In certain contexts a dancer has the same attitude and his movements reveal it. Whether the action is fast or slow, emphasis in phrasing is on arrival at a conclusion. Such arrival will usually fall on a strong beat in the music, frequently the strong beat immediately after a bar line.

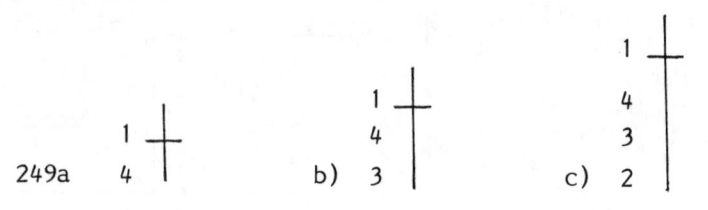

Any of the time patterns of Ex. 249a, b) or c) is suited to destinational movement, since each ends on the emphasized beat at the beginning of a new measure (bar). In 249a the movement on count four leads to the conclusion on count one. In 249b the movement phrase starts earlier making use of counts 3 and 4 of the previous measure, but the conclusion is still on count 1. Ex. 249c starts even earlier by using count 2 of the previous measure. Ending on a strong beat helps to produce a positive, conclusive statement. How long the resulting position is held may vary; usually the more definite and final the position, the longer it is held.

Space in Relation to Destination

Movement with an aim is by nature direct - why deviate when you know what your goal is? If the path, the progression itself, is not important, why embellish it? The movement tends automatically to go directly to the aim. Gestures which move out from the center of the body on a straight, spoke-like path, as in Ex. 250a, have a final limit - the extension of the limb in that direction.

The path of a movement can be extended, the limb can be carried further in space by including a movement of the body, as in the torso inclination of Ex. 250b. The arm can appear to continue to move spatially if the extending gesture leads into travelling, as in 250c. It must be realized that movement of the arm itself has ceased; the limb is moving only in the sense that it is being transported, much as we move through the countryside when we sit still in a car.

In many destinational movements both performer and viewer may be quite unaware of the path
of a movement which may have been so quick or
so vague that they are aware only of the final position reached.   This position is usually very definite, architecturally clearcut.   Strong destinations
make use of dimensional directions and those at 45°
angles to them, as in the following examples:

250d

250e

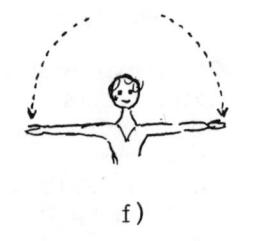

f)

g)

Taking the starting position of Ex. 250e we are not surprised by
the finishing position of 250f.   It is a location for the arms which is
familiar in most forms of dance and gymnastics.   Therefore we can register that point in space by a very brief pause before moving on to

the destination of Ex. 250g - another well
established placement.   But in the case of
250h the alignment is like an indistinctly
pronounced word; should it have been as in
250f?   Intermediate directions are used for
aesthetic reasons and, through repeated use,
become established as the 'norm', expected
destinational points.   Classical ballet uses
many intermediate directions for the arms.
Spatially they are not aligned with the major directions, but the extremities often relate to a particular part of the body, the
level of the eyes, the breast bone, the hips
and so on.

250h

Design or 'shape' poses, such as in 250i
occur in many Asian dances where the idea
of display, of presenting charming and often
intricate pictures, is predominant.   For
some choreographers picture making is their
prime aim, both for the individual dancer
as well as for group formations. Movement
occurs to change from one shape to another.
Pilobolus Dance Company has explored this
aspect of movement with astonishing results.

250i

Dynamics in Relation to Destination

For a destinational action a slight increase in energy at the moment of arrival serves as punctuation and gives emphasis to the termination. It has the effect of 'sealing' the end of the movement. Strong, dramatic gestures such as Ex. 251a are of this type.

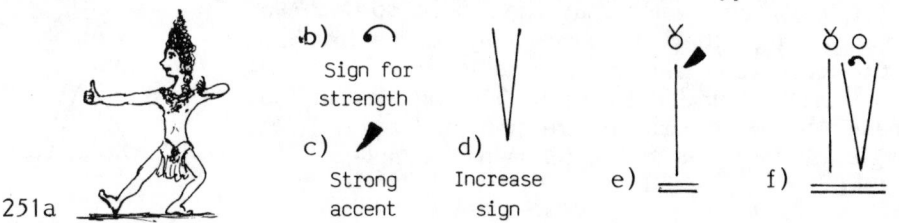

251a

b) Sign for strength

c) Strong accent

d) Increase sign

e)

f)

The pattern of impact, Ex. 251e, expresses this emphasis (or 'sealing') clearly. A strong accent, 251c, occurs at the end of the action. Such impact movements require a definite spatial pattern to be expressive, to establish a clear, strong message. The force may appear suddenly at the end of the action, as in 251e, or it may gradually increase during the 'life' of the movement up to its end, as in Ex. 251f. Note use of the sign for increase, 251d, combined with the sign for strength, 251b. The increase sign is derived from the music sign for crescendo: ◁——— .

MOTION

Dance is concerned with moving, with change, with passage from one situation to another. It is this passage which is the actual motion, "movement in flow", the 'going' of movement.

Consider an everyday example of motion such as would occur in the following situation: In a classroom students are already seated. The instruction is given: "Everyone get up and go to quite another part of the room and sit down". The first reaction is to rise (motion away from sitting); then there is uncertainty and hence various degrees of 'milling around' will occur as they decide where to go. A few may wait to see where others go and, while looking for a vacant spot, may move somewhat aimlessly, as in Ex. 252a. Once a destination is clear, the decision made, the nature of the movement changes; direct paths to a destination result, 252b. This experiment illustrates both how people tend to move when they have no immediate aim, no picture of where they should end up, and the change in movement that occurs once a destination is clear.

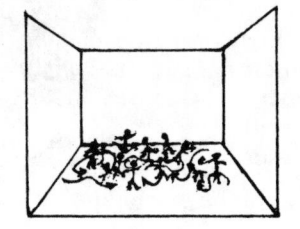

252a

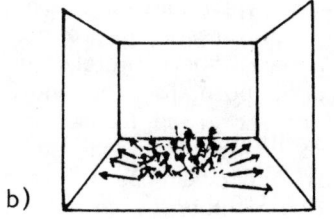

b)

Destination, Motion

What are the attributes of motion?

UNDECIDED — WANDERING — FREE TO GO — AIMLESS

One is reminded of the flight of birds, lifted by air currents, soaring, drifting, gliding, enjoying their passage through the air. Such motion cannot be captured in still drawings, hence no attempt at illustrations is made here.

It may be noticed that the above words seem to be of a negative type. Motion as an activity can be very positive. It is only that in many parts of the world society is goal oriented; we are expected to plan ahead. In some cultures, particularly those affected by hot climates, the indigenous movement styles enjoy many more flowing, ongoing patterns of movement.

In exploring motion we must relinquish the desire for a destination and be concerned with movement for its own sake. A good start is to wish only to move away, away from where you are. Where you go is not important; think only of a change. This 'going away' may be just of the limbs moving in space, or of the whole body moving across the floor, going from place to place - exactly where is of no consequence. A dramatic version of such going away is the idea of being chased, which allows for much improvisation both in paths and in gestural actions expressing the reason for fleeing, perhaps fear, perhaps teasing the pursuer.

While sitting on the floor one might decide to change position; perhaps stiffness is setting in and there is a desire to move. A change is wanted, but often no new shape or arrival point is in mind. In a lecture students may be given a few moments to get up, to stretch and move around after a spell of sitting. Stretching and any accompanying actions are usually pure motion performed and enjoyed for its own sake.

Motion may also be toward a destination but without an arrival. In the ballet *Lilac Garden* by Antony Tudor, Caroline sees her lover, moves toward him, but is drawn up short as she knows she must not be seen. Her pause is a cessation of movement toward her lover, not the establishment of a position, a placement of her limbs. A spatial design is the last thing on her mind, and if it were, if she felt the angle of her upper arm, lower arm and hand were important, it would ruin the dramatic effect cn the suspended motion.

What forms of movement best express motion? Some actions, such as turning, travelling, springing and falling are motions by nature. A turn can never be a position, though a body position can be held while turning. Turning is always an action of change; the destination of a turn, where it happens to stop, is not part of the turn itself.

Travelling only becomes destinational when a place of arrival is stated or the distance to be traversed is given. During a spring the limbs and torso may take a position, but the springing action is pure

Motion (continued)

motion limited only by gravity and arrival back on the floor. In loss
of balance it is the floor which provides a destination; falling itself, as
in parachuting, can go on for much longer.

Time in Relation to Motion

Because motion usually lacks purpose in the sense of arrival at any
spatial point there is frequently an enjoyment of time; there is a tendency to use more time, to be slower. A sense of hurry, of urgency,
is usually absent, though speed may be enjoyed in the passage through
space. Once movement is 'set in motion' it has the tendency to keep
going (the law of inertia). When a stop occurs it often results from a
petering out of the impetus which caused the movement; a new movement idea has not yet been formed, hence the stop. An abrupt stop
may be the result of a change of idea, a stopping in one's tracks to
surge off into another direction. Timing itself does not change the basic nature of motion; a slower pace allows more awareness and enjoyment of 'goingness'. T'ai-chi Ch'uan incorporates sustained enjoyment of limbs and body moving through space.

Space in Relation to Motion

Because motion is so often based on a positive aimlessness, the
enjoyment of an energy flow which carries the body into space, motion
has an affinity with indirect paths. When motion is enjoyed for its
own sake (not a by-product of another state) there is usually an enjoyment also of space. Movement is allowed to meander through kines-
pheric space as well as through the performing area. It is important
that no destination be expressed. In place of direct, spoke-like movements for which an aim usually exists from the start and for which
there is spatially a physical limitation, motion is better served by arcs,
curves and circles. If an arm rises from its normal situation at the
side of the body, Ex. 253a, how far will it rise? Where will it stop?
By use of continuous curves we may produce endless gestural movement, as in any circular pattern or figure-eight design, Ex. 253b,c).

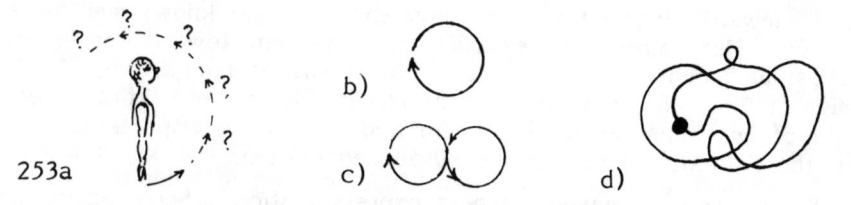

253a   b)   c)   d)

In such patterns there is no obvious destination, no built-in ending
point, no place where the movement HAS to stop. Ex. 253d shows a
curving path which could be started anywhere and go on endlessly. It
could be a three-dimensional path traced in the air or could be a path
walked across the floor as a floor design. The indulgence in space
which such a space pattern suggests is well suited to the type of
movement which stems from the concept of motion.

Dynamics in Relation to Motion

As we have seen with the idea of being chased, motion can be re-plete with energy, or, as in T'ai-chi, energy used may be almost mini-mal to produce gently flowing movements. The specific energy pattern which fits motion is that of <u>impulse</u>. From a center of collected en-ergy the movement flows out, or shoots out of the body. The energy in an impulsive movement may soon be dissipated. Ex. 254a shows an action which starts with a strong accent. In 254b an action starts with strength, the strength gradually diminish-ing, as shown by the 'going a-way' sign, 254c, which is re-lated to the musical sign for diminuendo: ⟩ .

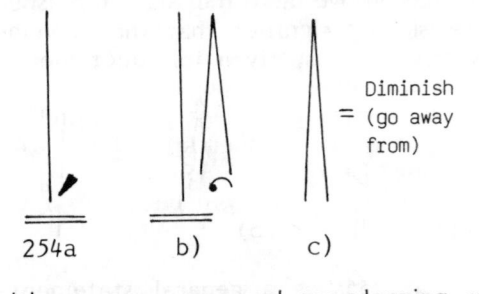

Diminish = (go away from)

254a   b)   c)

Pure motion, which occurs without awareness and pre-planning on the part of the mover, is less familiar than movement to a destination. In one way or another most movement training is goal-oriented. It would be desirable to give more illustrations of motion but pictures are static and even when arrows showing motion are used, the end of the arrow suggests a destination. One must return to the image of the passage of a bird enjoying the freedom of the air, floating on the air currents, <u>before</u> it spots a morsel of food or decides to return home.

Destinational Action Performed as Motion

A change of quality takes place when destinational patterns are performed with motion in mind. An inner feeling or desire affects the performance of material which is opposite in nature to this feeling. In classical ballet ports de bras and adage sequences require sustained, flowing movement but they are based on clear, established positions through which the limbs must pass or at which they must terminate. Too often the image of destination (a necessary image during the early training stages) produces a stilted quality of movement. With motion in mind the performer can observably change the manner of performing such established patterns. Conversely, movement patterns which should be flowing motion will be subtly changed if inner thought or feeling is concentrated on seeking a destination. Subtle changes occur which do not need to be 'spelled out' or analyzed fully. Long before any deep study of dynamics (the flow of energy in the body) is undertaken, ap-propriate images can produce a desired change in movement quality.

Indication of Destination, Motion

Our use of direction symbols for gestures has, up to now, been al-lowed a general interpretation. With the possibilities of destination or motion in mind we need to consider whether Ex. 255a, the indication for up, should mean upward motion, that is, movement upward from where the limb is, or whether it should mean arrival at the directional point stated, a destinational statement.

Indication of Destination, Motion (continued)

In the specific Structured Description of movement all direction symbols for gestures indicate the point of arrival, i.e. destination. In Motif Description the direction symbol by itself allows some freedom of interpretation; therefore some modification must be introduced in order specifically to state that destination or motion is intended. For destination we add the sign for 'specific'; this sign: ✳ resembles an asterisk and signifies that the movement indication is to be interpreted exactly, that is, given its exact meaning.

255a   b)   c)

Ex. 255a is a general statement of an upward movement for the right arm. In 255b the addition of the sign for exact performance will mean that the arm must arrive at the destination up, above the shoulder. Ex. 255c illustrates the right arm arriving at the point forward middle. The asterisk for exact performance is placed next to the sign it modifies. Once the transition has been made to Structured Description the asterisk is no longer needed; the description is automatically understood to be destinational.

Motion is indicated by combining the sign for toward or the sign for away with a direction sign or other appropriate indication such as an object, person or part of the room.

d) Sign for 'any'

Motion toward something (a state, object, direction, etc.)

e)

Motion away from something (a state, object, direction, etc.)

f)

255

In the above examples a very general statement has been made by use of 'any' with the signs for motion toward or away. The examples here show motion concerned with directional change. Ex. 255g is a motion toward down, 255h is moving toward side middle, while 255i and j) show motion toward and away from person 'P'.

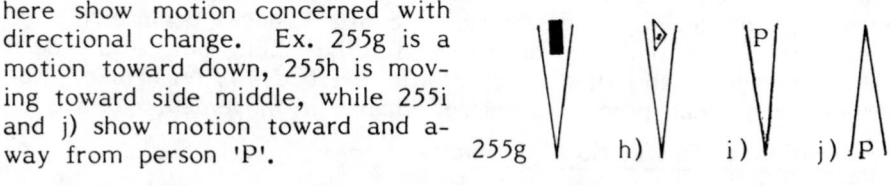

255g   h)   i)   j) P

Such indications are intentionally indefinite with regard to the exact movement to be produced. This is their value. Because of the lack of any clear result, i.e. a destination, these motions are hard to illustrate with figure drawings. They need to be explored through movement. Symbols for degrees of explicitness exist and are used in the Structured Description of movement.

Direction of the Progression

Another movement concept is to describe the path of a gesture in relation to the point of departure, the placement or situation of a limb before motion begins. In relation to the starting point the part of the body progresses forward, sideward, upward, and so on. This description of movement is exactly comparable to that used for ordinary walking, i.e. progression across the floor. For each step the direction is judged from the point where you are before the step begins. After the step is completed, a new point has been established from which the next step direction is judged. So it is when you describe the direction of progression for a gesture; the progression is judged from the extremity of the limb - the whole arm may move but one is conscious of the path taken by the hand.

An arrow, the sign commonly used to state "Progress from here to there," Ex. 256a, is used to indicate the direction of the progression. Ex. 256b shows the basic key for the concept of the direction of progression; 256c shows a progression up, 256d a progression down.

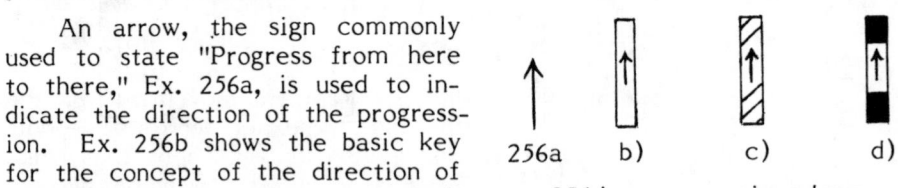

256a   b)   c)   d)

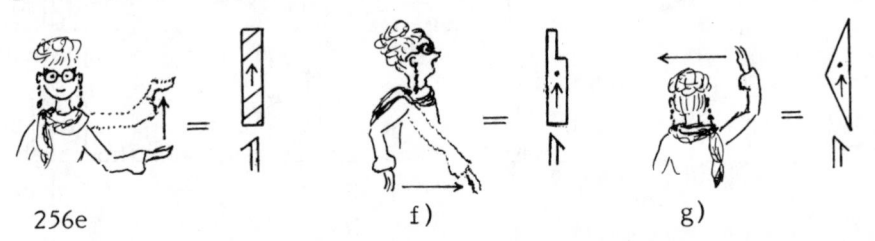

256e   f)   g)

Ex. 256e illustrates one setting for a progression vertically up; the arm as a whole rises but we are aware of the path of the extremity. In 256f the direction of the progression is forward horizontal while in 256g it is on a horizontal path to the left. For practical reasons the arrow placed within a direction sign *always points forward* regardless of the direction of the movement; thus it is a symbol rather than a pictorial indication.

Many steps travelling in the same direction are usually written in Motif Description with a path sign, Ex. 256h below. Thus a straight pathway and the direction of progression are, in fact, the same basic action. A path sign could therefore be written for such gestures.

Ex. 256i illustrates a sideward horizontal gesture for the right arm. In 256j this is written as a sideward direction of progression. A path sideward horizontal has been written in 256k. Either is correct but 256j is usually easier to read.

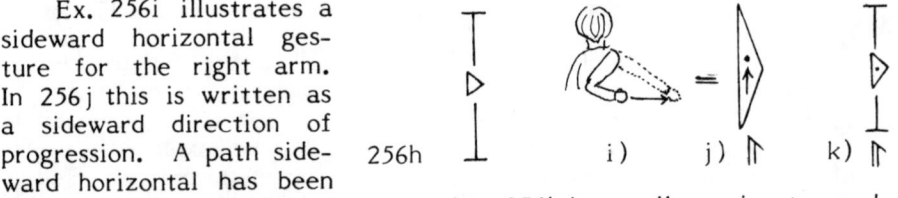

256h   i)   j)   k)

Reading Study No. 41

DESTINATION, MOTION

A study in motion toward a destination, arrival at a destination, and examples of the direction of progression. Note that one <u>arrives</u> at a directional destination and <u>achieves</u> a particular state of <u>flexion</u> or extension.

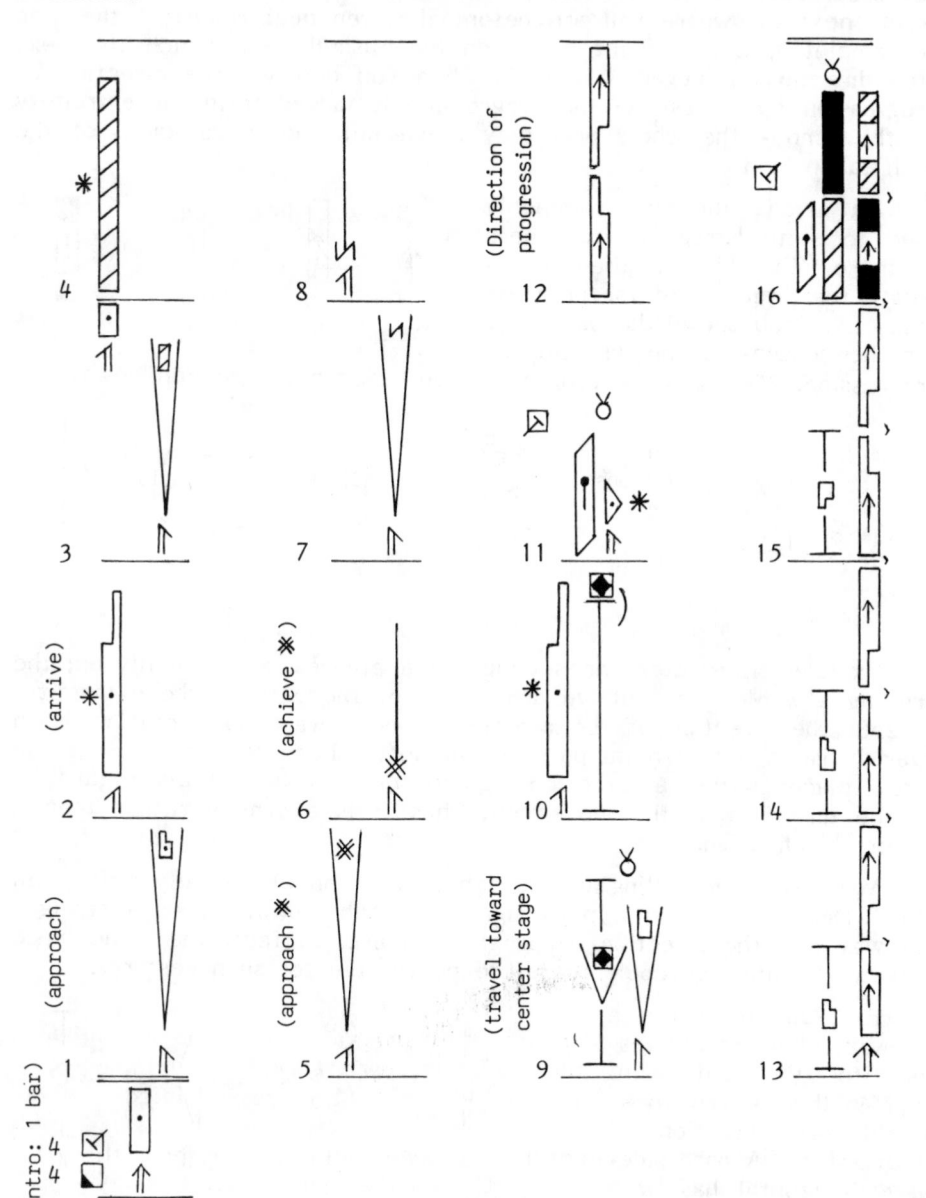

MOTION - MINOR DISPLACEMENTS

A directional change, a displacement in space, may be very small, a minor motion. The main ·direction symbols indicate major displacements, substantial movement. A pin shows a minor displacement away from a previous situation, a very slight change. For each of the main directions around the body there is an equivalent pin to show a spatially comparable minor displacement. In the charts below, each pin is placed next to the main direction symbol to which it relates.

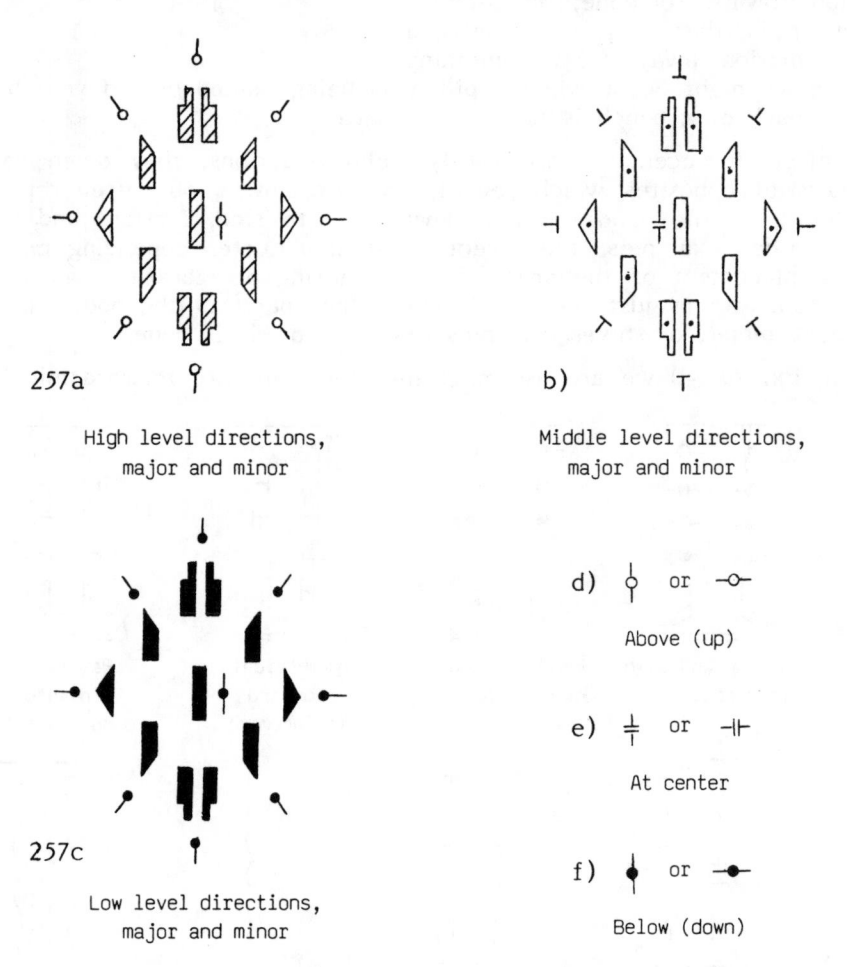

257a

High level directions,
major and minor

b)

Middle level directions,
major and minor

257c

Low level directions,
major and minor

d)   or

Above (up)

e)   or

At center

f)   or

Below (down)

The point of the pin indicates the direction; the head of the pin indicates the level. White pins indicate upward, high level minor displacements; straight pins (often called 'tacks') represent middle level minor displacements, and black pins represent low level minor displacements. For the vertical dimension - above, below or center - there is a choice in drawing the symbol. The choice depends on what is visually easier to read.

263

Motion - Minor Displacements (continued)

Minor directional changes, though small, may be very expressive. In Ex. 257g the arm (experienced mainly as the hand) moves upward, slightly above where it was before. In 251h the body (torso and head) moves forward, a slight displacement which may express a sympathetic motion toward someone, an interest in what is there, or conversely, a slight motion away from something

257g   h)

behind, as might occur when a pillow is being placed behind your back or the back of a bench is too cold or hard.

Minor displacements are rarely isolated actions, they often come in pairs of opposites which repeat, possibly slowly, but often rapidly. Fluttering of the hands up and down, side to side, forward and back are familiar examples, the direction of the flutter depending on the spatial placement of the arm. Such fluttering or vibrating can be of the whole arm or just the lower arm. Many parts of the body can vibrate, shimmer, or shiver; the pins describe how it is done.

In Ex. 257i-l) we are assuming that the arms are forward middle.

257i

Hands up and down
in opposition

j)

Hands up and
down in unison

k)

Symmetrical
sideward
displacement

l)

Parallel
sideward
displacement

257m

Shoulders in
opposition for-
ward and backward

n)

Shoulders in
unison

o)

Sign for
vibrato
(shaking)

p)

Rapid and repeated displacements can be shown to continue through use of a wavy vertical line, as in Ex. 257o. In 257p the knees are shown to be shaking.

READING EXAMPLES

Below are several pantomimic gestures for everyday actions which make use of motion (direction of the progression), of minor displacements and of palm facing. Note that a general cancellation is shown by the sign ʌ (a small 'away' sign) meaning the previous result is no longer in effect.

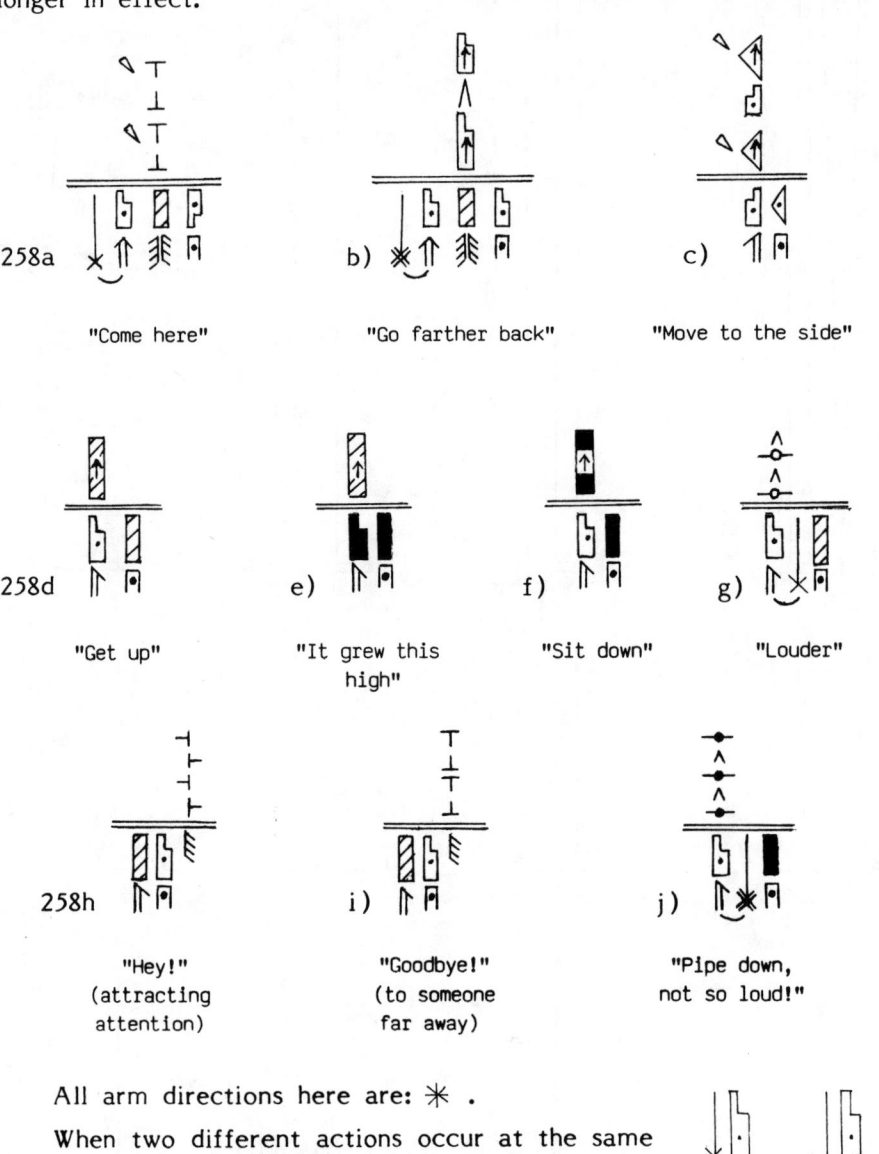

258a — "Come here"

b) — "Go farther back"

c) — "Move to the side"

258d — "Get up"

e) — "It grew this high"

f) — "Sit down"

g) — "Louder"

258h — "Hey!" (attracting attention)

i) — "Goodbye!" (to someone far away)

j) — "Pipe down, not so loud!"

All arm directions here are: ✳ .

When two different actions occur at the same time for the arm (or other part) the arm symbol can be centered below both movements, as in k), or a small horizontal bow can be used to link the additional action to the arm symbol, as in l).

258k   l)

265

K

MOTION, MINOR DISPLACEMENTS

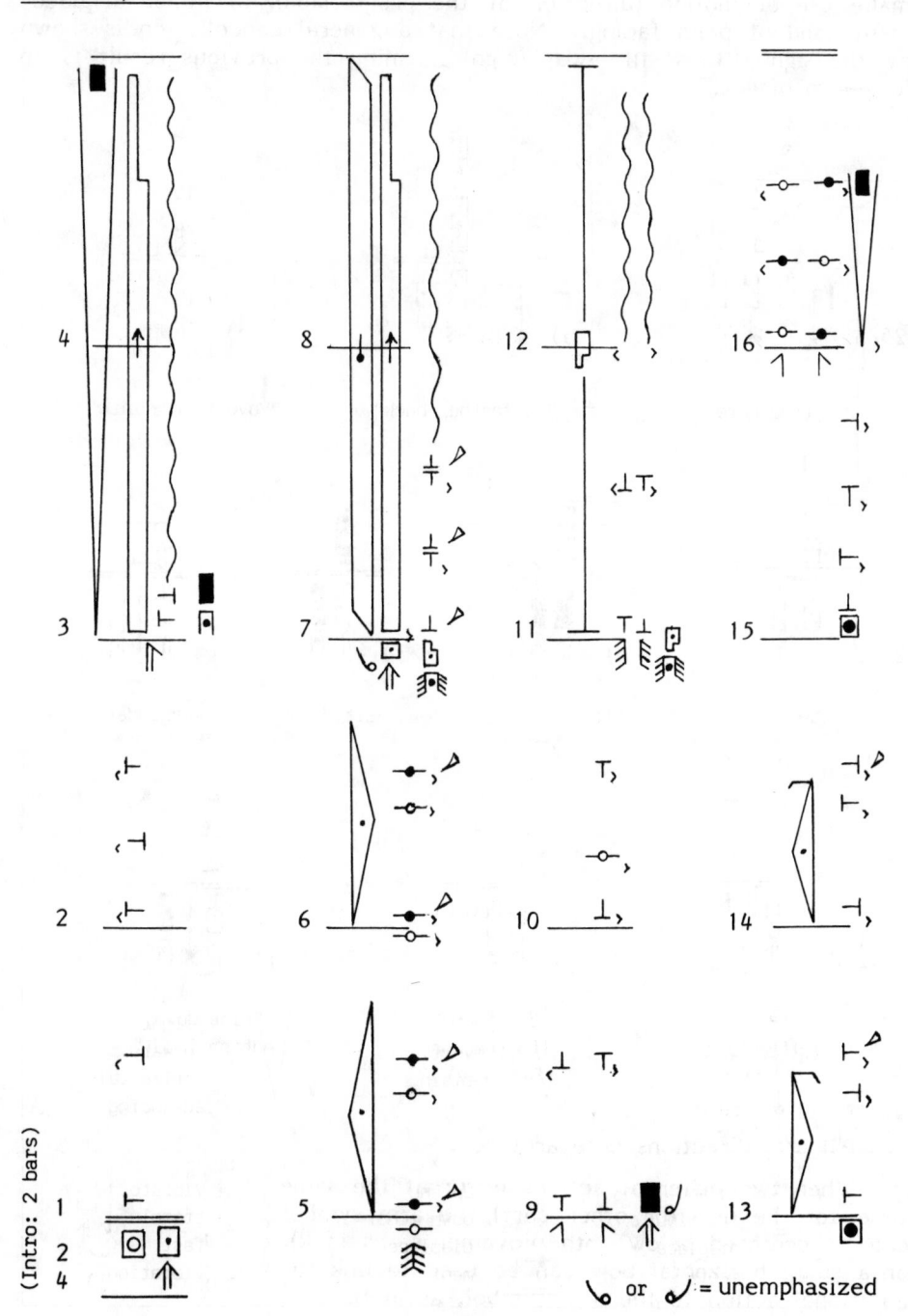

(Intro: 2 bars)

or = unemphasized

266

REVIEW FOR CHAPTERS SEVENTEEN AND EIGHTEEN

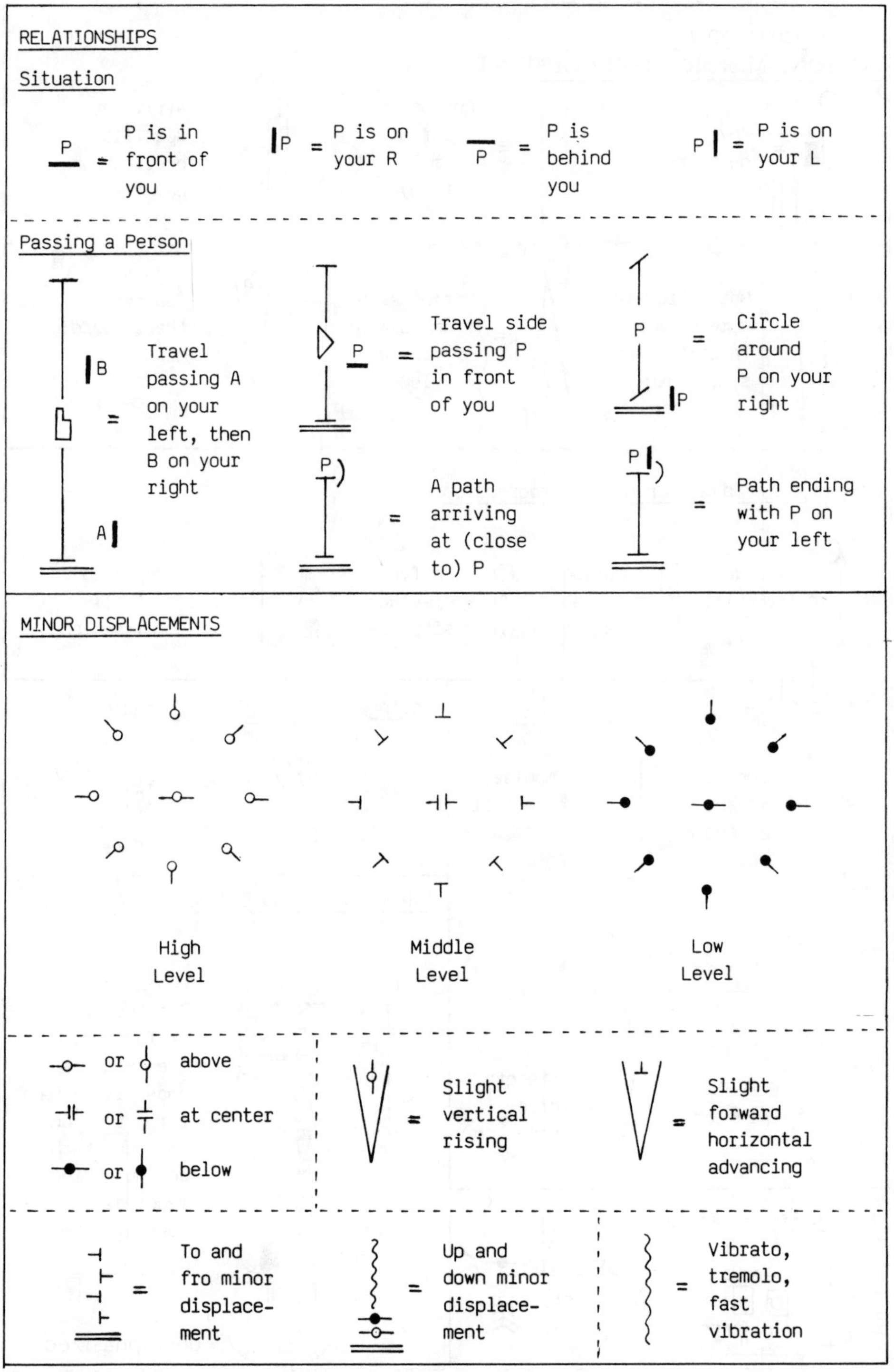
RELATIONSHIPS
Situation
P
= P is in front of you
P
= P is on your R
P
= P is behind you
P
= P is on your L
Passing a Person
B
A
= Travel passing A on your left, then B on your right
P
= Travel side passing P in front of you
P
= Circle around P on your right
P
P
= A path arriving at (close to) P
P
= Path ending with P on your left
MINOR DISPLACEMENTS
High Level
Middle Level
Low Level
or above
or at center
or below
= Slight vertical rising
= Slight forward horizontal advancing
= To and fro minor displacement
= Up and down minor displacement
= Vibrato, tremolo, fast vibration

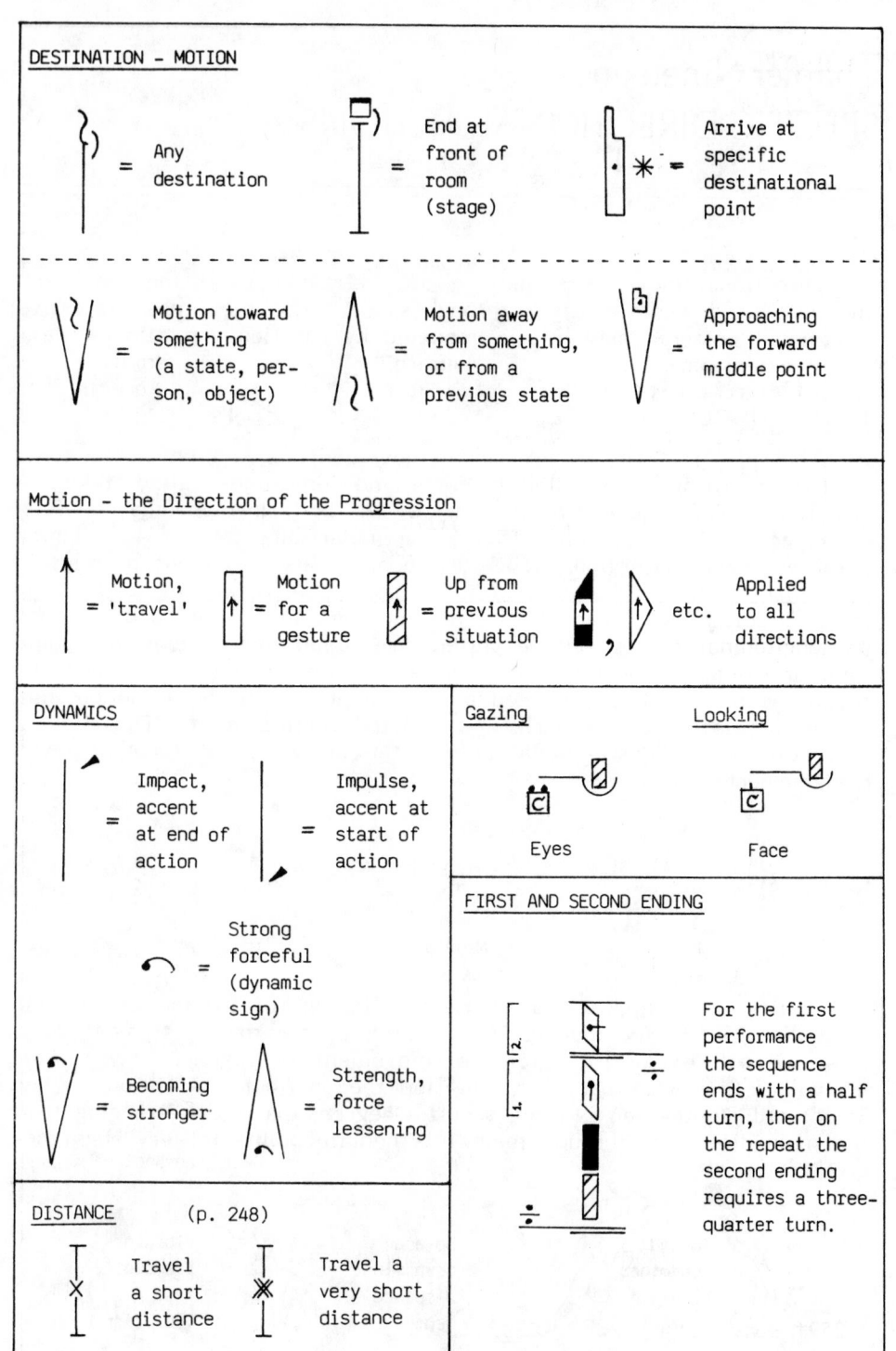

DESTINATION - MOTION

= Any destination

= End at front of room (stage)

= Arrive at specific destinational point

= Motion toward something (a state, person, object)

= Motion away from something, or from a previous state

= Approaching the forward middle point

Motion - the Direction of the Progression

= 'travel' Motion,

= for a gesture Motion

= previous situation Up from

etc. Applied to all directions

DYNAMICS

= Impact, accent at end of action

= Impulse, accent at start of action

= Strong forceful (dynamic sign)

= Becoming stronger

= Strength, force lessening

DISTANCE (p. 248)

Travel a short distance

Travel a very short distance

Gazing   Looking

Eyes   Face

FIRST AND SECOND ENDING

For the first performance the sequence ends with a half turn, then on the repeat the second ending requires a three-quarter turn.

Chapter Nineteen
SPECIFIC DIRECTIONAL ACTIONS

Directional movements may be of several kinds as the limbs and the body as a whole progress through space. For the limbs expressive directional gestures may be accompanied by rotation and also by flexion or extension.

TILTING, INCLINING

The specific form of directional movement for a limb or the torso is that of tilting, also called inclining and sometimes called 'taking a direction'. The free end of the part of the body involved may be seen or experienced as 'pointing' into a particular direction or as aligning itself with that direction. The idea behind this movement pertains in particular to the head and torso but is applicable to any part. By 'taking a direction' we mean placing the limb or part of the body so that its longitudinal axis is on the stated directional line. Below are some familiar examples for the arm. As can be seen in Ex. 259a-e concentration is on the line produced by the angle which the torso or limb makes in relation to the horizontal and the vertical axes. Thus 'taking a direction' is a destinational action, the design or 'picture' achieved being important.

259a   b)   c)   d)   e)

Tilting, inclining, 'taking a direction' can occur for the whole torso as in Ex. 259f-h, for the head as in 259i, or for the chest as in 259j. First we will explore this form of movement in a general way; later we will define what part is tilting and the particular direction. When Structured Description is used, specific degrees are shown, ranging from the main directions through their intermediate points to very slight degrees.

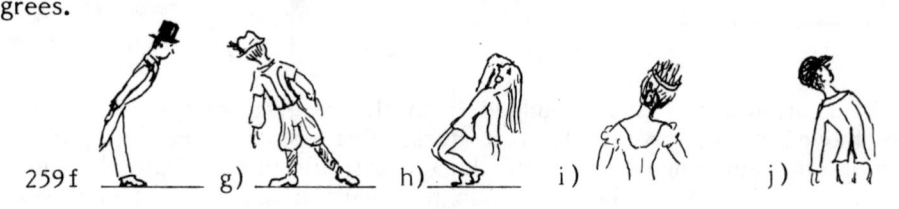

259f   g)   h)   i)   j)

Analysis of Tilting, Inclining

As an illustration of tilting, inclining, let us take a book and note its changing spatial alignment. From a vertical situation, Ex. 260a, the book can incline away to a slight or greater degree, as in 260b and c). If the book is lying down, as in 260d, a tilting (tipping) action occurs as it is being raised, 260e. The slanting line achieved in relation to the vertical or horizontal is important; the direction of the movement which produces the result is not of significance here.

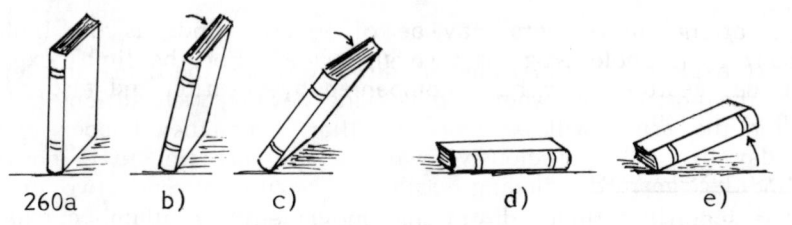

260a   b)   c)   d)   e)

Start with tilting actions for the head. This body area inclines through the flexibility in the neck, direction being judged from the base of the neck. The head is normally up (place high) when one is standing upright. From there it can easily incline forward, backward and sideward in high level (slanting upward from the base of the neck); for the head to achieve horizontal level the upper spine usually has to take part in the movement. Other levels are possible when the body is horizontal or upside down. Next explore possibilities for the whole torso, remembering that since the torso hinges at the hip joints direction and level are judged from there. Normally the torso is straight up, i.e. place high; only when it is horizontal, parallel with the floor, has it reached middle level. Experiment with forward or sideward low level tilts (slanting downward). From a standing position, backward torso tilts are limited. Inclining the chest (rib cage) can have the feeling of that part 'taking a direction', moving as a unit, as an area, rather than as a flexion of the spine, a curving of the vertebrae. Below are illustrations of tilting the torso, an analogy being made with tilting a chair. This same analogy applies to the head, chest and pelvis, although these are smaller units.

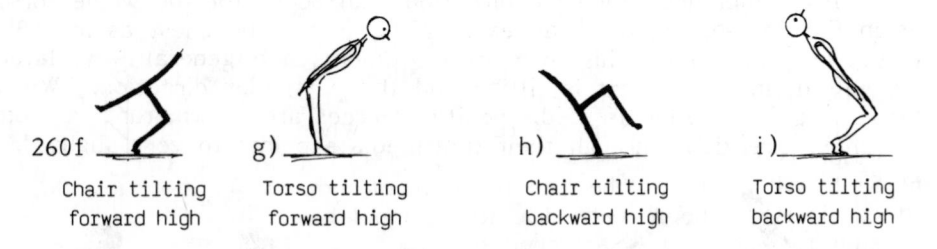

260f _____   g)_____   h) _____   i)_____
Chair tilting   Torso tilting   Chair tilting   Torso tilting
forward high   forward high   backward high   backward high

Direction for tilting is judged from the base, from the point where the movement originates; for the torso this point is the hip joint or joints. In 260i hinging is at the knee joint; for most people the hip is not flexible enough to produce such backward tilting without bent legs.

Specific Directional Actions

For horizontal tilts the longitudinal line (axis) of the part of the body must be parallel with the floor.

260

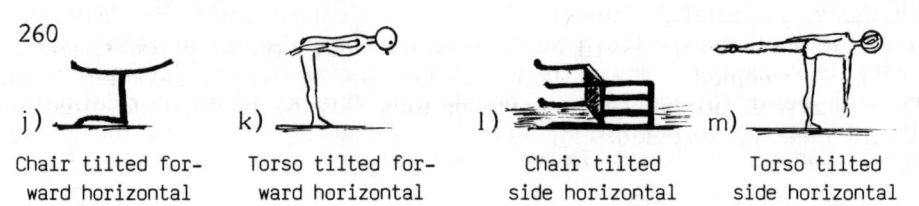

j)	k)	l)	m)
Chair tilted forward horizontal	Torso tilted forward horizontal	Chair tilted side horizontal	Torso tilted side horizontal

Next explore the full range of directions for the arms and legs including the possibilities when one is lying down. Such actions (particularly for the arms) will be more familiar since they happen often in every day life. Be consciously aware of the direction used, combining arm and leg gestures, finding variations in use of one, two or three limbs at the same time. Parts of the arms should then be explored, that is, directional placement for upper arm only, lower arm and hand - in isolation or in combination, using one or both arms. The parts of the leg may also have many directional placements; the range is extended through use of rotation and changes in body situation, as in lying down, a shoulder stand, etc.

Indication of Tilting, Inclining

The basic sign for tilting, taking a direction, is a rectangle (the sign for the vertical dimension) plus the stroke: \ to indicate away from that alignment, Ex. 261a. As the rectangle is also used as the basic indication for direction, as in 'any direction', it is appropriate that tilting, which is a directional activity, should have this rectangle as part of its sign.

Tilting, inclining, 'taking a direction'

261a

Although the basic sign of 261a suggests an action which inclines specifically off the vertical, the sign represents tilting as a basic type of action regardless of whatever spatial placement may result. Many actions in this category may result from rising toward the vertical rather than inclining away from it.

For tilting, 'taking a direction', a general interpretation of direction no longer applies. In Motif Description the right arm moving up, 261b, can still be interpreted in several ways. When an action is stated as one of taking a direction, the limb will arrive at the directional point indicated. It is as though each direction symbol has the sign for specific; ✳ attached to it.

261b

Reading Study No. 43

TILTING, INCLINING

This study explores tilting actions of body areas, of limbs, and of the two combined. For a limb 'taking a direction' is a better term. The limbs will probably be extended; they may be bent if the direction is still clearly expressed.

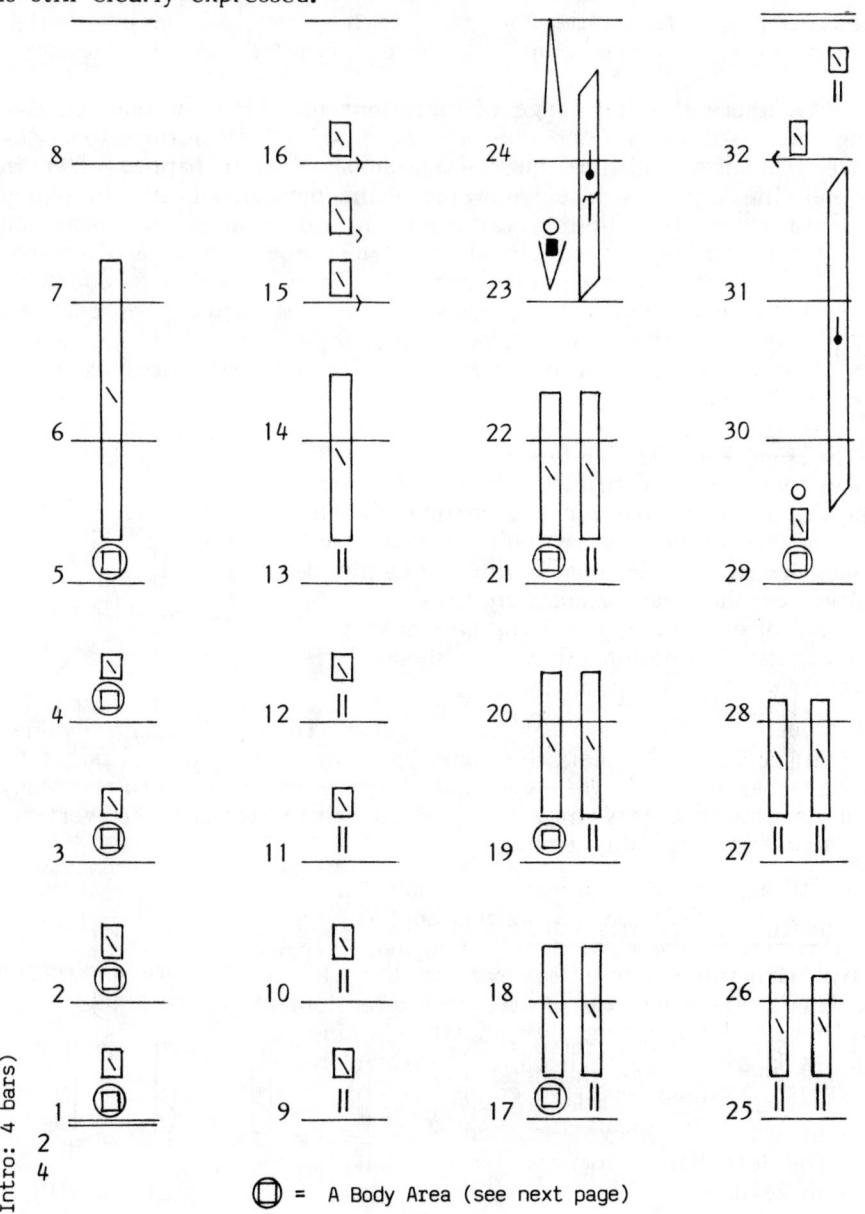

◫ = A Body Area (see next page)

Directions for Tilting, Inclining

In describing tilting the next step after freedom in choice of direction and part of the body is to state a specific direction. This is done by placing the slanting stroke: \ in the appropriate direction symbol. The following examples illustrate direction with no level stated.

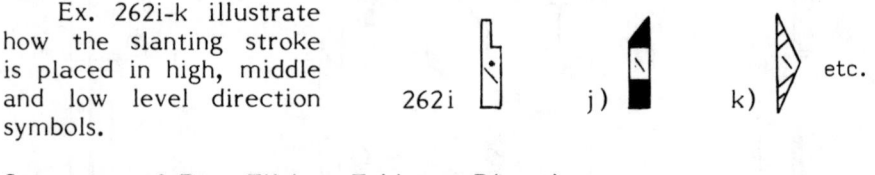

262a   b)   c)   d)   e)   f)   g)   h)

Indications of tilting, inclining, 'taking a direction', no level stated

When level is added to the general indication of tilting, inclining, room must be allowed within the symbol for the slanting stroke.

Ex. 262i-k illustrate how the slanting stroke is placed in high, middle and low level direction symbols.

262i   j)   k)   etc.

Statement of Part Tilting, Taking a Direction

The sign for a (any) body area, Ex. 263a, provides the choice as to which area (head, torso, pelvis or chest) to use. Ex. 263b is the sign for a (any) limb. If a caret: ⟨ or ⟩ is used, the pre-sign for an area or a limb need not be repeated for each indication.

263a ⬭ A body area

b) ‖ A limb

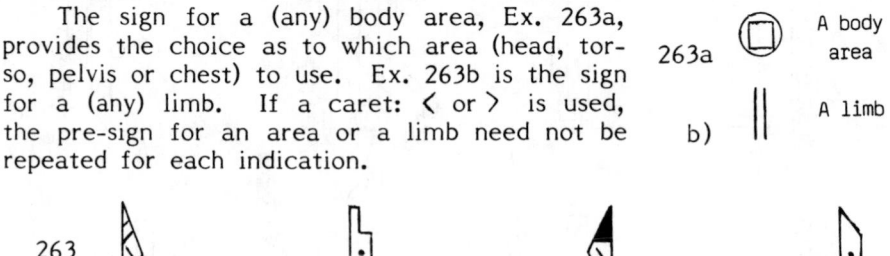

263

c) _____ An area tilts side in high level

d) _____ An area tilts forward in middle level

e) _____ A limb ends slanting left side low

f) _____ A limb moves to left front diagonal

Indication of Specific Part

By placing the appropriate part of the body sign before a direction symbol we state which part tilts, inclines, or 'takes a direction'.

Ex. 264a shows the torso tilting right side high; in 264b the head inclines forward high, while in 264c the right arm is up above the shoulder. The left leg is forward horizontal in 264d.

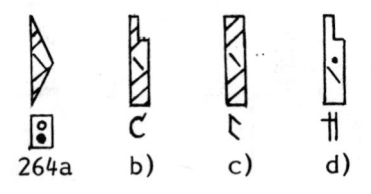

264a   b)   c)   d)

273

Reading Study No. 44

SPECIFIC TILTING, INCLINING

A 'Chinese Mandarin' dance - in no way authentic. Start with the arms folded across the waist. All directions for limbs are understood to be tilting (taking a direction) - note 'key' at start.

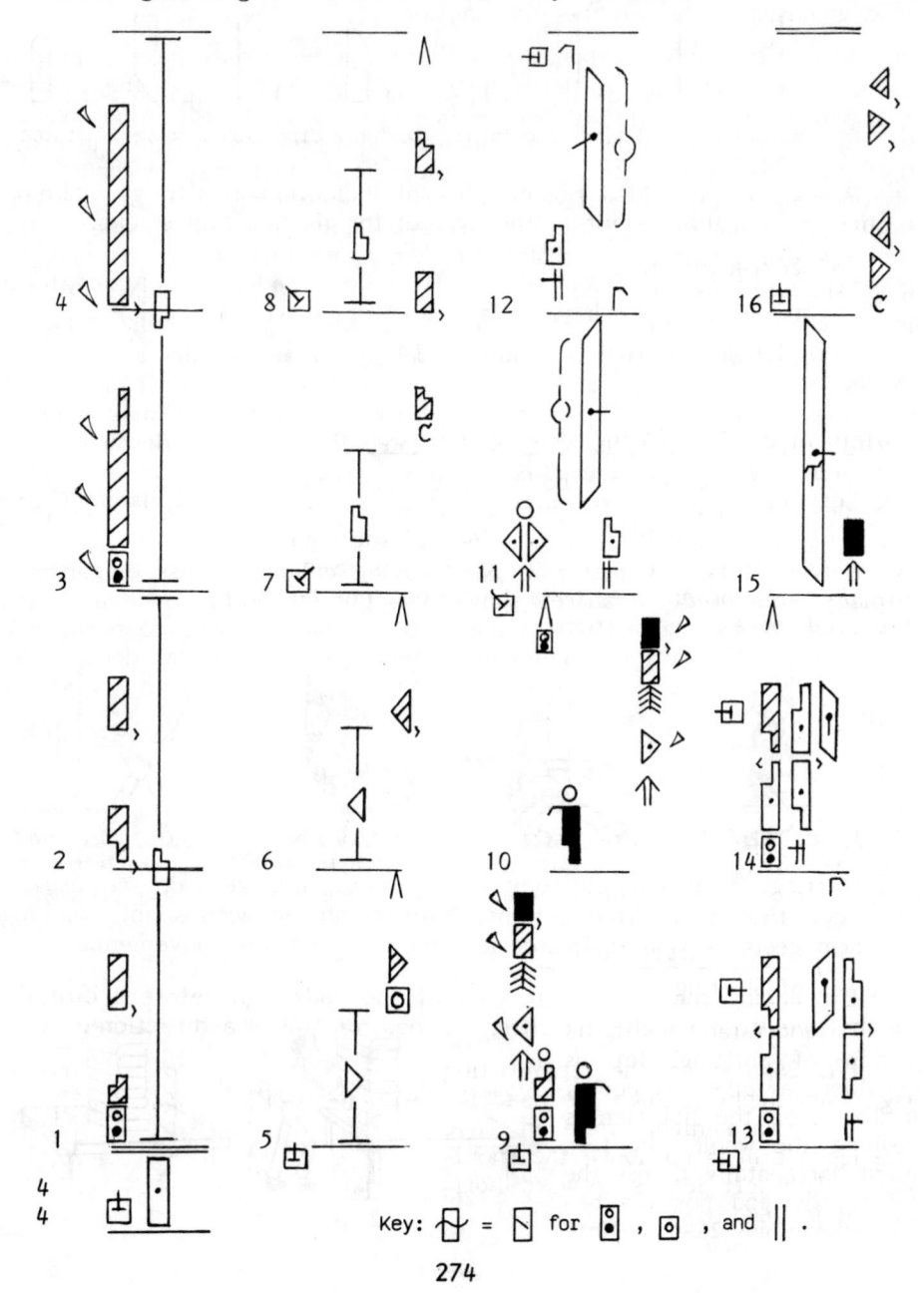

Key: (symbol) = (symbol) for (symbol), (symbol), and ‖.

SHIFTING BODY AREAS

The action of a body area shifting out of its normal alignment is usually a displacement on a straight path. The part in question may displace very slightly or a great deal. Shifts of head, chest and pelvis appear in modern jazz either in isolation - often with a particular rhythmic pattern - or as part of a general movement pattern serving to augment or embellish the main action.

What can shifting express? Shifting the head may have a practical function as when one peers forward to see better. In the theater a sideward head shift may be necessary in order to see when one is sitting behind a tall person. A sideward shift may also occur in order that one may hear better. A backward head shift may be caused by disapproval or by a negative reaction to something such as a nasty smell. A comic effect may be provided by the 'pecking' action of the head as it shifts forward and backward. Or shifting actions may be decorative, seductive, or may express valor or wonder, as in the lateral head shifts seen in East Indian classical dance.

Shifts of the chest may function for the same reasons as those of the head in that the chest often carries the head along as it shifts and thus may augment a head shift. A forward chest shift may express warmth toward a person who is in front of you. A sideward chest shift may occur to get out of someone's way or to reach for an object. The very fluid torso movements in certain African dances often include or center on chest shifts.

Pelvic shifts may result in hip swaying or in the less elegant hip displacements used in cabaret shows. In contemporary dance and jazz a hip shift may augment a lunging step, or may be used to produce a distortion in the natural alignment of the torso, an angular design.

265a   b)   c)   d)

Shifting movement of body areas, as in Ex. 265a-d, are usually practiced first as isolated actions, later combined with simple walking and arm gestures, and still later as part of composite movements.

Analysis of Shifting

To understand the basic action of shifting, let us consider a pile of books. In Ex. 266a the librarian is pushing the whole pile forward horizontally across the table, the end position being shown in 266b. Note

266a   b)

Analysis of Shifting (continued)

each book has travelled the same amount. In 266c the top books have been moved horizontally (shifted) while the bottom books have not moved. In 266d several books in the middle have been shifted while the top and bottom books remained

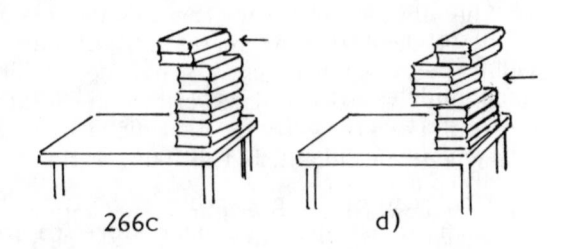

266c   d)

in place. How do these examples relate to movement of the body as a whole and to movements of its parts?

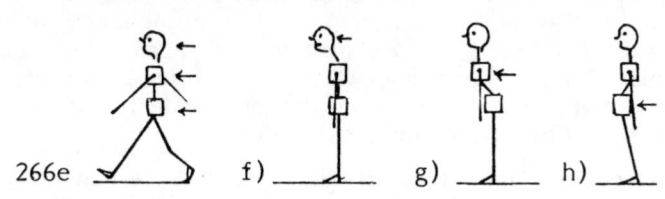

266e   f)   g)   h)

Ex. 266e illustrates a progression, a path forward for the body as a whole. Such moving to another place on a straight path occurs in walking and is comparable to Ex. 266b. In 266f only the head 'travels', shifting forward on a straight path while remaining upright. In 266g the chest has shifted, in this case carrying the head with it. A pelvic shift forward is shown in 266h, the chest remaining behind, comparable to 266d above. Degree of displacement for shifts varies according to the build of the body, that is, how a particular part is attached, and to the individual flexibility and training of the performer.

Indication of Shifting

Because a shift for a body area can be analyzed as a path (albeit somewhat limited in range) the movement could be (and sometimes has been) described with a straight path sign in which is placed the appropriate direction signs, as in Ex. 267b. However, because the point of reference for shifts is the natural body alignment to which the part will return, it is more appropriate to indicate the action as one in which each part of that body section is displaced spatially the same amount. In a tilting, inclining action, the free end of the torso or limb travels the greatest amount and each part that is closer to the base travels less, as illustrated in 267c for the torso and 267d for the arm.

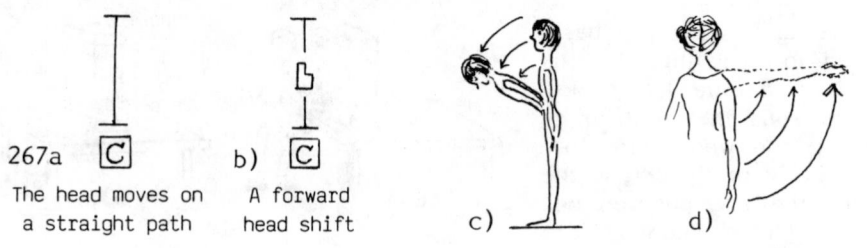

267a   C   b)   C   c)   d)

The head moves on   A forward
a straight path   head shift

Specific Directional Actions

Because in a shift each part of the body section moves an equal amount, the equal sign: = is placed within the direction symbol. Ex. 267e states shifting into any direction. In 267f head shifts to right and left are shown. A return to center after a shift is written with a place middle sign; this represents the normal situation, the point from which shifting directions are judged. In 267g the forward head shift is followed by a return to center. For horizontal shifts the equal sign is usually placed below the dot, Ex. 267h. For high or low level shifts (shifting upward or downward) space must be left within the symbol for the equal sign, 267i, j). Ex. 267k describes a clockwise circular shift starting forward. For shifting actions the sign for the area of the head: ⊡ is considered more appropriate than the ordinary sign for the head, ⊂, though this latter would not be wrong.

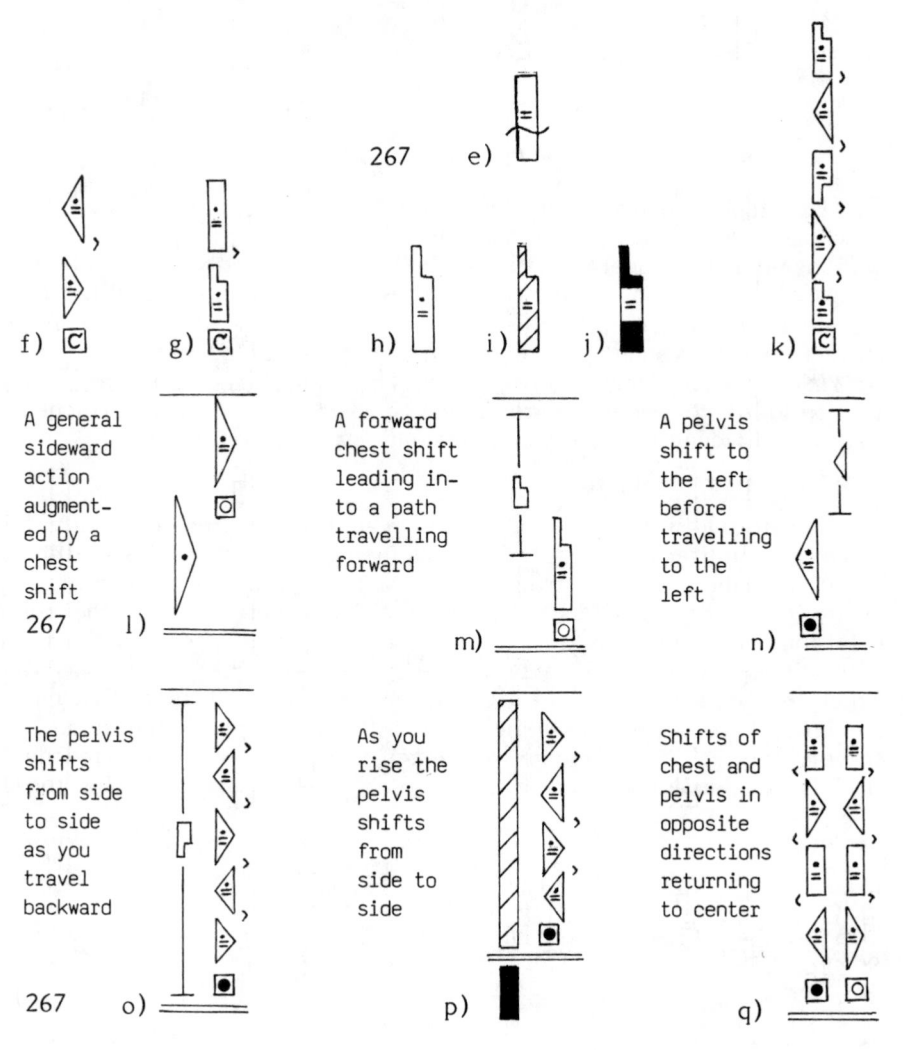

267   e)

f) ⊡   g) ⊡   h)   i)   j)   k) ⊡

A general sideward action augmented by a chest shift

267   l)

A forward chest shift leading into to a path travelling forward

m)

A pelvis shift to the left before travelling to the left

n)

The pelvis shifts from side to side as you travel backward

267   o)

As you rise the pelvis shifts from side to side

p)

Shifts of chest and pelvis in opposite directions returning to center

q)

277

Reading Study No. 45

SHIFTING BODY AREAS

When a shift is shown to return to center it is because that is an important action and not an incidental 'erasing' of a previous shift.

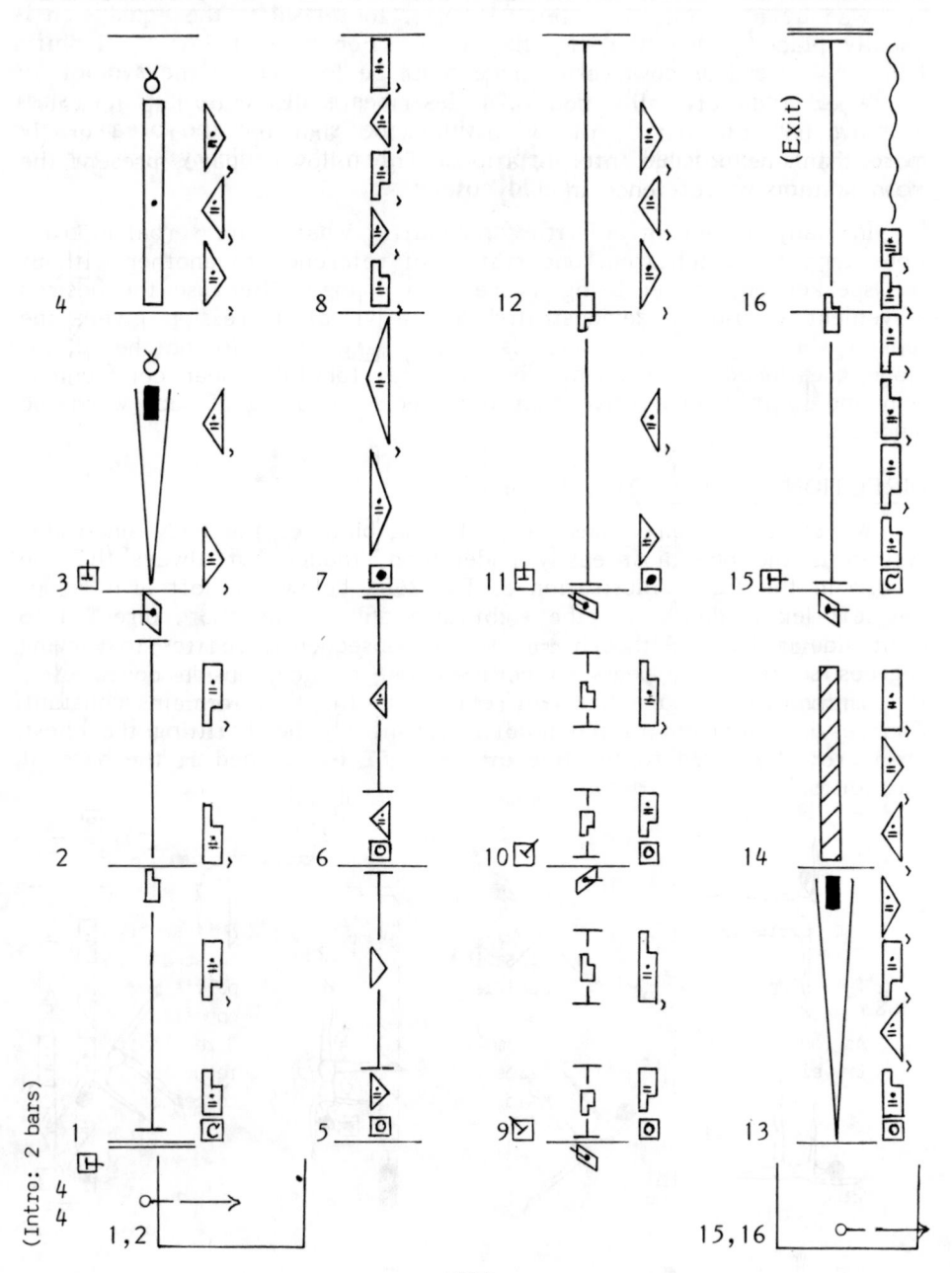

(Intro: 2 bars)

278

Chapter Twenty
DIRECTIONS: SYSTEMS OF REFERENCE

When a directional action is requested, for example "Leg forward" or "Arm up", to what do the words 'forward' and 'up' refer? There is more than one possible interpretation. The following pages present the main systems of reference in daily use.

In many movement activities, no matter what form, verbal instructions tend to switch from one system of reference to another without the speaker or listener being aware of a change. Because the desired movement is usually demonstrated and a visual impression given, the spoken words have only a secondary value and often are not heard, let alone questioned. But terminology is vital for full, clear communication and so it is imperative that the precise meaning of such words be pinned down.

DIRECTION - THE BODY CROSS:

We start with directions based on the build of the body since this system is the one most easily understood, though not always the one used. In the figure illustration of Ex. 268a below the left arm is up, the left leg is down, and the right arm and leg are both directed to right side middle. Although this figure subsequently rotates to varying degrees so that it appears to be lying on its side, upside down, etc., the configuration of the limbs in relation to the torso remains constant. Changes in placement of the limbs (inclining the head, tilting the chest, etc.) are all related to the line of the spine established at the base of the pelvis.

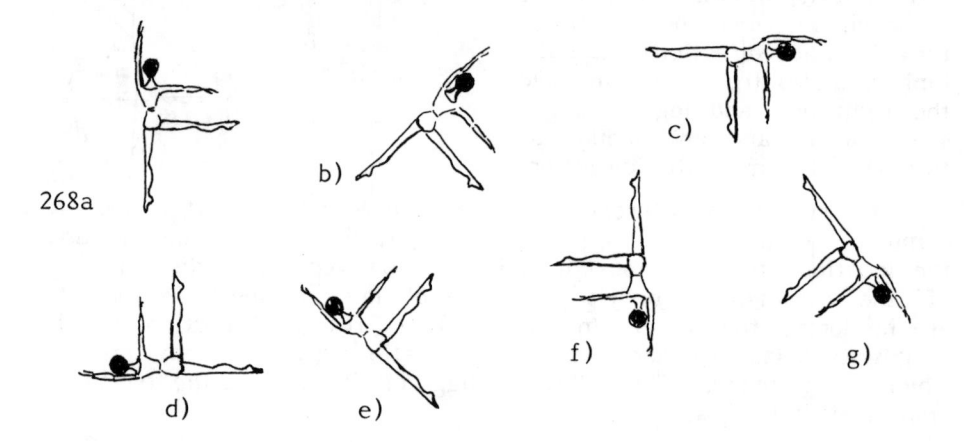

268a

b)

c)

d)

e)

f)

g)

Direction - The Body Cross (continued)

A directional reference to the Body Cross of Axes is based on the body build; there is no concern with outside points of reference, neither with the pull of gravity (a constant 'down') nor with a front established by a stage or classroom. It is the situation which astronauts experience when in the zero-gravity state. On earth we do not face this extreme since gravity is always with us; but there are many actions for which we find reference to directions according to the build of the body more convenient or more appropriate than to any other system.

The key for this system of reference: ⟃ is based on the idea of a circle representing the body aspects combined with a cross ┼ representing a cross of directions.

In general this key is most often used for the arms, head and chest when the torso tilts away from the vertical. When one is lying down, or upside down, the legs may also be described from this key.

DIRECTIONS - THE STANDARD CROSS: ⬤

Our concept of direction is habitually affected by our image of the vertical, upright standing or sitting position. Up is toward the ceiling; it is also past our head. Down is toward the floor; when we are standing it is also toward our feet. Right and left directions are established by the right and left sides of the body when we are standing. Forward and backward are determined by where the front and back surfaces of the body are facing in the normal, untwisted standing position. Since the pull of gravity is constant, up and down remain constant. We are aware of where our personal front is; thus the direction forward is easily determined. When a turn of the whole body takes place the direction forward is carried with us.

Upright Situation

Ex. 269a shows the right arm and right leg forward horizontal. Although in 269b the body has turned, this direction for the limbs remains the same. In 269c the right arm and leg are right side middle, and no amount of turning will change this direction.

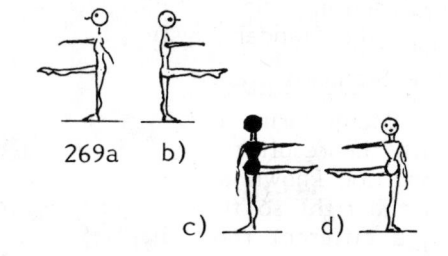

269a   b)

c)   d)

This system of reference is called the Standard as it is the most commonly used. When the body is upright, there is no question about the location of the various directions. However, when the torso tilts off the vertical, the body's physical 'up' and the line of gravity 'up' are no longer the same. In the Standard Cross of Directions the line of gravity holds firm and it is the designations given to body directions which are adjusted. The following diagrams illustrate some typical examples of this adjustment.

280

Torso off the Vertical

The following examples illustrate a progression in lowering to the ground indicating how the direction forward horizontal is maintained despite the change in torso direction and change in support. For many types of movement there is a strong need to relate to the Standard directions in such situations.

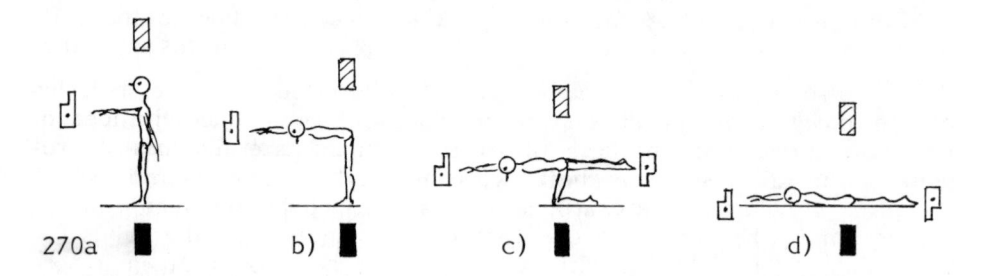

270a   b)   c)   d)

The next examples follow the same progression but show the sideward horizontal direction.

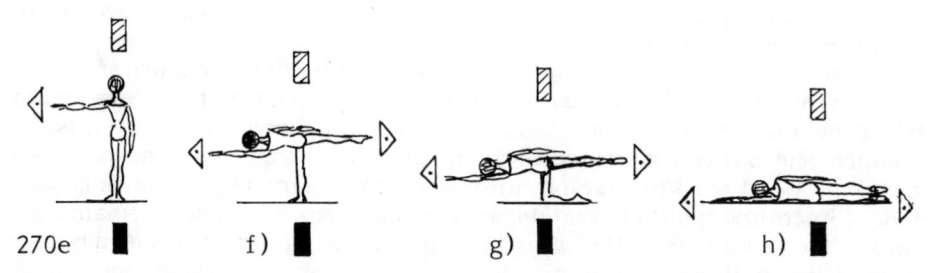

270e   f)   g)   h)

The key for the Standard System of Reference: ⟶ is based on the sign: + for the cross of horizontal directions combined with the sign ● representing the vertical line of gravity (the missing third dimension). Thus the Standard system has a constant gravity-based up and down.

The Standard Stance

Many forms of dance include strong twisting actions in the torso with the result that the upper and lower parts have different fronts, a condition known as 'divided front'. In Ex. 271a the chest has twisted to the right so that forward for the arms is in- to a different room direction from forward for the legs. In this twisting action the front of the chest clearly establishes the forward direc- tion for the arms. However, such twists some- times occur to give greater scope to arm ges- tures, to emphasize or color them without any sense of abandoning the previously established forward direction. There may be a considerable change in the shoulder line without a sense of a new forward direction having been established.

271a

St

The Standard Stance (continued)

271b   →St   c) St←   d)   Ṡt

In 271b a twist in the upper body has resulted from the inclusion of the body in the man's gesture reaching forward to touch the dog. Note the use of 'St' in these illustrations to indicate the direction of stance. Ex. 271c shows a chest twist in a stylized movement in which the arms are carried backward; stance is retained by the feet. In the next example the chest and one foot retain stance while the pelvis rotates taking the right leg with it, 271d. The head is often an important factor in retaining the previous front; usually the eyes project into the stance direction so that stance is held at both extremities, i.e. by the support and the head.

Definition of Stance

Stance is the main front, the forward direction established by the body as a whole. When parts of the body twist away from that front, the part that does not twist (usually the feet or a foot) retains the original front, the forward direction. In some dance forms the lower part of the body twists away while the upper part retains stance. Ex. 272a illustrates the legs and hips twisting away while chest, arms and head retain stance (in this case the direction facing the reader); 272b is a similar example.

Since direction for arm gestures is judged from the front of the chest (the shoulder line) and leg gestures from the front of the pelvis, we need an indication to state that, despite twists in the torso, forward is to be taken from stance. The sign for stance directions is a combination of the sign for retention in space: ◇ combined with the key for the Standard Cross of Directions: ✛ to produce the key: ◈ .

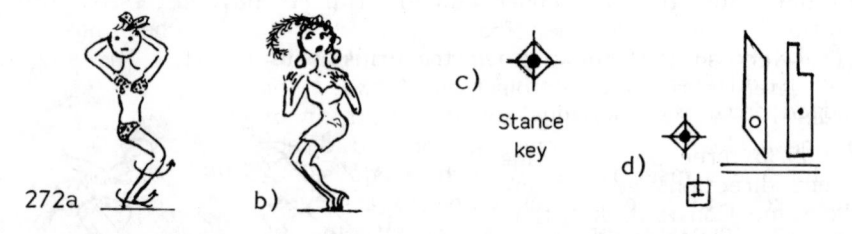

272a   b)   c)   ◈   Stance key   d)

Ex. 272d illustrates use of the Stance key. The general body twist to the left is accompanied by a general forward movement. Forward is understood to be toward the audience since such was the basic facing direction for the body as a whole at the start.

DIRECTION - THE CONSTANT CROSS: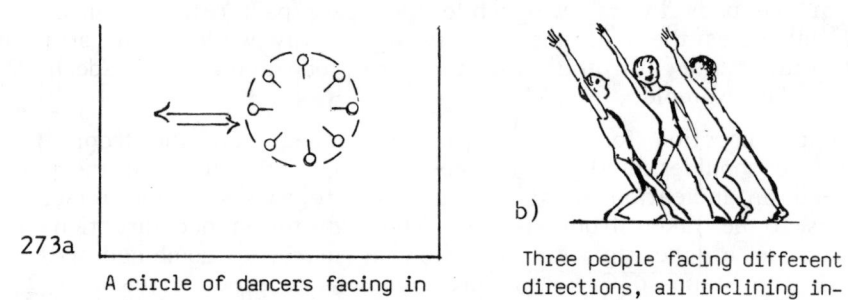

In any defined area it is usual for one side (one wall) to be designated as 'front'. On stage this front is obviously the audience. Whatever the location, once the room 'front' is set, directions based on the
Constant Cross remain constant: they neither turn with the performer
(as the Standard directions do) nor tilt with the performer (as Body-
based directions do). The idea of the Constant Cross of direction and
the key for it were introduced in Chapter Thirteen, page 185, in relation to the Front Signs. Here we are concerned with its use for movement.

The center of these Constant directions lies in the performer (not
in the center of the stage) and travels with the performer. Though he
or she may turn, as mentioned before, the Constant directions do not;
thus Constant 'forward' always remains into the same spatial direction
in the room. The established 'front' direction (the audience) is called
'Constant forward', which is not to be confused with the specific location of the center-front area of the room or stage.

When and why do movements need to be described in terms of the
Constant directions? There are two main needs. In a group in which
people are facing different directions and hence have different personal
fronts, the need may arise for all to move on parallel lines into the
same Constant direction. Stating this Constant direction avoids having
to describe the different step directions needed for each performer.

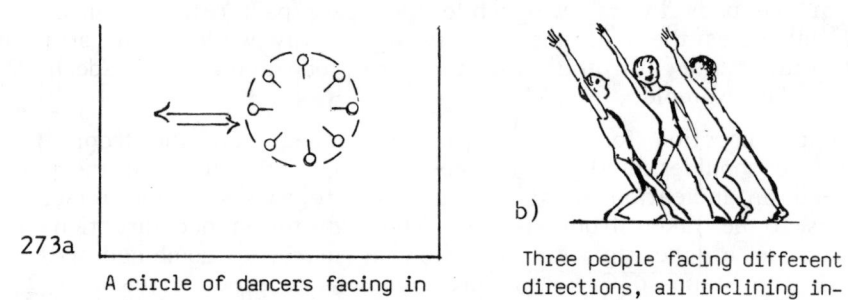

273a

A circle of dancers facing in
travels toward stage left.

b)

Three people facing different
directions, all inclining into the same room direction.

In Ex. 273a the whole group travels Constant left. The step direction is different for each person
as judged from the individual front.

In 273b three people facing
different directions gesture into the same Constant direction.
Another example, 273c, shows
three men pulling a rope into
the same spatial direction each
facing a different direction in
relation to the rope.

273c

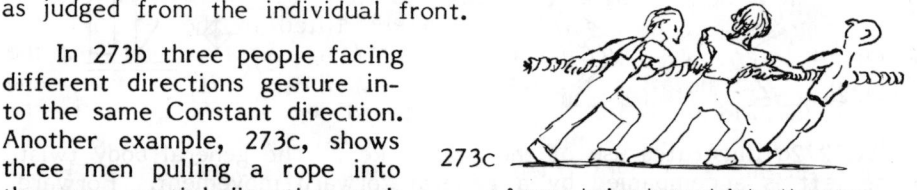

A rope being heaved into the same
direction by three men, each facing a different direction.

283

The Constant Cross (continued)

For a single person the need
for a Constant directional description arises when gradual turning
accompanies travelling, as in 273d.
Or a performer may be gesturing
undeviatingly into a Constant direction while turning.   For such
gestures a Standard or Body key
description is not satisfactory in
that neither directly describes the
movement idea.

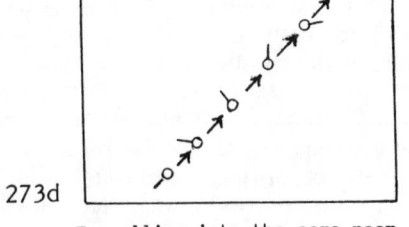

273d

Travelling into the same room
direction while slowly turning.

The sign for the Constant Cross of Directions is based on the sign
for an area: ☐ combined with a cross: ✛ representing a cross of directions.   Thus ⊞ represents the directions in an area, usually a room
or stage, but it could be any area in which one direction is designated
as front, the forward direction.

Use of Constant Directions Key

By placing the key for the Constant Cross before a direction symbol we indicate how that direction is to be interpreted.   In Ex. 274a
the instruction is to travel on the Constant right front diagonal; this
means that, no matter where the performers are facing, all will move
on parallel paths into the same Constant direction, as illustrated in Ex.
274b in which each performer is stepping into a different direction
judged from the personal front.

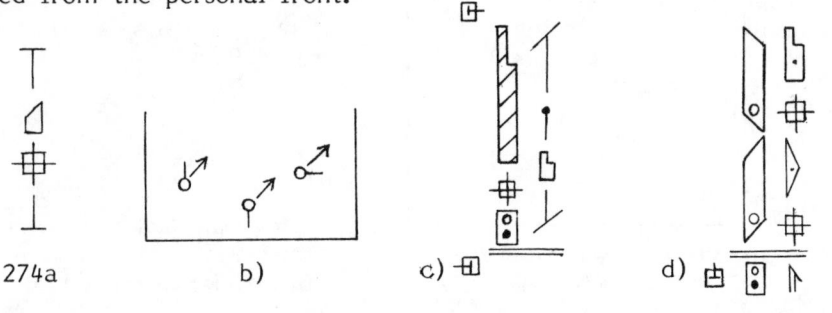

274a   b)   c) ⊞   d)

As an example of a gesture using a Constant Cross description, Ex.
274c shows the torso tilting to Constant forward while the performer
travels on a circular path.   Physically the torso will start tilting to the
right, progress over a forward tilt and end tilted to the left; but the
movement intent was to have the torso tilting constantly toward the
audience.   The notation of 274c describes this intention simply and
clearly.   In 274d torso twists of no specified degree occur, first to the
right, then to the left.   During the first twist the right arm gestures
toward Constant side right, then to Constant forward as the twist left
occurs.   Because degree of twist is not stated and a clear directional
result is desired, a Constant description is the most practical.   In jazz
dance where many twists in the body occur, spatial clarity for a group

often results from use of Constant directions, because degree of twist may vary slightly amony individual performers. For Constant direction descriptions levels for steps and gestures are determined as with the Standard key; a middle level gesture is horizontal, parallel with the floor, high level is slanting upward and low level is slanting downward.

Placement of Keys

The appropriate key for a system of reference may be placed before the direction symbol it modifies, as illustrated in the previous examples, or it may .be placed next to the direction symbol it modifies, as in Ex. 275a-c below. When several consecutive directions are to be modified by a key, the key is placed in a vertical bracket alongside the symbols, as in 275d.

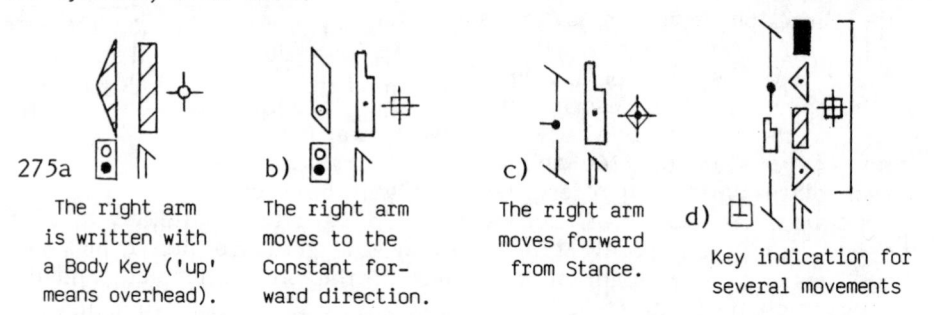

275a	b)	c)	d)
The right arm is written with a Body Key ('up' means overhead).	The right arm moves to the Constant forward direction.	The right arm moves forward from Stance.	Key indication for several movements

For a whole sequence the appropriate system of reference to be used (other than the Standard which is automatically understood to be in effect) may be stated as a key before the start of the piece. In 275e use of the Body system of reference is indicated. Ex. 275f gives the information that the Body key refers only to the arms.

Body Key for all gestures

275e

Body Key for arms only

f)

DETERMINING CHOICE OF KEY

How does one determine which system of reference to use at any particular time? Observation and experience indicate that the decision is based on recognition of a clearly defined direction, regardless of which key is involved. On looking at the destination of a limb, the mind immediately latches onto what is visually clear and so chooses the description which first comes to mind. There is no deliberate choice of key; whatever visually 'hits home' is chosen. The eye is impressed by directions which fall into dimensional directions according to ✛ , ✛ , or ⊞ , or into a 45° intermediate direction. The mind instinctively rejects descriptions which involve subtle intermediate directions whenever possible. Let us take some examples. What descriptions would you give to the following movement destinations for the right arm?

Determining Choice of Key (continued)

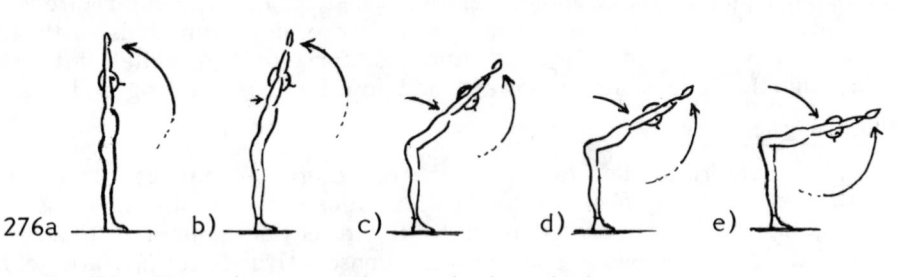

276a   b)   c)   d)   e)

In Ex. 276a the torso is vertical and the arm arrives up. There is no question about how to describe direction here; it is the same for ⊹ and ✦. In 276b the eye will see the torso slightly forward and the arm ending up from ⊹ , the line of the spine, so that description will come to mind. In 267c torso and arm are clearly forward high from ✦ . But in 276d and 276e the torso is at intermediate points; therefore the arm will be seen

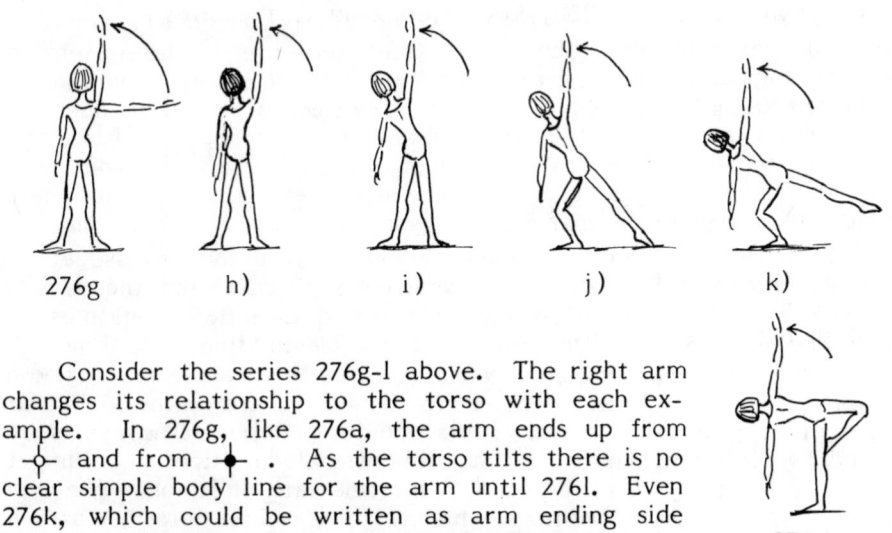

276f

to end up from ⊹ . If the torso is forward horizontal, as in 276f, the eye will probably revert again to judging the direction from ✦ , though some people might be conscious of the body alignment and call the direction up from ⊹ .

The above examples illustrate that the eye looks for clear spatial lines. In several cases the clear line existed only in the ⊹ key; thus Body directions came first to mind.

276g   h)   i)   j)   k)

Consider the series 276g-l above. The right arm changes its relationship to the torso with each example. In 276g, like 276a, the arm ends up from ⊹ and from ✦ . As the torso tilts there is no clear simple body line for the arm until 276l. Even 276k, which could be written as arm ending side high, is unlikely to be so described. What hits the eye is the vertical line from ✦ ; therefore this key will probably be the choice.

276 l

The following examples, seen as from bird's-eye view, illustrate determining choice of description in the forward direction.

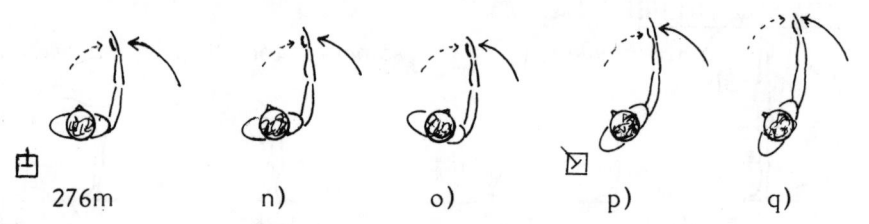

276m   n)   o)   p)   q)

In Ex. 276m the performer is facing ⬚ and the right arm ends forward from ✦ , ◇ and also ⊞ In 276n and 276o the slight change of front for the chest to one side or the other, produces an intermediate arm direction which is awkward to describe in relation to ✦ or ◇ but from ⊞ is the clear cut direction of forward middle. In 276p the arm is diagonal from ✦ and ◇ , but forward from ⊞ , so this last may be the first choice, depending on the sense, i.e. the idea in the movement context. Forward from ⊞ is the clear direction for 276q. In 276r the description can clearly be side from ✦ and ◇ . There would need to be a particular reason for preferring to call this destination forward from ⊞ .

276r

The examples given above have purposely been put into a series to illustrate the point. A far better test is to meet isolated examples with no related previous reference. It is important to become familiar with the three main keys and to be able to refer to them as needed. The Standard key is the one which is commonly preferred when circumstances do not demand another key. Consistent use of one system of reference facilitates quick giving and receiving of information; but if this system is not serviceable, then it is better to switch to another, using the key as an adjective as in 'Body' up, 'Constant' forward, and so on. In the classroom physical demonstration of a desired direction makes such adjectives superfluous. The eye sees, but no mental note is made as to what reference is being used and how this reference can affect the idea or intention of the movement. Improved movement education must include full awareness of how space is being used and for what purpose. Knowledge of how directions are determined and named should be part of every performer's equipment.

Reading Study No. 46

SYSTEMS OF REFERENCE

The music for this study is the same as for Reading Study No. 15 in Chapter Six.

Chapter Twenty One
DYNAMICS

Dynamics is an essential part of all movement. Movement cannot occur without some degree of energy, and dynamics concerns the ebb and flow of energy, how energy is used and to what degree. Dynamics is a specialized study which cannot be fully investigated in the basic explorations of this book. We have been concerned with the 'what' in movement, the kind of action to be performed, rather than with how that action is presented, the quality, texture, i.e. the dynamic content.

In exploring different kinds of movement we inevitably include some dynamic qualities; freedom in this respect was allowed throughout the experience of looking at basic actions. The movement studies in particular allow for a range of qualities; they were composed with a range of dynamics in mind and this range is reflected in the musical accompaniment. Dance is much affected by the music which accompanies it; the speed, weight, melody line, harmonies and particularly the rhythmic structure call forth different movement responses. Vigorous music encourages the performer to indulge in energetic actions; placid, languid music calls for sustained, flowing movement. This automatic response to music is part of the dance experience; dancing without the stimulus and framework of music to guide us is difficult; we are not trained to be self-sufficient in producing our own sustained rhythmic base, our own dynamic phrasing.

It is perhaps because of our hereditary dependence on music that certain aspects of movement, in particular dynamics, have never been fully investigated. We express what the music expresses. Relating to the music is in itself an education, but we never come face to face with the factors in movement that produce expression, how the body produces dynamic changes.

Expression in dance is a combination of subtle changes in the use of space, of parts of the body, of timing and of energy. All style in dance is composed of repeated use of characteristic patterns in minor spatial modifications, in subtle use of body parts, timing and energy. An investigation into expression and style also requires a degree of analysis beyond the scope of this book.

A word must be said about innate dynamics. Different types of actions require different degrees and patterns in use of energy. Jumping requires a greater degree of energy than walking. Either of these can be performed with a minimum amount of energy, i.e. just enough to produce the movement, no more. The result expresses lassitude, weariness, weakness, lack of enthusiasm, dullness. Yet the basic action is achieved. In contrast a performer bubbling with energy will walk vigorously, the excess energy appearing in how the feet are placed, the body held, the arms swung. Similarly excess energy in a spring will result in a higher bound into the air, a more vibrant use of the body, head and arms.

Innate movement dynamic variations result from changes in speed and distance. Very slow movements, whether transferences of weight or gestures, require control and guidance; the body's natural desire to move, once inertia has been overcome, must be held back. The slower the movement and the shorter the distance to be covered the more care and awareness of each moment of the movement are present. On the other hand, the need to cover a great distance in a short time will produce quite a different quality. Energy will rush into the muscles to get the body in motion to travel swiftly or, in the case of a gesture, the limb to arrive as fast as possible at the new destination.

The tempo of the accompanying music has a dramatic effect on movement. Consider a simple jumping sequence such as springing up and down with the feet together. If the music is too slow the jumps become heavy and earthbound; too much of the excess time must be spent on the ground, the performer waiting to rise into the air again in time with the musical beat. If the music is too fast the jumps become shallow and eventually end in a frenetic vibrating. The correct tempo for the individual performer will produce comfortable, fully realized rebound jumps. Another revealing movement pattern is an arm or leg swing. As the limb moves in an arc toward and away from gravity a comfortable tempo will allow a swift giving in to gravity and an increasingly sustained rising away from gravity, but extremes in tempo ruin this natural flow; tempi too slow and too fast will produce changes in the state of the body as a whole and in the particular limb which result in very different expressions.

A few dynamic indications have been used in the movement examples and studies; some additional explanations may be helpful.

ACCENTS

An accent, a momentary stress (increase in energy), is familiar in movement, in speech and in music. A sharp rise in energy and a slight increase or decrease in speed, both of which disappear immediately, are easy to produce - the performer need not analyze exactly what ingredients are needed to produce an accent.

An accent may be slight (light), using a slight rise in energy, or it may be strong, involving marked energy.

277   Slight accent   or   Strong accent   or

a)   b)

Earlier in this book we met the possibility of an accent occurring at the start of an action, at the end, or during a movement.

277 Accent at the start of an action   c)

Accent at the end of an action   d)

Accents during a movement   e)

An accent at the start usually sends a movement on its way, as in an impulsive action in everyday life. An accent at the end brings the movement to a strong conclusion; it produces an impact and gives the effect of a decisive movement statement. Accents also occur during the progression of a movement, 277e. Accents usually have a defined rhythmic pattern which adds interest to otherwise simple movement.

ENERGY SUSTAINED, INCREASED, DECREASED

A rise in energy level may be sustained for a while or the energy may gradually increase or gradually decrease.

Sign for strength   278a

Increased energy is sustained   b)

Increase in strength, energy   c)

Decrease in strength, energy   d)

The length of the vertical bracket in Ex. 278b indicates duration of the energy sustainment; the length of the increase or decrease signs, Ex. 278c,d, indicates duration of the energy change.

Unemphasized

When a particular movement should be of no importance, the indication for lack of emphasis is used. This sign, Ex. 279a, is related to the sign for relaxed, lowered energy, 279b, since it is a lowering of energy which makes a movement less noticeable. If a particular movement is to be stressed, the sign of 279c is placed next to the movement indication. As emphasis involves an increase in energy, the sign for emphasis is related to the sign for strength, Ex. 278a. The base of the signs for emphasized and unemphasized point in toward the indications they qualify.

279

a) ⟍ or ⟋

Unemphasized

b) ℮

Relaxed

c) ⟨ or ⟩

Emphasized

A full investigation into dynamics in movement has not yet been undertaken. In different areas of movement study some deep investigation has been undertaken, for example the various physical tests necessary to sending men to the moon, but none has concentrated on dynamics for dance - practical and expressive. A tremendous step forward was Laban's contribution in his development of Effort, but this work stopped short and more needs to be done. Many modern dancers have been concerned with dynamics; in isolated pockets much of value has been evolved but the great pull-together has yet to take place. The investigation into dynamics in human movement being undertaken by computer researchers promises a completely objective, scientific approach. As such investigation is being conducted in liaison with dance and movement specialists, there is promise of a factual body of knowledge emerging which will enrich future movement education.

REVIEW FOR CHAPTERS NINETEEN, TWENTY AND TWENTY-ONE

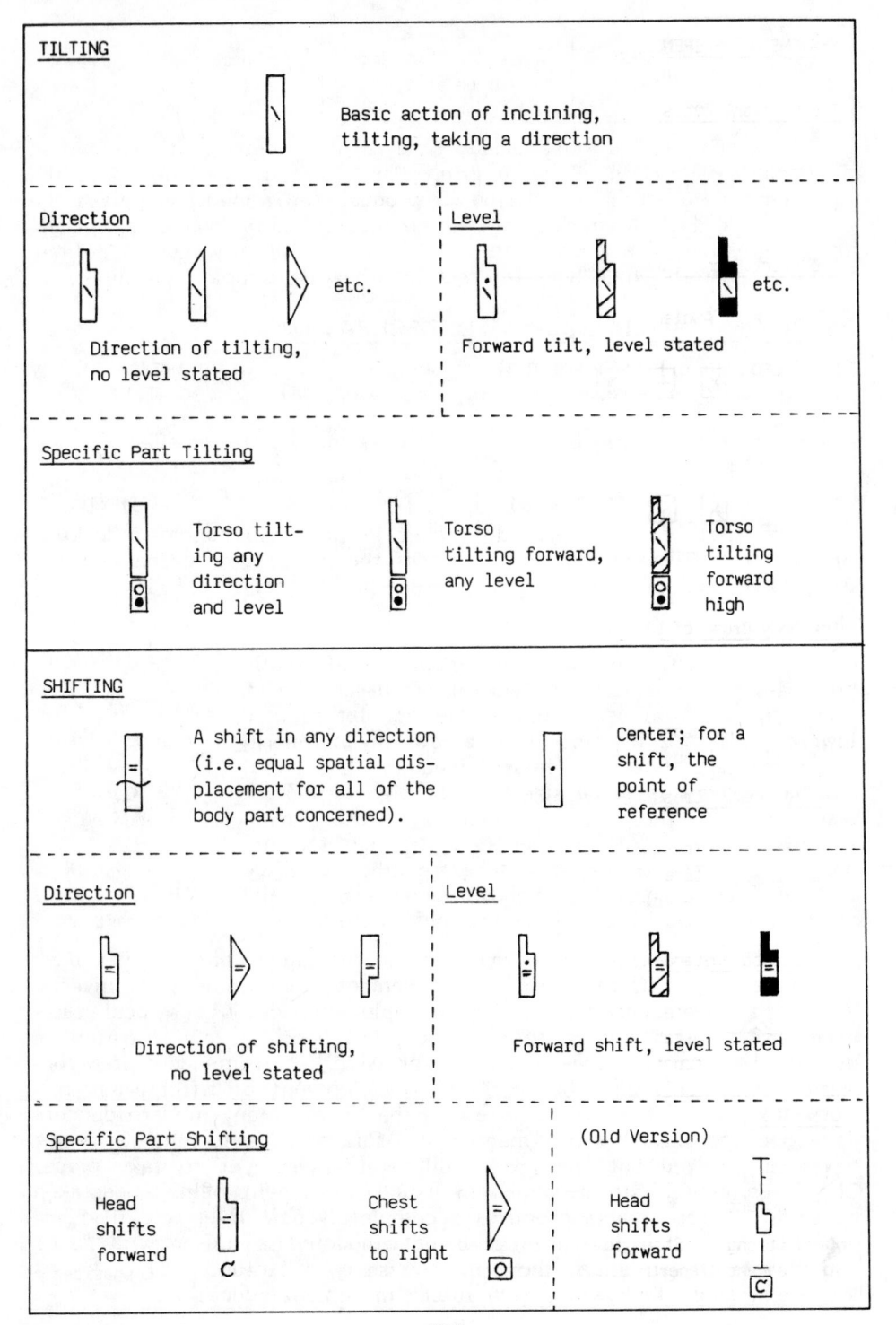

TILTING

Basic action of inclining, tilting, taking a direction

Direction

Direction of tilting, no level stated

etc.

Level

Forward tilt, level stated

etc.

Specific Part Tilting

Torso tilting any direction and level

Torso tilting forward, any level

Torso tilting forward high

SHIFTING

A shift in any direction (i.e. equal spatial displacement for all of the body part concerned).

Center; for a shift, the point of reference

Direction

Direction of shifting, no level stated

Level

Forward shift, level stated

Specific Part Shifting

Head shifts forward

Chest shifts to right

(Old Version)

Head shifts forward

REVIEW FOR NINETEEN, TWENTY AND TWENTY-ONE (continued)

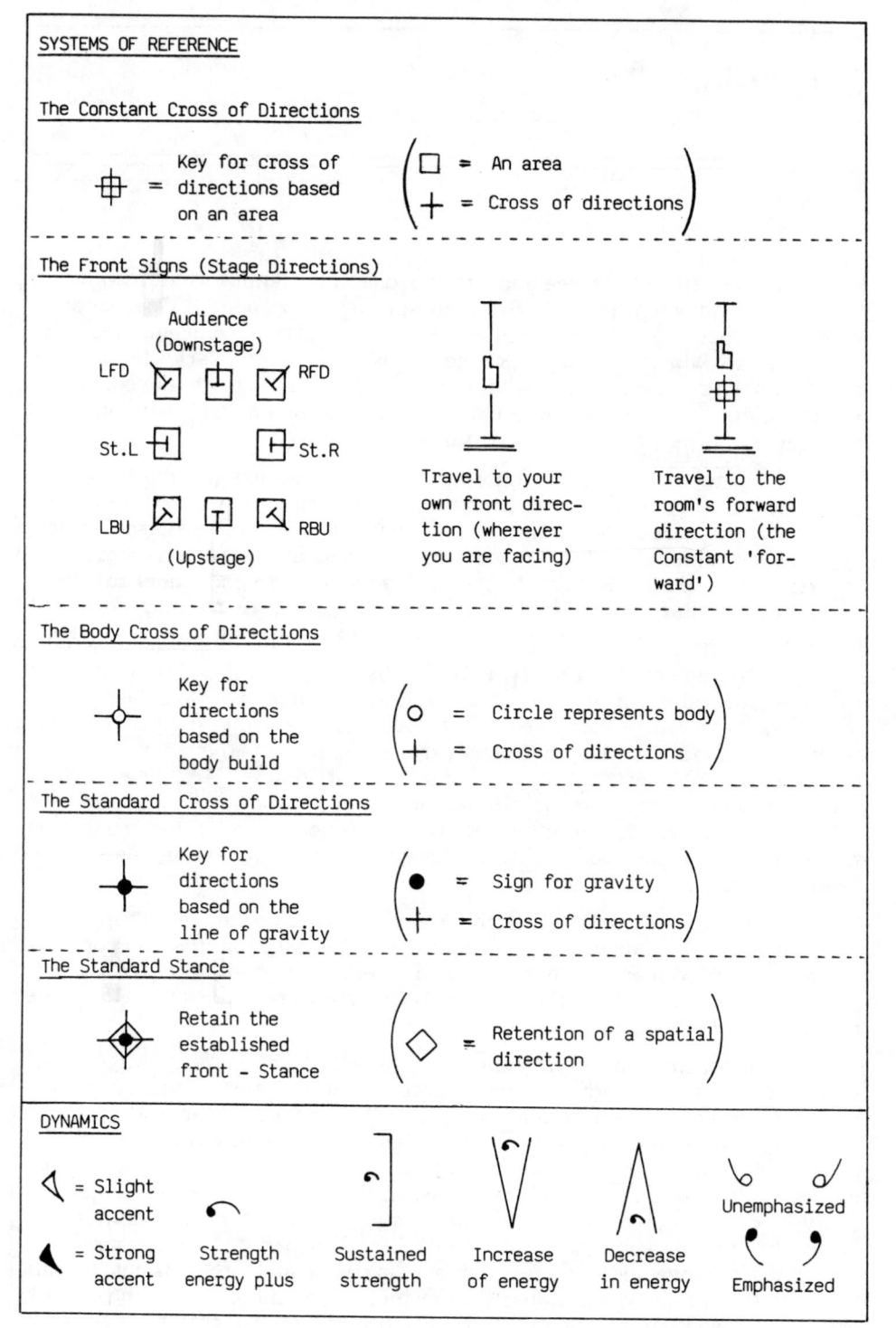

293

Conclusion

It is not enough to see movement; one must know what to aim for in moving and what to look for in observing movement. One needs to know and recognize what are the component parts of movement and be aware as to which of these are being used or particularly featured in any composite movement. Separation of the material of movement into its elements means recognizing those elements and naming them through use of a practical, universal terminology.

During the process of exploring and experiencing movement in the course of this book we have progressed from the most general concept and indication of a movement to a range of specific uses. No single type of movement study, no one style of dance has been favored; examples presented have been as general and open to individual interpretation as possible. This book leads comfortably into specific forms of movement study aimed at mastering physical and expressive techniques.

The Movement Family Tree of Verbs on pages 312-314 illustrates in an organized form the raw material with which we have been dealing. Our main focus has been on the actions themselves; thus it is the 'verbs' we have explored. 'Nouns' are the parts of the body, parts of the room, a partner, and any objects (props) in use. 'Adverbs', which are the 'how' in movement performance, include certain specific uses of time, of dynamics, of minor spatial variations and of the manner in which parts of the body initiate a movement. Some of these have been included in this book.

As has been evident from the material investigated in these chapters, many of our movement concerns are focussed on the aim or outcome of a movement. Thus we have needed to state directly the result of an action when this result is of greater importance than the movement which caused it.

The mechanics of movement may be analyzed in many ways - the sequence of muscle action, the degree of the angles produced at the joints by limb segments, and so on. The specific need dictates the form which the investigation (the analysis) will take. For the student mastering movement as an expression of the human condition or in order to gain specific movement skills, a balance between an objective analysis of movement structure and a comprehension of the content or intent of the movement is essential. It is hoped that for those who are new to movement studies the explanations and progressions in this book will have provided a basis on which to build and for those with previous movement training, a new insight into movement itself.

Appendix A
VALIDITY; ORGANIZATION OF THE NOTATION

Motif Description has very few rules. The main rule which needs to be known at once is that of validity, i.e. how long the result of a previous movement indication is to be in effect.

CANCELLATION RULE

Motif Description is concerned with movement: a full awareness of and involvement in a specified action. Because concentration is on each new movement in a sequence, importance is placed on the new material to be expressed, and not on retaining what has passed. There-fore automatic cancellation is the rule in Motif Description — do not retain the results of a previous activity.

Retention of a State

If a state, such as a twist, an extension, or a flexion, is to be re-tained maintenance is indicated by placing the sign for retention, Ex. 280a, immediately after the movement indication. The result of this movement will then be retained until the cancellation sign, Ex. 280b, is used. The sign: Λ , which is placed vertically above the indication it is to cancel, has the general meaning of "give up", "forget about it", "let it disappear". The timing of this cancellation can be fast, as in Ex. 280c, or slow, as in 280d. The length of the sign indicates dura-tion, the time it takes for cancellation to be achieved.

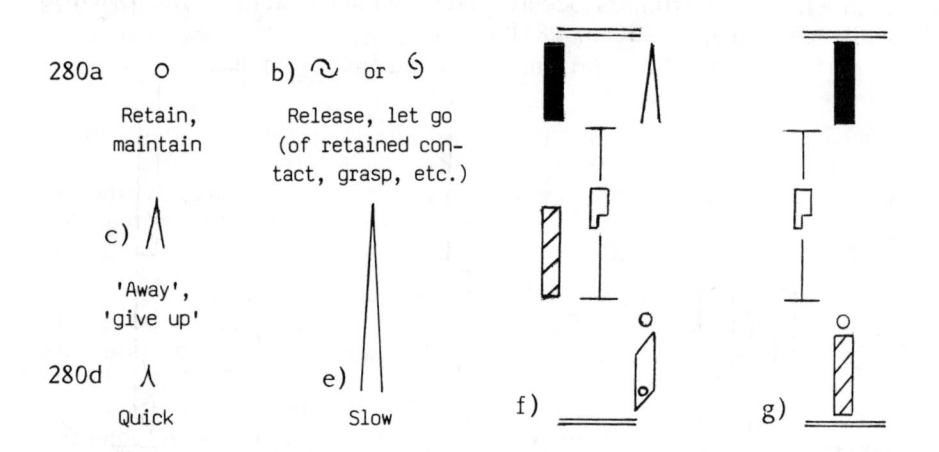

| 280a | o | b) ᔕ or ᔕ |
| Retain, maintain | | Release, let go (of retained con-tact, grasp, etc.) |

c) Λ

'Away', 'give up'

280d Λ   e)

Quick   Slow

f)

g)

In Ex. 280f the twist to the right is maintained while the perform-er is rising and travelling backward, but is cancelled when he starts sinking. Retained states are automatically cancelled by indication of the opposite kind of movement. In 280g, the upward movement which is held during the travelling is cancelled by the subsequent lowering.

295

PLACEMENT OF INFORMATION

Motif Description usually involves comparatively few indications. However, as we have seen, when two or more movement ideas occur at the same time, the indications appear more complex and a certain amount of organization of the material facilitates reading. Also, to a-void ambiguity certain basic guidelines need to be followed.

When more than one piece of movement information needs to be stated, the question arises as to how the symbols should be arranged.   Ex. 281a indicates one action, a turn.   In 281b extending occurs at the same time.   The two actions are placed side by side.   It does not matter which is placed on the right and which on the left, the meaning is the same.

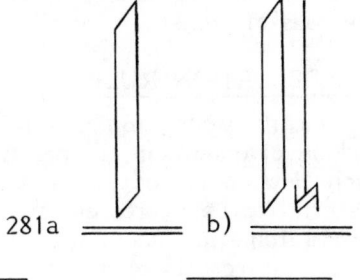

281a   b)

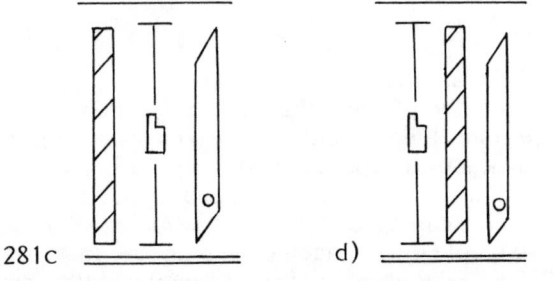

281c   d)   e)

In Ex. 281c three main actions are shown: travelling, rising and twist-ing.   It makes no difference if these are arranged as in 281c, as in d), or as in e).   When stillness occurs after combined actions its indication is usually centered, as in Ex. 281f below.

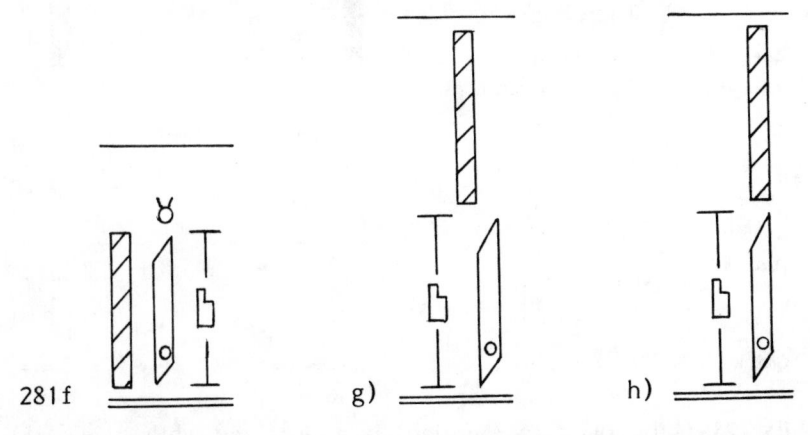

281f   g)   h)

After two simultaneous actions a single action is usually centered, as in Ex. 281g, though the placement of the symbols in 281h would be quite clear.

Ex. 281i illustrates two simultaneous actions following after three actions. Here again it would not matter if the two subsequent actions were placed slightly differently. The writer has only to be concerned with what seems logical and what facilitates reading. The turning sign in Ex. 281i logically follows after the twist into the same direction, just as in 281j the general movement down is placed above the previous movement up. Thus, for placement on the page, actions of the same category - flexion/extension, turning right/left, directional actions, paths - would logically follow one another in vertical placement.

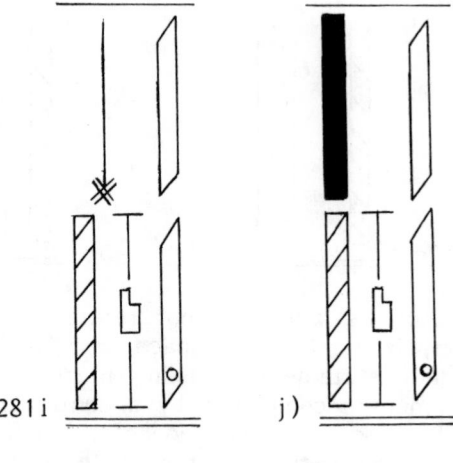

281i   j)

Right and Left Sides

Addition of the center line to indicate use of right or left side of the body poses the question of where this and other information should be placed.

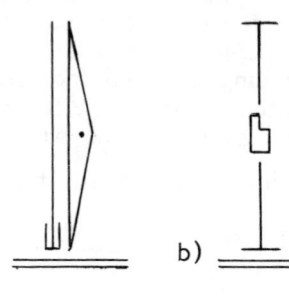

282a   b)   c)

Ex. 282a shows a simple statement of a sideward action for the right side of the body. In Ex. 282b a path travelling forward is added to the sideward movement; the instructions are quite clear. Ex. 282c illustrates a sideward action for the left side of the body during a turn to the right. Because of the 'left' and 'right' natures of these actions, there is a natural tendency to put them on the appropriate side. Ex. 282d shows turning to the right while upward and downward actions occur for the left and right sides of the body.

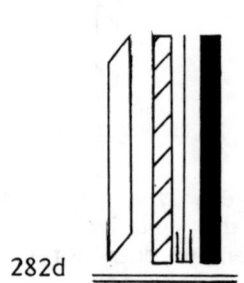

282d

L

Right and Left Sides (continued)

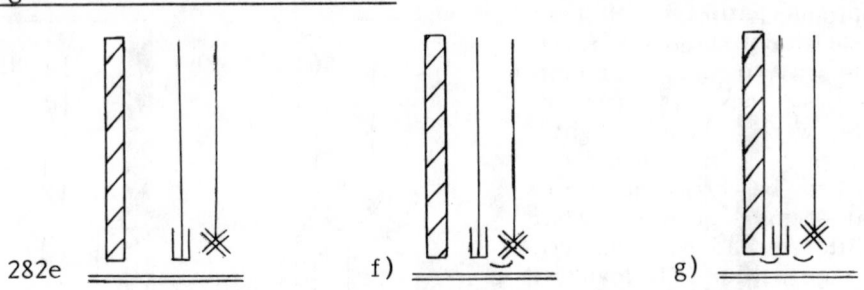

282e   f)   g)

Actions which do not relate to the center line should be placed apart, leaving enough space so that it is clear that a separate, independent statement is being made. Ex. 282e shows a general rising movement accompanied by a contraction on the right side of the body. In 282f use has been made of a small horizontal bow to tie the indication of contracting to the center line. In 282g both the rising and the contracting are tied to the center line indication; thus the example states that while the right side contracts, the left side is performing an upward movement. Use of this horizontal bow clarifies two simultaneous indications which belong together; however, use of a separation, as in Ex. 282e, is visually helpful.

Limbs, Parts of the Body

Main actions for the body as a whole are centered; actions for specific parts of the body (additional features) are placed adjacent on the right or left. Once certain placements have been established it is more practical for subsequent reading to keep indications of one kind vertically one after the other, rather than to switch placements. The degree to which this can be done may depend on what comes next.

If an action of a limb is the main movement, it is centered on the staff, as in Ex. 283a.

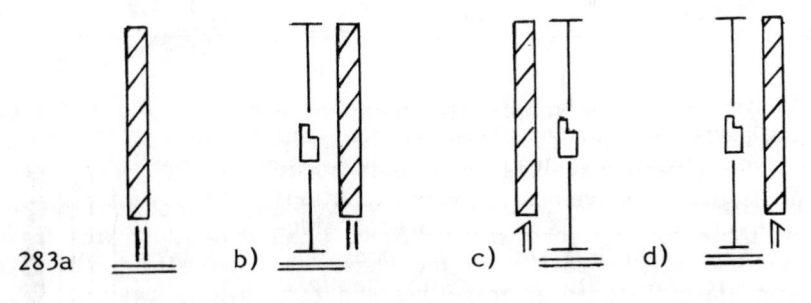

283a   b)   c)   d)

If there is a main general action, such as travelling, this is centered and the limb indication is placed alongside. In such cases right or left placement does not mean right or left limb; which side of the body is involved is still open. Ex. 283b states that 'a limb' moves up. In c) the limb is stated to be the left arm. Limbs for the right side of the body are placed on the right, those for the left on the left. Ex. 283d shows a path forward with the right arm moving up. In 283e two main actions, a twist and a lowering, occur in addition to the right arm gesture.

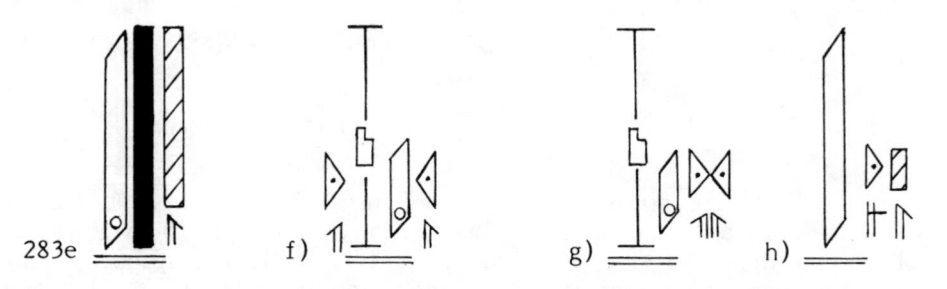

In Ex. 283f travelling forward begins with a twist to the right as both arms move across to the opposite side. When both limbs perform the same action, their signs may be placed next to each other to facilitate reading. In 283g the instructions for the arms have been placed together.

Placement on right or left applies to signs for the right and left limbs. In the case of indications for arm and leg of the same side, the arm is placed further out, as in 283h where, during the turn, the right leg is sideward and the right arm up.

Areas of the Body

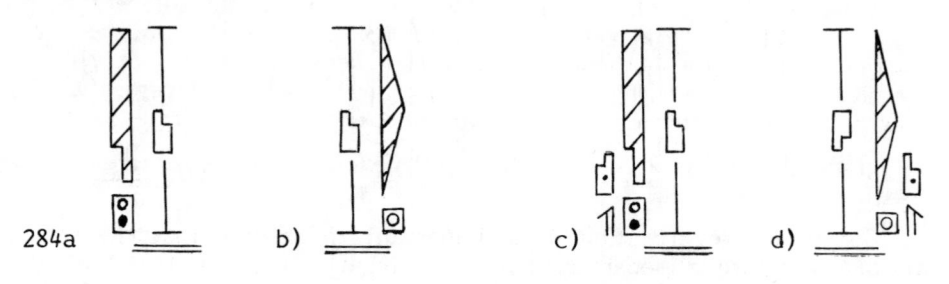

In the use of body parts, central parts such as the trunk (torso) and its parts, are placed closer to the center, while more peripheral parts (limbs, hands and head) are placed outside on the right and left.

Indications for the whole torso are usually placed on the left of center, those for the chest on the right. Ex. 284a illustrates travelling with a torso tilt; in 284b it is the chest which is tilting. In 284c the left arm starts forward as travelling and torso tilting begins. Ex. 284d indicates the right arm moving forward at the beginning of travelling backward combined with chest tilting.

For Structured Description of movement, placement of the various pieces of information is carefully organized on the three-line staff to provide ease in reading and in locating any particular movement detail.

Signs for Parts of the Body

Standard practice is to place the sign for a part of the body before the movement indication.

285a   b)   c)   or   d)   or   e)   f)   g)

Thus Ex. 285a states: "whole torso turns CW". Ex. 285b states: "right hand flexes" and so on. One knows at once the body part involved and then the kind of action it is to do. If the action is very quick the two indications can be placed side by side, as in 285c and 285d, but then they must be tied together with a small horizontal bow. Without the bow, as in 285e, the statement would be of some kind of flexion for the body as a whole, the meaning of the hand symbol not being clear — it appears that a movement indication for the hand has been omitted by mistake. Ex. 285f shows a quick rotation (twist) for the right arm, while in 285g there is a quick inward rotation for the left leg.

Leg Rotation, Whole Body Rotation

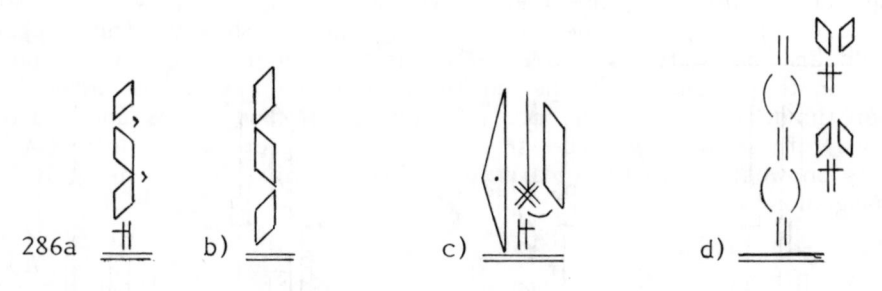

286a   b)   c)   d)

Concerning leg rotation, it is important to observe that the action of 286a is quite a separate movement from a rotation (turn) of the body as a whole, 286b. For a turn of the whole body, the performer is usually supporting on one or both feet while turning. Rotation of the free leg in or out (or even the supporting leg in or out) exists quite separately from a pivot turn. Exact use of leg rotations belongs more to Structured Description, where it is important to record any slight change in the rotational state. In Motif Description leg rotations are usually the focal point of an action, rather than an additional, subordinate factor. In Ex. 286c a general sideward movement to the left is accompanied by the right leg turning in and flexing. We presume the right leg to be gesturing. Such flexion and rotation could, however, occur for a supporting leg; but if these two actions are to be featured a gesture is more appropriate. In 286d two consecutive jumps occur. The first lands with legs turned in, the second with legs turned out.

Supports

When we write changes of support which involve use of a specific part (foot, knee, hip, etc.) indication for the part of the body taking over the weight is placed at the end of the action stroke. The length of an action stroke which terminates in a new support gives the time during which the transference of weight is to be achieved. It is only at the end that weight is fully on the new support, Ex. 287a.

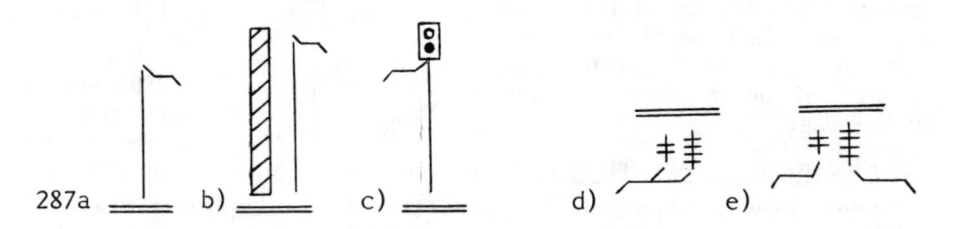

287a   b)   c)   d)   e)

In Ex. 287b there is a change of support during a rising action. This very open statement allows for the weight to be taken on any part of the body you wish. Because of the accompanying upward action it is likely that certain parts will be chosen in preference to others; however, the change of support could be onto the shoulders, the legs performing the movement up. Ex. 287c states a slow action at the end of which you are lying down (supporting on the whole torso). In 287d supporting on one foot and one knee is shown. This support could also be written as 287e. As this notation is of a starting position (note placement of the double horizontal line), it is understood that timing is not shown, only the appropriate body signs and support bows. These bows may be drawn to the right or to the left, choice rests on what is visually clearer in a given context, the meaning is not changed.

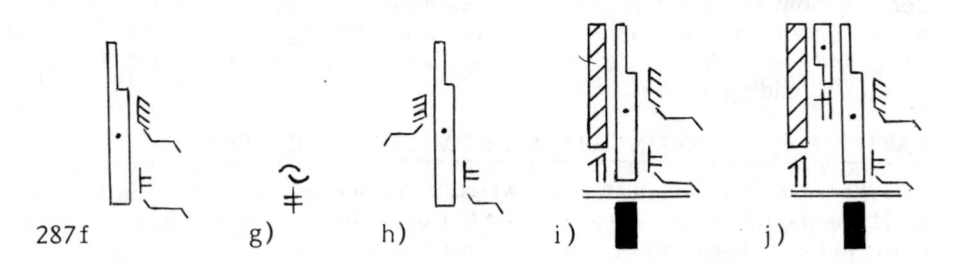

287f   g)   h)   i)   j)

In Ex. 287f a forward action is accompanied by supporting first on the right knee, then on the right hand. It is expected that the knee support will remain until other movement indications cause it to be replaced, or until a specific indication to release the knee is given, as in 287g. Ex. 287h is similar but weight is taken on the left hand, the sign logically being placed on the left side. Ex. 287i illustrates the movement of 287f with the addition of a starting position and an upward gesture for the left arm. In 287j a backward leg gesture has

Supports (continued)

also been added. Gradually the action is becoming more structured, although there is still much leeway for interpretation.

The pathway forward in 287k is achieved by supporting on the knees, right, left, right, and left. Placement of the signs on their appropriate sides facilitates reading, though 287l clearly indicates the same thing and has the advantage of being more compact on the page.

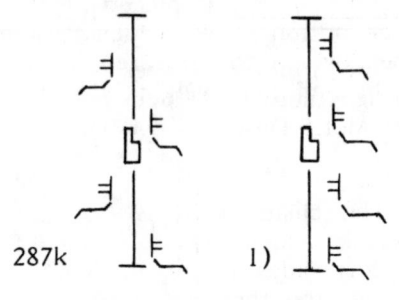

287k 1)

Placement of Supporting Bow

Some leeway is possible in placement of the supporting bow; it is also possible to use the other form of the bow, Ex. 288a, particularly when lying on the ground. If supporting on a particular surface of the torso, let us say the front, is to be shown, the supporting bow can be written as in 288c or 288d. It is not necessary to connect the bow to the 'tick' which marks the front surface; the torso sign with indication of the desired surface is a unit and thus 288e or 288f would also provide the same message.

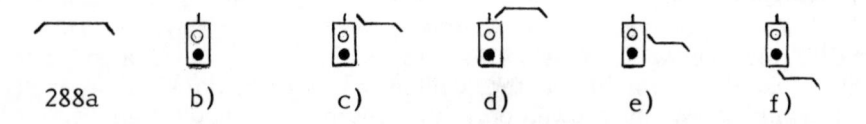

288a b) c) d) e) f)

Even though gaining writing skills is not included in the exploration of movement covered in Your Move, certain questions will arise concerning how movements are to be expressed on paper. When recording a movement sequence one usually aims at getting the information down first and then, with the next copy, arranging the indication logically to make reading easier.

PATH SIGNS - CONTINUATION FROM STAFF TO STAFF

When a circular path sign written in one staff needs to extend into the next staff, the path sign is repeated in the new staff and a caret is used at the top of the first staff and at the bottom of the second staff to indicate that this sign is 'the same'. Information on the amount of circling or direction of travel is placed in the first part of the path sign unless this part is too short, in which case the information appears in the second part. In Ex. 289 the clockwise circling takes three measures to complete.

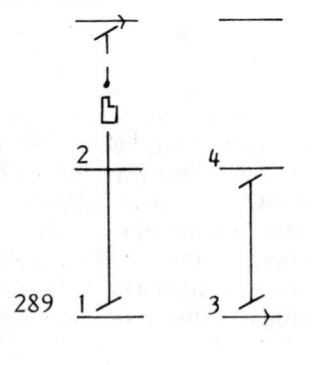

289

Appendix B
TRANSITION FROM MOTIF TO STRUCTURED DESCRIPTION

The following pages are designed to illustrate the transition in writing rules and placement of symbols which occurs in progressing from Motif Description (MD) to Structured Description (SD).

STAFF

The basic staff, Ex. 290a, to which is added indication of right and left sides of the body, 290b, becomes the three-line staff of Ex. 290c. This staff provides columns for the main parts of the body, the movement indications being placed in the appropriate columns.

Ex. 290d shows the full staff with identification of the columns. The dotted lines, marked here for explanatory purposes, are not usually included; for visual clarity only the three vertical lines are used. Within the three-line staff are columns for the body, arms and head.

The center line divides right and left. Use of the columns is:

1 - supports (usually on the feet)
2 - leg gestures (not taking weight)
3 - body (torso, etc.)
4 - arms
5 - hands
6 - head (placed away from other indications).

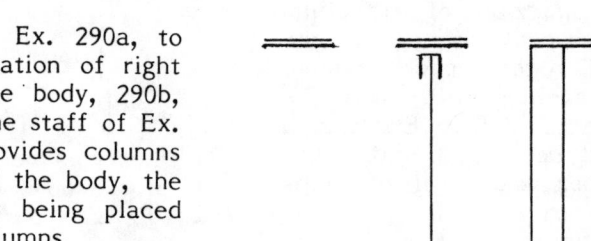

290a   b)   c)

290d   L | R

STEPS

Stepping, which, as an action ending in a new support on right or left foot, was written as 291a or the abbreviation of 291b, is now shown by indications in the right and left center columns in the full staff, 291c. The center columns are for supports on the feet unless otherwise indicated.

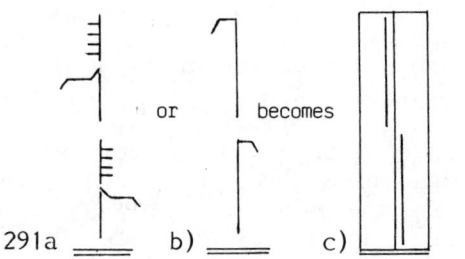

or   becomes

291a   b)   c)

303

Steps (continued)

For steps into a specific direction, as in Ex. 291d which states right step forward, left step side, the direction symbol is placed in the appropriate support column, as 291e.

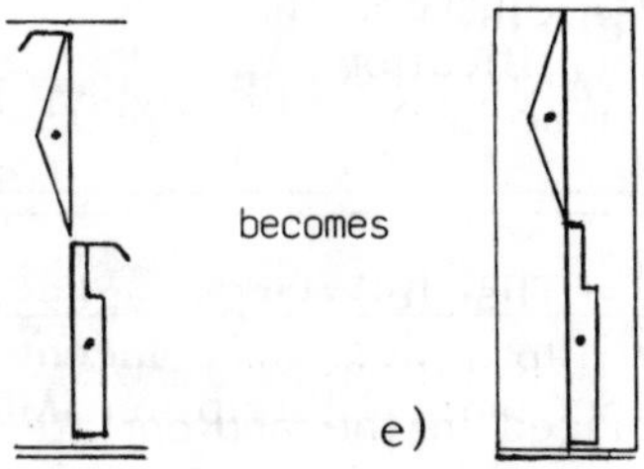

becomes

291d

e)

TRAVELLING

Direction of travelling is shown by direction of the steps in the support column. If travelling starts with the right foot, then Ex. 292a,b could become 292c,d. The number and level of steps used are not stated in the notation of 292a or b).

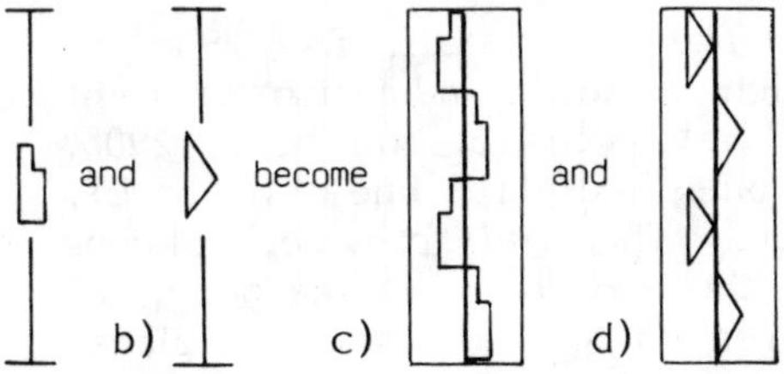

a) and b) become c) and d)

292

For circular paths the direction of travelling is shown in the support column, while the action of circling is placed outside, alongside the steps. Ex. 292e becomes 292f.

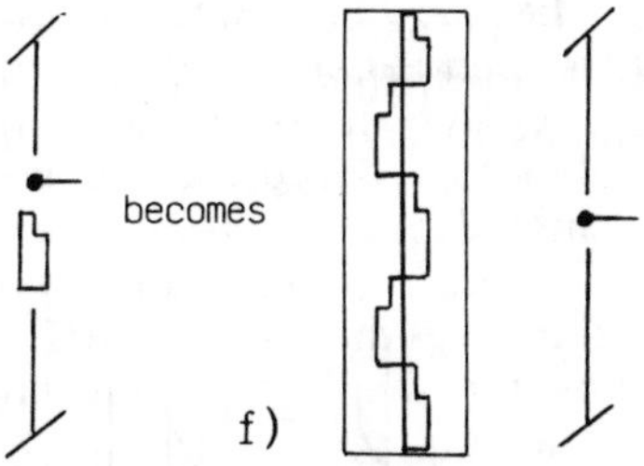

becomes

292e f)

TURNING

General turning, pivoting, Ex. 293a, becomes specific by placement of the turn sign in the appropriate support column, according to where the weight is placed, e.g. on the right foot, Ex. 293b, on the left, c), or on both feet, Ex. 293d.

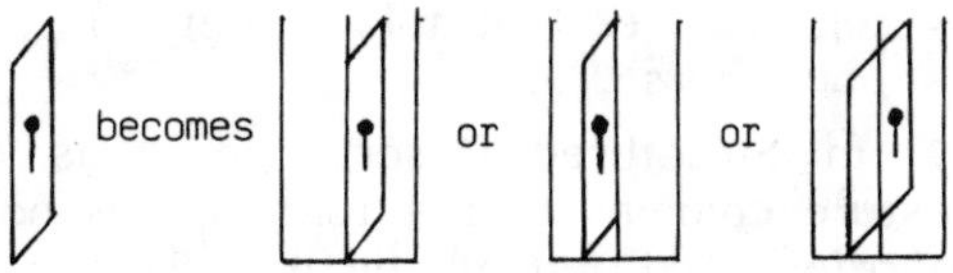

293a becomes b) or c) or d)

Turning on the spot through steps in place may be shown by placing the turn sign outside the staff to refer to the body as a whole, Ex. 293e, or a circular path sign may be used, as in f), the logic being that the feet are making a circle, even though a very small one. Should it not be clear that the turn sign refers to the whole

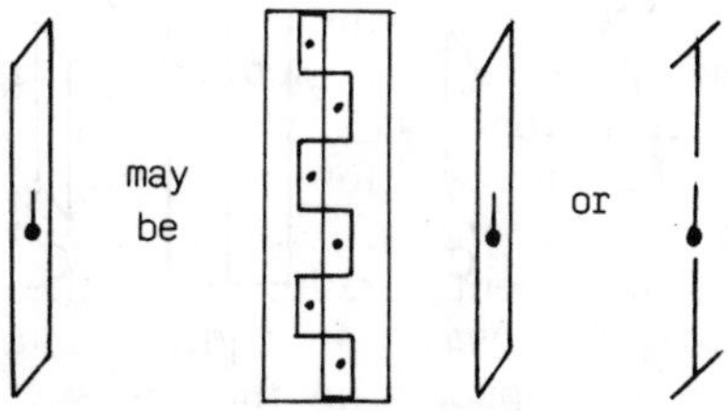

293 may be e) or f)

body and not to some other part recently mentioned, the sign for the body as a whole: ⊔ can be used for identification, Ex. 293g.   (The need for such a use is rare).

293g ⊔

Turning: Rotations, Twists

Rotations and twists of the areas and limbs of the body are now placed in the appropriate columns.   Arms and legs have their own columns; thus Ex. 294a becomes b) and c) becomes d).

294a   b)   c)   d)

The parts of the torso are placed in the body columns but are still identified for practical purposes.   Thus 294e becomes f), g) becomes h) and i) becomes j).

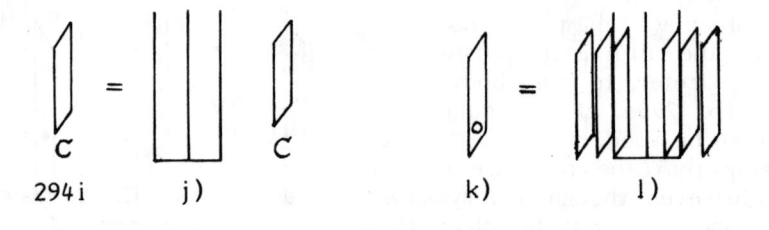

294e   f)   g)   h)

In Structured Description it is clear from placement within the gesture columns that a turn sign is not a turn for the body as a whole; therefore addition of the hold sign: o within the turn sign to show rotation or twist of a limb is not needed.   The sign of 294k becomes a plain turn sign within the appropriate columns, Ex. 294l).

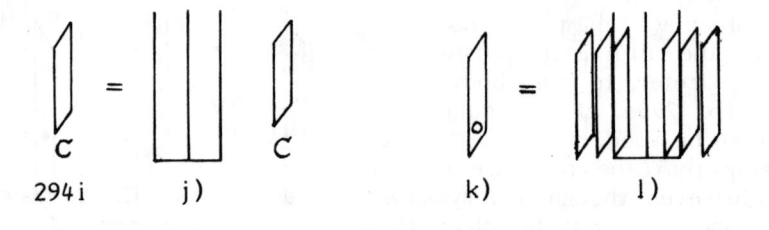

294i   j)   k)   l)

305

AERIAL STEPS

For the general indication of 'any spring into the air' no form exists in SD; the general statement must now become specific. Below are the specific forms shown first with no direction indicated.

In SD a gap (space) in the support column means that there is no support, you go into the air, i.e. a spring.

295 a)

295 b)   c)   d)   e)

295 f)   g)   h)   i)

Directions for Aerial Steps

Specific directions shown in MD for the take off or for the landing is translated directly into the support column in SD. The same is true of directions indicated for the legs while in the air.

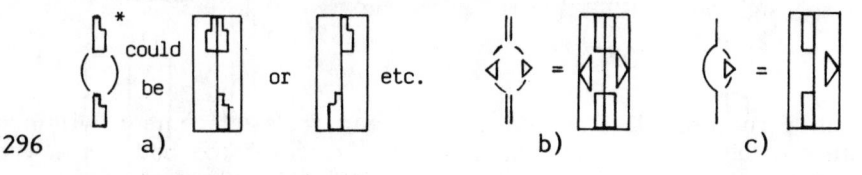

296 a)   or etc.   b)   c)

(MD does not state exact form.)

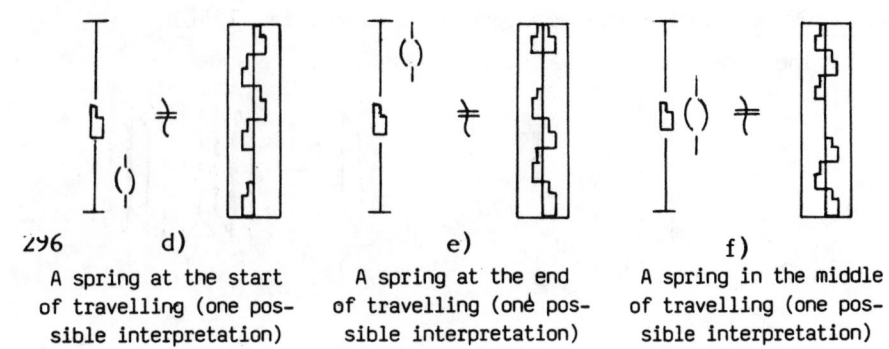

296   d)   e)   f)

A spring at the start   A spring at the end   A spring in the middle
of travelling (one pos-   of travelling (one pos-   of travelling (one possible interpretation)   sible interpretation)   sible interpretation)

306

TILTING, TAKING A DIRECTION

Tilting indications for specific parts of the body are placed in the appropriate column. For the torso and its parts, the specific body sign is still used. Ex. 297a becomes b), c) becomes d), e) becomes f).

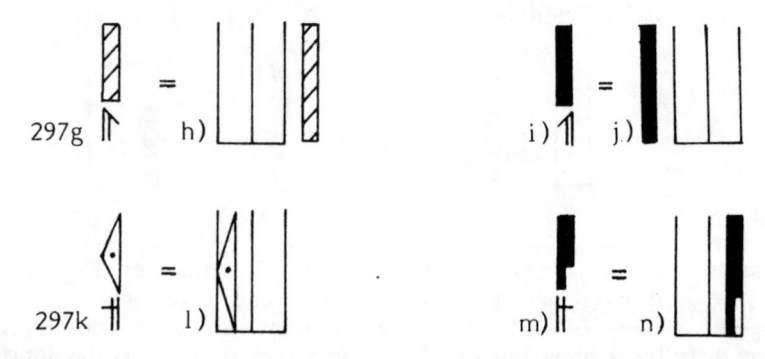

297a   b)   c)   d)   e) C   f) C

Gestures of the limbs to a directional destination are written by placing the required direction symbol in the appropriate column. Thus Ex. 297g becomes h), i) becomes j), and so on.

297g   h)   i)   j)

297k   l)   m)   n)

SHIFTING

In SD 'any level' for shifting movements is not expected; therefore the sign without level is taken to be middle level.

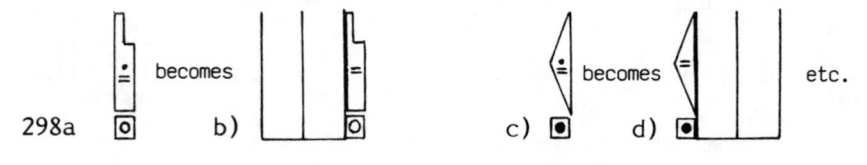

298a   b)   becomes   c)   d)   becomes   etc.

DIRECTION OF PROGRESSION

For the direction of progression middle level is understood in SD.

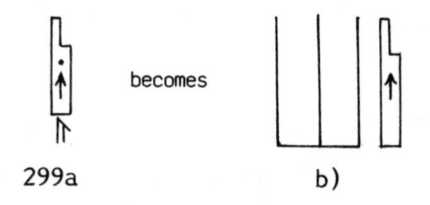

299a   becomes   b)

FLEXION, EXTENSION

Flexion and extension of the limbs and trunk are written in the appropriate columns. For the arms, 300b is the Structured Description of 300a; for the legs 300c becomes 300d.

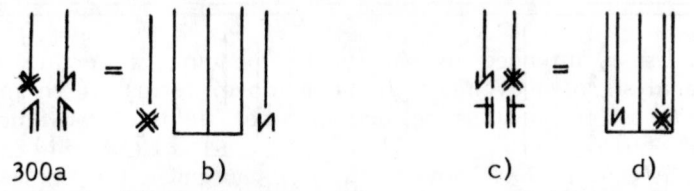

300a   b)   c)   d)

Flexion and extension which occur at the same time as a directional change are combined in SD, the flexion or extension indication being placed before the direction symbol in the same column. Ex. 300e becomes f) and g becomes h).

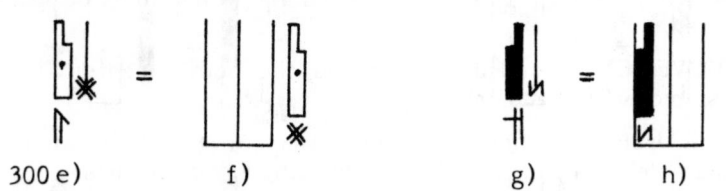

300 e)   f)   g)   h)

This survey of the transition from Motif to Structured Description reveals the logical relationship between the broad intentions stated in MD and specific identification of the movement which is the function of SD. For a fuller exposition of SD consult the textbook Labanotation by this author, published by Theatre Arts Books, New York.

Appendix C
TERMINOLOGY

This list is intended to clarify the meaning of certain words used in the analysis of movement in Your Move, terms which may not be familiar to all or not thus defined in other fields of movement study.

ACTION, AN ACTION - movement of a particular type or with a particular purpose or content.

ANATOMICAL TERMS - terminology used in the study of anatomy.

ASPECTS OF MOVEMENT - the different 'sides', 'views' of movement on which attention may be focussed or which may be particularly featured.

AXIAL MOVEMENT - movement around the body's center (in contrast to locomotor movement).

BREATH PAUSE - a fleeting interruption of the flow of movement comparable to a singer taking a breath during an aria.

CONCEPTS OF MOVEMENT - ideas and comprehensions of movement from which movements are 'conceived' and viewed.

CONTRACTION - the form of flexion concerned specifically with drawing in a limb toward the center, the extremity approaching the base of the limb on a straight path. The term is used in its anatomical sense and does not refer to the stylized movement of the torso met in certain contemporary dance techniques.

EXTENSION - this 'parent' term includes actions of lengthening (elongating, stretching), unfolding, and spreading (separating). It is not used in the sense of meaning given to it in anatomical terminology.

FACTOR - one of the elements or influences that contribute to produce a result, a component part.

FORM - the shape, type, or kind to which a movement belongs. In general parlance the word 'form' is applied in many ways. Forms of movement may be gymnastics, games, dance, etc. Forms of dance may be ballet, Spanish, Javanese, etc. Forms of locomotion can be running, skipping, sliding. Forms of flexion are contracting, folding, joining (closing in laterally or sagittally), and so on.

GESTURE - a non-weight-bearing movement. Gestures are usually of the limbs but may also be of the head, torso and its parts.

HOLD - the retention of a state or situation.

HORIZONTAL PLANE - the plane which is parallel with the floor when one is standing and which divides the body into upper and lower halves (also called the 'table' plane).

KINESPHERE - the sphere within which we move, its boundaries being defined by 'reach space', i.e. the distance limbs can reach without any travelling occurring.

LANGUAGE OF DANCE - the means through which dance is communicated, not only by performance of the movement itself - the act of dancing - but through a sound analysis of movement content, the presentation and communication of which is facilitated by a universally based terminology supported by written representation in notation of the facts and motivations.

LATERAL - pertaining to the sideward directions.

LATERAL PLANE - the lateral-vertical plane in the body dividing front and back (also called the frontal plane, or 'door' plane).

LOCOMOTOR - movement which produces travelling of one form or another, usually on the feet.

MOVEMENT - motion of any kind. In this book this word is used as a general term when no specific action or particular content is intended, but just a general change of some kind.

MOTIF DESCRIPTION, STRUCTURED DESCRIPTION - see page xxii.

PERSONAL SPACE - space within the kinesphere surrounding each person which is psychologically their personal 'property'.

PRIME ACTIONS - the elements of movement, the root actions. Like prime numbers, these actions cannot be further reduced into component parts. (See page xxiii.)

RETAIN - the maintaining of a state (as in a touch) or of an activity (as in continuous sliding).

ROTATION - a turning as a unit of the body-as-a-whole or of a part of the body.

SAGITTAL - pertaining to the forward-backward body directions.

SAGITTAL PLANE - the sagittal-vertical plane dividing the body into right and left halves (also called the 'wheel' plane).

SIGN, SYMBOL - indications on paper representing the many component parts of movement. Major indications are usually termed symbols, minor indications called signs.

STILLNESS - absence of change in which the expression, the 'feel', the 'reverberation' of the movement which has just ceased is continued.

TURN(ING) - the general term used for parts of the body when the specific form (rotation in one piece or twisting) is not important or is not to be stated.

TWIST - a turning of the body or a part of the body in which the extremity (the free end) produces the greatest degree of turn and the base (the fixed end) none at all.

Appendix D
VERBS

The Prime Actions (the raw material of movement) with which we have been dealing are like 'parents' in that the subdivisions and variations of each are like 'children' and 'grandchildren'. To illustrate this and show the relationship between various subdivisions, a chart is provided on the next three pages. This 'Movement Family Tree' is concerned with movement 'words of action', i.e. the 'verbs'. Two other charts, the Family Tree of Nouns ('what' is being moved or is involved in a movement) and the Family Tree of Adverbs ('how' an action is performed, the quality, dynamics) are not included in this book. Their value relates more directly to Structured Description.

The Movement Alphabet given on page xxiii indicates the prime actions and concepts of which movement is comprised. This alphabet provides a basic reference for the material to come. The chart of Verbs leads on from the Movement Alphabet. Numbers in the corner of key boxes in the Family Tree of Verbs refer to the items so numbered in the Movement Alphabet. Once the prime actions have been explored, reference to the Verbs chart is a valuable guide and an aid to clarification in teaching the material covered in Your Move. As details on the various forms of movement are presented, the chart is a help in providing perspective on how new material relates to what has gone before. Many people like to know the extent of the material under investigation and to have a clear idea of the relationship of the individual parts. The Family Tree of Verbs is a visual aid in mentally organizing and thus better understanding the movement facts and ideas.

Some items on the Verbs chart may be met more frequently in Structured rather than Motif Description. Although they may not be explored in this book, knowledge of their existence is helpful in obtaining a total picture.

The Movement Family Tree of Verbs progresses from the simplest indication - an action of some kind - to the more sophisticated concepts of filling a shape or penetrating space. The concept of destination in contrast to motion is listed before specific forms of movement are introduced. Anatomical possibilities are then considered, the different forms of flexion, extension and rotation made possible by the nature of the joints of the body. These physical actions produce spatial changes in placement of the limbs and body parts. How we move in and travel through space is a 'multicolored' category. Concern with support, the placement of weight, is essential in almost all movement description; transference of weight and balance are an important consideration. The chart ends with indication of the results of actions, the many forms of relationship and concern with visual design.

311

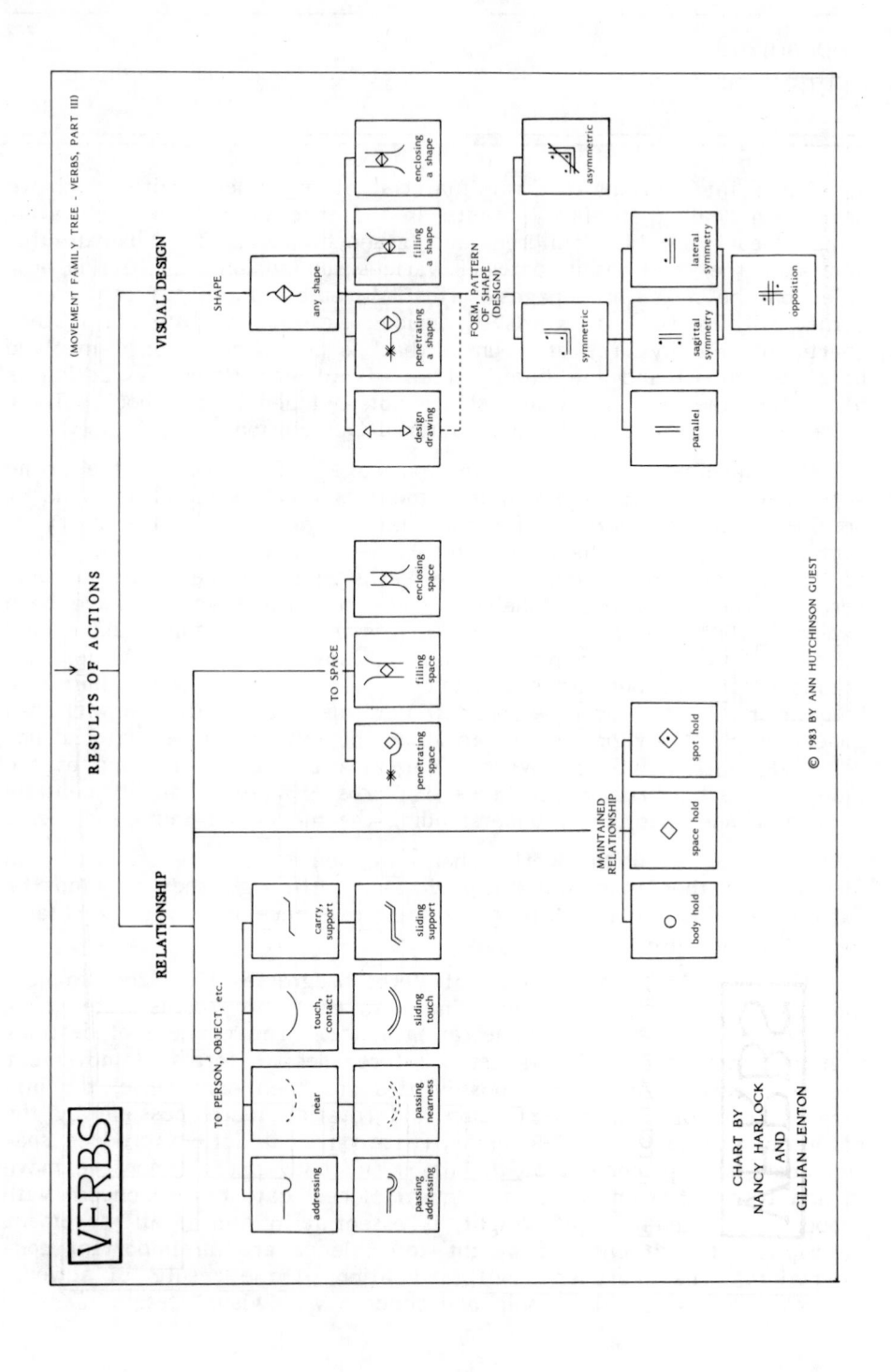

(MOVEMENT FAMILY TREE - VERBS, PART I)

VERBS

BY

ANN HUTCHINSON GUEST

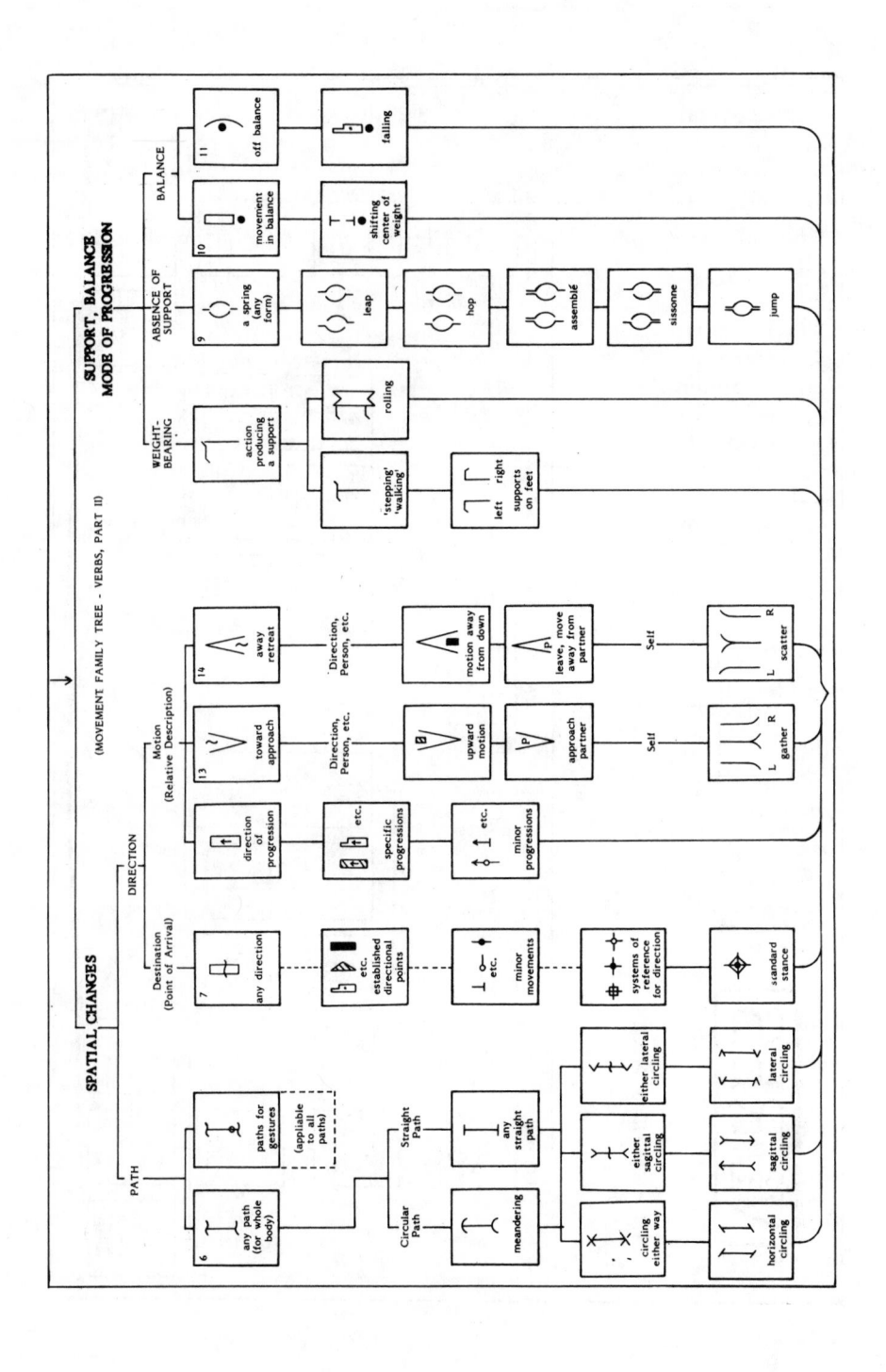

Index

Alphabetization is by main words; disregard lesser words such as 'of', 'for', 'with', etc. Page numbers for main references are under-lined. Entries include movement discussion on the topic, indication in notation and use in the Reading and Practice Studies.

The following abbreviations are used only where needed:

C of A - Cross of Axes
contr - contraction
destin(at) - destination
diff - different
dim(ens) - dimension(al)
dir - direction(s)
exten - extension
flex - flexion
indic(a) - indication(s)
individ - individual

interpr - interpretation
measur - measurement
mvt - movement
perf - performance
relat - relationship
ref - reference
S.D. - Structured Description
separat - separation
w - with

315